Preface

Momentous changes have occurred in the Soviet Union and Eastern Europe since the second edition of *Europe Since 1945: A Concise History*; these changes have necessitated a major revamping of the third edition. An entire new chapter 13 concentrates on the reforms of Mikhail Gorbachev in the Soviet Union and their impact on Eastern Europe and the West. Morever, the book traces reforms throughout the former "Soviet bloc" to longer-term opposition to the Stalinist and Leninist economic and political systems within each country, not merely as a response to Gorbachev's initiatives. Also of great significance since the second edition has been the retreat from nationalization and extensive welfare systems in the West, inspired to a large extent by British prime minister Margaret Thatcher. Finally, an increasing number of historical monographs treating the postwar period have provided a wealth of detail and interpretation for this text that was not available when the first two editions were written. Although the third edition is no longer as concise as the earlier editions, it now has a richness of detail that many readers desired. This new edition is not then merely an updating; it is a major renovation of the original work.

Europe Since 1945 is organized both chronologically and thematically. While chapters on politics provide the basic chronological structure, other chapters, primarily thematic, are located at points where comprehension of their arguments will enhance the understanding of the chapters that follow. For example, the first two chapters (on a bipolar world and on the Cold War and the Sovietization of Eastern Europe) are fundamental to an understanding of the third chapter (on European politics from 1945 to 1948). The chapters on politics are tied to the other chapters by an underlying socioeconomic theme that is viewed as the major determinant of political change or continuity.

Developments in postwar Europe are seen as the culmination of a chain of events stretching back to the turn of the century. However, the enormous impact of World War II is not overlooked in shaping the postwar world. For example, the Cold War confrontation between the Soviet Union and the United States is explained as resulting in part from the growth of non-European power centers, beginning with the emergence of Japan and the United States in the late-nineteenth century, and from the struggle between communism and capitalism that had been at work in domestic and international politics since 1917. The incorporation of Europe within a bipolar world after 1945 is, according to this interpretation, primarily the result of the attainment of superpower status by the United States and the USSR during this century. And coverage of the lessening of German power is important in order to understand the power vacuum created in Central Europe that could only be filled by the two superpowers. The analysis of the end of European empire moves outside the European-centered interpretive framework to explain the emergence of independent Third World countries in the postwar period as a three-stage revolutionary pattern stretching over nearly a century. When the impact of decolonization has an extensive domestic impact on a colonial power, as in the case of French Algeria, it is also dealt with in the chapters on domestic politics.

In the chapters on economic and social developments, demographic and statistical data are interwoven with theories that have been advanced to explain postwar European society. Such phenomena as changing occupational structures, the spread of affluence, and the persistence of distinct social classes and governing elites are treated in depth. In dealing with these themes, special attention is given to the smaller European states, as they have often been forerunners in the development of the postwar welfare state. It is, for example, to Scandinavia that one must look in order to understand the impact of socioeconomic policies that have been pursued by most Western European states since World War II. Also examined is the effect of economic modernization and communism on Soviet and Eastern European societies.

Throughout the study, conciseness is favored over excessive attention to detail in order to highlight significant patterns and theses. Much of the statistical material is incorporated in the many tables located throughout the book. Seven maps help students grasp the full significance of political and economic developments. An annotated list of selected readings at the end of each chapter guides students in research and further study.

I wish to thank Professors Philip Cook, Louisiana Tech University; Laura Gellott, University of Wisconsin, Parkside; Loyd E. Lee, State University of New York, New Paltz; M. C. Rosenfeld, Southeastern Massachusetts University; Paul Scherer, Indiana University, South Bend; Irwin Wall, University of California, Riverside; and John Willertz, Saginaw Valley State College, for their reading and helpful suggestions for the third edition. A special debt of gratitude is owed my student assistants at the University of Notre Dame, Craig Stillwell, John Quinn, and Carolyn Huber, for helping me track down recent works for possible inclusion in the Further Reading sections. Finally, I want to express my thanks to Don Reisman and Beverly Hinton Beers of St. Martin's Press for seeing *Europe Since 1945* through to its final form.

J. ROBERT WEGS

Contents

1 A Bipolar World

> There are on earth today two great peoples, who, from different points of departure seem to be advancing towards the same end. They are the Russians and the Anglo-Americans.
>
> Alexis de Tocqueville, *Democracy in America*, 1835

Contemporary history tends to exaggerate the influence of recent events—the impact of World War II on Europe's role in world affairs, for example. Long-term developments—the growing economic and political importance of the United States, Japan, and the Soviet Union or the demographic patterns that began to reduce Europe's proportion of the world's population after 1930—do not receive the attention given to a recent cataclysmic event such as World War II. Europe's weakened condition, especially the collapse of the German center, made the U.S. and USSR military might appear even more formidable. Much of the history of the postwar years will involve a European recapturing of some of the worldwide hegemony it had in 1900 but lost in 1945.

The Emergence of the Superpowers

This is not to minimize the enormous consequences of World War II. But it was only one of many influences that led to the polarization of world affairs around the activities of the United States and the Soviet Union, which emerged as superpowers after the war. The eclipse of the European balance of power system seems on the surface to be primarily a result of the war. But in fact the origin of that eclipse can be traced to the prewar emergence of power centers outside Western Europe. Even before the war, the countries rimming the Pacific Ocean had begun to shift the power balance away from Europe and to usher in an era of global politics.

The meeting of the American and Soviet armies on the Elbe River in 1945 merely symbolized the changes that had been going on in the world's power relationships for over half a century. In World War I, Great Britain and France had already had to call on the United States to restore the

1

Table 1-1 Growth of Industrial Production in Western Europe and the United States, 1901–1955

	Index of Industrial Production (volume) (W.E. 1938 = 100)		Index of Industrial Production (per capita) (W.E. 1955 = 100)	
	WESTERN EUROPE	UNITED STATES	WESTERN EUROPE	UNITED STATES
1901	44	35	37	74
1913	69	66	51	109
1929	86	124	60	165
1937	102	127	67	160
1955	177	291	100	285

Source: *Carlo M. Cipolla*, The Economic History of World Population, *3rd ed. (Baltimore: Penguin Books, 1965), p. 69. Reprinted by permission of Penguin Books, Ltd.*

power equilibrium in Europe. In the interwar period, the growing economic strength and political importance of the United States and the Soviet Union were for the most part ignored because of the American policy of isolation from European affairs and the Soviet concentration on internal problems.

As indicated in Table 1-1, the United States had overtaken Western Europe in industrial production in the interwar years. By 1939, the United States was producing one-third of the world's most important metals, one-third of its coal and electrical energy, two-thirds of its oil, and three-quarters of its automobiles.

Despite this rapid growth, between 1929 and 1938 the U.S. share of the world's industrial output had actually declined from 42.2 to 32.2 percent. This decline resulted from the Great Depression of 1929 and the growth in the Soviet share of world production from 4.3 to 18.3 percent during the same period.

That such accelerated growth would ultimately have a far-reaching impact on world affairs did not escape the attention of some Europeans. It apparently convinced Adolf Hitler that Germany had only a short time to secure the territorial basis for competing in a world of superpowers. In 1928, Hitler wrote: "With the American Union a new power of such dimensions has come into being as threatens to upset the whole former power and order of rank of the states." The defeat of Germany and Japan in 1945 and the switchover to the production of war materiel in the United States and the Soviet Union brought about the concentration of power in the hands of the superpowers that Hitler had feared.

Although many had predicted the awesome military power exercised by the Soviet Union and the United States in 1945, few foresaw the collapse of power in Europe that brought about the Soviet-American confrontation. The Allied demand for unconditional surrender made it impossible for Germany or Japan to seek a compromise peace. Leaders in both countries realized what fate awaited them and therefore exhausted their countries' resources in the hope that a last-minute miracle might avert defeat. Hitler put his hopes in German rockets, jet planes, and the possibility that the United States and the Soviet Union might come to blows before the defeat of Germany. With German resistance continuing until the fall of Berlin in May 1945, Germany lay in ruins. France, weakened by defeat, occupation, and internal divisions, was incapable of assuming leadership in Europe. Only Great Britain seemed to offer an alternative power center.

But World War II had, in an economic sense, been a hollow victory for the British. The nation that had ruled a quarter of the human race in 1914 was no match for the superpowers in 1945. The second largest creditor nation in the world in 1939, Britain became the largest debtor as a result of World War II. While expenditures increased fivefold during the war, exports were reduced to only 60 percent of the prewar total. To meet its wartime obligations, Britain had to liquidate more than a billion pounds in foreign assets.

The relative decline of Britain had begun even before the war. Its territorial base shrank as its colonies and territories gained independence or became autonomous members of the empire. Nor could it any longer tap the resources of colonies as it had done in the nineteenth century. As the empire was transformed into a commonwealth of nations in the two decades after the war, Britain was reduced to a small island nation whose population and resources were inadequate to compete with the superpowers. Although recently declassified documents have shown that Britain played a major role in shaping Western policy immediately after the war, British foreign policy in the postwar years became increasingly dependent upon U.S. economic and military power and the American view of world affairs. When Britain tried to act independently, as it did at Suez in 1956, American disapproval and limited British resources thwarted the attempt.

With no possibility of restoring a European power equilibrium because of the military preponderance of the Soviet Union, Western leaders were fearful that all of Europe would be at the mercy of what they saw as Soviet expansionism. A prostrate Europe appeared to offer Soviet expansionists tempting bait. Yet did Soviet leaders actually desire an extension of Soviet hegemony over all Europe? Or, as American radical revisionists such as Gabriel Kolko and William A. Williams believe, were Soviet actions a response to the United States' attempt to use its economic and military superiority as a basis for global hegemony? Or are these positions extremist and unsupported by the evidence? The answers to these questions are to be found in Soviet and American objectives and actions.

The Soviet Union at War's End

At the end of World War II, the Soviet Union controlled most of Eastern Europe, Manchuria, northern Korea, northern Iran, and threatened to expand into Turkey. Despite Soviet military preponderance in these areas, which was soon to be of fundamental importance in determining postwar spheres of influence, Joseph Stalin, as leader of the victorious Soviet forces, was awed by the enormous economic and military might of the United States and anxious about his role at home.

Stalin's fears for Soviet security, bolstered by serious weaknesses in the Soviet economy and growing suspicion and hostility abroad, were not unfounded. Twice within the previous twenty-five years Russia had suffered extensively from foreign invasions. Nearly 20 million Soviet citizens died as a direct or indirect result of World War II. Large sections of the country were laid waste by German and Soviet armies. Cities such as Kiev and Minsk had been devastated and had to be completely rebuilt; Leningrad suffered severe damage during nine hundred days of siege and bombardment, and 1 million of its inhabitants—one-third of the city's population—starved to death during the siege. In many industries, production had been halved because of the shortage of personnel and raw materials and the war damage to factories.

On the other hand, Stalin was keenly aware of American economic strength because of the vast amounts of U.S. material shipped to Europe and the Soviet Union during the war and used by U.S. and Allied forces, including his own, in both the Pacific and the European war zones. Equally disturbing to him was the size of American military forces at the end of the war, numbering 12 million as compared to the Soviet Union's 11 million. Stalin was aware that in an economic sense his country was not a superpower in comparison to the United States. To restore its economic strength, he hoped to obtain American aid and expected to acquire indispensable industrial equipment and raw materials from Germany and the countries of Eastern Europe. U.S. opposition to these goals was to be one of the major causes of the Cold War between East and West.

Stalin's feelings of insecurity both at home and elsewhere in the Communist world had a direct impact on his foreign policy. His opposition to independent Communist-led revolutionary movements, such as those in China and Yugoslavia, revealed his fear of outside rivals. His opposition to the leftist forces in the Greek Civil War and to Yugoslav support of the rebels reflected his fear that President Tito of Yugoslavia might establish a Balkan Communist confederation big enough to challenge Stalin's preeminence in Eastern Europe and his domination over the Eastern European Communist parties. It was his dislike of Tito's independent course that led to Yugoslavia's ostracism from the Soviet-dominated Communist bloc in 1948 (see chapter 2).

Within the Soviet Union, Stalin had been excessively concerned with the possible ideological contamination of Soviet citizens because of their contacts with Western Europe during the war. After the war, his desire to keep the West unaware of Soviet economic weakness and to avoid further "contamination" from Western ideas led to the curtailment of contacts with the West for all but a few Soviet nationals. By preventing Western knowledge of Soviet domestic affairs, Stalin only increased the mystery concerning life in the Soviet Union and promoted Western abhorrence of what came to be known as *Stalinism*—the dictatorial exercise of state power by a small elite to bring about certain Marxist-Leninist objectives. Widespread fear among nations of the West that such a system might spread beyond the Soviet sphere of influence provided considerable support for the eventual United States policy of containment of communism.

It was in order to achieve the national security against a resurgent Germany that he felt the West was not willing to provide that Stalin tried, during the war and after, to gain control over Eastern Europe. He had become convinced of Western hostility toward the Soviet Union long before the Cold War. He well remembered the West's attempts to defeat bolshevism after World War I, the sellout of Czechoslovakia in 1938 at the Munich Conference, and the failure to side with the Soviet Union against Germany before the war. In order to avoid an immediate war with Germany and gain control of additional territory, Stalin felt it advantageous to sign the Nazi-Soviet Nonaggression Pact in 1939. The pact restored territories lost as a result of World War I, Bessarabia and White Russia, and permitted the annexation of the Baltic countries (Latvia, Lithuania, and Estonia). While this pact gave the Soviet Union two more years to prepare its armies for the conflict with Hitler, Stalin apparently considered it to be a more permanent protection against Nazi attack. Both Nikita Khrushchev's unofficial memoirs and Marshal Zhukov's unedited memoirs contend that Stalin was so shocked by the invasion that he was unable to act for over a week.

East-West Relations during World War II

Stalin's suspicions concerning Western intentions were not allayed by Western actions during the war. His actions were therefore determined by traditional balance of power considerations aimed at obtaining strategic and economic benefits for the Soviet Union after the war. As early as the Moscow Conference in December 1941, Stalin offered Great Britain whatever security arrangements it wanted in France, the Low Countries, Norway, and Denmark if the Western Allies would grant the Soviet Union similar rights in Eastern Poland, Finland, and Romania.

Anthony Eden, at that time British foreign minister, later wrote of the conference: "Russian ideas were already starkly definite. They changed little during the next three years, for their purpose was to secure the most

During World War II, cities on both sides were ravaged by bombing raids. However, Leningrad, which was under siege for two years, suffered especially severe damage and loss of life. In this photo, taken in 1942, fire has broken out following bombardment of the city by the Germans. (Novosti from Sovfoto)

tangible physical guarantees for Russia's future safety.'' Only because of President Franklin D. Roosevelt's objections—British prime minister Winston Churchill had already accepted—were these East European riders excluded from the subsequent Anglo-Soviet Treaty of Alliance of May 1942.

Serious rifts began to develop among the Allies in 1942. Since Stalin was bearing the brunt of the German attack, he wanted his Western allies to open a second front in Western Europe to divert some German forces from the Russian front. The inability of the West to launch the Normandy invasion until June 1944 fed Stalin's suspicion that the West hoped to weaken Soviet forces by prolonged conflict in order to reduce Soviet strength in the postwar period.

Stalin's suspicions of Western intentions were further borne out, in his mind, when the United States and Great Britain tried to exclude the Soviet Union from any control over liberated southern Italy. Stalin's demands to be given a voice in Italian affairs prompted the Western Allies to form an Advisory Council for Italy with French as well as Soviet participation. However, this council proved to be powerless. Real jurisdiction in Italy was lodged in an Anglo-American Control Commission and the military forces on the scene. A noted American historian, W. H. McNeill, astutely observed: "Having excluded Russia from any but nominal participation in Italian affairs, the Western Allies prepared the way for their own exclusion from any but a marginal share in the affairs of Eastern Europe."

Teheran, Yalta, and Potsdam

Since Soviet domination of Eastern Europe eventually became one of the major reasons for East-West hostility, an understanding of the wartime diplomacy that facilitated Soviet control sheds much light on later Soviet actions in the area. Even before the Big Three meetings of U.S., Soviet, and British leaders at Yalta and Potsdam—often viewed as the meetings that led to Soviet control of Eastern Europe—three factors had led Stalin to believe he would have a free hand in that area: The first factor was the Soviet military occupation of Eastern Europe. The second was the Anglo-American decision not to invade Germany through the Balkans. This decision, reached by the Big Three at the Teheran Conference in November 1943, left only Soviet forces and troops from Balkan nations to clear Eastern Europe of Axis troops. Churchill wanted to invade Europe through Greece and the Balkans for political reasons: to prevent Soviet domination of Eastern Europe. But his proposal was considered militarily inappropriate by U.S. military experts at Teheran, who felt that a single concerted attack across the English Channel would achieve much faster results. By recognizing Soviet supremacy in an eastern zone of operations, the Teheran meeting limited the West's participation in the postwar political affairs in that area.

The third factor that convinced Stalin he would have a free hand in the Balkans was the October 1944 agreements he negotiated with Churchill. When Soviet troops liberated Romania and Bulgaria in August–September 1944, Churchill decided to head off further Soviet expansion into Greece and Yugoslavia by reaching a *modus vivendi* with Stalin. At this meeting Churchill and Stalin agreed that the Soviet Union should have 90 percent control over Romania and 75 percent control over Bulgaria. With Soviet armies firmly in control of both countries, Churchill felt he was sacrificing little. Yugoslavia and Hungary were to be controlled equally. In return, Churchill got what he wanted—90 percent Western jurisdiction over Greece. While these percentages were vague, each side understood that control belonged to whoever had over 50 percent jurisdiction.

Although Churchill was later severely criticized for such horse trading, the Western Allies could have expected little more in the Balkans. Even though President Roosevelt never approved these agreements, Churchill's acquiescence apparently convinced Stalin that the West would accept Soviet predominance in these areas. Moreover, Churchill believed Stalin had upheld the agreement when the latter permitted the British to defeat the Communist forces in Greece during the first stage of the Greek Civil War in 1944. But it is also true that Stalin realized that the power balance in Greece favored Britain and the United States and that Greece was hardly essential to Soviet security. As the postwar vice president of Yugoslavia Milovan Djilas related in *Conversations with Stalin*, Stalin told a Yugoslav delegation, "What do you think, that Great Britain and the U.S.—the U.S., the most powerful state in the world—will permit you to break their line of communication in the Mediterranean Sea! Nonsense. And we have no navy. The uprising in Greece must be stopped, and as quickly as possible."

The Yalta Declaration and the United Nations During the Yalta Conference in February 1945, Stalin's *Realpolitik* confronted Roosevelt's utopian view of postwar politics across an unbridgeable gulf. Stalin wanted to resolve issues before the war ended, but Roosevelt wanted to put off making decisions in order to avoid East-West acrimony that might doom his pet scheme of a postwar worldwide organization. By postponing final decisions on such issues as German borders and reparations, and by making some concessions to Stalin over Eastern Europe, Roosevelt avoided a direct confrontation that might in his opinion have led to a Soviet refusal to join the United Nations.

Roosevelt was convinced that, having obtained Soviet approval for the formation of the United Nations at Yalta, he could assure the world's nations that they would have a forum for the resolution of all postwar problems. After returning from the Yalta Conference, he told a joint session of Congress that the agreements at Yalta

> ought to spell the end of the system of unilateral action, the exclusive alliances, the spheres of influence, the balances of power, and all the expedients that have been tried for centuries and have always failed. We propose to substitute for all these, a universal organization in which all peace-loving nations will finally have a chance to join.

When Stalin agreed to the Yalta Declaration on Liberated Europe that would provide governments responsive to the will of the people, he thought it an American propaganda weapon for home use. The 1944 agreements with Churchill and the presence of Soviet armies in Eastern Europe reassured him that the declaration was only for public consumption. He believed foreign affairs should be settled in private among government leaders, not decided in open forum. One month after signing the declaration, Stalin forced Romania and Bulgaria to accept governments "friendly" to the Soviet Union.

In retrospect, the Yalta Declaration must be seen as a rather naive document. To expect the Soviet Union to withdraw its troops from Eastern Europe and permit free elections was unrealistic. Yet perhaps Roosevelt expected that world opinion, centered in the United Nations, could actuate the Soviet Union to carry out the agreements reached in the declaration. Roosevelt was surely aware the West would have a majority in the U.N. Security Council (in which the five permanent members could exercise a veto) since Great Britain, France, and China could at that time be expected to side more with the American viewpoint.

Stalin obviously viewed the United Nations with great suspicion. After having long been denied membership in a similar world organization, the League of Nations, and then having been expelled from it in 1939 for invading Finland, the Soviet Union could not be expected to view the United Nations, where the West would have a four-to-one majority in the Security Council, as a guarantor of Soviet security. So Stalin continued to strengthen Soviet control over Eastern Europe and at the same time reluctantly permitted his foreign minister, Vyacheslav Molotov, to sign the United Nations charter in April 1945. Although the USSR would be in the minority in the United Nations, its veto power in the Security Council could block any proposals that it considered detrimental to Soviet interests.

Germany: Reparations or Dismemberment? Disagreements among the Allies over Germany also originated before the wartime conferences at Yalta and Potsdam. Allied failure to reach firm commitments on postwar German reparations and boundaries before the end of the war led to Germany's division and contributed mightily to the development of the Cold War. The Allies' inability to resolve the German problem had its immediate cause in differing Soviet and Western attitudes toward reparations. But the reparations question stemmed from the earlier disagreement over Germany's future. The Soviet Union and France desired not only the destruction of Germany's war-making potential but also its dismemberment. On the other hand, the United States and Great Britain wanted to destroy Germany's war-making potential but retreated from the idea of dismemberment when it was discussed at the Quebec Conference in September 1944.

At Quebec, U.S. secretary of the treasury Henry Morgenthau presented his plan to dismember Germany, to eliminate all heavy industry in the newly constituted areas, and to leave Germany under the occupation of the Soviet Union and France. The plan was the major topic of discussion. Stalin already suspected that the West's late opening of a second front against the Germans was a prelude to the establishment of a German bulwark against the Soviet Union. To reassure him that they were not going to adopt a lenient policy toward Germany, Roosevelt and Churchill did not reject the Morgenthau Plan outright.

Soon after the Quebec Conference, however, Western actions and statements indicated that the West was indeed going to adopt a policy of leniency. To avoid specific guarantees to the Soviet Union on the amount of reparations it would receive, the British and American leaders now sought to postpone any discussion of Germany's future until after the war.

Roosevelt seemed to repudiate the Morgenthau Plan completely in December 1944 when he told his new secretary of state Edward Stettinius that Germany should be permitted to "come back industrially to meet her own needs" after the war and that the United States would not allow the imposition of reparations. Roosevelt was apparently able to overcome his fear of a resurgent Germany when confronted by the specter of an all-powerful Soviet Union. He also believed that support of the Morgenthau Plan would steel German resistance, lengthen the war, and possibly cost him some support in the coming presidential elections.

At the Yalta Conference in February 1945, Stalin directly challenged Western attempts to avoid specific agreement over reparations or dismemberment. Stalin wanted to have a specific dismemberment clause in the German surrender terms. He was opposed by Churchill and circumvented by Roosevelt, who was against such a clause but wanted Soviet help against Japan after victory was achieved in Europe. The only agreement reached was that the Allies would undertake the "complete disarmament, demilitarization and the dismemberment of Germany as they deem requisite for future peace and security." In other words, each ally could interpret the clause as it wished once Germany was defeated. An Allied Control Council agreed to at Yalta in order to provide and implement uniform policies throughout the separate zones of occupation proved to be ineffective.

When the topic of discussion at Yalta switched to reparations, the impasse between the Soviet and Anglo-American views was even more readily discernible. Stalin wanted to set specific reparation sums; Churchill and Roosevelt opposed the idea. Roosevelt maintained that no precise amounts could be agreed on until after the war, when it could be determined how much Germany could pay. Churchill agreed with Roosevelt that no specific sums could be decided and that no specific percentage of total reparations for the Soviet Union could be set. Ultimately, it was decided at Yalta to instruct a Reparations Commission, to be set up in Moscow, that a total reparations bill of $20 billion—of which 50 percent should go to the Soviet Union—should serve as a basis for discussion after the war. Underlying the practical obstacles to reaching specific reparations figures was the Anglo-American desire not to weaken Germany to the extent that Central Europe would be easy prey to Soviet expansion into the heart of Europe. Immediately after the Yalta Conference, Churchill said he wanted to postpone the question of "dismembering Germany until my doubts about Russian intentions have been cleared away."

Equally indecisive were the discussions concerning Germany's postwar borders. At Moscow in October 1944, Churchill had acceded to the Soviet

Winston Churchill, Harry Truman, and Joseph Stalin shake hands after a meeting in the prime minister's residence at Potsdam in July 1945. (Camera Press—Globe Photos)

desire to internationalize the Saar and Ruhr areas. Now, more concerned about Moscow's intentions, he sought to delay any agreements that would be binding after the war. Concerning Germany's eastern borders, the most the conference could agree on was that Poland had the right to expand north and west but that the final borders should not be established until a postwar peace conference was held. Stalin was willing to accept postponement of the Polish-German border issue since he knew his armies would control that territory at the war's end. Moreover, the division of Germany into occupation zones, agreed to at Quebec by Churchill and Roosevelt and at Yalta by the Big Three, put Eastern Germany, and thus the Polish-German border area, under Soviet jurisdiction.

Since no major postwar peace conference was held because of the animosity among the Allies, both Germany's borders and the reparations issue were finally determined by the occupation zones set up at Yalta and confirmed at the Potsdam Conference in July 1945. Fears that the United States would not keep its troops in Europe for long led Churchill to demand and obtain a zone of occupation for France in order to counter the Soviet presence in Europe. At Potsdam the Big Three agreed to permit each occupying power to remove German property from its own zone but not so much as to jeopardize a tolerable German standard of living. In addition, the Soviet Union was to get 25 percent of the dismantled industrial equipment from the Western zones, since most German industry was located there, in exchange for food and raw materials from the Soviet zone. The conference participants also agreed to establish the Polish-German border along the Oder and western Neisse rivers, thus moving Poland two hundred miles to the west, and permit the Soviet Union to retain the areas annexed in 1939. Little else was achieved at Potsdam owing to the growing intransigence between Stalin and Western leaders.

President Harry Truman, who had replaced Roosevelt at the conference table, was emboldened by America's explosion of the first atomic bomb in July 1945 and angry at what he considered to be Soviet betrayal of the Yalta agreements over Eastern Europe. Churchill was equally convinced that this new atomic weapon gave the West irresistible power. But the bomb never became as significant a factor in East-West negotiations as Churchill or Truman expected. Stalin was well aware that the United States would have few atomic bombs and would permit their use against the Soviet Union only under the most extraordinary provocation. He told a United Press correspondent, "Atom bombs are designed to scare those with weak nerves, but they cannot decide wars because there are not enough of them." Although the bomb was used only as a threat in diplomatic negotiations, its existence did significantly inhibit the actions of both East and West because of its destructive potential. As we shall see, it was instrumental in restraining both the Soviet Union and the West during the Berlin crisis of 1948–1949.

Despite these growing differences over Germany, Truman still hoped to resolve East-West differences by establishing a personal relationship with Stalin in late 1945. John Gaddis's recent book, *The Long Peace*, has established that Britain and France were much more distrustful of Soviet actions than was the United States. Truman opposed setting up an American sphere of influence in Europe before 1948 even though he was constantly pressed to do so by the Europeans. But the continued Soviet resort to unilateral actions gradually led Truman to a policy of confrontation and eventually containment of "communism" by 1947–1948.

The Occupation of Germany

At the war's end, France and the Soviet Union hoped to rebuild their own economies and destroy Germany's war-making potential. To do so they immediately began to strip their zones of industrial plants and material. But the exchange of industrial equipment for food and raw materials between the Soviet and Western zones led to endless acrimony because the Soviet Union and the West put different values on those goods and arrived at different estimates of a minimum tolerable level of industrial capacity for Germany. The United States maintained that the permissible industrial capacity would have to be raised in the American zone because of the influx of refugees from the Soviet Union. The Soviets refused to ship stipulated quantities of food from their zone to the Western zones because, they maintained, insufficient industrial equipment was being sent from the Western zones. This led the Western Allies to refuse, in May 1946, to continue dismantling and shipping industrial material from their zones to the Soviet Union. Only if both sides had been completely trusting and cooperative could an amicable settlement have been reached over the exchange of goods. Great Britain and the United States, faced with severe food shortages and economic chaos in their zones, stopped sending reparations out and began bringing food in.

Soviet policy in the Soviet zone contributed to the political impasse. East German Communist party leader Walter Ulbricht, who had been in exile in Moscow since Hitler's destruction of the Communist party in Germany, returned to the Soviet zone even before the war ended. After the war the Soviet Union permitted other parties to exist, although the Communist party was clearly favored. But when local elections went against the Communists in early 1946, the Soviet Union decided to eliminate all other political parties; even the Socialist party was forced to unite with the Communists in a new Socialist Unity party (Sozialistische Einheitspartei Deutschlands or SED) in April 1946. Stalin's policy toward the Soviet zone was guided by his threefold desire to keep Germany weak, to use it to help rebuild Soviet industry, and to prevent the emergence of any groups, political or otherwise, that might challenge Soviet jurisdiction.

It was Western distrust of Soviet intentions as well as the economic misery in the Western zones that prompted the United States and Britain to change their occupation policies. Secretary of State James Byrnes's call for a revival of the German economy in September 1946 was soon followed by the fusion of the American and British zones into a single economic and administrative unit called Bizonia. France refused to merge its zone with the British and American zones at this time since it opposed any measures that might lead to a unitary and therefore more powerful German state. It was still possible in 1946, however, that some sort of amicable settlement would prevent the division of Germany. East-West opposition had not yet reached the fever pitch that marked the relationship after 1947 and prevented any diplomatic solution.

The Iron Curtain Descends

The announcement of the Truman Doctrine and the Marshall Plan, and Stalin's reactions to them, split the world into two hostile camps in 1947.

Until then, several important issues had been resolved between the superpowers. The Soviet Union withdrew its support of the Iranian Separatist movement in May 1946 when the issue was brought before the U.N. Security Council. Determined Western opposition, epitomized in Churchill's denunciation described below, apparently convinced Stalin that the attempt to incorporate northern Iran into the Soviet Union would lead to a major East-West confrontation. Moreover, the Soviet Union accepted its failure to obtain an oil concession when the Iranian Parliament refused to ratify the withdrawal agreement. The Soviets also gave up their claim for a base in the straits connecting the Black Sea to the Mediterranean when the Turkish government, bolstered by the dispatch of an American naval contingent, rejected their demands.

While these issues were being resolved according to traditional power considerations, anticommunism gained importance in the confrontations. Although Truman and his secretary of state James Byrnes remained ambivalent in their attitudes toward the Soviet Union, the British moved earlier under the influence of Foreign Secretaries Anthony Eden and Ernest Bevin toward a policy of firm opposition to Soviet aspirations. Truman's shift toward confrontation was heavily influenced by Foreign Policy Advisor George F. Kennan's famous telegram in February 1946 in which he first sketched out the theory of containment, i.e., opposition to what he depicted as ideologically driven Soviet expansionism. Then, in March 1946, at Westminster College in Fulton, Missouri, Churchill delivered a stinging attack on the Soviet Union. With Truman at his side, Churchill declared:

> A shadow has fallen upon the scenes so lately lighted by the allied victory. Nobody knows what Soviet Russia and its Communist international organization intends to do in the immediate future, or what are the limits, if any, to their expansive and proselytizing tendencies. . . . From Stettin in the Baltic to Trieste in the Adriatic, an iron curtain has descended across the continent.

He warned that many nations, including Italy and France, were imperiled by Communist parties or fifth columns that constituted "a growing challenge and peril to Christian civilization."

Concern about a worldwide Communist peril increased in 1946 as the forces of Mao Tse-tung (Zedong) gained strength in China and economic conditions deteriorated in Europe. Communist parties in France and Italy were seen as fifth columns ready to seize power when the economic collapse came. The decisive events that propelled the United States into a worldwide struggle against communism in 1947 were Communist support for the leftists in Greece and the British announcement that it could no longer afford to extend economic aid to Greece and Turkey. The fact that it was Yugoslavia that supported the Greek leftists against Stalin's wishes was either not known or was purposely misrepresented by the Truman administration, since it would be easier to secure congressional approval of aid to Greece and Turkey if Yugoslav aid to Greek rebels was depicted as an aspect of Communist expansionism.

Since the Truman administration had previously drawn up plans for economic and military aid to Greece, Truman in February 1947 asked Congress for $400 million in aid to Turkey and Greece "to support free peoples who are resisting subjugation by armed minorities or by outside pressures." Arthur Vandenberg, chairman of the Senate Foreign Relations Committee, advised Truman "to scare the hell out of the country" if he wanted congressional approval for what later would become known as the Truman Doctrine. Truman therefore stressed in his message to Congress that the aid was necessary to maintain freedom throughout the world. He did not mention the more legitimate foreign policy goal of protecting Western interests in the eastern Mediterranean because he realized that such an objective was unlikely to sway the public. Identifying as a Soviet aim the spread of communism, rather than traditional Russian imperialism, the Truman Doctrine committed the United States to a global crusade to stem that tide.

The military and economic might of the two superpowers and Truman's ideological campaign against "totalitarian communism" forced many nations to line up with one superpower or the other. A nation's support for either side was now equated with ideological commitment to the American or Soviet worldview, irrespective of its domestic politics. Congress, convinced even before Truman of the specter of Communist subversion, overwhelmingly approved $400 million of U.S. aid for Greece and Turkey. This was a turning point not only for the United States but also for Great Britain. A dominant power in 1939, Britain was now forced into dependence on the United States, for only through cooperation with the United States could Britain hope to obtain the financial aid needed to overcome its severe domestic problems and maintain its empire.

Even more alarming to Washington was what appeared to be the imminent economic and political collapse of Western Europe itself. The immediate goal was to provide for German economic recovery within a general European recovery program so that it would be acceptable in Europe and the United States. Fear that Communist parties in Italy and France would gain power in the event of economic chaos was enough to convince Americans that massive aid was necessary. The U.S. response to Europe's economic needs, unlike the Truman Doctrine, was not couched in ideological terms. As formulated by Secretary of State George Marshall and a policy planning staff directed by George F. Kennan, the Marshall Plan was, in Marshall's words, "directed not against country or doctrine, but against hunger, poverty, desperation, and chaos." But Under Secretary of State Dean Acheson, arguing that the Marshall Plan was to provide aid to "free people who are seeking to preserve their independence and democratic institutions and human freedoms against totalitarian pressures, either internal or external,'' viewed it as another tool in the battle against Soviet totalitarianism.

This European Recovery Program, the official name of the Marshall Plan, was ostensibly formulated to help all European countries, including the Soviet Union and its so-called satellites in Eastern Europe. Marshall and Kennan had opposed the sharp ideological tone of the Truman Doctrine and did not want the United States to appear to be responsible for the final division of Europe between East and West. Still, it was extremely doubtful that Marshall Plan aid would have been extended to the USSR. If Stalin rejected the program—as he did in July 1947—the onus of Europe's division would be shifted to the Soviet Union.

Stalin rejected the Marshall Plan because he thought it would increase U.S. influence in Europe, including Eastern Europe, and thereby threaten Soviet hegemony in those areas he considered essential to Soviet security. Whatever its needs, the Soviet Union would not accede to the requirement that participating countries reveal their financial needs to an all-European conference that would determine the total amount required from the United States. Furthermore, Stalin did not expect that Europe would recover and believed it better to have a weak Western Europe that posed no threat to Soviet security than a revitalized Europe under the influence of the United States. When Stalin forbade the Eastern European satellite countries to accept Marshall Plan help, he completed the division of Europe into two antagonistic parts.

The Rift Widens

Realizing that an accommodation with the United States was impossible after the Truman Doctrine and Marshall Plan, the Soviet Union launched an offensive in 1947 to bring territories it occupied more firmly under its control (see chapter 2 for details). Soviet leaders instructed Eastern European Communist parties to remove all non-Communists from their governments and all National Communists (those who would not follow Moscow's direction) from the Communist parties. Diversity within the Communist camp was no longer tolerated as it had been from 1945 to 1947 when Stalin thought there might be a resolution of East-West problems.

The Comintern (Communist International) had been set up by Lenin to promote Communist revolution throughout the world and had been disbanded during World War II to please Stalin's Western allies. In its place a new organization, the Cominform (Communist Information Bureau), was established in September 1947. The Cominform's principal aim was to pressure Communist countries into strict obedience to Moscow to prevent them from being seduced into cooperation with the West. Terming the Marshall Plan and Truman Doctrine ''an attack on the principle of national sovereignty,'' Andrei A. Zhdanov, the major Soviet delegate to the Cominform Conference, instructed Western European Communist parties to "take up the standard of defense of the national independence and sovereignty of their countries."

The Soviet Union had reversed its hands-off policy in Western Europe by instructing Communist parties in the West to "bend every effort" to defeat the Marshall Plan. In May 1947, Communists were expelled from the governments of Italy, France, and Belgium. Now Communist parties in Western Europe were instructed to discontinue their support of coalition governments and follow an obstructionist course. Beginning in November 1947, poor economic conditions in Western Europe led to numerous strikes instigated by the Communist parties, thus lending credence to earlier U.S. assertions that the Communist parties represented a threat to Western European governments.

Several events were to intervene before Europe was divided into two extremely hostile camps. The first was the Communist coup d'état in Czechoslovakia in February 1948, which brought Czechoslovakia firmly within the Soviet camp (see chapter 2). The heated reaction in the West portrayed the Czech coup as merely another step in the worldwide expansion of communism rather than a Soviet move to strengthen its control over Eastern Europe.

Although the Czech coup convinced the United States Congress to approve the Marshall Plan, it was hardly unexpected in Washington. George Kennan, the formulator of the U.S. policy of containment of communism, supports the revisionist historians who insist that the administration knew the coup was not an indication of new Soviet aggressiveness. He wrote in his memoirs that the coup "had nothing to do with any Soviet decision to launch its military forces against the West," and that Soviet action "flowed logically from the inauguration of the Marshall Plan Program, and was confidently predicted by U.S. government observers six months in advance of the event."

Nevertheless, Truman said the Czech coup proved that the Soviet Union intended to expand communism "to the remaining free nations of Europe." His response to the coup and the previously formed Cominform was to introduce a bill in Congress for universal military training and a return to conscription. Panicked British and French leaders pressed the United States for a military alliance, and the foreign ministers of Great Britain, France, Belgium, Holland, and Luxembourg signed a treaty in March 1948 establishing the Western Union for their collective defense against armed attack on any member nation. The West further held the London Six-Power Conference (excluding the Soviet Union) to discuss further integration of the Western occupation zones in Germany, which led ultimately to the first major East-West confrontation in Berlin in June 1948.

London Conference representatives announced in a communiqué of March 6, 1948, that agreement had been reached on a plan for a federal form of government and the further economic integration of the Western zones. This provoked an angry reaction from the Soviet Union. Stalin realized that successful implementation of the London communiqué would end his hopes of keeping Germany neutralized and weak. Two weeks later Soviet marshall Sokolovsky ended the charade of East-West cooperation concerning Germany by walking out of the Allied Control Council deliberations in Berlin. Next, Stalin ordered a meeting of the Second People's Congress in the Soviet zone of Germany in March to create a People's Council (later the People's Chamber of the German Democratic Republic) for the Soviet zone. He also began restricting access to Berlin on March 31, apparently in the belief that this would divide the Western powers and force a retreat from their plans. But France, now receiving Marshall Plan aid, finding no support for the plan to keep Germany dismembered and weak, and confident that the United States and Britain were going to be in Germany indefinitely because of the Soviet threat, had less reason to fear the unification of the Western zones. On June 18, 1948, France agreed to fuse its zone with Bizonia, the Anglo-American zone. Now Stalin was presented with a solid Western front.

The Berlin Blockade   When the West decided to reform Germany's currency by introducing a new deutsche mark on June 20, 1948, Stalin realized that a strong German currency under Western sponsorship would destroy the weak German currency in the Soviet zone. The Soviet Union therefore responded four days later by introducing a similar currency reform in its zone. At the same time it initiated a blockage of all land traffic into and out of Berlin, which was deep inside the Soviet zone. Stalin hoped the blockage would be a bargaining weapon to prevent the establishment of a strong German state under Western auspices since the French had not yet decided to merge its zone with the Anglo-American zones. But this plan was thwarted when the Western powers instituted an airlift that kept Berlin supplied with food, fuel, and medicines for nearly a year.

Stalin knew he had lost. Recognizing that a Soviet attack on Western aircraft would mean war, denied the bargaining leverage he had sought, and fast losing face in what appeared to be an attempt to starve 2.25 million residents of Berlin into submission, Stalin had to call off the blockade in May 1949. This first major East-West confrontation made vividly apparent the limits of Soviet power when faced with the West's air superiority and nuclear monopoly. Stalin could not use his massive land superiority against Berlin to force the West to bargain because of the West's ability to destroy Russian cities with airpower and nuclear weapons.

The New West German State   The Berlin blockade speeded up the West's plans for the establishment of a separate German state comprising the three Western zones. After the West founded the German Federal Republic on May 21, 1949, the Soviet Union responded by establishing the German Democratic Republic in October of the same year. The first

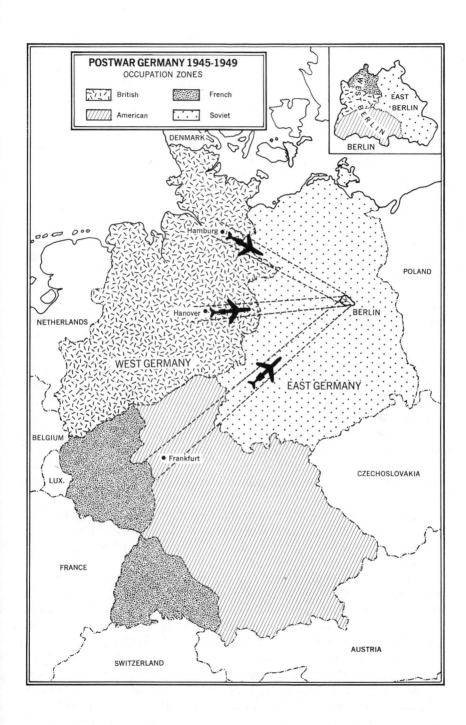

POSTWAR GERMANY 1945-1949
OCCUPATION ZONES

British
American
French
Soviet

DENMARK

Hamburg

POLAND

NETHERLANDS

Hanover

BERLIN

WEST GERMANY

EAST GERMANY

BELGIUM

LUX.

Frankfurt

CZECHOSLOVAKIA

FRANCE

AUSTRIA

SWITZERLAND

WEST BERLIN

EAST BERLIN

BERLIN

parliamentary elections in West Germany produced a Christian Democratic (CDU) majority with Konrad Adenauer as the chancellor. Having gained fame for his resistance to nazism, Adenauer was a popular choice. He also represented almost everything the West desired in a German leader: cooperation with the West; rapprochement with Germany's traditional enemy, France; a federal structure rather than the highly centralized Nazi state; and, after 1948, an active anti-Communist posture.

The United States distrusted the other major German party, the Social Democrats (SPD). SPD leader Kurt Schumacher's call for the nationalization of industry and banks, combined with the growing Western fear of the Soviet Union, had prompted active Western support for the CDU prior to the Berlin crisis. Although the CDU had a slim seven-seat advantage over the SPD in the legislature, Adenauer put together a coalition with the Free Democratic party (FDP) that excluded the SPD from any role in the government.

U.S. Military Might in Europe   The Berlin crisis provided a powerful stimulus for the integration of Western Europe into a military alliance dominated by the United States. Negotiations began in July 1948 after the U.S. Congress dropped the traditional American opposition to alliances with foreign powers. In April 1949, eleven European countries joined with the United States in forming the North Atlantic Treaty Organization (NATO). Thus began the return of American military might in Western Europe and the division of Europe into two armed camps.

Military cooperation among Western countries seemed even more imperative in 1949, when the Soviet Union developed its own nuclear capability. Western Europe was now more than ever economically and militarily dependent upon the United States. Economic aid from the United States was often tied to military and political cooperation (see chapter 3). Western European nations were made aware that the reduction of Communist influence in their governments was necessary if they were to achieve economic recovery.

Western Europe now moved toward integration under the auspices and encouragement of the United States. Containment of the Soviet Union became official U.S. policy. One way to achieve this goal was to restore Europe's economic vitality and integrate it further in a Western economic and military bloc. Sixteen nations of Western Europe established the Organization for European Economic Cooperation (OEEC) to dispense American aid. At the same time, the United States allocated $5.3 billion to meet the needs of OEEC members in the first year of the Marshall Plan. The economic recovery of Western Europe had begun.

By 1949, the iron curtain that Churchill had described in 1946 had become a reality. With the buildup of American strength there, a power equilibrium had been restored in Europe that could not be disrupted short of all-out war. Since both sides now portrayed the East-West conflict as an ideological struggle, there was little possibility of resolving conflicts

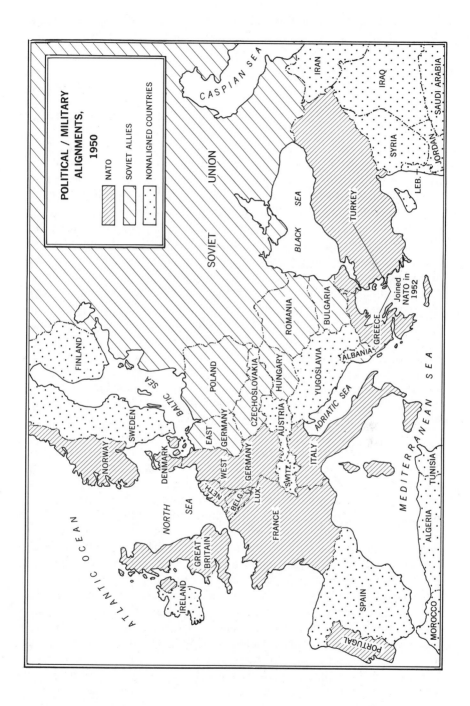

POLITICAL / MILITARY ALIGNMENTS, 1950

NATO

SOVIET ALLIES

NONALIGNED COUNTRIES

through normal diplomatic procedures. Each side was now in a struggle to protect freedom, either from "Western imperialism" or from "Soviet communism," throughout the world.

The Korean Conflict

Because of the global nature of the Cold War and Europe's increasing dependence on the United States, events in the Far East soon had a direct impact on Europe. The triumph of the Communist forces in China in 1949 was viewed in the West as another demonstration of the threat of world-wide Communist expansion. When the Soviet-backed Communist regime in North Korea attacked the American-supported South Korean government in June 1950, the United States immediately assumed that the Soviet Union was behind it. President Truman charged, "The attack upon the Republic of Korea makes it plain beyond all doubt that the international communist movement is prepared to use armed invasion to conquer independent nations." While it appears likely that the North Korean decision to invade stemmed largely from local causes, it is probable that the invasion would not have been launched without Stalin's permission since the Soviet Union trained and supplied the North Korean military.

One possible explanation for the invasion is offered by revisionists and supported by Kennan. They suggest that the peace treaty being negotiated between the United States and Japan, providing for American naval and air bases in Japan, might have persuaded Moscow to establish a Communist government throughout Korea before the United States could bring a preponderance of power to the area.

Public statements by American leaders had led the North Koreans and the Soviet Union to believe that Korea was not essential to America's "perimeter of defense" in Asia, leading them to expect an easy victory. But the specter of Communist regimes dominating the entire Asian continent and threatening a disarmed Japan brought a sudden reversal of U.S. policy in Asia. Moreover, the United States realized that its desertion of South Korea after the North Korean attack would bring into question American commitments throughout the world. The United States, envisaging a worldwide struggle against communism, committed itself to a policy of containment in Asia as well as in Europe.

Faced with the task of mobilizing sufficient forces to both repel the North Korean invasion and maintain Western strength in Europe, the United States began a substantial buildup of Western military strength that included a call for the rearmament of West Germany. In September 1950, Great Britain agreed to the recreation of an army for the German Federal Republic. Stalin's view that Western hostility toward the Soviet Union knew no bounds was borne out, in his own mind, by the call to rearm this traditional foe. Kennan's warning to the United States government that rearmament would divide Germany permanently into Soviet

2 The Cold War and the Sovietization of Eastern Europe

This war is not as in the past; whoever occupies a territory also imposes his own social system. Everyone imposes his own system as far as his army can reach. It cannot be otherwise.

Joseph Stalin, in *Conversations with Stalin* by Milovan Djilas

The modern history of Eastern Europe is a history of encirclement by more powerful empires and nations. Before and during the eighteenth century, this area fell victim to the expansionist drives of the Russian, Prussian, Austrian, and Ottoman empires. Although Greece, Romania, Serbia, and Bulgaria gained independence in the nineteenth century, theirs was a perilous existence that resulted from the compromises and machinations of the major powers. Since no major power gained a decided military advantage until after World War II, conflicts in Eastern Europe tended to be limited.

World War I came about partially as a result of a changed power relationship at the turn of the century. The alliance of Germany and Austria-Hungary, combined with the military weakness of the Ottoman Empire, convinced the first two that they could dominate the Balkans and reduce or eliminate Russian influence in Eastern Europe. Their failure in World War I led to the collapse of the German, Ottoman, Austro-Hungarian, and Russian empires and produced a power vacuum in East-Central Europe that permitted the establishment of independent states throughout Eastern Europe. The newly established Soviet Union, weakened by internal civil war, could not take advantage of the defeat of its former rivals to gain supremacy in East-Central Europe.

The revival of German and Soviet military power in the 1930s again placed Eastern Europe at the mercy of its stronger neighbors. With the other great powers uninterested in or incapable of intervening, the fate of Eastern Europe now rested in the hands of Hitler and Stalin. In 1939, the two states briefly resumed the collaborationist policy that had characterized their relationship to Eastern Europe in the eighteenth and nineteenth centuries.

Confronted with Western indifference to the threat of German expansion, made clear in Stalin's mind by the acquiescence of Britain and France to the dismemberment of Czechoslovakia at Munich in 1938, Russia chose to join with Hitler in the Nazi-Soviet Pact of 1939. This agreement gave Stalin the opportunity to regain much of the territory lost during World War I and the Russian Civil War in Eastern Europe—the Baltic states, Bessarabia, and some Polish and Finnish territory.

Again, war was to have momentous consequences for Eastern Europe. The defeat of Germany and the exhaustion of France and Great Britain in World War II left a power vacuum in East-Central Europe that was filled immediately by Soviet armies. Roosevelt had informed Stalin at Yalta that American forces would be withdrawn from Europe after the war, and Churchill had acquiesced to Soviet domination of much of Eastern Europe in 1944, leading Stalin to expect that Soviet hegemony in Eastern Europe would not be contested.

Although the West objected to Soviet actions in Eastern Europe, Soviet military might was overwhelming. Almost all the Eastern European states reached whatever terms they could with Stalin. In 1944–1945 the terms rested on several major factors: the role those states played in the German invasion of the Soviet Union, the Soviet assessment of the area's strategic importance, Stalin's relationship with the former leaders of the various states, local conditions, the ability and willingness of the states to oppose Soviet power, and Stalin's objectives in Eastern Europe.

Soviet Goals in Eastern Europe

As summarized in chapter 1, Stalin wanted Eastern Europe to be a buffer zone between the Soviet Union and German territory. Some have criticized this goal as an expression of paranoia, considering the condition of Germany and the Soviet Union at the end of the war. But only Stalin was aware of the severe Soviet economic weaknesses in 1945, and he was distrustful of the West's intentions in Germany. By controlling Eastern Europe, he could prevent those states from participating in an attack or again becoming a staging area for an attack on the Soviet Union.

In addition, Eastern Europe became an indispensable aid to Soviet economic development, an area to be exploited. States that fought against the Soviet Union were forced to pay reparations. The entire area was integrated in the Soviet economic system as a source of cheap goods, especially raw materials. Countries were forced to sell goods to the Soviet Union at low prices to keep Soviet manufacturing costs low and profits high. Many Eastern European companies were compelled to include the Soviet Union as a partner in their operations. Strict adherence to these conditions was equated with political orthodoxy. Charges of political deviation were hurled at those attempting economic independence as well as at those guilty of ideological heresies.

In the immediate postwar years, the Soviet Union appeared to permit considerable political autonomy in some East European states as long as they seemed to pose no threat to Soviet security or Soviet leadership among Communist nations and as long as they continued to cooperate economically. Coalition governments were permitted for a time in countries such as Hungary and Czechoslovakia. But the recent arguments of Charles Gati indicate that Hungarian autonomy may have been a "Polish trade-off" to reduce resistence from the West while Stalin eliminated all opposition in Poland. By categorizing the East European states as "people's democracies," a form of state between Western bourgeois democracy and the "mature" socialism of the Soviet Union, Stalin could justify their subordination to the Soviet Union on ideological grounds while maintaining the appearance of a democratic multiparty system. Also, any move toward a Western-style government or any failure to cooperate economically with the Soviet Union could be opposed on ideological grounds.

Stalin opposed precipitate Communist takeovers in areas other than Poland and East Germany for several reasons: First, he did not want to provoke the Western powers to intervene in Eastern Europe. Second, he wanted to avoid violent resistance to communism in Eastern Europe since it would necessitate large Soviet forces to contain the unrest and it would also destroy the Soviet argument that the Communist parties in Eastern Europe were popular. Third, he still hoped for financial aid from the United States. Stalin believed a loan to the Soviet Union might actually help the United States by putting former soldiers to work in order to meet the Soviet demand for goods; therefore, he thought that the United States might supply the desperately needed finances. Finally, Stalin believed it was still possible to resolve the conflict with the West over German reparations and thereby gain additional funds.

As to Stalin's long-term goals in Eastern Europe, a major difference of opinion exists between orthodox and revisionist writers. The orthodox view, represented by such studies as Hugh Seton-Watson's *The East European Revolution*, discerns a three-stage pattern of conquest by Soviet-backed Communist parties. The conquest begins with a coalition government including non-Communist representatives, then proceeds to a second-stage persecution of non-Communist groups and Communist domination of the important state offices such as the premierships and interior ministries. The final stage is the elimination of all non-Communists from the governments and the inclusion of the state within a monolithic Communist bloc headed by the Soviet Union.

The revisionists reject this concept and insist that Stalin would have permitted the coalition governments to continue indefinitely and would have relaxed Soviet control in Eastern Europe if Western hostility and the Cold War had not forced him to clamp down in 1948.

Both views overlook several important factors: The orthodox view presents an overly deterministic Stalinist blueprint for Soviet domination of Eastern Europe and underestimates the impact of the Cold War on Stalin. The revisionists, in turn, fail to understand Stalin's goal of a monolithic Communist area of control in which Soviet objectives prevail. In cases such as Czechoslovakia, the Cold War did indeed determine the timing of the Soviet crackdown in Eastern Europe. But this does not mean that Stalin would not have acted at some other time to maintain the economic integration of the area, to halt the movement toward an independent form of national communism in the various states, or to prevent countries from endangering Soviet security by becoming too closely associated with the West. A closer examination of Soviet actions in the different East European states will clarify these points.

Poland's Coalition Government

Where Stalin felt Soviet security was seriously threatened, as in Poland and the Soviet zone of Germany, the coalition governments he allowed could only be described as shams. Traditional Polish-Russian enmity, reinforced in the twentieth century by the Polish attack on the Soviet Union after World War I and the hostility of interwar Polish leaders, convinced Stalin that Poland must be subordinated to Moscow.

East-West acrimony over Poland had been building during the war. Remnants of the Polish government and army had fled to France and finally to Britain after Poland was attacked first by German and then by Soviet armies in 1939. Throughout the war Stalin sought approval from the exiled Polish government in London for the incorporation of eastern Poland into the Soviet Union. Stalin felt that his claim to the territory was valid because the bulk of the population of eastern Poland was ethnically either Ukrainian or White Russian and because eastern Poland had been taken from the Soviet Union during the Russian Civil War in 1920. But the London Poles were reluctant to approve the loss of eastern Poland, which the Soviet army had conquered while Poland was in the midst of a life-or-death struggle with Germany. Furthermore, the London Poles feared that their acquiescence would cost them the support of the Polish Home Army, which adamantly opposed ceding eastern Poland. Therefore, the London Poles adhered to the position of the Polish Underground, as articulated in a February 1944 resolution rejecting the Soviet incorporation of eastern Poland and expressing their determination "to fight the new Soviet aggression." However, the same resolution accepted an extensive enlargement of Poland's western boundaries at Germany's expense. This attitude undoubtedly contributed to Stalin's decision to destroy the Polish Underground in 1944–1945.

Stalin had already been provided with a pretext for liquidating the Polish Underground by the attitude of the London Poles concerning the massacre of over 4,000 Polish officers in the Katyn Forest during the war. The London Poles called for a neutral investigation of the massacre by the

International Red Cross, which implied that they felt that Soviet rather than German forces might have been responsible. Although the Soviet Union admitted in 1988 that it had been responsible for the massacre, Stalin not only refused to accept blame but used the accusation to his advantage. Charging that the Polish government in London had "sunk so low as to enter the path of accord with the Hitlerite government," Stalin broke off relations with the London Poles in April 1943. Then, in July 1944, he announced the creation of a Polish Committee of National Liberation, composed primarily of Polish Communist functionaries and leftist intellectuals in the Soviet Union and Communists involved in the Polish Resistence in Poland, to replace the exiled Polish government.

Stalin eliminated the other major source of opposition when Soviet forces allowed the Germans to destroy the bulk of the underground Polish Home Army when it attempted to liberate Warsaw in late 1944. As Soviet troops advanced across Poland, they vanquished most of the remnants of the Polish Home Army. Thus at the end of the war, the Soviet-backed Committee of National Liberation had no opposition inside Poland and the support of the Soviet forces. On January 1, 1945, this committee designated itself the Provisional Government of Poland.

At the Yalta Conference in February 1945, the West recognized the Provisional Government with the conditions that it include a few "London Poles" and that it hold free elections soon. Stalin's response was to permit four of the London Poles to join sixteen Communists in a new government. Subsequent Western demands for a democratic government and elections met stiff Soviet resistance. Stalin judged correctly that "any freely elected government would be anti-Soviet, and that we cannot permit."

The illusion of a coalition government continued when Stalin permitted the Polish Peasant party leader Stanislaw Mikolajczyk to join the coalition. However, Stalin had no intention of letting the Peasant party become a viable political force. As the major non-Communist organization in Poland, it had been extremely popular among the predominantly peasant population in the interwar years, and Stalin knew that it could outbid the Communists for support. Communist intimidation and Mikolajczyk's own political blunders soon splintered the Peasant party and rendered it ineffective. In the January 1947 rigged parliamentary elections, the Peasant party gained a mere 27 seats compared to 392 seats for the government bloc of Communists, Socialists, dissident Peasants, and a so-called Democratic party. Mikolajczyk was dropped from the cabinet and fled the country in October 1947.

The other rival to the Communist party, the Polish Socialist Workers party (RPPS), proved equally troublesome. In 1946 the RPPS claimed correctly that they had more popular support and a larger membership than the Communists and were the leading party in the government coalition and demanded a greater role in the cabinet. But such popularity meant little in the face of opposition from Stalin and the authority welded by the Polish Communists. The RPPS leaders were summoned to Moscow twice in 1946 and were forced to cooperate with the Communist party in the January 1947 elections in return for the promise that the RPPS would be allowed to retain its separate identity. Then they were forced to purge themselves twice in early 1947, to join the Communist party in declining participation in the Marshall Plan, to purge themselves again in September 1948, and then in December 1948 to merge with the Communists in the Polish United Workers party. Since Communists filled eight of the eleven seats in the Politburo of the party, the RPPS had been rendered ineffective. Although the Cold War may have speeded up the pace of events in Poland, it is clear that Stalin would not have permitted the Socialists a separate existence for much longer. He was distrustful of their independence and their contacts with Socialist parties in Western Europe.

Romania's Coalition Government

The Romanian case was similar to that of Poland in terms of its strategic importance as well as its previous hostility toward the Soviet Union, made clear by its participation in the German invasion of Russia. Stalin's insistence on a government friendly toward the Soviet Union, which initially was supported by Churchill and Roosevelt, conflicted with the later Western demand for democratic governments and free elections in Eastern Europe. As in the Polish case, a freely elected government in Romania would have been hostile to the Soviets.

Because King Michael had gained widespread popularity when he overthrew the pro-Nazi regime of Marshal Ion Antonescu in August 1944 and declared war on Germany, Stalin had to proceed slowly so as not to cause a massive insurrection and further exacerbate East-West relations. Not only did King Michael retain his throne, but he was awarded the Soviet Order of Victory after the war.

Rightly fearing that Michael's popularity would decrease support for the Romanian Communist party, in March 1945 Stalin pressured the king to appoint a National Democratic Front Coalition, including Communist representatives. Although the Communists held only three ministries, the new government was headed by the pro-Communist leader of the Ploughman's Front, Petru Groza. The presence of Soviet occupation forces would have made it possible to enforce acceptance of a Communist government, but Stalin proceeded slowly in order to build up support for the Communist party. The Popular Front government was undoubtedly a temporary expedient to enhance Communist support and to end Western criticism.

The coalition immediately gained popular support by confiscating and redistributing all land holdings exceeding 120 acres. An election in November 1946, marked by considerable intimidation of noncoalition parties, gave the Democratic Front an overwhelming victory. Even though the Communist party held only one-sixth of the seats in Parliament, the presence of a Soviet Army of Occupation gave them considerably more authority than their numbers warranted. By the spring of 1947, the Communists began to act openly against the opposition parties. Accused of complicity with American imperialism, opposition party members were tried and sentenced to long prison terms. The popular Peasant party leaders were imprisoned and their party disbanded. King Michael had to abdicate in December 1947, and Romania became a People's Republic the following spring. Groza continued as puppet premier, with Communists heading all the other important government offices. By March 1948, the Communist party had disbanded or absorbed all other parties into the

Romanian Workers' party. Premier Gheorghe Gheorghiu-Dej assumed direction of the economy, and Ana Pauker, a Communist trained in Moscow, became foreign minister. At this point, the nationalization of industry and collectivization of agriculture began in earnest.

Soviet Relations with Bulgaria

Despite the fact that Bulgaria had been allied with Germany in World War II, it had not participated in the German attack on the Soviet Union. Instead of animosity, the Bulgarian-Russian relationship had always been marked by friendship. Owing their liberation from the Turks in the nineteenth century to czarist Russia and from the Germans in 1944 to the Soviet Union, most Bulgarians looked to their mighty northern neighbor as a benefactor. As they had built the Alexander Nevski Church in honor of czarist armies, they now constructed monuments to Soviet forces.

The Bulgarians had overthrown their pro-Fascist government as Soviet armies were marching toward Bulgaria in 1944. But the fact that Bulgaria had been a German ally provided the Soviet Union with the pretext for invading Bulgaria and establishing a Soviet-supported Fatherland Front coalition government in September 1944. The subsequent participation of the Bulgarian army in the attack on Germany removed much of the stigma of the earlier association with Germany. In contrast to his policy toward Romania and Hungary, Stalin demanded no reparations from Bulgaria.

Although the Fatherland Front did not become openly Communist dominated until 1947, the non-Communist members of the coalition had lost their effectiveness by the preceding year. At first, Communist domination of the important state offices was challenged by opposition groups and by the Peasant and Socialist parties, led by Nikola Petkov and Kosta Lulchev respectively. Encouraged by Anglo-American support, Petkov and Lulchev demanded that the Communists relinquish their control of the interior and justice ministries. Although a compromise was reached at the Allied Foreign Ministers' Conference in Moscow in December 1945, whereby two members of the opposition were to be admitted to the government, Petkov and Lulchev would not back down from their demand that the positions be ministers of the interior and of justice.

Confronted with a crisis that appeared to threaten Soviet domination, and with the Bulgarian Communist party already having worked out a compromise with Petkov and Lulchev, Stalin decided to eliminate the opposition groups. In July 1946, leadership of the Bulgarian army was transferred from a non-Communist member of the coalition to the entire cabinet, and the army was purged of possible opponents. A plebiscite in September 1946 changed Bulgaria from a kingdom to a republic and forced the abdication and exile of seven-year-old King Simeon. Once the United States ratified the Bulgarian Peace Treaty in June 1947, eliminating the Control Commission for Bulgaria and thus ending direct American participation in Bulgarian affairs, Stalin ordered the elimination of the political opposition. Petkov's Peasant Union was dissolved in August and he was arrested and, in September 1947, hanged.

Throughout this period the Communist party was led by Georgi Dimitrov, who had served as secretary-general of the Communist International headquarters in Moscow and was a close friend of Stalin. Firmly in control of the country by 1948, Dimitrov ousted all non-Communists from the government, forced the Socialist party to merge with the Communist party, instituted a Soviet-style constitution, and began the nationalization of industry and the collectivization of agriculture. Bulgaria now became the most avid supporter of Stalin's attempt to overthrow Yugoslav leader Marshal Tito. On the ground that Tito wished to incorporate Bulgaria into an enlarged Yugoslavia, all pro-Yugoslav Communists were either executed or driven from the country.

Hungary's Coalition Government

Because of Hungary's strategic importance as well as its participation in the German attack on the Soviet Union, Stalin would have desired a government completely under Soviet control. But Stalin was forced to proceed slowly because of the presence in Hungary of an Allied Control Commission, because of the Churchill-Stalin agreement to divide jurisdiction equally in Hungary, and because Stalin wished to quiet Western fears concerning his actions in Poland by a more moderate policy in Hungary. Therefore, the Provisional National Government of Democratic Hungary, set up under Soviet auspices in December 1944, was a true coalition government headed by a former member of the interwar conservative government of Admiral Miklós Horthy. Stalin did not immediately demand, as he did in the other Eastern European countries, that a Communist occupy the important cabinet post of minister of the interior. The only posts held by Communists were the ministries of trade and agriculture.

However, possession of the agriculture ministry permitted the Communist party to build its popularity in Hungary. Under the moderate Communist Imre Nagy, the agriculture ministry expropriated the large Hungarian estates and monastic lands and distributed them among 642,000 formerly landless peasants. Collectivization of the land was not begun immediately in order to gain popular support.

In November 1945, relatively free elections gave the agrarian Smallholders party 60 percent of the parliamentary seats compared to 17 percent for the Communist party. But before the election the head of the Allied Control Commission, Marshal Kliment Voroshilov, had pressured members of the coalition to agree that the Smallholders party could hold no more than half the cabinet posts in a coalition government. Apparently now fearful that this Hungarian subterfuge had gone too far, Stalin summoned Matyas Rakosi to Moscow and instructed him to undermine the Smallholders party. Two deputy premiers, one of them Rakosi, aided the new Smallholder premier, Zoltán Tildy. Tildy appointed Ferenc Nagy as prime minister in January 1946 when he was elected president of the republic. When the Communist Imre Nagy became minister of the interior in November 1945, as a result of Soviet and Communist party pressure, the Communists gained control over the police. This ministry soon passed to the more ruthless Communist Lásló Rajk, who intimidated or discredited most of the members of the Smallholders party by 1947. Power soon passed to Rakosi who, as first secretary of the Hungarian Communist party and deputy prime minister, combined Communists and Socialists into a United Workers' party in June 1948. The final step was the proclamation of a Hungarian People's Republic in 1949.

Czechoslovakia's Coalition Government

Stalin permitted Czechoslovakia a true coalition government at first, even though Communist-dominated people's committees were in control of the country when it was liberated by Soviet forces in 1945. Because of Stalin's special friendship with prewar Czech president Edvard Beneš, he permitted the exiled Czech government in London to return to Prague in May 1945. Unlike the London Poles, Beneš avoided provoking Stalin by entering into negotiations with him concerning his postwar government in Czechoslovakia and by surrendering the province of Ruthenia to the Soviet Union. Knowing that the Czech Communist party had been popular before the war, Stalin realized that a freely elected government would not necessarily be hostile toward the Soviet Union. It appears that Stalin had no predetermined plan for the eventual communization of Czechoslovakia and that he wished to use it, as he did Hungary, to divert attention from his policies in Poland.

A free election in May 1946 gave the Communist party 38 percent of the vote, the Socialist party 18 percent, and the Peasant party 16 percent. Communist party leader Clement Gottwald, who became premier of the United Front government, believed that the Czech Communist party could dominate the country without intimidating or persecuting the other parties. Until 1947, the Czech Parliament held free and open debate and the press had considerable freedom to criticize the government. But Communist tactics changed in 1947 when Marshall Plan aid was offered and when decreasing popular support for the Communist party, as revealed in opinion polls and in the rapid growth of other parties, appeared to threaten Communist domination of the government. Stalin was also angered by the May 1947 exclusion of the Communists from coalition governments in Italy and France.

Czech acceptance (including the Communists) of an invitation to a preliminary conference on the Marshall Plan in July 1947 marked the begin-

A battle-scarred wall in Budapest, Hungary, covered with Communist campaign posters for the 1948 election. A smiling peasant (top) promises more bread and a better life if the Communists are elected. Communist deputy premier Matyas Rakosi is pictured at bottom left. The other poster shows the three great national heroes, Rákóczi, Kossuth, and Petofi. (United Press International Photo)

ning of the end for the coalition government. Stalin forbade the Czechs to attend the conference and denounced the Czech Communists at the Cominform meeting in September 1947 for their moderation. Stalin feared that the Czechs would develop a Western-style parliamentary government and be drawn into the U.S. orbit if the country accepted Marshall Plan aid. Such an eventuality obviously would threaten Soviet security. The alignment of Czechoslovakia with the West would divide Soviet Eastern Europe into two parts and give the West a common border with the Soviet Union. The establishment of a social democratic government, which Stalin thought would be inevitable, would also set a dangerous precedent for other East European countries.

By early 1948, Gottwald, under pressure from Stalin, had established one-party control of Czechoslovakia and silenced all possible opponents. Jan Masaryk, the foreign minister and son of the first president of Czechoslovakia, was killed in a suspicious fall from a government building window. President Beneš resigned in June 1948, since he found it impossible to approve the new Communist-inspired constitution. While the timing of the Soviet crackdown in Czechoslovakia was partially a result of Cold War events, the weakening of the Czech Communists internally was also a major contributing factor.

The Revolt of the First Secretaries

By 1947, Stalin was faced with a more direct problem than Western animosity: nationalism, or what the Communists termed *national deviation*. Immediately after the war, all Eastern European Communist parties contained members extremely loyal to Moscow, usually referred to as Muscovites, who had spent considerable time in the Soviet Union. But the parties' memberships also included Communists whose first loyalty was to their native lands and who were influenced less by the Soviet Union. Thus the parties were split between those who envisioned their parties as part of a monolithic Communist world and those who placed their own countries above any international or ideological considerations. One of the leading Nationalists, Władysław Gomułka of Poland, sought to enhance his party's following by identifying it with national goals. He avoided terror tactics, refused to alienate the peasantry through premature collectivization, and associated the party with Polish nationalism. Explaining the Polish rejection of collectivization, he said, "Our democracy is not similar to Soviet democracy, just as our society's structure is not the same as the Soviet structure." This stance of Nationalist leaders was termed by one expert the "revolt of the first secretaries" of the Eastern European Communist parties.

The most serious first-secretary challenge to Stalin came from Marshal Tito of Yugoslavia, who Stalin feared might set up a Yugoslav-dominated federation of Balkan states that would result in two centers of Communist authority. Since Tito had led the Communist Underground Resistance in Yugoslavia that had helped defeat the Nazi forces before Soviet troops arrived, Stalin could not dominate Tito as he did other Communist leaders. Tito told Western correspondents in June 1947 that the Balkan states should form a "strong monolithic entity." After several visits with Bulgarian leader Dimitrov, Tito claimed in November 1947 that "the cooperation was so close that the question of federation will be a mere formality." Tito also threatened to incorporate the tiny country of Albania into a greater Yugoslavia. Only strong Soviet support for Tito's opponents in Albania combined with a national revulsion against Yugoslavian encroachments permitted the Albanians to maintain their independence. Moreover, because of Tito's support for Communist revolutions throughout the world, Stalin feared that ideological leadership of the Communist world would shift to Tito.

While Stalin had been engaged during and after the war in political horse-trading over Eastern Europe, Greece, and Trieste, Tito had been busy promoting the worldwide Communist movement by aiding the leftist forces in Greece. Tito was unwilling to accept the united front government in Yugoslavia desired by Stalin and the Western Allies. Not only did he establish a one-party dictatorship but by prematurely proclaiming Yugoslavia a people's democracy he appeared to place Yugoslavia ahead of the Soviet Union in the transition to a true Communist society. Added to Tito's challenge to Soviet primacy in the Communist world was the distant challenge of Mao Tse-tung's successful Communist movement in China. Stalin had withheld aid from Mao because he was afraid of a strong rival Communist movement.

The People's Democracies

In order to establish Soviet supremacy in the Communist world, Stalin launched a concerted offensive that continued from 1948 until his death in 1953. He first sought to deter the West from any further involvement in Eastern European affairs by making plain the Soviet Union's determination to defend its interests. The Soviet blockage of all land-access routes to Berlin on April 7, 1948 (see chapter 1), was the opening salvo in this offensive. To further occupy the West, he ordered Communist parties everywhere to foment unrest and governmental instability. However, the rapid economic recovery of Western Europe as a result of Marshall Plan aid prevented any serious economic-political problems in the West.

It was to Eastern Europe that Stalin directed most of his efforts. He began by setting up so-called people's democracies modeled on the Soviet Union in each country. All coalition governments were to be replaced by one-party dictatorships. All non-Communists, such as Edvard Beneš in Czechoslovakia, were to be excluded from the governments.

The parties were now forced to model their constitutions on that of the Soviet Union and to stress rapid industrialization and the collectivization of agriculture. Countries such as Poland that had spurned collectivization were now compelled to begin it. All Eastern European countries adopted economic planning, usually five-year plans that were coordinated with the Soviet Five-Year Plan.

Although forced industrialization promoted rapid economic growth, it generated enormous problems. As heavy industry and armaments were stressed, the production of agricultural machinery declined. The resultant drop in agricultural output left the countries short of food. As for the cities, the growth of industry brought with it a characteristic shift in population to the urban centers, which resulted in overcrowding, housing shortages, and inadequate services for the population.

Soviet-Yugoslav Split

Central to the effort to reestablish Soviet supremacy in the Communist world was a stepped-up campaign to discredit and bring down Tito's government. When Stalin founded the Cominform in September of 1947, he established its headquarters in Belgrade partly in order to intimidate and spy on Tito and undermine his support within the Yugoslav Communist party.

Tito was accused of being anti-Soviet because of his failure to accept Moscow directives on industrial and agricultural policies. Stalin expected that his campaign would soon bring Tito to his knees, for he told Nikita Khrushchev, "I will shake my little finger—and there will be no more Tito, he will fall." But with Tito, Stalin was to experience a foretaste of that national communism that was to weaken the Soviet Empire severely in the 1950s and 1960s. Primarily because of the national issue, Yugoslav Communist party members remained loyal to Tito. Unable to create divisions within the Yugoslav Communist party or to make Tito recant, Stalin had the Cominform expel Yugoslavia in 1948.

Stalin expected that the separation from Eastern European economic affairs would spell disaster for the Yugoslav economy. The Council for Mutual Economic Assistance, or Comecon, had been formed in January 1949 in part to carry out the economic embargo against Tito. When it excluded Yugoslavia from East European trade, Tito again proved his resourcefulness by opening up trade ties with the West and by obtaining an American loan that helped Yugoslavia through a period of acute economic peril.

An important aspect of the split between the Soviet Union and Yugoslavia was the Soviet determination to keep its satellites dependent on it for manufactured goods and to make them serve as reservoirs of raw materials for Soviet factories. Soviet attempts to postpone Yugoslav industrial development exasperated Yugoslav leaders, who felt that they had been extremely cooperative with the Soviet bloc countries. By 1947, Yugoslav trade with the Soviet bloc had increased to 52 percent of imports and 49 percent of exports. However, as the Yugoslavs pointed out, the bulk of the exports were raw materials, whereas the imports were primarily higher priced manufactured goods.

The Yugoslavs had also dutifully adopted the Stalinist economic model of centralization, nationalization of all industry, and emphasis on heavy industry. Soviet leaders, fearing that Yugoslavia might become a better example of a Socialist society than the Soviet Union, complained about their uncritical acceptance of the Soviet model.

Expulsion from the Cominform and the trade embargo by all Soviet bloc countries had serious consequences for Yugoslavia. By 1949, a year after the expulsion, Yugoslavia's imports from the Soviet bloc had declined to 3.2 percent and its exports to 7.7 percent of its foreign trade. Since Yugoslavia had been actively anti-Western, supporting the Greek Communists and adopting a belligerent attitude toward the United States, ostracism from the Soviet bloc left it balanced precariously between East and West. The Yugoslavs were too Marxist to identify closely with or to depend on the West, yet they could not return to close cooperation with the Soviet bloc. They were therefore forced to alter their practices in order to convince their critics that they were ideologically purer than the Soviet Union.

Attempting to prove that it was not Yugoslavia but the Soviet Union that was following a deviationist course, the Yugoslavs attacked the Soviet bureaucracy as a serious obstacle between the government and the people. To reduce the power of the central bureaucracy, Yugoslavia gave local party officials more authority in 1952. The party, renamed the League of Communists, was no longer the sole authority at the local level. Despite the retention of most decision making in Belgrade, the government increased the authority of local agencies. The alienation of the people was furthered, the Yugoslavs maintained, by Soviet state capitalism that deprived the worker of a share in the management of the Socialist economy. According to Yugoslav propaganda, the Eastern European states had been placed in a position of dependence similar to that of the Soviet people.

To reduce their bureaucracy, the Yugoslavs began a policy of decentralization through workers' councils and communes. Decision making was increasingly assumed by local communes and the workers' councils in industry after 1950. The workers' councils became Tito's primary ideological weapon against the Soviet Union. Even though they did not give workers total control of the factories—power was shared with the Communist party and the local commune—they gave workers a greater voice in the management of their factories than was the case anywhere else in

Among the stipulations of the United States' agreement to supply Yugoslavia with imports and foreign aid during the Soviet economic blockade was that U.S. observer teams be permitted to verify that food was being equitably distributed. Here, two U.S. army jeeps pass through Yugoslav Customs en route to a food distribution center. (Pictorial Parade)

the world. Workers not only helped choose their factory managers but also helped choose and often served on the managing board of their enterprise. Needless to say, the managing board was made up primarily of Communist party members since they were usually the most activist of the workers.

The effectiveness of a factory was no longer to be determined by its achievement of production quotas set by the central government but by capitalistic laws of supply and demand and profit. The Yugoslavs termed it a Socialist market economy. Factories now competed against one another for the domestic market as well as for foreign sales. As the communes and workers' councils gained more jurisdiction, the central government would presumably wither away. Although it took years to institute the changes, Yugoslavia's impact on the Soviet satellites became damaging to Soviet bloc unity in the 1950s. With Titoism there were now two roads to socialism.

Placed between two antagonistic powers and in need of development funds, Yugoslavia had no choice but to turn to the West. United States financing helped Yugoslavia through the extremely difficult years (1949 to 1952) of the economic blockade by the Soviet bloc. Tito then abandoned his stance as an advocate of world revolution and began to advocate peaceful coexistence with the West.

Imports and foreign aid from the United States comprised 34 percent of Yugoslavia's total imports, reflecting the U.S. conviction that this was an excellent opportunity to weaken the Soviet bloc. Thus the collapse that the Soviet Union had expected was averted. Yugoslav leaders had no idea in 1948 that their country would become a model for many developing countries as well as the primary model of national communism in Eastern Europe.

National Deviationism Ends

Although Tito was indomitable, Stalin was able to eliminate national deviationism elsewhere in Eastern Europe. Native Communists were ostracized one after another, and many were executed after being humiliated in show trials: Lucretiu Patrascanu in Romania, Koce Xoxi in Albania, László Rajk in Hungary, Traicho Kostov in Bulgaria, and Vladimir Clementis and Rudolf Slanski in Czechoslovakia were discredited and liquidated. Some of the more powerful leaders, such as Poland's Gomułka, were dismissed from their posts and arrested but never executed.

Even Muscovites who stepped out of line were forced to recant: after proclaiming in 1948 that Communist countries should develop independently, Bulgarian Communist party leader Dimitrov was forced to surrender to Stalinist ideological conformity in 1949. By 1950, the Soviet Union had an iron grasp on the countries of Eastern Europe. In the Soviet Union and outside it, Stalin's opponents were afraid to take a stand against him. Soviet agents made sure that no deviationism occurred. But neither Stalin nor his agents could prevent mass discontent and unrest. Labor riots in Czechoslovakia in June 1953, followed a week later by a youth rising in East Germany precipitated by the lowered standard of living and shortage of food brought about by forced collectivization and economic emphasis on heavy industry, indicated that discontent may have been suppressed but not eliminated.

One institution that was battered but not broken by the Stalinist onslaught was the Catholic church. In Poland the church even gained support due to the Poles' identification of the church with Polish nationalism. Some Catholic church officials, such as the Hungarian cardinal Mindszenty, were forced to endure show trials and imprisonment; others, such as the Polish cardinal Wyszynski, were imprisoned without trial. Monastic orders were dissolved, except in Poland, and most religious schools disbanded.

The motives behind Soviet policy during this period were a mixture of practical and ideological considerations. The practical necessity, in Soviet eyes, to strengthen Soviet defenses against Western hostility was one such consideration. A second was Stalin's personal desire for total control within an Eastern European sphere of influence and for ideological conformity among Communist parties. For the most part, Soviet moves to increase its authority in Eastern Europe and to enhance the position of the East European Communist parties began before the announcement of the Truman Doctrine and the Marshall Plan. In the case of Yugoslavia, Stalin felt that any surrender to Yugoslav Communist party independence would weaken Soviet authority throughout Eastern Europe. Khrushchev's policy of diversity in Eastern Europe and the resultant revolution in Hungary in 1956 (see chapter 7) were precisely what Stalin thought would happen if Soviet control was relaxed. Only in the case of Czechoslovakia does the Soviet-Western hostility appear to have been a decisive event in the Soviet crackdown.

FURTHER READING

Two outstanding recent studies of events in Eastern Europe after the war are Joseph Rothschild, *Return to Diversity: A Political History of East Central Europe since World War II* (1989), and J. F. Brown, *Eastern Europe and Communist Rule* (1988). Both authors perceive that events in Eastern Europe did not result from any preconceived blueprint but from a combination of Stalinist goals and local conditions. For a more opinionated description of Soviet policies in Eastern Europe, see Zbigniew Brzezinski, *The Soviet Bloc, Unity and Conflict* (1960, rev. ed. 1967). Brzezinski rejects the revisionist argument that the imposition of Stalinist conformity in Eastern Europe came about because of the Cold War. Ghita Ionescu's *The Break-up of the Soviet Empire in Eastern Europe* (1965) is a valuable early analysis of the establishment and "break-up" of the Soviet bloc. Joseph Rothschild's earlier work, *Communist Eastern Europe* (1964), found that the enforcement of Soviet primacy in Eastern Europe was a result, first and foremost, of Stalin's desire to maintain a monolithic Communist bloc subservient to the Soviet Union. Hugh Seton-Watson, in *The East European Revolution* (1950, rev. ed. 1957), takes the position that Stalin and the East European Communist parties had a preconceived plan to communize Eastern Europe. McCagg and Mastny's studies, cited in the Further Reading section of chapter 1, contend that Soviet policy was primarily an outgrowth of Soviet internal policy rather than the Cold War.

The most comprehensive study of Stalin is Adam B. Ulam's *Stalin: The Man and His Era* (1973). Ulam sees the socialization of Eastern Europe as a result of Stalin's paranoia and believes that the Cold War had only a limited impact on Soviet policy. Isaac Deutscher's *Stalin* (1961) remains an important study of the Soviet leader. In the absence of Soviet documentation, Milovan Djilas's *Conversations with Stalin* (1962) and Nikita Khrushchev's *Khrushchev Remembers* (1970) are two of the few sources containing statements by Stalin as to his motives and policies. Roy Medvedev's anti-Stalinist, pro-Leninist *Let History Judge* (1971) and *On Stalin and Stalinism* (1979) provide further insights into Stalin's policies by revealing information that was not available to Western scholars. For more works on Soviet foreign policy, see the bibliographies following chapters 1 and 7.

The Soviet-Yugoslav split is described in Robert Bass and Elizabeth Marbury, eds., *The Soviet-Yugoslav Controversy, 1948–1958: A Documentary Record* (1959). Vladimir Dedijer, in *Tito* (1953) and *The Battle Stalin Lost* (1971), provides a personal account of the Soviet-Yugoslav confrontation. Dedijer points out Stalin's unwillingness to accept any potential rivals in Eastern Europe. A balanced view of the controversy is presented in Adam Ulam's *Titoism and the Cominform* (1952). Important information on Tito and national communism can be found in Paul Zinner, *National Communism and Popular Revolt in Eastern Europe* (1957).

Coverage of the Communist coup in Czechoslovakia can be found in Josef Korbel, *The Communist Subversion of Czechoslovakia, 1938–1948: The Failure of Coexistence* (1959); Morton Kaplan, *The Communist Coup in Czechoslovakia* (1960); Paul Zinner, *Communist Strategy and Tactics in Czechoslovakia* (1963); and Walter Ullmann, *The United States in Prague, 1945–1948* (1978). Kaplan's and Zinner's studies are more balanced than Korbel's, which views the coup as a premeditated plan. Kaplan sees the coup as an unplanned and somewhat hasty response to the Marshall Plan and the declining strength of the Czech Communist party. Ullmann believes that U.S. failure to aid the non-Communist forces weakened them in the face of growing Communist pressure. The U.S.'s failure to comprehend Czechoslovakia's problems and to develop a consistent, long-term policy contributed to American weakness in the area.

Polish affairs can be studied in Hans Roos, *A History of Modern Poland* (1966), and Richard Hiscocks, *Poland: Bridge for the Abyss* (1963). A recent study by Richard C. Lukas, *The Strange Allies: The United States and Poland, 1941–1945* (1978), concludes that the United States sympathized with Poland's plight but gave little support to the Poles. For information on Romania, see Ghita Ionescu, *Communism in Rumania, 1944–1962* (1964), and Stephen Fischer-Galati, *The Socialist Republic of Rumania* (1969). An outstanding recent study of Hungary is Charles Gati's *Hungary and the Soviet Bloc* (1986). Also valuable for descriptions of the immediate postwar period in Hungary are Bennet Kovrig, *The Hungarian People's Republic* (1970), and Ferenc Nagy, *The Struggle Behind the Iron Curtain* (1948). Stephen Kertesz's *Between Russia and the West: Hungary and the Illusions of Peacemaking, 1945–1947* (1984) is an excellent insiders study of the immediate postwar years.

3 From Left to Right: European Politics, 1945–1948

> There were a few who simply wanted to return to the institutions of the [French] Third Republic. But, to the great majority, this *ancien régime* was doomed.
>
> Charles de Gaulle, in *De Gaulle* by Alexander Werth

When the Second World War drew to a close in Europe in May of 1945, even the victors had little to celebrate. With approximately 14 million deaths in Western and Central Europe, one-half of them civilians, and the transplanting of another 16 million during and immediately after the war, few families escaped the war's suffering. The specter of economic ruin and famine threatened much of the continent. In Great Britain, wartime debts and postwar shortages cut short the victory celebrations. In France, the destruction of large areas of the northeast as well as chaos in internal social and political affairs boded ill for the nation's future. For the defeated, Germany and Italy, the future seemed even bleaker. In Germany the survivors would have to live with widespread destruction, famine, and an economy that had ground to a halt. Germany also had to absorb around 16 million ethnic Germans who had fled or were driven out of Eastern Europe. Countries that had been caught between the major belligerents, such as Belgium and Holland, had also suffered severely from the war.

Before Europe could begin to put the pieces together again, political life had to be restored. In Germany and Italy this meant monumental changes. New constitutions had to be written and new leaders had to be found.

The immediate problem was to find individuals capable of establishing democratic governments who had not been associated with previous regimes. Not uncommonly, this search led the occupying powers and European leaders to those who had been on the left of the political spectrum in the prewar years. The popularity of parties on the left, Communists and Socialists, resulted from their wartime opposition to fascism. After the German attack on the Soviet Union in 1941, Communists had played a major role in the various Resistance movements.

Parties on the right had little support in the immediate postwar period. The extreme right had been compromised by its prewar association with fascism and the Conservative parties by their association with depression and economic want during the years between the two world wars. Few people still favored the Conservatives' economic liberalism with its laissez-faire economic philosophy.

Widespread support for economic planning and the nationalization of industry had developed during the war. Only by such measures, many thought, could the economic experiences of the interwar period be avoided. Communist and Socialist parties cooperated in coalition governments in most European countries in the period immediately after the war. But by 1948, on the Continent and 1951 in England, parties of the center and right—usually Christian Democratic parties—had regained power in most countries, and the left was in retreat. The major reasons for this change were the rapid economic recovery of Europe, the adoption of the welfare state concept even by Conservative parties, and the Cold War. The right now seemed more progressive than it had been in the interwar period, and many now associated the left with Soviet expansionism.

Great Britain: The Welfare State Begins

With the only Labour party in power among major European countries, Great Britain seemed to be the country in which the most fundamental economic and social reforms would be instituted. Indeed, postwar shortages and wartime promises did compel the government to increase social services and to nationalize certain industries and utilities. During the war the Beveridge Report, introduced in the House of Commons in 1942 to boost morale, had promised all citizens a minimum income and a comprehensive system of social welfare. The report was given wide coverage by the press and accepted by the public, then it was shelved for the duration of the war.

Once the war was over, questions of social welfare became the focus of public attention. An opinion poll taken during the first postwar election campaign showed that the respondents were most concerned about housing, full employment, and social security.

The election campaign reflected the primacy of social issues over foreign policy considerations. When Winston Churchill, the standard-bearer for the Conservative party, warned that a vote for the Labour party was a vote for totalitarianism, Labour countered with a comprehensive program of social welfare. Despite widespread admiration for Churchill, the voters associated the Conservative party with the prewar depression, with its soup lines and widespread unemployment. Labour, on the other hand, by filling the home ministries in the wartime National Government coalition, had gained widespread admiration and support for its mobilization of the home front.

On July 5, 1945, Churchill and the Conservatives were dealt a resounding defeat by the British public. The Labour party, with a minority of 145 votes in the House of Commons, was free to enact its program. The decisive defeat of the Conservatives indicated that during the war large sections of the middle class had become convinced that the government would have to assume responsibility for the less-privileged members of society.

Contrary to Churchill's warnings, the Labour party leadership, with its diverse social composition, proved to be reformist rather than revolutionary. Most of the leaders were interested in pragmatic short-term reforms rather than a complete revamping of the society and the economy. Clement Attlee, the new prime minister, had gained valuable experience as deputy prime minister during the war. He was hardly the flamboyant leader one might have expected from a Labour government, but his low-keyed, pragmatic style of leadership was what Britain needed to overcome its serious postwar economic and social problems.

The right wing of the Labour party was represented by the new foreign secretary Ernest Bevin, who was a part of the trade union faction of the party. The left wing was led by Sir Stafford Cripps, head of the Board of Trade and later chancellor of the exchequer, and by Aneurin ("Nye") Bevan, minister of health. Cripps was an upper-middle-class lawyer, while Bevan had been a miner in his youth.

The economic and social program enacted by the Labour party clearly shows the divisions within the party. Revolutionary minded critics described the Labour measures as the cautious revolution or half-revolution. Certainly the legislation enacted by the Labour government stopped short of being revolutionary in the eyes of the left wing of the party and among most European Socialists as it did not bring about the expected redistribution of wealth. Moreover, while the government reduced the private sector's share in the direction of the economy, it did not go as far as France or Italy in adopting a plan for long-term development (see chapter 4). Government investment and planning tended to be short-term rather than long-term.

But Labour's establishment of the welfare state and its nationalization of major industries and utilities were no small steps. The Bank of England and civil aviation were nationalized immediately; the coal and steel industries, public transportation, electricity, and gas followed. Nationalization of only one industry, iron and steel, was strongly contested by the House of Lords and the Conservative party. (The Conservatives denationalized it in 1951, only to have it renationalized in 1967 by Labour.) The Lords' opposition was overcome by the passage of an amendment to the Parliament Act of 1911, reducing the power of the Lords to delay legislation to one session. (The 1911 act had abolished the Lords' right to veto money bills passed by the Commons and permitted the Commons to pass *any* bill if it obtained Commons' approval in three successive sessions over a period of at least two years.) Some of the nationalizations, particularly of the Bank of England and of public utilities, were less than revolutionary since the government had already exercised considerable control over their activities. In addition, Labour refused to assume full responsibility for the direction of nationalized industries and instead placed them under the direction of autonomous corporations rather than government agencies, as was done in France and Italy.

The initial legislation providing for the creation of the welfare state consisted of the National Insurance Act and the National Health Service Act, both passed in 1946. The National Insurance Act set up a comprehensive social security program and nationalized medical insurance companies so that the state now subsidized the unemployed, the sick, and the aged. The National Health Service Act instituting socialized medicine faced greater opposition but was also in effect by 1948. Doctors and dentists were forced to work with the state hospitals, where the bulk of the patients were going, but they were permitted to retain a private practice. Although the system was very costly—it was the second highest governmental expenditure—it was so widely accepted by the time the Conservatives came to power in 1951 that more than 90 percent of the medical profession was cooperating with it, and there was no significant effort to repeal it.

No sooner had Labour instituted its program than it began to lose popularity. Although the welfare programs helped deplete the British Treasury, many of the economic problems were beyond Labour's control. Inherited from the interwar years and the war were a huge debt and an outdated industrial plant that made the balance of trade increasingly unfavorable.

Britain's need to import a large percentage of its foodstuffs and raw materials compelled it to export large quantities of processed goods to pay for them. Unfortunately, the loss of markets during the war and the inability to compete with more modernized foreign industries in the postwar period further reduced its exports and inflated its deficits. Britain had had to sell off many foreign investments during the war and no longer had large returns on such investments to offset the huge trade imbalance. Only with the help of loans from the United States could the government be bailed out.

Economic recovery was hampered in the postwar period by the outlay of large sums in support of foreign policy. Until U.S. president Harry

Truman's 1947 proclamation of the Truman Doctrine, which provided economic and military aid to Greece and Turkey, Britain bore the brunt of the effort against the leftist forces in the Greek Civil War. At the same time, British troops were caught up in the hostilities between the Jews and the Arabs in Palestine and between the Hindus and the Muslims in India (see chapter 6). To add to these woes, Britain spent $60 million in 1946 and another $60 million in the first quarter of 1947 to feed the Germans in its occupation zone.

To carry out these far-flung commitments, Britain still had 1.5 million soldiers in 1947. The decisions to leave India and Palestine in that year and to cut off aid to Greece and Turkey stemmed from economic necessity more than from a genuine desire to retreat from empire. Labour foreign secretary Ernest Bevin had in fact long held out against the pressure to withdraw from these areas.

Even the elements seemed to be against Britain during its financial plight. The coldest winter in sixty-six years, with snow piling twenty feet high in some areas, brought the nation to a standstill in 1946–1947. The resulting fuel shortages necessitated increased imports of fuel and at the same time cut factory output, which in turn cut exports. The government had no choice; it devalued the pound from $4.03 to $2.80. Although devaluation increased exports and stabilized the value of the pound, the move was unpopular because it increased the price of imported goods and made foreign travel more expensive. Labour's decreasing popularity became apparent when the 1950 elections reduced its lead over the Tories to a mere seventeen seats.

The issue that finally drove the Labour party from power was rearmament. It caused a battle in the party between a right wing that wanted to rearm and cooperate with the United States and a left wing that wanted to follow a neutral course and not rearm. Ernest Bevin, disillusioned by his dealings with Moscow and convinced that Britain had no choice but to cooperate with the United States, led the rearmament forces to victory. In 1951, in response to the financial demands of the Korean War, the majority of the Labour party decided to cut health care, notably dental and optical payments, and to spend more for rearmament. This shuffling of priorities was apparently done to convince the United States of the Labour government's loyalty. In response, Aneurin Bevan, the minister of health, resigned from the cabinet and was followed by a number of others from the left wing of the party. The election of October 1951, called by Attlee to increase the Labour majority, instead produced a slim Conservative victory. Labour would not return to power until 1964.

France: The Fourth Republic

The difficulties facing postwar France were even more complicated than those facing Great Britain. Not only did France have serious financial

World War II hero General Charles de Gaulle of France being welcomed by an admiring crowd at Chartres. (Robert Capa—Magnum Photos)

problems, for which it was dependent on U.S. aid, but it also was faced with more wartime destruction, social dislocation, and political turmoil. For example, the destruction of four-fifths of its railway rolling stock hampered transportation. The political division between supporters of the wartime Vichy government and members of the Resistance had no parallel in Britain. The purge of Vichy collaborators, which took thousands of lives, and the inability of the new provisional government to establish its authority outside Paris until October 1944 brought the country close to anarchy. Some Frenchmen used the occasion to carry out vendettas against personal enemies. Over 5,000 collaborators were killed by partisans before the new provisional government reestablished the legal system.

The leader of the provisional government, General Charles de Gaulle, had not been in France since June 1940, when German troops moved in. A little-known secretary of state for the army at the time of the defeat, de Gaulle was soon to become one of the most influential and controversial leaders in the world. As the organizer of the Free French movement in exile, his leadership was eventually accepted by the Underground Resistance movement in occupied France. Embarrassed by the quick defeat of France in 1940, he sought throughout his life to restore French grandeur. The Anglo-American refusal to acknowledge him as leader of the French government in exile, partially due to Roosevelt's and Churchill's personal dislike of his vain and domineering character, was a humiliating experience for him.

But Churchill and Roosevelt had to recognize his leadership after the Free French movement was established in liberated Algiers in 1943 and de Gaulle had the acceptance of the French Underground, including the Communists. Three days before the Allied invasion of Normandy on June 6, 1944, a provisional government was set up in Algiers with de Gaulle at the helm. When he returned to Paris on August 25, 1944, General Dwight D. Eisenhower permitted de Gaulle to take Paris with the Second French Armored Division, Parisians gave him an enthusiastic welcome. In two weeks he set up the French provisional government, then sent large French forces into the battle against Hitler. But stable political life could not be restored until the provisional government could establish its authority throughout the country.

Political turmoil was avoided during the provisional government period because of the cooperation of the Communists and de Gaulle. The political right was completely discredited because of its collaboration with Germany and its association with the puppet Vichy government.

The postwar cooperation of the left and de Gaulle was an outgrowth of the wartime coordination of military efforts between the Soviet Union and the Western Allies. The leaders of the Communist party, Maurice Thorez and Jacques Duclos, who were responsible for the cooperation, were both Moscow Communists and followed orders from the Kremlin. Whatever their ultimate goals, they chose initially to support a parliamentary government with de Gaulle as its leader. The Communist party cooperated with de Gaulle in disarming the Resistance forces that might have been used by the left to gain power in France. At this point, the Communists apparently hoped to come to power in France as part of a left coalition. Some have suggested that without the Cold War and the subsequent polarization of international politics, the Communists would soon have become a genuine national party with no ties to Moscow. While the party's reformist stand and anti-Soviet pronouncements in the 1960s and 1970s tend to support this view, its renewed orthodoxy in the late seventies reject it.

Equally important in promoting national harmony in the postwar period was a consensus emanating from the war and especially from the Resistance movement. A Resistance charter, accepted by Resistance leaders in March 1944, advocated major economic and social changes when peace was restored. In order to rid the country of "economic and financial feudalism," the charter called for nationalization of key industries and services, economic planning, and the establishment of economic and social democracy. Sharing with the left many Resistance ideas, de Gaulle carried out some nationalization (e.g., the coal mines, the four largest banks, civil aviation, and a few industries) and initiated economic planning.

By October 1945, sufficient order had been established to hold the first postwar election. The three parties representing the major Resistance forces—the Communists, Socialists, and *Mouvement Republicain Populaire* (MRP)—gained 461 of the 586 Assembly seats. At this point the Communists, with 26 percent of the vote, and the Socialists, with 24 percent, were still cooperating. Both wanted a new constitution that would provide a strong Assembly with the power to choose and reject a premier.

De Gaulle, seeing in a strengthened Assembly a return to the weak Third Republic form of government, hoped for a constitution with strong powers for the executive. The other major Resistance faction, the Christian Democratic MRP, also wanted a strong executive. Although asked to stay on as premier and president, de Gaulle soon realized that the Communists and Socialists who dominated the new Constituent Assembly were writing a leftist constitution that would strip him of much of his power. He was also aware of the opposition of most parties to his desire for increased military expenditures. Therefore, on January 20, 1946, de Gaulle retired from active political life for the first of three times.

The search for a new premier revealed the growing divisions in the tripartite coalition of Communists, Socialists, and MRP. The Communist party proposed a Communist-Socialist government with the Communist Thorez as premier. The Socialists, fearful of being dominated by the Communists, refused to support any premier who did not have MRP approval. The MRP, distrustful of the Communists, refused to support *any* Communist for premier. To break this deadlock, Félix Gouin, the Socialist president of the Constituent Assembly, was named to head the government. Gouin, who was an ineffective leader, was described by a centrist magazine as a "man of goodwill rather than will."

The Constituent Assembly's attempts to formulate a new constitution brought about a clash between those who wanted a strong legislature and those who wanted a powerful executive. Essentially the right (MRP, de Gaulle) wanted a strong executive in the American fashion and the left desired an all-powerful legislature. Primarily on the basis of MRP opposition, the first constitution was defeated by a national referendum in May 1946 because it did not provide for a strong executive. Another election the following month, necessitated by the defeat of the constitution, made the MRP the largest party in the tripartite coalition, and its leader, Georges Bidault, was chosen premier, replacing Gouin. When the second constitution, providing for a stronger executive and an upper house in the legislature, was accepted by a national referendum in November 1946, the Fourth French Republic came into existence. The new representative bodies, the National Assembly and the Council of the Republic, resembled the legislative bodies of the interwar period. Dissatisfied with this new constitution, one-third of the electorate abstained from the referendum. The major flaw in the new constitution centered on the selection of a premier: after being nominated by the president, a premier had to present and defend a program before the National Assembly. It proved difficult to find a premier who could gain and then maintain approval from the Assembly. Searches for new premiers produced extensive party bickering and repeated government inactivity. New governments came to power only after elaborate party negotiating to put together a coalition acceptable to the National Assembly.

In the November elections the popularity of the Communists once again made the French Communist party (PCF) the largest party in the tripartite coalition (see Table 3-1).

The selection of a new premier after the November elections, the exclusion of the Communist party from the tripartite coalition in May 1947, and the massive strike wave in November–December 1947 revealed how inextricably French domestic affairs were entangled with international affairs. As the largest party, the PCF hoped that its leader, Thorez, would become the new premier. But the absorption of the left wing of the Polish Socialists by the Communist party of Poland and the return to France of the anti-Communist Socialist leader Léon Blum from Moscow increased the distrust between the two left parties.

Blum's dislike of the Communists grew out of his association with them in the interwar Popular Front government. He felt that any Communist-dominated government would produce a leftist dictatorship and asserted, "Without socialism, democracy is imperfect; without democracy, socialism is helpless."

Without Socialist support the Communists had little chance of gaining the premiership, so in January of 1947 they agreed to accept the Socialist

Table 3-1   Seats Won in French Elections, 1945–1946

Party	October 1945	June 1945	November 1946
Communist (PCF)	161	153	183
Socialist (SFIO)	150	126	105
Christian Democratic (MRP)	150	169	167
Radical	28	32	43
Conservative	64	67	71
Other	33	36	49

Source: *Philip M. Williams,* Crisis and Compromise: Politics in the Fourth Republic, *3rd ed. (Essex, England: Longman, 1964), p. 532. Copyright Philip M. Williams, 1958, 1964. Reprinted by permission of Penguin Books Ltd.*

Paul Ramadier as the new premier. PCF efforts to keep the tripartite coalition alive were thwarted by three major crises of the Ramadier government: the Indochina War, the Cold War, and a domestic labor dispute.

The Indochina War   It was inevitable that France's colonial policy would eventually become an issue in the developing Cold War. Until 1947 the Communist party supported the government's attempt to reimpose its control over Indochina. But only six days after the enunciation of the Truman Doctrine on March 12, 1947, the PCF withdrew its support of France's Indochina policy. Up to this point, Stalin, in keeping with the spirit of Allied wartime cooperation and distrustful of any strong Communist parties outside the Soviet Union, had directed the PCF to cooperate with the other political forces. Now, clearly, the position was reversed. It appears that Stalin told the French Communists to stop supporting a colonial war.

The Cold War   At the heart of the conflict among the coalition parties was the Cold War. Before 1947 the French government had tried to adhere to a neutral position between Moscow and Washington, but the steady deterioration of relations between the two superpowers and the French need of economic aid made this policy impossible.

As late as April 1947, Bidault, now minister of foreign affairs, tried to get Soviet support for the separation of the Ruhr from Germany, French occupation of the Rhineland, integration of the Saar with France, and a decentralized German state. However, after being snubbed by Stalin and Molotov at the Moscow Conference in March–April 1947, he turned to the United States.

Accepting U.S. help meant giving up plans to strengthen France by incorporating German territory and accepting American and British plans for the economic revival of Germany. Even before this, some French politicians had recognized the advantages of cooperating with the United States. Pierre Mendès-France, the later Radical party premier of France, said, "We must keep up this indispensable Communist scare" since the United States was making a great effort to aid those threatened by communism.

The End of Tripartism   Ramadier's economic policies precipitated a crisis that resulted in the expulsion of the PCF from the government coalition. The Communist party had denounced strikes as anarchist even through the largest labor union was under its control. But Ramadier's policy of low wages and high prices to promote business recovery precipitated a massive strike at the government-owned Renault automobile factory in April 1947, forcing the PCF to support the workers against the government. After winning a vote of confidence on his economic policy in the Assembly, Ramadier demanded that the Communist deputies resign, and tripartism came to an end.

Although the developing Cold War helped undermine the PCF in

France, domestic affairs were even more important in excluding the PCF from power. Despite a moderate, conciliatory Communist policy after being excluded from office, the Socialists abandoned their coalition with the PCF in October 1947 in the municipalities. As a result, Communist mayors lost 842 mayoral seats when they had lost only 3 percent of their vote in the municipal elections. The PCF now turned toward more resolute support of worker's economic demands. PCF support for the massive strikes throughout France in November and December 1947 led to a further defeat for the party. Workers had to return to work when the Socialist minister of the interior called in the army and threatened workers with the loss of their social security benefits. After another attempt to gain a share of power in 1948, the PCF turned to a closer working relationship with Moscow and the Cominform. It approved the Communist coup in Czechoslovakia and the Stalin-directed expulsion of Yugoslavia from the Cominform in 1948.

While the Socialists were engaged in their offensive against the Communists in 1947–1948, a new political party of the right appeared. This party, the Rally of the French People (RPF), led by de Gaulle, sought but failed to gain support from the United States as France's bulwark against communism. De Gaulle's arrogant attempt to make the government call a national referendum on his return to power was decisively beaten back, and for the second time de Gaulle had to retire from the political arena. By the spring of 1948, the MRP-led government of Robert Schuman, supported by Marshall Plan funds and stabilized by domestic economic recovery, was firmly in control.

Italy: A Policy of Muddling Through

Like France and Great Britain, Italy experienced a wartime and postwar resurgence of the left. Again it was the left anti-Fascist activities that were responsible for its popularity. The Fascist Grand Council and King Victor Emmanuel III replaced Benito Mussolini with Marshal Pietro Badoglio in July 1943, following the Allied invasion of Sicily. However, Badoglio had to flee to liberated southern Italy when German troops took control of northern Italy (including Rome). In the liberated south, a coalition of anti-Fascist parties called the Committee for National Liberation (CLN) challenged Badoglio's claim to the post of head of the Italian government.

The CLN, most of whom wanted a republic, clashed with Badoglio over the fate of the monarchy. Under pressure from the Allies, King Victor Emmanuel III promised to step aside in favor of his son, Umberto, who would act as lieutenant governor until a postwar national referendum could decide the fate of the monarchy. Only the Communist leader Palmiro Togliatti's approval of the king's action, apparently a continuation of Soviet-Allied wartime cooperation, convinced the remaining CLN parties to accept Umberto. With the liberation of Rome in June of 1944, the CLN forced acceptance of Ivanoe Bonomi as head of a new government.

Meanwhile, military and political activities in the north had taken a politically more radical turn because of the German occupation. Resistance fighters formed the Committee of National Liberation for Northern Italy (CLNAI) centered in Milan. The CLNAI, dominated by the left of center—the Communist, Socialist, and Action parties—desired a far more radical republic than the Bonomi government in the south was willing to institute. The CLNAI opposition to Bonomi was sufficiently strong to have the leader of the Action party, Ferruccio Parri, appointed premier by Lieutenant General of the Realm Umberto.

In May and June of 1945, immediately before Parri came to power, the weakening of the political left set the pattern for the postwar development of Italy. Throughout the north the leftist-dominated CLNAI permitted the participation of workers in the management of industrial enterprises through so-called management councils. The CLNAI also launched attacks on big business to penalize it for cooperating with fascism and to begin the process of destroying what were considered to be the reactionary forces in Italy.

That the left was unable to take full control can be attributed in part to Allied intervention. The left realized that any outright attempt to seize power would be opposed by American and British forces that were then in the country. As the left attempted to gain Allied acceptance by adopting a moderate reformist position, its basis of strength was systematically destroyed by the Allies. Leftist Resistance groups were compelled to surrender their arms. Workers' councils were disbanded; factory managers were urged to reassert their authority; and local committees of liberation, invariably leftist, were replaced by military government for a few months.

Parri, convinced of the need for radical reforms in postwar Italy, was thus handicapped from the start. His attempts to institute policies favoring small and medium-size business rather than big business and to redistribute wealth through a more effective tax were defeated by the Liberals and Christian Democrats in his cabinet, who considered his policies too radical. After only six months in office, Parri resigned, blaming the Liberals and Christian Democrats for sabotaging his program. His fall signified the end of radical social and political change in postwar Italy and condemned Italy to a policy of muddling through.

With Parri's fall began the postwar domination of Italian politics by the Christian Democratic party that has lasted almost to this day. Although the Christian Democrats, led by Alcide de Gasperi, were forced to share power with the Socialists and Communists, they clearly dominated the coalition. It was fairly easy for the coalition to accept a public referendum

The piazza of Montefiasconi, a village in Italy, during the 1948 election campaign. Almost every available space is covered with election posters and party slogans. (David Seymour—Magnum Photos)

in June 1946 ending monarchy in Italy but much more difficult for it to reach decisions on complex economic and social problems. The establishment of regional governments, provided for in the 1948 constitution of the Italian government, was not fully implemented until 1970 due to Christian Democratic fears that they would create Communist governments across north-central Italy.

While the Communists and Socialists wanted to nationalize some industry, De Gasperi preferred an essentially private enterprise policy with some state financial subsidization. Although government-owned corporations such as IRI (see chapter 4) extended public ownership to large sectors of industry, de Gasperi and his fellow party members, especially the Catholic clergymen, saw the Communist and Socialist parties as threats to the church. De Gasperi's attempts to oust the Communist and Socialists from the coalition were helped along by a split in the Socialist party between those, like Pietro Nenni, who favored cooperation with the Communists and those who did not. The latter, led by Giuseppe Saragat, broke away from the Socialist party in January 1947 and formed the Social Democratic party (PSDI).

With the left opposition divided, de Gasperi used the growing anti-Communist sentiment stemming from the Cold War to exclude the Communists from the coalition government in June 1947. Coming one month after the Communist coup in Czechoslovakia, the April 1948 parliamentary elections became a battleground between the People's Bloc of Communists, supported by Nenni Socialists, and de Gasperi's Christian Democrats. During the election campaign, the Vatican and the United States energetically supported de Gasperi. The United States warned that a Communist-Socialist government would not receive any economic aid and the Central Intelligence Agency actively supported the Christian Democrats. With the Italian electorate anxious about a possible Communist government and the economic consequences this would entail, the Christian Democratic party obtained sufficient votes in the 1948 election, 48.5 percent of the vote, to govern alone. De Gasperi astutely included representatives of the Social Democratic, Republican, and Liberal parties in his ministry, leaving the Communist and Socialist parties isolated on the left. The PCI-staged general strike of July 1948, following the attempted assassination of Togliatti, failed when the Communist trade union leaders folded when confronted with the government threat to use military force.

Since 1947 the Communist party and its working-class supporters have been excluded from governing coalitions in Italy. However, the Communists managed in the 1960s and 1970s to gain power in many provinces and municipalities. Their popularity in recent elections has won them important positions in the legislature. (This resurgence will be explored in chapter 14.) Because the basis of support for the Christian Democrats has come from the Conservative upper and middle classes and the southern peasantry, there has been little support for meaningful economic and social reforms.

Spain: An End to Ostracism

A swing to the left was impossible in Spain and Portugal, where strong dictatorships prevented any free political activity. General Francisco Franco had clapped tight police control over his leftist opposition after his victory over the Popular Front government in the Spanish Civil War in 1939. Strong support by Spanish Nationalists—and bitter opposition between his opponents, Communists and anti-Communist Republicans— made Franco's task much easier. With a government composed of military men and members of Nationalist groups, Franco retained the pragmatic authoritarianism that he had established during the civil war. He feared that the establishment of any clear-cut ideological basis for his regime would alienate some of his Nationalist support. Therefore, he opposed the Falange's (Spanish Fascist party) attempt to transform his government into a purely Fascist movement.

Concerned that the European democracies might turn on Spain for its adherence to the Fascist Anti-Comintern Pact of 1939, Franco declared

Spanish neutrality at the outset of World War II. But the swift German victory over France produced a marked pro-German attitude among Spanish leaders. Only economic hardships and the possibility that a close identification with the Fascist powers would bring crippling economic sanctions kept Spain from openly supporting Germany and Italy at the beginning of the war.

The Nazi attack on the Soviet Union in 1941 caused Franco's vehemently anti-Communist regime to send a force of 20,000 Spanish volunteers to help Germany on the Russian front. But Spain's enthusiasm waned with the Soviet victories at Moscow and Stalingrad and the United States' entry into the war.

From this point on, Franco maintained strict neutrality despite the protestations of the pro-Fascist Falangist party. Spain's neutralism began to bear fruit when the Allies launched their invasion of French North Africa in 1942. At that time President Roosevelt offered assurances that the invasion was not directed at Spanish holdings in Africa and that the Allies would not intervene in Spanish internal affairs.

Franco overcame the immediate postwar problems by again cautiously adapting his policies to satisfy both internal and foreign opponents. At home, he shored up support among his military, church, and Monarchist supporters by reducing the influence of his Falangist party followers. The Spanish left, still divided and still closely watched, offered little opposition. On the right, no strong conservative alternative existed to challenge Franco, and the military continued to support him. Heated foreign opposition to his regime had little impact since government propagandists portrayed it as an anti-Spanish rather than an anti-Franco campaign. Franco further strengthened his regime in 1947 by declaring Spain a kingdom with himself as regent and by having it confirmed by a national plebiscite. Although he did not permit the return of the king, he promised that the country would be ruled by a king upon his death or retirement. In 1955, he permitted the pretender's son, Prince Juan Carlos, to return to study.

Another factor that helped Franco hold his domestic critics at bay and overcome international ostracism was Spain's growing usefulness to the United States and its allies in the Cold War. In the event of war with the Soviet Union, the United States began to see that the value of military bases in Spain would be immeasurable. By 1948, most of the anti-Communist West had reopened diplomatic contacts with Spain, and the United States had begun to provide Spain with financial aid to overcome its serious economic problems. No longer ostracized so completely (Spain was still excluded from NATO) and beginning to recover economically, Franco did not have to alter his internal policies to please Republican opponents.

Portugal: Uninterrupted Peace

Before the outbreak of World War II, Portugal had a dictatorship that was long established and ideologically more consistent than that of Spain. A professor of political economy at the University of Coimbra, Antonio de Oliveira Salazar, had been brought into the military government in 1928 to resolve the acute financial difficulties, and by 1933 Salazar had become dictator of the military regime. The Portuguese accepted his strong, authoritative leadership primarily because of a yearning for peace and security after suffering through twenty-three antigovernment revolts between 1910 and 1928.

Salazar overcame the Portuguese Fascists, called National Syndicalists, by offering his brand of Catholic corporatism and by concentrating political power in a single government Party of National Union. To provide order and stability he set up a consultative corporate chamber in place of a senate and brought labor under the jurisdiction of government syndicates.

By providing transportation and communication facilities to Franco, Salazar's regime proved to be a valuable aid to the Nationalist forces in the Spanish Civil War. But he refused to aid Franco directly and adhered to the international nonintervention agreement. During World War II, Salazar initially adopted a policy of strict neutrality. Fearing that the war might bring about a polarization of forces within Portugal, he carried out a comprehensive program of civic nationalism. A youth organization, an auxiliary militia system, political purges of suspected opponents, and a government loyalty oath were among the tools used to stamp out all opposition to the regime.

Owing to Portugal's longtime friendship and Treaty of Alliance with Britain, Salazar was never so pressed as Spain was to enter the war on the side of Germany and Italy. This friendship led Salazar to change his policy of neutrality and to grant the United States and Britain use of military bases in the Azores in 1943 and to stop the shipment of strategic material to Germany in 1944.

After the war, Portugal escaped much of the international anti-Fascist campaign because of its wartime cooperation with Western Allies and because it retained a parliamentary form of government. Moreover, Salazar instituted a liberalization program to satisfy both foreign and domestic opponents. The program included the restoration of freedom of the press, amnesty for political opponents of the regime, and new parliamentary elections. However, a reduction in the number of persons eligible to vote and a boycott by the opposition made a sham of the elections.

Although some political unrest was evident in the late 1940s, Salazar was able to maintain his authoritarian rule. Serious economic problems were avoided when his regime received economic aid from the Marshall Plan. Membership in NATO gained Portugal international support. By

1950 Salazar's opposition was limited to a few students and intellectuals, a small group of military men, and some members of the middle class.

The Small Nations: Restoring Order

With the exception of Greece, the smaller European countries concentrated on domestic affairs in the postwar period. Many had suffered extensively from the war and were faced with considerable reconstruction problems. Large sections of Holland, especially Rotterdam, had been destroyed by German bombs. Although Belgium had suffered less war damage, it was in the throes of internecine political-cultural conflict between the politically radical, anticlerical, French-speaking Walloons and the politically conservative, Catholic Flemish.

Among the Nordic countries, only Norway and Finland experienced serious wartime losses. Norway lost one-half of its merchant fleet. Finland suffered through a Soviet invasion in 1939, the loss of some territory to the Soviet Union, and the burden of heavy reparations in the postwar period. Nevertheless, the Finns managed to retain their political democracy and won admiration throughout the world for their stout resistance to Soviet domination. The Socialist and the Agrarian parties successfully resisted Communist attempts to gain control of the country. In Norway and Denmark, thousands of German collaborators were arrested at war's end. As in Finland, the Socialist and Agrarian parties dominated the governments as Communist strength waned following the war.

Forced to cooperate with Germany under threat of invasion, Sweden remained neutral during the war and did not, therefore, have to face the problems of economic reconstruction and political restoration confronting most European countries. The Swedish Socialist party continued to dominate domestic politics as it had done before the war.

Austria, as an ally of Germany, had suffered extensively from Allied bombing. Not only did Austria have to recover from serious economic destruction and dislocation but it also had to endure a four-power occupation until 1955, when it became an independent, neutral state.

Greece: From Occupation to Civil War

Greece suffered through four years of German occupation (1941–1944) and a destructive civil war before political peace was obtained. A Communist-led National Liberation Front (EAM), with its People's Army (ELAS), challenged the exiled Government of National Unity for leadership when Greece was liberated. The ELAS force could have seized power when the Germans withdrew in October 1944, but it refrained because the Churchill-Stalin agreements assigned Greece to Western jurisdiction and because Stalin issued direct orders not to overthrow the British-backed Government of National Unity.

But in December 1944, encouraged by Tito against Stalin's wishes, the ELAS seized power when the government threatened a reorganization that would equalize the Communist and non-Communist military forces in a new national army. British troops compelled the EAM-ELAS to capitulate in February 1945. In the anti-Communist reaction that followed, government security agents and vigilante groups hunted down Communists. Again in March 1946, the Communists tried to seize power. Despite guerrilla activity, parliamentary elections were held in March as scheduled. As the Communists had feared, the pro-Royalist parties won 206 of the 354 seats in the legislature. This trend continued in the September referendum, when 70 percent of the voters cast their ballots in favor of a restoration of the monarchy.

The Communist guerrillas, with support from Yugoslavia, Albania, and Bulgaria, could not be dislodged from their mountain retreats until funds provided under the Truman Doctrine, totaling $250 million, permitted the buildup of the Greek army in 1948. When the Communist forces shifted from guerrilla warfare to conventional warfare in 1949, they were wiped out by the Greek army.

After nine years of warfare, large sections of Greece were devastated. With support from the Marshall Plan, Greece was able to begin a modest recovery from economic misery. But internal political troubles and the lack of economic resources kept it a poor and troubled country.

Stalin had ordered Tito to stop his support of the Greek guerrillas, and Tito's failure to comply was one of the major reasons for the Stalin-Tito rift in 1948. Yugoslav support for the guerrillas ended in July 1949, when Tito had to concentrate his efforts on resisting Soviet pressures. In any case, Tito could ill afford to support a guerrilla war that might well spill over into Yugoslavia. He was also desperately in need of economic aid himself, as a consequence of the economic embargo of Comecon.

Popularity of the Left

With the exception of Spain and Portugal, the political left was popular everywhere among the smaller European states. As in France and Italy, leftist parties had led the Resistance in the occupied territory or had been popular in the interwar period. The postwar governments of both Belgium and Denmark contained Communists. Without Allied intervention, a left coalition would undoubtedly have come to power in 1944 in Greece. In Belgium, a Communist attempt to gain power in 1944 was beaten back by Allied troops. However, the popularity of the far left waned quickly because of its identification with the Soviet Union.

The more successful moderate left embodied in the Socialist and Social Democratic parties that came to power jointly or separately in Austria,

Switzerland, Denmark, Norway, Sweden, and in Belgium, the Netherlands, and Luxembourg (the Benelux countries) never suffered the political decline experienced by Social Democratic parties in Germany, Italy, and France after 1946. The resilience of the Social Democrats in northern Europe resulted both from their interwar popularity and from the absence of strong Communist scares in the postwar period; in the 1950s, Social Democrats were in power, as in Scandinavia, or shared power, as in the Netherlands, Belgium, and Austria.

In retrospect, the year 1948 seems to mark a breaking point in the postwar history of Europe. By this time, left-of-center parties were out of power in the major continental European countries. Only the more reform-minded Labour party in Britain managed to cling to power until 1951. It was also 1948 when foreign funds, primarily through Marshall Plan aid, started the economic recovery of Europe.

Moreover, 1948 and 1949 were the years of the division of Europe into two hostile camps. Beginning with the formation of NATO in 1949, for a decade European countries had to follow the dictates of either the United States or the Soviet Union in foreign affairs.

But 1948 was also a hopeful beginning for Western Europe. It was in that year that economic recovery began. And that year also marked the inception of long-term plans for economic cooperation that eventually developed into the European Common Market.

FURTHER READING

For sympathetic treatments of the British Labour government, see Kenneth O. Morgan, *Labour People* (1987); Keith Hutchinson, *The Decline and Fall of British Capitalism* (1951); C. R. Attlee, *As It Happened* (1954); Maurice Bruce, *The Coming of the Welfare State* (1961); and Emanuel Shinwell, *The Labour Story* (1963). Details on British industry under the Labour government can be found in Arnold A. Rogow, *The Labour Government and British Industry* (1955); W. A. Robson, *Nationalised Industry and Public Ownership* (1960); and Andrew Shonfield, *British Economic Policy since the War* (1958). For more critical accounts, see Ernest Watkins, *The Cautious Revolution* (1950); R. H. S. Crossman, *New Fabian Essays* (1952); and Richard Titmuss, *Income Distribution and Social Change* (1962). An important source for the nature of British politics is Samuel Beer, *British Politics in the Collectivist Age* (1965) and *Britain against Itself* (1982).

For standard thorough accounts of the first years of the French Fourth Republic, see Philip M. Williams, *Crisis and Compromise: Politics in the Fourth Republic* (1964); Alexander Werth, *France, 1940–1955* (1956);

François Goguel, *France under the Fourth Republic* (1952); and Dorothy Pickles, *French Politics: The First Years of the Fourth Republic* (1953). A highly critical account of the first postwar leaders can be found in Ronald Matthews, *Death of the Fourth Republic* (1954). A study by Catherine Gavin, *Liberated France* (1955), heaps most of the blame for the failures of the Fourth Republic on de Gaulle. A thorough recent study of French politics is provided by Jean-Pierre Rioux's *The Fourth Republic, 1944–1958* (1986). George Ross provides a sound analysis of the French Communists in his *Workers and Communists in France: From Popular Front to Eurocommunism* (1982). Irwin Wall, *French Communism in the Era of Stalin* (1983), offers an important reassessment of the postwar Communist party. Wall argues that the PCF did not desire revolution but integration into a broadly based democratic coalition. His *L'Influence Americaine sur la Politique Française* (1989) argues that American influence on postwar French politics was much less than previously believed.

Thorough accounts of postwar Italian politics include M. Grindrod, *The Rebuilding of Italy: Politics and Economics, 1945–55* (1955); Norman Kogan, *A Political History of Italy: The Postwar Years* (1983); Giuseppe Mammarella, *Italy after Fascism: A Political History, 1943–1963* (1964); H. Stuart Hughes, *The United States and Italy* (rev. 3rd ed., 1979); F. Spotts and T. Wiesner, *Italy: A Difficult Democracy* (1986); and Joe LaPalombara, *Democracy, Italian Style* (1987). For Italian neo-Fascist movements, see Leonard B. Weinberg, *After Mussolini: Italian Neo-Fascism and the Nature of Fascism* (1979). Joan Barth Urban's *Moscow and the Italian Communist Party, from Togliatti to Berlinguer* (1986) argues that the Italian Communist party began its independent course from Moscow already in the immediate postwar years. For the United States' role in Italian affairs, see John L. Harper, *America and the Reconstruction of Italy, 1945–1948* (1986), and James G. Miller, *The United States and Revolutionary Italy, 1940–1950* (1986).

For the smaller European countries, see W. B. Bader, *Austria between East and West, 1945–55* (1966); and William T. Bluhm, *Building An Austrian Nation* (1973). The Scandinavian countries are treated in Ander O. Fritof, *The Building of Modern Sweden: The Reign of Gustav V, 1907–1950* (1958); D. A. Rustow, *The Politics of Compromise: A Study of Parties and Cabinet Government in Sweden* (1955); Alice Bourneuf, *Norway: The Planned Revival* (1958); and Harry Eckstein, *Division and Cohesion in Democracy: A Study of Norway* (1966).

Postwar Spain is given a balanced treatment in Stanley G. Payne, *The Franco Regime, 1936–1975* (1987). Sheelagh M. Ellwood's *Spanish Fascism in the Franco Era* (1987) provides a useful summary of falangism. Portugal is treated in Hugh Kay, *Salazar and Modern Portugal* (1970), and Charles E. Nowell, *Portugal* (1973). The Greek Civil War is competently covered in E. O'Ballance, *The Greek Civil War, 1944–49* (1966), and W. H. McNeill, *The Greek Dilemma: War and Aftermath* (1947). John O. Iatrides treats the first stages of the civil war in *Revolt in Athens: The Greek Communist "Second Round," 1944–1945* (1972). Jon V. Kofas's *Intervention and Underdevelopment: Greece during the Cold War* (1989) provides coverage of the postwar period.

4 Economic Recovery in Western Europe

To present the postwar growth as one of history's unpremeditated happenings would be most unhistorical. For what distinguishes the postwar era from most other periods of economic history is not only its growth but the extent to which this growth was "contrived": generated and sustained by governments and the public.

M. M. Postan
An Economic History of Western Europe, 1945–1960

In the two decades following 1948, revolutionary economic changes laid the groundwork for what many observers termed the New Europe. By 1960 Europe had regained its place as the leading trading area in the world, with nearly one-quarter of the world's industrial output and 40 percent of the world's trade.

Few expected the economic recovery to proceed as rapidly as it did. When the United States was providing some of the initial financing for European recovery through Marshall Plan aid, no one envisioned that a decade later we would be studying the rapid European growth rates in order to find some means to stimulate the U.S. economy.

Equally unexpected was the integration of much of Europe, including some former enemies, in one large economic entity known as the European Economic Community or, more familiarly, the Common Market, which went into effect January 1, 1958. Although the Common Market failed to achieve all that was expected of it at first and European economic growth rates slowed appreciably in the late 1960s, by the 1980s some of the highly developed European countries surpassed the wealth and affluence of the United States on a per capita basis.

Characteristics of European Economic Recovery

The war, in numerous ways, stimulated economic growth. Amid the rubble that covered large areas of Europe at the end of World War II were numerous factories that needed only minor repairs before they could resume operations. Only about 20 percent of Europe's factories were demolished or seriously damaged.

In some cases the destruction wrought by bombing provided the impetus for long-term economic growth. The systematic bombing of residential areas necessitated the reconstruction of entire cities, which served as a stimulus to the building trades. Moreover, the productive resources of the World War II belligerents had increased immensely during the war. A team of German researchers estimated that, after damages and dismantling, fixed assets in German industry increased by 7 billion German marks from 1936 to 1945. With this increased productive capacity and the shortage of consumer goods throughout Europe, an absence of financial resources remained the only serious obstacle to rapid economic growth.

Wartime destruction of plants, equipment, and capital goods proved to be an added benefit; it permitted a modernization that made European industry highly competitive. The destruction of a portion of Europe's transportation network prompted the complete modernization of a number of national railway systems. France closed down unnecessary lines, eliminated prewar bottlenecks, and electrified one-fifth of its rail network. Now French trains are considerably longer and faster than British trains and can thus ship goods at lower cost.

Marshall Plan Stimulus to Recovery

Some of the capital necessary to finance the initial reconstruction and modernization of European industry was provided by the United States. Western Europe's desperate need for funds in 1947 to keep recovery underway was provided by Marshall Plan aid. Without this aid, ambitious economic expansion programs begun in 1945 would have been disrupted. The United States offered aid with the objective of achieving European economic as well as political integration in order to fend off a perceived Communist threat.

There was a considerable amount of self-interest in the decision since a financially sound Europe would provide a large market for U.S. products. But there was also compassion for those suffering from wartime losses as well as the realization that the European countries would have to be helped more than they had been after World War I. By 1947, the United States had already provided $15.5 billion in aid to Europe, $6.8 billion of that being outright gifts. But the bulk of American aid, $23 billion, was provided by the Marshall Plan from 1947 to 1952.

By 1949, when the United States entered a recession, Europe was able to finance its own industrialization. Contributing to this economic recovery was the rapid growth of exports, especially in West Germany. In 1949, German exports doubled over the previous year, and the following year they increased another 75 percent.

Few expected the rapid economic growth to be more than a short-term phenomenon. But as Table 4-1 indicates, growth rates through the early 1960s were not significantly lower than those of 1948 to 1954. The cyclical fluctuations of boom and bust typical of prewar economic growth were not characteristic of postwar Europe. It was this long-term sustained growth that was later studied in the United States with the objective of raising its own growth rates above the 3 to 4 percent annual rate of the 1960s. Although some economists have sought to single out one or two primary causes of the high growth rates, there appear to have been a multitude of reasons.

Trade Stimulus to Recovery

Although Marshall Plan aid was an important early stimulus, the ever-increasing foreign trade provided the most important stimulus to economic growth after 1949 by raising foreign sales, personal income, and domestic demand. In the 1950s, the exports of Germany, Italy, and the Netherlands rose more than 10 percent annually compared to a 6.4 percent growth rate for world exports. Much of the increase resulted from the worldwide relaxation of trade restrictions.

Most important for Europeans was the easing of trade restrictions under the auspices of the European Payments Union (1950), the Coal and Steel Community (1951), the Common Agricultural Policys (1950) and the Common Market after 1958 (see chapter 8). However, Common Market membership was not indispensable for rapid economic growth. One country outside the Common Market, Austria, experienced a growth of industrial output second only to that of West Germany. Even if there had not been a Common Market, the worldwide increase in trade would probably have been sufficient to stimulate European industrial recovery. But the Common Market did provide a number of advantages. It gave European agriculture a much larger internal market and protected it with uniformly high tariffs against foreign, especially U.S., imports. French agricultural exports to Common Market countries increased during the 1950s from about 15 to 41 percent of the country's total agricultural exports.

Demographic Stimulus to Recovery

Demographic changes provided another important impetus for the rapid economic growth following the war. A rising birthrate coupled with the influx of refugees and foreign workers swelled the population of Western Europe from 264 million in 1940 to about 320 million in 1970. In the immediate postwar years, refugees from Eastern Europe provided much of the labor for West German industry. More jobs were available than there were people to fill them after 1948, and each additional laborer added to European output and demand. The refugees constituted a large supply of cheap labor, encouraging investment in industry since it assured industrialists that manufacturing costs would remain low and Europe's exports would remain highly competitive in the market. When the flow of refugees stopped, foreign workers came from southern Europe and then from southeastern Europe, north Africa, the Iberian Peninsula, and Turkey to man the Western European factories.

Refugees had increased the West German population by 4 million, and foreign workers had added another 3.6 million by 1962. But it was in France that the demographic change was most marked. After more than a century of remaining steady, the French population increased from 42 million in 1950 to about 50 million in 1966, and de Gaulle hoped for a France, including colonies, of 100 million people by the year 2000. Although some of this increase was the result of immigration, most of it was brought about by a rise in the birthrate.

Beginning in the interwar period, French leaders tried to encourage population growth by raising family allowances. In the postwar period, France increased family allowances and added rent subsidies because the French leaders saw population growth as a way to revitalize the country. Foreign workers came to France primarily from Algeria, Spain, Portugal, and Italy. In Switzerland and Luxembourg, one-third of the labor force came from the less-industrialized areas of Europe.

A growing population with the wherewithal to buy new housing and a severe shortage of housing units provided a long-term impetus to industrial expansion. Especially in Germany and Holland, entire cities had to be rebuilt. From 1953 to 1964 Germany had the highest per capita housing construction in the West: half a million units a year. Some economists see housing construction as the major reason that Europe did not experience a business recession for so long after the war. These economists predicted an end to the building boom and considerably lower growth rates. But massive government support for the building trades prevented a slump in construction on several occasions following World War II and was used during the 1970s to lessen the impact of Europe's worst postwar recession.

At the center of European economic resurgence is the automobile. As one of the leading economic sectors, it has promoted growth in the steel industry, road building, service stations, and countless associated industries. From a production of about 500,000 vehicles in the late 1940s, European vehicle output reached 9 million units a year in the 1970s before encountering Japanese competition in the late seventies. The age when the theft of a bicycle was a tragedy for the European family has passed. Europeans' love for their cars and for driving speeds rivals that of American adolescents. The automobile was as much a status symbol in Europe in the 1960s as it was in the United States a decade earlier, and Europeans now buy new cars before they improve their housing. Such status seeking has also led to a decline in the European's love affair with the Volkswagen "beetle" and a growing desire for larger, faster cars. Only the rise in gasoline prices brought about by the increased price of Middle East oil

An automobile factory in Turin, Italy, which helped meet the growing consumer demand for passenger cars in postwar Europe. (Karl Gullers—Camera Press London)

dampened the enthusiasm for larger, more prestigious cars. Cheaper oil in the eighties has brought a renewed surge in large-car sales.

The New Capitalism

The fact that European economic growth was not seriously affected by economic slumps in the 1950s as it was in the prewar period resulted from the retreat of laissez-faire economics and the growth of government intervention in the economy. Postwar economic problems were of such magnitude that governments had to intervene to provide basic foodstuffs and raw materials and to prevent unemployment. Reconstruction tasks could often be carried out only by the government. In some cases, governments decided to nationalize industries that were considered indispensable: railroads, airlines, public utilities, and some heavy industry.

Called modern capitalism or neocapitalism, it has been characterized by a mixture of private and government initiative in what is essentially a free enterprise system. Government control of banks and budgetary policies had permitted governments to determine the rate of growth of their economies. Now, when European economies seem headed for recession or inflation, governments step in to regulate the economy by manipulating the monetary system as well as supply and demand.

Despite some variations, the new capitalism entailed government acceptance of Keynesian economics and economic planning. Keynes's *The General Theory of Employment, Interest and Money,* written in 1936, provided the theoretical groundwork for neocapitalism. In recasting the traditional free enterprise system, Keynes contended that full employment led to high consumption and increased productivity. Full employment could be attained, he said, through governmental manipulation of taxation and expenditure that would sustain the demand for goods and services at a high level. He rejected the generally accepted theory that governmental stimulation of the economy would lead to inflation and rising prices, which would in turn lead to economic chaos. Keynesian economists take the position that if workers are provided with high wages, they will consume more and industry will prosper. If labor and management accept such policies, class conflict should diminish as the two sides decide on appropriate wages to maintain economic expansion.

In practice, some countries implemented full employment policies and established wage guidelines and income policies that met most labor demands. The implementation of Keynesian economics helped governments avoid fluctuations in the business cycle that brought unemployment and recession. By stimulating demand during periods of recession, governments were able to prevent serious depressions. On the other hand, inflation was kept in check by restricting credit and raising taxes.

The policy of full employment was soon supplemented by a policy of economic growth. In order to meet the steadily growing expenditures for social services and armaments, as well as the public demand for improvements in the standard of living, governments adopted a policy of rapid economic growth. And now that economic progress was being equated with high annual growth rates, various forms of economic planning had to be adopted in order to direct investment to those economic sectors that would maximize growth.

To achieve maximum economic growth, most countries drew up long-term plans and centralized planning in government agencies. By 1960, France, Belgium, Austria, Italy, Sweden, Norway, and the Netherlands had instituted some form of long-range economic planning. Western planning did not specify production quotas or allocate all raw materials and investment funds, as was done in Eastern Europe and the Soviet Union, but set general guidelines for future economic development and provided financial aid to sectors that would stimulate growth.

The amount of interference in the economies varied considerably in Western Europe. In France the precedents for planning were set under the Popular Front government in the decade before World War II. After the war the new planning agency, set up under Jean Monnet, became another arm of the government. The Monnet Plan aimed to use German coal and coke to make the French steel industry internationally competitive. Once France realized that the Ruhr coal and iron ore resources were not going to be internationalized but returned to German control, the Monnet Plan logic necessitated a close working relationship with Germany in order to obtain coal and coke. This plan led naturally to Robert Schuman's European Coal and Steel Community proposal to integrate the heavy industrial resources of the later Common Market countries.

Great Britain, because of its historic dedication to laissez-faire principles, was slow to institute economic planning. Only after serious economic difficulties compelled repeated government intervention did British leaders become convinced in 1961 that long-term planning was necessary. Soon after the war, Sweden set up a Labor Market Board in which employers and labor plan construction and investment in order to sustain full employment. The one partial exception in this era of planning is Germany. As a reaction to Nazi intervention in the economy, and at the urging of the Allies, postwar West German leaders sought initially to divest the government of control over industry. Yet the government did intervene in the economy every time it granted subsidies, low-cost loans, or tax breaks to favored enterprises.

One economist has described West German industry as "organized private enterprise." Huge industrial corporations commanding enormous sources of capital remain highly competitive in the international market. Instead of government planning, the Federation of German Industry engages in investment planning and long-term forecasting of supply and demand. The federation is dominated by three large banks that obtain agreements among industrial enterprises to avoid competition. Bankers hold important seats on the supervisory boards of the major West German corporations, the big three banks holding more than half the seats.

Industrial Concentration and Nationalization

Planning was made easier throughout Western Europe by the concentration of industry and by government nationalization of important industries. Once a government nationalized the large enterprises in an industry, smaller competitors were forced to cooperate. Compliance with government planning usually brought with it tax relief, state contracts, and loans. These advantages and nationalization have promoted the development of huge industrial corporations.

One such corporation, the *Société Générale* of Belgium, dominates the Belgian economy. As one of its directors put it, "The *Société* is not too large; it's just that Belgium is too small.'' By 1960, it had under its control 40 percent of the iron and steel industry, 30 percent of coal, 25 percent of electrical energy, and 70 percent of the insurance companies.

Four huge corporations—Royal Dutch Shell, Unilever, Philips, and AKU—dominate the Dutch economy. The annual income of only one, Royal Dutch Shell, is larger than that of Switzerland.

In Italy, monopolization and state control permitted the government to participate extensively in long-range industrial planning. Some of the firms that were nationalized during the Fascist period became enormous industrial conglomerates. By 1963, the government-owned IRI (*Istituto per la Ricostruzione Industriale*) consisted of 120 companies with 280,000 employees. Financial resources were firmly under the control of the government; the major commercial bank was nationalized, and the IRI controlled over four-fifths of the capital of the next three largest banks. The IRI and the other great public corporation, ENI (*Ente Nazionale Idrocarburi*), were responsible for more than one-third of all capital investment in manufacturing, transportation, and communications by 1964. Both ENI and IRI established the necessary infrastructures (inexpensive energy sources, producer goods, and roads) that permitted the growth of huge private companies: Fiat, Perelli, Olivetti, etc.

In Austria, the nationalized industries accounted for 24 percent of industrial production and 27 percent of exports in the sixties. Government control extended also to finance.

In France, jurisdiction over the most important French banks, the *Caisse des Dépôts* and the *Crédit National*, gave the French government control over credit.

A noneconomic factor that has contributed mightily to postwar recovery is the belief among industrialists and civil servants alike that economic expansion is not only desirable but attainable. Despite the tendency of some French and English to avoid rapid economic growth lest they be forced to take unnecessary risks to sustain the growth rates, most European industrialists and civil servants have become supporters of what M. M. Postan calls growthmanship. For example, the director of ENI in Italy, Enrico Mattei, while successfully developing Italy's natural gas deposits, pushed production to the point of exhausting Italian resources. As important as the attitude of the managers is the attitude of the general public that economic growth is necessary and achievable. Europeans became willing in the sixties to make long-term investments in their economies instead of hoarding their money or sending it abroad in search of profits.

Agricultural Developments

Changes in agriculture have rivaled the revolutionary transformation of industry. Many European countries have made the transition from small-scale subsistence agriculture before 1945 to agricultural production aimed primarily at the much larger urban market. Despite the rapidly growing demand in Europe, a technological revolution in agriculture began to produce massive surpluses by the 1970s.

In 1974, 40 percent of the bumper 1973 wine crop had to be distilled into alcohol. And the EEC was also compelled to either buy up or dispose of especially large surpluses of dairy products and meat.

Increased mechanization, greater use of fertilizers and insecticides, improved seed, and modern equipment have produced the surpluses; the number of tractors in the countries of the EEC rose sixfold, from 370,000 in 1950 to 2,330,000 in 1962. The number of farm animals has been increased through artificial insemination, while their size and quality have improved by better feed and selective breeding.

The development of larger, more efficient agricultural units has not kept pace with technological changes primarily because of government policies. Lest they antagonize agricultural voters, governments have subsidized agriculture and have thus preserved many small high-cost farms. In France, Germany, and the Benelux countries, strong organizations of farmers mobilize their members to prevent any change in this policy. Armed with pitchforks, farmers have opposed all EEC attempts to alter their privileged status.

The Common Market perpetuated the system of government protection and high agricultural prices. High tariffs were set against foreign products as tariffs between the EEC members were slowly reduced. To offset lower international prices, an EEC agricultural fund subsidized members' exports. Such protection places a disproportionate burden on the mass of consumers, who have to pay considerably more for their food than consumers in the rest of the world. Third World countries accused the EEC of being a rich man's club because of its exclusion of foreign agricultural products. As a result, many agreements have been reached with Third World countries in order not to exclude their products.

One of the major obstacles to British entry into the EEC was Britain's agricultural sector, which is on a larger scale and more productive than those on the Continent. British farms average two hundred acres each, compared to a continental average of about forty acres. But the small total acreage in Britain, necessitating large imports of food, was a sufficient enticement to EEC members once Britain promised it would slowly stop purchasing lower-priced products from its Commonwealth partners.

Membership in the EEC has brought about a major transformation in Italian agriculture. Many peasants who farmed marginal land in the south and central parts of Italy were drawn to the industries in northern Italy, Switzerland, Germany, and France. This migration put an end to the tillage of marginal land and thus reduced Italian agricultural output. Italy must now import more food from its EEC partners—at the much higher supported prices—than is produced by the remaining peasant population.

While this rationalization of industrial and agricultural production is one of the EEC goals, it has placed a special burden on Italy's balance of payments. In 1974, France felt it necessary to subsidize its exports to Italy when Italy had to reduce food imports to overcome a severe financial crisis. However, Italian firms have profited enormously from the larger European market and began to overcome the imbalance of payments in the eighties.

France: Economic Development

Beneath the surface similarity of postwar economic development there are many national differences. Even within each state there are considerable regional differences and conflicts over the rapid growth of industry. Nowhere is this more apparent than in France. The French economy was encumbered with small businesses and their centuries-old attitude, "What I have may be small but it is mine." Small-business opposition to the concentration of French industry was centered in the PME (Unions of Small and Medium-size Business) and the Poujadist movement. Before the PME accepted the so-called new France in 1958, it constantly opposed the concentration of business and industry and upheld the small family enterprise as typically French.

More violent in its support of a static France and in its opposition to the modernization of French industry was the Poujadist movement. Led by a small grocer, Pierre Poujade, the movement opposed the Common Market, fought higher wages for labor, resisted higher taxes, and sought government support for small businesses. Although Poujadism itself faded, the movement lived on. In the early 1970s, Jean Royer, who was both the mayor of Tours and France's minister of commerce and small business, became the new champion of the small businessman. A bill he proposed gave small businessmen who sat on municipal councils the power to veto the building of huge chain stores or supermarkets in their areas. In 1974, serious clashes occurred in France between the local municipal councils and employees of supermarkets that were prevented from expanding.

But there is the other France, dominated by the new citizenry bent on economic modernization. This is the France of the Caravelle, Concorde, Renault, and the Plan. It is also the France of Robert Schuman and Jean Monnet, the architects of Western European economic integration. It is the France of those teams of industrialists, the *missions de productivité*, who studied in the United States after the war to prepare themselves to put France on a modern economic footing. Although Schuman proposed the European Coal and Steel Community primarily to rid Europe of its internecine wars, particularly those between Germany and France, he was also aware of its great economic potential. Jean Monnet's first economic plan concentrated on the long-term reconstruction of basic industries rather than on the alleviation of the housing shortages.

This is also the France that has been renowned for its technical creativity since the nineteenth century. A prime example of this creativity was the conception and production of an excellent jet passenger plane, the Caravelle, long before a similar plane flew in the United States. This creativity also characterized the building of the first supersonic passenger plane, the Concorde, in the 1970s. This is, of course, the France that is responsible for the dramatic social and cultural changes that threaten the individualism and uniqueness of the old France. Laurence Wylie's study of change in the small French village of Roussillon, *Village in the Vaucluse*, indicates that this new France has won out over the France of the PME and Poujade. In the 1950s, peasants refused to plant orchards lest they be destroyed in World War III. In the 1960s, the peasants were going into debt to plant olive trees that would not mature for twenty years.

Before Charles de Gaulle returned to power in 1958, the French economic miracle was well under way. As Table 4-1 shows, the French gross domestic product had been increasing at over 4 percent a year for a decade. Nevertheless, the stability provided by the de Gaulle regime and the

Table 4-1   Compound Rate of Growth of Gross Domestic Product in Selected Countries, 1949–1963 (percentages)

	1949–1954	*1954–1959*	*1960–1963*
West Germany	8.4	6.6	7.6
Austria	5.7	5.7	5.8
Italy	4.8	5.6	6.0
Spain	6.4	5.7	
Switzerland	5.7	4.6	5.1
Netherlands	4.9	4.1	4.7
France	4.8	4.1	4.6
Portugal	4.2	4.0	
Norway	4.2	2.7	3.5
Sweden	3.5	3.2	3.4
Denmark	3.7	3.4	3.6
Belgium	3.7	2.5	3.2
United Kingdom	2.7	2.3	2.5
United States	3.6	3.3	
Canada	4.2	4.4	

Source: *David S. Landes*, The Unbound Prometheus: Technological Change and Industrial Development in Western Europe from 1750 to the Present *(Cambridge: Cambridge University Press, 1970), p. 497. Reprinted by permission of Cambridge University Press.*

propitious timing of the devaluation of the franc in 1958, immediately before a rapid expansion of world trade, increased the nation's exports dramatically. Gold and foreign exchange reserves jumped from a mere 10 million francs in 1959 to 28.6 billion by late 1966.

West Germany: Economic Development

A superficial view of the West German economy might leave one with the incorrect impression that postwar German economic growth was solely the result of laissez-faire economics. While it is true that the German government does not engage in long-term planning as the French government does, other institutions in Germany do engage in short-term planning.

As we have seen, the Federation of German Industry, in concert with the banks, manipulates investment in order to regulate industrial output and control prices, and the German government constantly intervenes in the economy by means of taxation and subsidies. One example of this tactic is the 1951 Investment Aid Act, which taxed German business a billion marks in order to finance reconstruction in heavy industry and to develop energy sources. Another measure, the Housing Act of 1950, provided public-subsidized housing projects for low-income families and housing projects with tax preferences for the builders. As a result, before 1961 the government financed more than half the housing construction by direct capital investments and tax reductions granted to builders.

The role of German banks in German industry has grown immensely since 1945. Immediately after the war, the Allies divided Germany into eleven states, each with its own budget and taxing power. To prevent the concentration of banking typical of the Nazi period, ties between the banking services of the various states were prohibited. However, the Allied decision to fortify West Germany so as to counter the presumed threat from the Soviet Union led directly to the removal of economic barriers between the German states and the reconcentration of German banking. By 1950, the Deutsche and Dresdner banks were again in control of all their branch banks, and the remaining member of the Big Three, the Commerz Bank, regained control of its branch banks in 1958. Two years later these three banks controlled about 56 percent of German industrial shares. The Deutsche Bank, according to a London banker, was equivalent in size already in the sixties to the English Midland, Barclay's Hambro's, Baring's, Rothschild's, and Cazenove's all rolled into one.

The banks and industry cooperate extensively to regulate output and avoid destructive competition. By occupying almost one-fourth of all seats on corporate boards of directors, eleven German banks discourage investments that they consider unproductive or that they think will increase competition among firms associated with them. They have been able to convince companies to produce products cooperatively and have prevented the overproduction of goods. While such regulation by banks, firms, and trade associations is never as comprehensive as the national planning in France, it does permit a division of production that is not typical of a true laissez-faire state.

The postwar concentration of industry has permitted closer control. By 1960, the one hundred largest firms accounted for 40 percent of industrial production. Seven West German firms were among the twenty largest European enterprises in the 1960s: Volkswagen, Siemens, Thyssen-Hutte, Daimler-Benz, Farbwerke-Hoechst, Farbenfabriken Bayer, and Krupp.

Nationalized until 1961, Volkswagen epitomized the resurgence of German industry. The car that the British considered too ugly and noisy to achieve mass acceptance was one of the major factors in West Germany's favorable balance of trade since the early 1950s. In 1967, Volkswagen sold more cars in the United States than in Germany. Cleverly merchandised—"Your second car, even if you haven't got a first"—Volkswagen faced little serious competition from European car manufacturers until the 1960s. Then it was challenged by producers of larger family cars, primarily Fiat, and its European sales slipped below those of Fiat.

Volkswagen was also falling victim to the status consciousness of Europeans, who no longer thought the beetle an appropriate status symbol. In the United States it was challenged by smaller American cars that offered similar economy. Although Volkswagen's sales remain high because of the production of new models and continued high foreign sales, it has been unable to raise its sales in recent years. In 1974, VW was offering 7,000 marks to any worker who would quit. Of course, the sales of German luxury cars, Mercedes and BMWs in particular, have kept the German automobile sales high. Such luxury cars have become a necessary status symbol among many Americans.

Britain: Economic Decline?

Compared to the high economic growth rates on the Continent, the British economy experienced a relative decline after 1945. As Table 4-1 indicates, the growth of gross national product from 1949 to 1963 was three times as high in West Germany as it was in Great Britain. French, Italian, and Austrian growth rates were about twice as high. This situation led one British critic to castigate his country as "the stagnant society."

Another indication of the relative economic decline was a very low average annual percentage increase in exports of 1.8 percent compared to increases above 10 percent in Germany, Italy, the Netherlands, and Norway and above 6 percent in most other Western European countries. However, when British growth rates are compared to the lower increases of the United States, her economic performance does not appear so bleak. Unquestionably, there has been a relative decline, but it should be pointed out that Great Britain has sometimes been unfairly compared to countries that were much more in need of massive postwar reconstruction—Germany, Italy, and Japan.

A large share of the responsibility for Great Britain's discouraging economic performance rests with the government. Both the postwar Labour and Conservative governments were reluctant to interfere in industry. Nationalization was viewed not as a means to enhance efficiency but as a last-ditch effort to save stagnant industries. The vast majority of British firms received little support or direction from the government. Lurking in the back of every Labour and Conservative minister's mind was the conviction that the free enterprise system, which had served Britain so well in the past, would be sufficient for the future. Therefore, contrary to the continental experience, long-term planning was rejected in favor of haphazard short-term intervention in the economy.

One example is a Labour decision to reduce industrial investment in the belief that it would ease the pressure on the external balance of payments. The expectation was that industrial imports would be reduced and more capital equipment would be exported. But instead, output went down and more consumer goods had to be imported.

In some cases, large British firms prevented government intervention in the economy. Development councils, proposed by the Labour government to aid research and promote exports, were rejected by large enterprises on the assumption that small firms would dominate the councils and that the councils were a step toward nationalization.

Industrial management hindered economic growth in other ways. Managers failed to modernize their factories and make their products internationally competitive. One study has shown that American-controlled firms in Great Britain yielded 50 percent higher returns than the British-managed firms because of lower administrative costs, better salesmanship, higher productivity, and greater concentration of capital investment.

The British automobile industry represents a clear example of Britain's inability to capitalize on its postwar potential. With the continental car companies unable to meet European demand, the British had an excellent opportunity to break into the European market. But English car manufacturers resisted mergers and continued to produce a huge variety of automobiles, none of which could capture a large share of the continental market. Even after two companies merged in 1951 to form the British Motors Corporation, the new firm continued to produce the same old cars. Eventually it did turn out the Mini, thereby breaking the tradition of heavy, rugged cars typical of British automakers. But by this time, other European car manufacturers were meeting the European demand.

A 1968 merger of BMC and Leyland Motors into one huge enterprise called British Leyland Motors, coupled with Britain's entry into the Common Market, did not raise the sales of British automobiles as many expected. Foreign sales of British cars are restricted to a few Europeans and Americans who consider ownership of a Rolls Royce, Jaguar, or Rover a status symbol.

Italy: Economic Development

Despite a slow beginning, since 1954 the Italian economic growth rate has exceeded those of all other EEC states except West Germany. However, this growth was restricted to the north, where Italians enjoy a standard of living similar to northern Europeans. Except for small pockets of industrialization, southern Italy has remained an underdeveloped area.

In the early 1970s, a large portion of EEC development money was still going to southern Italy. Italian politicians and industrialists were at first more intent on developing their markets within the EEC than on developing the south. Fiat, the largest automobile manufacturer in Europe, refused to open plants in the south on the ground that industry had to be concentrated in order to meet modern competition.

To be sure, the concentration of industry and banking has been a major reason for Italy's rapid industrial expansion. The fact that IRI controls a number of banks and 120 companies makes possible a concentration of capital for investment purposes, a reduction of domestic competition, and a focus on the European market. The concentration of oil and gas resources permits ENI to compete with the large American petroleum companies for foreign markets and petroleum resources. Plentiful supplies of labor have kept wages low and Italian products highly competitive in Europe and the international market. In 1966, Italian wages were only about half those in West Germany and Great Britain. Serious labor unrest was avoided through the employment of thousands of southern Italian laborers in Germany, Switzerland, and France.

A rapidly growing domestic and foreign demand and an internal concentration of industry have created a number of mammoth firms. In the 1960s, Italy was producing most of the refrigerators used in the Common Market, and Fiat had become the largest automobile manufacturer in Europe. Within Italy the demand for cars continually outstripped the supply. In 1960, one out of every twenty-one Italians owned a car; in 1968, one out of seven. And Olivetti became one of the world's largest producers of office machines.

Postwar Development Patterns

By the end of the 1960s, Europe was divided among a variety of economic organizations and exhibited a multitude of economic faces. Wide differences existed between the advanced industrialized west and north and the predominantly agrarian underdeveloped south. Economic change was beginning to transform Spain, but Portugal and Greece had undergone little economic modernization.

Immigration to the labor-hungry factories of the north provided a measure of relief for a small segment of the population, and worker remittances to their families provided some stimulus to the south, but this could not be a long-term substitute for economic modernization at home. In some cases emigration tended to thwart modernization by siphoning off skilled professionals and laborers. In agriculture, emigration often brought improvement by removing surplus population from the land, but sometimes large areas were virtually depopulated, agricultural output dropped, and costs rose as food had to be imported. In the 1970s it became apparent that the benefits of emigration were short-term when a Western European economic recession forced many migrant workers to return to their native countries.

Western Europe itself was shocked by the high inflation rates and reduced growth rates of the early 1970s, as detailed in chapter 14. The Keynesian manipulation of the economy no longer produced immediate results, as it had done in the 1950s and early 1960s. European optimism flagged as growth rates dipped and unemployment figures climbed. Countless economic conferences were held to ascertain the problems and provide the remedies for economic stagnation.

But the slump was probably unavoidable. The growth rates had been extremely high for nearly two decades but could not be sustained indefinitely. With consumption levels approaching those of the United States, Western Europe began to experience similar economic difficulties. There were limits to the demand that could be stimulated in order to perpetuate high rates of growth. Europe was more dependent on exports than the United States, but was now facing competition from areas of high output and low labor cost such as Japan. Rising unemployment held down domestic demand. The advanced states of Europe will undoubtedly be hard put to attain the economic growth rates of the past and will have little choice but to endure a certain amount of unemployment. As John Kenneth Galbraith pointed out, demand can be artificially stimulated by convincing people that they must buy unnecessary commodities, but there is a point beyond which the market becomes satiated. Chapters 8 and 14 will take up economic activities in the seventies and eighties.

FURTHER READING

The best recent study of postwar reconstruction is Alan S. Milward, *The Reconstruction of Western Europe, 1945–51* (1984). Milward challenges all those who claim that the successful economic and political reconstruction of Western Europe resulted from the idealism of statesmen, by arguing that it grew out of the pursuit of narrow self-interest by all the countries involved. The Marshall Plan resulted from American self-interest, and European economic integration was primarily the outcome of French self-interest.

An excellent older survey of European industrialization with coverage of the postwar period can be found in David S. Landes, *The Unbound Prometheus* (1970). Another survey, Sidney Pollard's *Peaceful Conquest: The Industrialization of Europe, 1760–1970* (1981), stresses the British industrial experience. Indispensable examinations of the postwar period are Andrew Shonfield, *Modern Capitalism: The Changing Balance of Public and Private Power* (1969); M. M. Postan, *An Economic History of Western Europe, 1945–1964* (1967); and A. Maddison, *Economic Growth in the West* (1964). A stimulating analysis of the role of labor in promoting postwar growth can be found in Charles P. Kindleberger, *Europe's Postwar Growth: The Role of Labor Supply* (1967).

For details of French planning see J. and A. M. Hackett, *Economic Planning in France* (1961), and Pierre Masse, *Histoire, Methode et Doctrine de la Planification Française* (1962). An outstanding recent study of France's economy in the twentieth century is Richard F. Kuisel's *Capitalism and the State in Modern France: Renovation and Economic Management in the Twentieth Century* (1981). Kuisel stresses the role of long-term planning in French economic growth.

The British economy is treated in J. C. R. Dow, *The Management of the British Economy, 1945–1960* (1964); Andrew Shonfield, *British Economic Policy since the War* (1958); Martin J. Wiener, *English Culture and the Decline of the Industrial Spirit, 1850–1980* (1981); M. W. Kirby, *The Decline of British Economic Power since 1870* (1981); and G. B. Stafford, *The End of Economic Growth? Growth and Decline in the U.K. since 1945* (1981). Wiener believes that the adoption of a low-growth mentality by the British elite in the nineteenth century has hampered economic development ever since. Kirby provides a summary of reasons previously advanced for Britain's slow growth after 1945. Stafford presents a survey of the literature of the two main economic theories that have influenced British economic practice: the neoclassical and the Keynesian. For Germany, see Henry C. Wallich, *Mainsprings of German Revival* (1955), and Frederick G. Reuss, *Fiscal Policy for Growth without Inflation: The German Experiment* (1963). For Sweden, see Holger Heide, *Die Langfristige Wirtschaftsplannung in Schweden* (1965). For Italy, see Vera Lutz, *Italy: A Study in Economic Development* (1962), and George A. Hildebrand, *Growth and Structure in the Economy of Modern Italy* (1965).

In *The Marshall Plan: America, Britain, and the Reconstruction of Western Europe, 1947–1952* (1987), Michael J. Hogan argues that the United States wanted to "refashion Western Europe in the image of the United States." John Gimbel's *The Origins of the Marshall Plan* (1976) argues that it was France that blocked four-power agreement over Germany rather than the United States or the Soviet Union. Gimbel claims further that Marshall Plan aid was not a result of the Cold War but was a way to integrate Germany economic recovery with a general European recovery.

Among the many publications of economic statistics are the Organization for Economic Cooperation and Development's annual surveys of all member states, the OECD *Observer*, the United Nations Statistical Yearbooks, and the United Nations' annual economic surveys of Europe.

5 Western European Politics, 1948–1965

France intends to once again exercise sovereignty over her own territory, at present infringed upon by the permanent presence of Allied military forces and by the use which is being made of her airspace, to end her participation in the integrated command, and to no longer place her forces at the disposition of NATO.

Guy de Carmoy
Les Politiques Etrangères de la France, 1944–1966

The rapid economic growth in Western Europe and improved East-West relations determined the course of political development from 1948 to 1965. Spared serious economic crisis after 1948, the politically moderate and right-of-center forces in the major Western European countries were not challenged seriously by the left. Growing economic affluence, combined with government extension of social welfare services and full employment policies, stilled demands for truly revolutionary political change. Parties on the left, kept from office by the improving economic conditions and their own revolutionary rhetoric, began to adopt reformist rather than revolutionary policies. Moderate reformers, such as Willy Brandt in West Germany, emerged as the new leaders of Socialist parties.

Only the Communist parties of France and Italy, which attracted primarily working-class support, continued to pay lip service to revolutionary objectives. But even their revolutionary zeal was dampened by the Soviet Union's suppression of the Hungarian Revolution in 1956. Social Democratic parties gained or shared government office in the 1960s in Italy and Germany only by compromising their former ideals or by breaking away from their revolutionary associates and becoming reformist parties similar to the British Labour party and the Scandinavian Social Democratic parties. In foreign affairs, Europe's economic resurgence and a reduction of Cold War tensions led to a gradual restoration of European self-confidence and the reduction of United States influence in Europe, especially in de Gaulle's France.

Italian Political Affairs

The impact of economic improvement and the Cold War is clearly discernible in Italy during this period. As described in chapter 3, the Cold War and United States influence had led the Christian Democratic party (DC) to drive the Communist party (PCI) from the government in 1947. That same year the reformist issue split the Socialist party into a reformist Social Democratic wing under Giuseppe Saragat and the still revolutionary Socialists (PSI) under Pietro Nenni and Lelio Basso. In a quadripartite government coalition held together only by the parties' shared hostility toward communism, Saragat found that there was considerable opposition to his reformist ideas, especially since the dominant Christian Democratic party based its strength on the Catholic church, big business, big landowners, the lower middle class, and the peasantry.

Eventually, with the aid of the left wing of the DC led by Alcide de Gasperi, some of the Saragat-backed reforms were begun. In 1949 and 1950, a few large estates totaling 20 million acres were expropriated in the south and sold to the peasants. But after the initial redistribution, the DC failed to push further agrarian reform. Only mass immigration to the industrial areas in the north temporarily relieved the situation. As a result, in the 1953 elections the Communist party gained a million votes in the south. Meanwhile, Nenni had led the Socialist party into close cooperation with the Communist party. But Nenni, never comfortable with this alliance, offered to break with the Communists in 1953 and enter a coalition government with the DC if his PSI were given important cabinet positions. Rejecting this offer, de Gasperi and then a succession of premiers put together bare majorities that reduced the government to immobility for the next five years. Heavily factionalized, the Christian Democrats had to rule as a minority party or find partners among the small center parties since they would not seek a coalition with a left or right party. Governments changed rapidly as one or another faction gained predominance in the DC. Only domestic prosperity and decreasing international tension made such government inaction tolerable.

A leftward trend in successive elections in 1953, 1958, and 1963 resulted from decreasing Cold War tensions, rapid economic growth, and the moderating position taken by Palmiro Togliatti, leader of the Communist party. The Communists were responding to a growing sense of economic well-being that was reflected in Labor's selection of more moderate factory and labor union officials. Shocked by the Soviet Union's crushing of the Hungarian Revolution in 1956, Togliatti became convinced that his rightward shift was the proper course.

When Nenni's PSI decided in 1957 to break with the Communist party and seek a coalition with the DC, Togliatti led the PCI even further to the right in order to restore the left coalition. Despite this, Nenni continued to seek a role for the PSI in a coalition with the DC. The attempt to gain PSI approval for the coalition failed in 1957 when the left wing of the party gained a majority against Nenni. When he finally gained a majority for his position, his left-wing opponents within the PSI broke away and formed the Socialist Party of Proletarian Unity or PSIUP.

Nenni's efforts finally succeeded in 1962 when DC leaders agreed to a center-left coalition with the PSI. The left wing of the DC, led by Aldo Moro and Amintore Fanfani, had been trying to arrange an "opening to the left" since 1958. Although there was considerable opposition within the DC to a coalition with the PSI, public support for it was growing. A strong trend to the left in the 1958 parliamentary elections indicated that Italians were finding the parties on the left more acceptable and were becoming discontented with the government's immobility.

Adding immensely to the public's acceptance of the Socialists and their desire for social reform was the papacy's acceptance of the welfare state in the 1960s. This momentous change in papal policy was a direct result of the election of Angelo Roncalli as Pope John XXIII in 1958. A product of humble beginnings himself, Cardinal Roncalli had gained further knowledge of the world's ills on diplomatic missions to the Balkans and as papal nuncio to France. When he became pope he was determined to bring the church into line with modern political and social change. This meant a reversal of the papacy's century-old opposition to all forms of socialism and, in the 1960s, adjusting to the institution of the welfare state throughout Europe. In the 1961 papal bull *Mater et Magistra* (Mother and Teacher), Pope John expressed the papacy's approval of the mixed economy, economic planning, and social justice. A second major papal encyclical, *Pacem in Terris* (Peace on Earth), confirmed this new papal attitude only a few weeks before the 1963 elections.

Within the DC, Moro maneuvered his party closer to the PSI by encouraging DC-PSI coalitions at the local level. With the support gained from forty such coalitions, Moro and Fanfani convinced the majority of the party to accept the PSI in 1962. The PSI had to accept a pro-Western position, including continued membership in NATO and the EEC, and the DC accepted the PSI plan for the nationalization of electric power and the establishment of more regional governments. The DC had originally opposed the regional governments, fearing the left would control most of them. When the left made further gains in the 1963 elections, indicating an increased desire for reforms, Moro was able to convince the recalcitrant DC deputies that his course was necessary in order to keep the DC in power. After some initial difficulties, Moro put together a center-left cabinet with Nenni as vice premier. This leftward trend continued into the 1970s as Cold War tensions declined and the Communist party became even more reformist.

The selection of Willy Brandt, the popular Social Democratic mayor of West Berlin, to head the party sealed the victory of the reformers. In their eyes, their choice of course was proved right in the 1961 parliamentary elections when SPD seats in the *Bundestag* increased from 169 to 190 and CDU seats dropped from 270 to 242.

The 1961 elections indicated further that the CDU was beginning to lose its hold on the German electorate. A measure of the disenchantment could be attributed to the slowing of economic growth and the onset of a mild recession, but other factors were political infighting in the CDU and Adenauer's increasingly authoritarian behavior. In 1959, Adenauer had agreed to take the post of president and give up the chancellorship to Ludwig Erhard. When he realized that Erhard, whom he personally disliked, would be the real ruler in Germany and the presidency would be only a titular post, Adenauer went back on his word. This type of behavior was tolerated when economic growth was rapid and Germany's future was in doubt; now it became intolerable.

After the election losses in 1961, Adenauer managed to gain support for his plan to form a new cabinet only by promising to retire before the 1965 elections. But before he retired he became involved in another incident that was to blemish his own reputation and that of the CDU. Adenauer's defense minister, Franz Josef Strauss, irritated when the magazine *Der Spiegel* published what he considered to be secret military information, arrested five members of the editorial staff. When both Strauss and Adenauer refused to take responsibility for the affair, the Free Democratic party members of the cabinet threatened to resign and thus bring down the government. Strauss was eventually forced to resign, and Adenauer promised to resign in the fall of 1963.

This incident brought into question Adenauer's, and indirectly the CDU's, commitment to democratic government. It tarnished Adenauer's reputation and made the ministry of his successor, Erhard, much more difficult. Throughout West Germany it unleashed a spate of criticism of many CDU programs. Critics contended that Germans had not received the proper education in the principles of democracy because of Adenauer's authoritarian government. The criticism further indicated that the German public did not want a return to arbitrary government.

When Erhard failed to stem the economic recession and the Free Democrats quit the coalition government in 1966, the way was paved for the SPD to share power with the CDU in 1966 and gain power in a coalition with the Free Democrats in 1969.

French Political Affairs

The changes in French socialism and politics have been as dramatic as those in West Germany. As early as 1945, the Socialist party (SFIO) accepted the Western orientation of French foreign policy and coalition with the Christian Democrats (MRP). Socialist leader Ramadier refused to support the candidacy of Communist leader Thorez for French premier. The exclusion of both Communists and Gaullists from the government after 1947 produced an extremely fragile center-left coalition of the SFIO, the MRP, the moderate-liberal Radicals, and the Moderates. This quadripartite coalition, held together primary by a shared dislike for the PCF and de Gaulle, could not agree on a unified economic or colonial policy.

The nineteen different governments between 1948 and 1958 prevented France from dealing resolutely with its domestic or foreign policy. Only the eight-month government of Pierre Mendès-France can claim much success. This government paralyzation, called *immobilisme* in France, resulted from the internal divisions between right and left that prevented a legislative-based executive from acting resolutely over an extended period of time. On the right, traditional Conservatives, Gaullists, Colonialists and radical-rightist Poujadists battled for the vote. The left was divided by the Communists and the two Socialist parties. The center parties failed to maintain any long-term voter support. For example, The centrist MRP gradually lost support as its left-wing supporters shifted to the Socialists and its right-wing joined with Moderates or Gaullists. De Gaulle's political support was also not dependable. The national movement he established in 1947, the Rally of the French People (RPF), gained 40 percent of the vote in the October 1947 municipal elections but then faded as its Conservative supporters switched to traditional right-wing groups. The RPF managed to become the largest party in the 1951 parliamentary elections by altering the proportional election system to permit a party or coalition that won a majority in any constituency to take all the seats in that area. But the RPF's turn to traditional party politics in the early fifties led de Gaulle to retire from the political arena for the second time in 1955. This change in the electoral system led to the displacement of the MRP and the Socialists as the dominant parties by the right-wing Radicals and even more conservative Independents. The MRP lost about half of its following to the RPF in the 1951 elections.

Governments fell rapidly in the fifties as colonial problems multiplied, but even successes in colonial policy were not always sufficient to ensure government stability. Premier Pierre Mendès-France had ended French involvement in the Indochina War (see pages 116–117) and granted autonomy to Tunisia in 1954, but he fell from office the following year when he was unable to change his Radical party's economic policies from laissez-faire to economic planning. A reform-minded Radical-Socialist coalition government of 1956, led by Mendès-France's reformist Radicals and Guy Mollet's Socialists, was overthrown by rightist opposition. It fell in early 1957 when its attempts to reform the tax system were defeated by Conservative opposition.

By the midfifties, foreign policy—the EDC, Indochina, Suez, and particularly Algeria—inflamed political exchange and pushed domestic issues off center stage. The Algerian rebellion brought down the Fourth Republic, returned de Gaulle to power, and enabled him to change dramatically the French tradition of a dominant legislature. It also thrust de Gaulle and France into a position of European dominance that prompted some observers to dub European history from 1958 to 1968 "the de Gaulle era." For Europe as a whole, de Gaulle's resolution of the Algerian problem instilled a new confidence and respect that enabled Europe to chart a more independent course.

The Fourth Republic was split over Algeria. The right, including the Gaullists, strenuously opposed any concessions to the Algerian rebels. Support for the right came from more than a million French settlers (*colons*), four-fifths of them born in Algeria, and from a large segment of the French army. The loss of Indochina in 1954, the failure of the Anglo-French force against Egypt's Nasser in 1956, and the granting of independence to Tunisia and Morocco in 1956 (see chapter 6) made French rightists and the army determined to keep Algeria. The army, numbering nearly half a million in Algeria by 1957, had concluded that the French government could not be trusted to "save" Algeria for France. Attacks from the right diminished the stability of the Fourth Republic and led to a steady decline in its control over the army.

Ironically, a decisive attempt to resolve the Algerian issue by the normally indecisive Fourth Republic brought about its downfall. On the last day of January in 1956, an Algerian reform bill, providing for regional autonomy and equality of voting for Muslims and Europeans in Algeria, was rendered unworkable by French military action against the Algerian rebels, who now refused to accept the bill. When the Fourth Republic selected a ministry headed by Pierre Pflimlin (MRP) in May 1958, a man the army and the *colons* expected would offer concessions to the Algerian rebels, French army units with *colon* support occupied the palace of the governor-general in Algiers in May 1958 and set up a Committee of Public Safety with General Jacques Massu at its head. The rightists and certain army officers then began to prepare a paratroop attack on Paris.

This anarchic situation enabled the Gaullists to demand the return of de Gaulle to prevent a civil war in France. After a round of negotiations with President René Coty, the National Assembly approved de Gaulle as the new premier on June 1, 1958. When de Gaulle told the French Assembly that he had formed a government to preserve the Republic, one skeptical deputy warned, "Today, chamber music. Tomorrow, a brass band."

The crisis atmosphere gave de Gaulle the opportunity to institute the kind of government that would provide the strong executive authority he desired. Never wavering from his conviction that the French government should not be dominated by the legislature, de Gaulle pushed through a constitution that increased the power of the executive and reduced the authority of the Assembly. The constitution that set up the French Republic, approved by 80 percent of the voters on September 28, 1958, permitted the president to appoint the premier and to dissolve Parliament. Although the premier and the cabinet theoretically shared executive authority with the president, de Gaulle now wielded power comparable to that of the American president.

Elections in November further solidified de Gaulle's position by giving the Gaullist UNR (Union for the New Republic) 189 of the 576 seats in the National Assembly. A return to the Third Republic electoral system, which required a run-off election in districts where no candidate received a majority, succeeded in reducing the representation of the Communists and their allies from 150 deputies to only 10. De Gaulle was selected as president by an overwhelming 78.5 percent of the votes from an electoral college of over 80,000 voters.

In 1958, de Gaulle's objectives were not yet clear even in his own mind. He was influenced by foreign criticism and the possibility that a United Nations' vote of condemnation might thwart his objective of restoring French prestige in the world. Now, armed with the new powers given him by the new constitution, he could tackle the Algerian problem with increased confidence and bring the army back under the control of the government.

To gain military support, de Gaulle at first kept his aims vague, thus leading the army to believe that he would keep Algeria French. Although he wanted to retain Algeria, he realized by 1959 that the Algerian rebels, led by the FLN (National Liberation Front), would not accept continued French suzerainty. His offer of Algerian self-determination in September 1959 was refused by an ever more confident FLN leadership and violently opposed by the French army leaders in Algeria, who now felt betrayed. In January 1960, a mass uprising against de Gaulle's policies, the Barricades Revolt, failed when metropolitan France rallied to his side.

When de Gaulle began to speak about a possible Algerian Republic after November 1960, the French army and *colons* in Algeria adopted yet more violent tactics. A Secret Army Organization (OAS) was set up in Algeria to intimidate those who would support a free Algeria and to bring down de Gaulle's government by means of terrorism and assassination. In April 1961, the army generals in Algeria rebelled, took over the government of Algeria, and threatened military action against metropolitan France. Only de Gaulle's immense prestige made defeat of the generals possible. Supported overwhelmingly in France, he appealed directly to military units not to support the generals. When the air force and the navy chose to follow him, the army generals had to surrender.

De Gaulle was now determined to resolve the Algerian problem and end military disobedience by granting independence and bringing the army home. On March 18, 1962, negotiators for the FLN and the French government met at Évian-les-Bains and decided to grant Algeria its full independence on July 3, 1962. These Évian Accords granted the *colons*

Algerians celebrating their hard-won independence in the place du Gouvernement.
(Paris Match)

equal rights and provided compensation for the property of those who
wished to leave Algeria. Despite widespread OAS terrorism to keep the
French settlers in Algeria, within a year only 100,000 remained. With the
Algerian problem resolved and the French army firmly under his control,
de Gaulle could now turn to his goal of making France the leader of
Europe.

To increase French prestige and strength, de Gaulle believed the authority of the president had to be increased further and the power of the
political parties had to be reduced. He viewed political parties as divisive
forces and therefore tried to circumvent them by appealing to the populace
through national referendums. To strengthen the office of the president
he held a referendum in 1962 on the direct election of the president. Despite the opposition of the National Assembly, which had not approved
the referendum, it won the support of 67.7 percent of the voters.

Now de Gaulle no longer had to please the electors, who were associated with political parties, in order to stay in power. When the Assembly
censured his ministry, with Georges Pompidou as premier, de Gaulle dissolved the Assembly and called new elections. Often he threatened to

resign, and often he warned of the weaknesses of parliamentary government. These ploys helped the Gaullists to gain 250 of the 480 seats and an absolute majority in the Assembly.

Despite the election success, de Gaulle's popularity soon began to decline. Many resented his blocking of British entry into the EEC in 1963. Others shifted their support away from de Gaulle when it became apparent that he wished to reduce French democracy to a facade. A growing number felt that France should not try to develop an independent French military deterrent—as we shall see—but should concentrate on domestic problems. The vote in the 1965 presidential elections reflected a shift toward the left. In the first popular election of a president since 1848, de Gaulle captured only 44 percent of the votes; François Mitterrand, candidate of the newly formed Left Federation (Socialists, Communists, and Radicals), carried 32 percent; and the other major candidate, Jean Lecanuet, representing a centrist coalition, received 16 percent. France was not yet ready for a Socialist president, however. In the run-off election against Mitterrand, de Gaulle gained 54.4 percent of the vote. Despite this victory, popular resentment against de Gaulle would soon reduce Gaullist support and steadily increase the strength of the left in French politics.

Even before de Gaulle had resolved the Algerian problem he began to implement another of his major goals, the reduction of United States influence in Europe. Since de Gaulle was little influenced by ideologies, except for his dislike of the French left, he did not believe in a struggle between communism and capitalism for world dominance. He viewed Soviet actions in terms of old-fashioned balance-of-power considerations rather than from the American perspective. In other words, he felt that Soviet expansionism was limited to Eastern Europe and therefore posed no threat to Western Europe. What is more, he believed a reduction of American influence in Western Europe would not lead to a sovietization of Western Europe but would enhance French power in Europe.

In March 1959, de Gaulle began to withdraw French naval units from the NATO Mediterranean Command as the first step in the French withdrawal from NATO. The United States' humbling of the Soviet Union in the Cuban missile crisis in 1962 and subsequent United States/Soviet steps toward détente convinced de Gaulle that his perception of the Soviet "threat" was accurate.

In order to establish France as an independent third force between the two superpowers, de Gaulle undertook the development of an independent French nuclear force. In 1964, he refused to sign the Nuclear Test Ban Treaty sponsored by the United States and the Soviet Union since it would prevent France from developing its own nuclear force. In 1965, France pulled out of the Southeast Asia Treaty Organization (SEATO) and refused to participate in NATO military maneuvers. In 1966, French forces were withdrawn officially from NATO, and its headquarters was transferred from Paris to Brussels. Contributing to this show of independence was an economic upsurge that brought France a $6 billion gold reserve by 1965.

Despite these actions, de Gaulle was unable to resolve European-Soviet differences unilaterally. By this time, Soviet leaders were more interested in dealing directly with the United States to resolve world and European problems. Still, de Gaulle had begun the gradual loosening of United States/European ties, and other countries followed suit in the late 1960s and 1970s as the United States became mired in the Vietnam War.

British Political Affairs

After defeating a divided, ideologically confused Labour party in 1951, Great Britain's Conservative party retained office until 1964 through the acceptance of the welfare state, the impact of several periods of rapid economic growth, and the continued division in the Labour party. Returning to power at the age of seventy-seven, Winston Churchill changed little of the previous Labour government's programs. Improving economic conditions permitted Churchill to end food rationing, an issue that had contributed to Labour's defeat, and to carry out the Conservative campaign promise to build more than 300,000 houses a year to relieve Britain's housing shortage and stimulate the economy.

Now convinced that the British wanted the welfare state, Churchill did no more than increase medical fees slightly and reverse Labour's nationalization program only in the iron and steel industry and in road transport. The Conservatives did, however, change Labour's policy of raising income taxes to achieve a more equitable distribution of wealth. The Conservatives hoped that the reduction of income taxes would also stimulate the economy.

When a heart attack forced Churchill to retire in 1955, Anthony Eden became prime minister. A business boom in 1954 and 1955 and another reduction in income taxes put an even larger Conservative majority into the House of Commons in the 1955 elections.

Within a year after Eden assumed power he was called upon to deal with Egyptian leader Gamal Abdel Nasser's nationalization of the Suez Canal (see chapter 6). Backed by the majority of the Conservative party and by France, Eden tried to force a reversal of Nasser's policy. In the face of stiff United States' and United Nations' opposition, Britain was forced to back down. Before the crisis had passed, Eden suffered a nervous breakdown and was replaced by Harold Macmillan.

"Supermac" proved to be a more capable leader than Eden. Supported by improving economic conditions, Macmillan spent little time on domestic affairs. He traveled more than 80,000 miles in eighteen months in an attempt to ease Cold War tensions and restore British respectability after the humiliation of Suez. At home, his government slowed investment in the economy and restricted credit in order to avert another devaluation of the pound. Although these measures eventually put the brakes on economic growth and added to the unemployment rolls, a renewed business boom in 1958 and 1959 gave the Conservatives an even larger majority in the House of Commons in the 1959 elections. Labour's support for an expansion of welfare programs apparently contributed to its resounding defeat.

The Labour party was plagued by divisions over social welfare and rearmament throughout the decade. Led by Aneurin Bevan, the left continued to demand more attention to social welfare. The right, under the leadership of Hugh Gaitskell, a former Oxford University economics don, and Clement Attlee, opposed an extension of welfare and the growth of the bureaucracy it would bring about. After the 1959 elections, the right wing convinced the party to jettison nationalization in favor of expanding economic growth through full employment and periodic stimulation of the economy.

Leftist intellectuals writing for the *New Left Review*, shocked by the Soviet suppression of the Hungarian Revolution, began to emphasize democratic socialism in place of class conflict and economic controls. The Labour support for British development of the hydrogen bomb in 1957 produced a new left movement, the Campaign for Nuclear Disarmament (CND). The CND and the left wing of the party finally got Labour to reverse its stand on nuclear weapons but not its drift toward a more moderate political and social program.

An economic downturn after 1959, reflected in a growing inflation rate and an unfavorable balance of trade, undermined Conservative support. Although Macmillan resorted to a wage freeze, increased indirect taxes, and initiated some very unconservative economic devices to overcome the economic downturn—even including a modified form of economic planning—he was unable to turn the economy around.

The economic malaise stemmed from a variety of shortcomings in the British economy described earlier (see chapter 4), as well as from growing competition from the continental European countries and Japan. Adding to Conservative woes in 1963 was de Gaulle's veto of British entry into the Common Market. Although Britain's entry would certainly not have brought immediate relief to the British economy because of the dislocations accompanying entry, it was a severe blow to Macmillan's much-publicized plans for British entry.

Then Macmillan's secretary of state for war, John Profumo, became the subject of a scandal. As banner headlines reported day after day, he was involved with a call girl, and she had been asked by a naval attaché of the Soviet Embassy to get all the information she could from Profumo on Britain's nuclear arsenal. Although Macmillan demanded and got Profumo's resignation, he was himself compelled to take some of the responsibility. This scandal and his increasing bad health led Macmillan to tender his resignation.

Macmillan was replaced by Sir Alec Douglas-Home. Even though Douglas-Home lacked the charisma of Macmillan and of the Labour candidate Harold Wilson, he won the election by a slim four-seat margin. Despite all the Conservatives' problems, there was still considerable anxiety about a Labour government.

Nordic Political Affairs

There was little anxiety about left-of-center governments in Scandinavia. With the exception of Finland, where the Agrarian and Socialist parties shared power, the Scandinavian countries had Socialist-dominated governments from the end of the war until the mid-1960s. Only Denmark had a brief interruption, from 1950 to 1953, of Social Democratic or Labor party leadership. The Social Democrats might have gained power in Finland were it not for the Soviet Union's preponderant influence and its distrust of the Social Democrats. As the Conservative parties in Western Europe had profited from the postwar economic resurgence, so did the Socialist parties in Scandinavia.

Economically, Western Europe had been divided into two blocs, the European Economic Community (France, Italy, West Germany, and the Benelux countries) and the European Free Trade Association or EFTA (Austria, Denmark, Great Britain, Norway, Portugal, Sweden, and Switzerland). This caused some economic dislocations, but in general, the Scandinavian countries profited from the expansion of both. In 1960, about one-third of Swedish exports were going to partners in EFTA and another one-third to the EEC. Denmark, always a major exporter of farm products, managed to bring its industrial exports abreast of its agricultural exports by means of a concerted industrialization program coupled with tariff reductions among EFTA countries.

The Norwegian Labor party and the Swedish and Danish Social Democrats, which had been in power since the interwar years, increased their popularity during the rapid economic expansion by extending social welfare services. Sweden adopted compulsory health insurance and pension plans, family allowances, and other social measures that cost the country $3 billion a year (see chapter 9). By 1965, Denmark and Norway had similarly become social welfare states.

The economic resurgence had contributed to Socialist success in the 1950s, and the economic downturns in the 1960s undermined their leadership. An economic slowdown in Denmark in the mid-1960s, caused by the high tariff walls erected by the EEC, resulted in a devaluation of the kroner. Adding to the Socialist woes were exceedingly high direct and indirect taxes, needed to support the welfare state, that were increasingly resented by the population. When both the Social Democrats and their coalition partner, the Socialist People's party, lost votes in the 1968 elections, a group of center parties formed a governing coalition.

Labor's thirty-year rule in Norway, weakened also by the EFTA-EEC split, ended when the Conservative, Liberal, and Center parties formed a coalition cabinet. However, these changes had little effect on domestic policies since all Scandinavian parties accepted the welfare state.

Benelux Political Affairs

Politics in the Benelux countries are incredibly complex because of the plethora of parties—ten parties won parliamentary seats in the 1963 elections in the Netherlands—and because ethnic and religious differences intrude into the political arena.

In Belgium the division between Flemish (Dutch)-speaking Belgians and French-speaking Belgians (Walloons) often cuts across party lines. In general the Flemish support the Catholic party—the Social Christians— whereas the Walloons favor the Socialists and the Liberals. State support for Catholic schools became a major issue in the 1950s and was resolved only through a compromise that permitted the state to supplement the salaries of teachers in church-sponsored schools. Controversy over Louvain University (the Flemish wanted it to be exclusively Flemish) was resolved only by a division of the university into separate Flemish and Walloonian institutions.

Relatively slow economic growth—the gross national product, or GNP, grew at a rate of only 2.7 percent in the 1950s—exacerbated the ethnic-linguistic division. The Walloons, who had dominated the country in the interwar period, suffered most from the economic stagnation. Most new industry was built in the Flemish region because of its superior transportation facilities, and the southern Walloon area bore the brunt of the economic decline because the coal resources in that area had been exhausted. When the government tried to revitalize industry in 1960 by applying austerity measures, including reductions in welfare benefits and public works as well as various aids to industry, a twenty-seven-day general strike brought down the government.

In the 1960s, the Flemish-Walloonian division continued to inhibit government attempts to resolve the nation's economic problems. Ministries fell in 1965 and 1968 primarily over the language issue. There was some relaxation of tension late in the decade as EEC aid ended the economic stagnation and encouraged a greater sense of community. Moreover, the economic impact of losing the Belgian Congo and Ruanda-Urundi was offset by the improving economic conditions. The creation of dual ministers for education, culture, economy, and community problems further reduced the Flemish-Walloon acrimony.

Despite the multiplicity of parties in the Netherlands and the division of most institutions along religious lines, rapid economic growth has tended to keep the turmoil down to manageable proportions. Although the Netherlands had suffered severely from German bombardment during the war, its geographic location at the mouth of the Rhine and its traditional focus on commerce contributed to its rapid recovery as world trade picked up and German industry expanded. Rotterdam has become the leading seaport in Europe and the Dutch the major EEC shipping nation. The loss of Indonesia in 1949 had little effect on the Dutch economy, as evidenced by the doubling of industrial output from 1954 to 1964 and by the growth of commercial activities.

The Catholic People's party and the Labor party dominated the political scene throughout the 1950s and 1960s. A Labor and Catholic People's party coalition ruled the country until 1958, when Labor lost support by its unorthodox policy of wage fixing. After 1958, the Catholic People's party, in coalition with two Protestant (Calvinist) parties, took over the premiership. Both major parties lost votes and suffered internal splits in the mid-1960s, but they continued to dominate the coalition governments or renew their association, as they did in a ministry in 1965 and 1966.

Austrian Political Affairs

The easing of Cold War tensions, coupled with rapid economic growth, had a singular impact on Austrian political affairs. Occupied by the wartime Allies since World War II, Austria had had no chance to regain its national sovereignty during the Stalin era because Stalin considered Austria to be of strategic importance in Central Europe. But in 1955, Khrushchev, in a move to reduce Cold War tensions, agreed to end the occupation of Austria in return for an Austrian pledge of permanent neutrality.

At first, Austrian politics was changed little by the sudden end of occupation. The Social Democrats and Christian Socialists, who had shared political office and civil service jobs in direct proportion to their votes since the occupation began, continued their coalition for eleven years after the occupation ended. Both parties were cautious about resuming normal political activities lest there be a dangerous polarization of the kind that had erupted in civil war during the 1930s. However, rapid economic growth and the Social Democrats' adoption of a reformist rather than revolutionary course soon stilled fears of political chaos. With the restoration of political confidence, the coalition was ended in 1966 when the Christian Socialists gained sufficient votes to rule independently.

Iberian Political Affairs

In southern Europe, where economic transformation was minimal, political affairs remained authoritarian. Spain and Portugal, under the dictatorships of Francisco Franco and Antonio Salazar, stoutly resisted political and social change into the 1960s. Opposition political parties continued to be banned in Spain, but Franco was unable to prevent them from forming or put a stop to their clandestine activities. Despite opposition to his regime among the citizenry, Franco continued to receive support from the Catholic church, the army, and the Falange (the official party of the regime).

When opposition developed within the church and the army, Franco was obliged to permit limited reforms. Liberals among the Catholic clergy grew more outspoken in their opposition to Franco's authoritarianism; and young army officers, eager for faster promotions and economic modernization, agitated for change. A group of militant Catholics in the Opus Dei movement, including some government ministers, urged both economic modernization and closer association with the EEC. Bolstered by a strong position it won in the universities after the war, the Anti-Socialist–Pro-Monarchist movement sought to modernize Spain through a rejection of corporatist autarchy favored by the Falange and the adoption of capitalism. After gaining Franco's support in 1957, Opus Dei technocrats directed Spain toward economic incorporation within the Western economic system. Spain's application for membership in the EEC in 1962 owed much to the Opus Dei insistence that Spanish modernization demanded Western capital, trade, and expertise.

Franco's strongest opposition came from Separatists in the northern Catalan and Basque regions, who increasingly resorted to violence to achieve more autonomy. But the opposition groups, including the political parties, were unwilling to undertake a cooperative challenge of the regime. In the 1960s, Franco weakened some of his opposition when he granted limited reforms. He relaxed press censorship, abolished military courts, gave the minorities greater rights, divided the executive powers between himself and Parliament, and permitted the free election of one hundred members of the six hundred-member Parliament.

The regime was further strengthened when the long period of economic stagnation was brought to an end. Increased investments by the United States, Germany, and France provided the necessary industrial capital. In return for permitting American bases in Spain, Franco received both economic and military aid. And as an added fillip, the Spanish economy got a boost from the flood of tourists who came to savor the sunny Mediterranean beaches and low prices.

The Economy in Political Affairs

As the Cold War's significance in domestic politics dwindled, economic factors predominated as determinants of political success or failure. While rapid economic growth in the 1950s had kept the right in the ascendant in the major European countries and had sustained social democracy in the Scandinavian countries, economic downturns in the mid-1960s generated strong and sometimes successful challenges from political

One of many travel posters encouraging tourism in Spain.

adversaries. Labour replaced the Conservatives in Great Britain and
the German Social Democrats gained a share of the Christian Democrats'
political power.

Although the Italian Christian Democrats remained the dominant political party, they faced a growing challenge from parties to their left.
Since the French economy did not begin a serious downturn until the late
1960s, and since de Gaulle's diplomatic successes were still fresh in the
minds of the French up to that time, the Gaullist-led UNR remained strong
until then. But center and left coalitions formed, and de Gaulle's margin
in 1965 was much narrower than expected, heralding the beginning of the
challenge to Gaullist political dominance. In Scandinavia, only the Swedish Social Democrats managed to stay in power in the 1960s. The ruling
Norwegian Labor party and the Social Democrats in Denmark fell from
power primarily as a result of economic issues.

A particularly significant factor in the changing political fortunes of

Europe's ruling parties was social welfare. In many of the major states, the electorate was demanding extended welfare programs and reforms, whereas in Scandinavia the electorate was demanding a halt to the extension of even more elaborate welfare programs. In countries where social welfare and an economic downturn were combined issues, the parties in power were seriously weakened or were supplanted as the dominant parties.

FURTHER READING

Important studies of British politics are Samuel H. Beer, *British Politics in the Collectivist Age* (1965) and *Britain against Itself: The Political Contradictions of Collectivism* (1982); R. Rose, *Politics in England* (1964); and R. M. Punnett, *British Government and Politics* (1968). Valuable analyses of the relationship between politics and the social structure of Britain are provided in Kingsley Martin, *The Crown and the Establishment* (1963); D. V. Glass, *The British Political Elite* (1963); and Anthony Sampson, *Anatomy of Britain Today* (1965). British elections are treated in the studies of David E. Butler, *The British General Election of 1951* (1952) and the *British General Election of 1955* (1956); David E. Butler and Richard Rose, *The British General Election of 1959* (1960); and David E. Butler and Anthony King, *The British General Election of 1964* (1965). Conflicting studies of the British Labour party are Barry Hindess's *The Decline of Working Class Politics* (1977) and Tom Forester's *The British Labour Party and the Working Class* (1976). Forester rejects Hindess's thesis that the British Labour party experienced a deradicalization and increasing control by the middle class.

Valuable background studies of the development of French political ideologies and alignments and the relationship between society and politics can be found in Gordon Wright, *France in Modern Times* (1981); and David Thomson, *Democracy in France* (1958). Postwar French politics are analyzed in Philip Williams, *Crisis and Compromise: Politics in the Fourth Republic* (1964); Philip Williams and Martin Harrison, *Politics and Society in de Gaulle's Republic* (1971); Lowell G. Noonan, *France: The Politics of Continuity in Change* (1970); Stanley Hoffmann (ed.), *France: Change and Tradition* (1963); Raymond Aron, *France: Steadfast and Changing* (1960); Jacques Chapsal, *La Vie Politique en France depuis 1940* (1966); and François Goguel and Alfred Grosser, *La Politique en France* (1964).

Valuable studies of de Gaulle are Alexander Werth, *De Gaulle: A Political Biography* (1966); J. M. Tournoux, *La Tragédie du Général* (1967); and Brian Crozier, *De Gaulle* (1973). Crozier's study is a lengthy and valuable synthesis that is critical of de Gaulle. French communism is treated in Charles A. Micaud, *Communism and the French Left* (1963); George Lichtheim, *Marxism in Modern France* (1966); J. Fauvet, *Histoire du Parti Communiste Français* (1965); and Irwin M. Wall, *French Communism in the Era of Stalin: The Quest for Unity and Integration, 1945–1962* (1983). For further information on Christian Democracy, see Mario Einaudi and François Goguel, *Christian Democracy in Italy and France* (1952); and M. P. Fogarty, *Christian Democracy in Western Europe* (1957).

The best studies of Italian politics are Giuseppe Mammarella, *Italy after Fascism: A Political History, 1943–63* (1964); Norman Kogan, *A Political History of Post-war Italy* (2 vols., 1966 and 1981); Joseph LaPalombara, *Interest Groups in Italian Politics* (1963); and Donald Sassoon, *Contemporary Italy: Politics, Economy and Society since 1945* (1986). The Italian Communist party is competently treated in Donald Blackmer's *Unity in Diversity: Italian Communism and the Communist World* (1968). The Christian Democratic party is covered in Mario Einaudi and François Goguel, *Christian Democracy in Italy and France* (1952); and M. P. Fogarty, *Christian Democracy in Western Europe* (1957).

For further information on the nature of West German politics, see Lewis J. Edinger, *Politics in Germany* (1968); Edward Pinney, *Federalism, Bureaucracy and Party Politics in Western Germany* (1963); and Uwe W. Kitzinger, *German Electoral Politics* (1960). For a comparisons of East and West German politics, see Arnold J. Heidenheimer, *The Governments of Germany* (3d ed., 1971) and Henry A. Turner, Jr., *The Two Germanies since 1945: East and West* (1987).

The workings of the West German Parliament are treated in Gerhard Loewenberg, *Parliament in the German Political System* (1967). The transformation of the Social Democratic party is analyzed in Douglas A. Chalmers, *The Social Democratic Party of Germany: From Working Class Movement to Modern Political Party* (1964). Two important studies of Adenauer are Arnold J. Heidenheimer, *Adenauer and the CDU: The Rise of the Leader and the Integration of the Party* (1960), and Richard Hiscocks, *The Adenauer Era* (1966). A more critical and controversial treatment of Adenauer and German politics is presented in Ralf Dahrendorf, *Society and Democracy in Germany* (1969). Two important studies of German foreign policy are David Calleo, *The German Problem Reconsidered* (1978), and Wolfram Hanrieder, *Germany, America, Europe. Forty Years of German Foreign Policy* (1989).

Valuable surveys of Franco's Spain are Stanley G. Payne, *Franco's Spain* (1967); Max Gallo, *Spain under Franco* (translated from the French by Jean Stewart, 1974); and Raymond Carr and Juan Pablo Fusi Aizpurua, *Spain: Dictatorship to Democracy* (1979). Political dissent under Franco can be studied in José Maravall, *Dictatorship and Political Dissent: Workers and Students in Franco's Spain* (1978). Maravall shows how attempts to grow and develop through more liberal and open policies while maintaining authoritarian institutions led to worker and student dissent.

For the small states of Western Europe, see D. A. Rustow, *The Politics of Compromise: A Study of Parties and Cabinet Government in Sweden* (1955). Norway is treated in Harry Eckstein, *Division and Cohesion in Democracy: A Study of Norway* (1966). For the Netherlands, see Arend Lijphart, *The Politics of Accommodation: Pluralism and Democracy in the Netherlands* (1968). Hugh Kay, *Salazar and Modern Portugal* (1970), and Charles E. Newell, *Portugal* (1973), cover Portugal during this period. For Austria, see W. T. Bluhm, *Building an Austrian Nation* (1973), and Kurt Steiner, *Politics in Austria* (1972).

6 The End of European Empire

We prefer self-government with danger to servitude in tranquillity.

Kwame Nkrumah, *Autobiography*

During the two decades following World War II, Europe lost its Asian and its African empires. The Asian Empire was the first to go because of national liberation movements that began before World War I. By 1965, most of Africa had followed the Asian countries to independence. Over forty countries with one-quarter of the world's population had overthrown colonialism in this brief span of time.

Although World War II had provided a powerful stimulus to the independence movements, many of the liberation struggles, especially those in Asia and the Middle East, were well under way before the war. Japan's successful challenge of Russian imperialism in the 1905 Russo-Japanese War provided an early impetus to Nationalist groups throughout Asia by convincing them that the European powers were not invincible.

During World War I, the European powers weakened themselves by promoting Nationalist movements against each other: Germany encouraged Arab nationalism against the French in the Maghreb; and the British and French promoted nationalism in the Middle East against Germany's ally, Turkey. Wartime promises of concessions in return for aid against their enemies further loosened the grasp of Europe's nations on some colonies. As World War I drew to a close, the anti-Imperialist propaganda campaign launched by Lenin after the Bolshevik Revolution in November of 1917 instigated a countermovement in the West. U.S. president Woodrow Wilson's support for self-determination in his Fourteen Points was followed by Briton David Lloyd George's pledge in 1918 that self-determination was applicable to the colonies as much as it was elsewhere.

But World War I also provided a stimulus to the victors who enlarged their colonial empires. During the interwar years, Europe's dominance was challenged by colonial elites in some areas but not broken. The economic strain of World War II and the postwar years would force the colonial powers to relinquish their dominance, due primarily to a lack of resources and the growing strength of the anticolonial forces. The colonial powers' responses to the decolonization movements varied. The British put up less resistance than other powers because of the postwar economic exhaustion. Still, the Labour government tried to hold on to areas such as the Middle East through a policy of "partnership" with the elites. The French refused to grant the colonial elites any share of power and clung tenaciously to their colonial empire. Only military defeat (Indochina), savage guerrilla warfare (Algeria), and worldwide pressure (Suez) forced France to quit her colonial possessions. The responses of Britain, France, and other colonial powers to the anticolonial movement were, indeed, so different that no single pattern exists. Their very different responses are discussed in this chapter and chapter 5.

Stages on the Road to Independence

National independence movements commonly passed through three stages before independence was achieved. During the first stage, traditional elites tried to stave off westernization and preserve the native culture and institutions. Tribal chieftains in Africa, for example, engaged in ineffective protests against the vastly superior military might of the colonial powers. Only in Ethiopia and Morocco did leaders of this first, so-called proto-Nationalist stage manage to retain power after independence.

The second, or bourgeois, stage was a direct result of Western modernization of native economies and societies. Except where it was deliberately held back, as in Vietnam, a Western-educated middle class emerged to challenge and in time replace the traditional native elites. In order to destroy the old social order, the colonial powers usually encouraged these middle-class groups, in the expectation that they would remain loyal because of their acceptance of Western ideas, techniques, and institutions. World War I led to a rapid expansion of this Westernized elite.

When the colonial powers concentrated all their efforts on World War I in Europe, a native industrial class grew rapidly. This new elite occupied an ambivalent position in the colonial countries. Despite superior training, the members of the group were allowed to fill only the subordinate positions in the colonial administrations. Denied equal status with the European administrators on the one hand and separated from the traditional society on the other, they were often frustrated in their attempts to bring about the changes they desired or find positions that fit their training. India's Jawaharlal Nehru, who later adopted a more revolutionary posture, aptly described their ambivalent feelings: "Indeed, I often wonder if I represent anyone at all, and I am inclined to think that I do not, though many have kindly and friendly feelings toward me. I have become a queer mixture of the East and West, out of place everywhere, at home nowhere.''

Although the members of this group eventually demanded independence for their countries, their social base remained narrowly middle class. They refused to appeal to the masses of workers and peasants for support, thus generally permitting leadership of the independence movements to pass to more revolutionary countrymen. Independence came during this second phase of the liberation struggle only when the colonial powers withdrew because of financial and international pressures, as in Nigeria and Tanganyika.

For the most part, national liberation movements succeeded during the third, or mass revolutionary, stage. Nationalist leaders such as Mahatma Gandhi and Jawaharlal Nehru in India, Mao Tse-tung in China, Ho Chi Minh in Vietnam, Kwame Nkrumah in Ghana, and Achmed Sukarno in Indonesia mobilized the masses of peasants and workers to overthrow their colonial overlords. Gandhi's policy of massive civil disobedience, adopted in the 1920s, presented the colonial powers with an insurmountable obstacle to their continued rule and provided subsequent Nationalists with techniques that were invaluable in their own liberation struggles. Both Gandhi and Mao established elaborate ties between the masses and revolutionary leaders that were adopted by Nationalists elsewhere. While this three-stage struggle went on for more than a half century in India, it was telescoped into less than fifteen years in Africa, due primarily to the debilitating impact of World War II on the colonial powers.

India's Independence Movement

The parent of all independence movements was clearly that of India. Beginning in 1885 with the Congress party movement, India provides one of the best examples of the three-stage division of Nationalist movements. The first leader of the Congress party, G. K. Gokhale, accepted British rule and asked only for greater integration of educated Indians in the colonial administration. After 1905, a Western-educated elite led by B. G. Tilak rose to leadership in the party. This is the group that ultimately rejected piecemeal reforms and British suzerainty and demanded independence. However, the group's failure to appeal to the Indian masses left the independence movement in the hands of students and a few middle-class leaders. Britain had, in fact, promoted the buildup of a Western-educated elite to support it against the traditional Nationalists.

World War I and its aftermath irretrievably weakened the British hold on India. From this point on, the British could only engage in delaying tactics as they watched the Nationalist movement gather momentum and pass into the third stage. To maintain their influence, in 1917 the British promised the gradual development of self-governing institutions; and in 1919, they committed themselves to internal self-government by installments. But the British massacre of Indians at Amritsar in 1919 showed that internal self-government would not come soon. By this time the Congress party was demanding independence on its own terms.

When Gandhi organized the party on a mass basis with the Nagpur Constitution of 1920, it had a chain of command stretching to the district and village level. His policy of massive civil disobedience stymied the British despite their superior resources. Congress's other leader, Nehru, overcame rightist opposition within the party and pushed through a social reform program that tied the masses to the new leadership. Winston Churchill seriously misread the Congress party's new revolutionary program and its impact on the masses when he said in 1931: "They merely represent those Indians who have acquired a veneer of Western civilization, and have read all those books about democracy which Europe is now beginning increasingly to disregard."

Other British leaders had by 1935 become sufficiently convinced of the strength of the Congress party to pass the Government of India Act, which provided for the election of provincial legislatures and the establishment of provincial cabinets. By granting local rights and maintaining control over foreign affairs and other national issues, Britain hoped to stop the independence movement. But the Congress party would now be content with nothing less than complete independence.

Efforts to secure Indian cooperation against Germany during World War II finally convinced British leaders that they had no choice but to grant India its independence. When Britain requested Indian aid in 1939, the Congress party not only refused but also withdrew its representatives from the provincial parliaments. Britain responded by jailing many of the Congress leaders. However, the Japanese march through Indochina and Burma forced the British to seek an accord in 1942.

For its cooperation, the British representative, Sir Stafford Cripps, offered India full dominion status within the British Commonwealth after the war. Gandhi, mindful of earlier promises that went unfulfilled as well as of Britain's predicament in the war against Germany, would not compromise. Instead, the party passed a Quit India Resolution that promised cooperation if independence was granted or massive resistance if it was refused. Again Congress leaders were put in jail, where they remained until the end of the war.

The absence of the major leaders of the Congress party permitted the Muslim League, led by Mohammed Ali Jinnah, to build up its strength. Street clashes between Muslims and Hindus increased in number and intensity as the Muslim League pushed for its own separate state once independence was achieved.

With the Labour party victory in the 1945 British elections, independence for India awaited only the resolution of the Muslim-Hindu dispute. In the elections for a Central Legislative Assembly set up by a sympathetic Labour party, the Muslim League and the Congress party captured most of the seats. But the Muslim League refused to take part in a cabinet headed by Nehru.

While the British engaged in fruitless attempts to bring the two sides together, continued street clashes divided the two sides even further. Convinced by February 1947 that a unitary Indian state could be achieved only if the two factions were compelled to resolve their differences, Britain announced that it was pulling out of India by June 1948. Realizing that no compromise was possible, in July 1947 Britain passed the India Independence Bill that set up two independent states: India and Pakistan.

After a massive migration of Muslims and Hindus and considerable bloodshed, India and Pakistan became independent states in August 1947. Both were given the option to turn their backs on the British Commonwealth; both decided to remain within it. Despite the partition, India became a powerful symbol for countries still under colonial domination. After studying Gandhi's policies, Nkrumah said it "could be the solution to the colonial problem." In fact, many Nationalist leaders adopted the same policy of passive resistance and appeal to the masses. Shortly after India gained its independence, Nationalist pressures in Ceylon and Burma, in combination with financial problems at home, led Britain to relinquish its jurisdiction over these two countries.

China's Independence Movement

Although China remained independent during the imperialist period, it was unable to prevent the European powers and Japan from establishing hegemony over most of its coastal areas' major cities. The three-stage Nationalist pattern is associated in China with three people: Kang Yu-wei, Sun Yat-sen, and Mao Tse-tung.

In Kang's time (the late 1800s), China was ruled by the Manchus, a Mongol people who had invaded in 1643 and had stayed on to found the Manchu dynasty. As if that were not enough of foreigners, in the Sino-Japanese War of 1894–1895 China had suffered defeat at the hands of Japanese forces. Furthermore, before the turn of the century, Western powers were clamoring for economic concessions.

Kang stirred up popular sentiment against aliens and promoted enthusiastic but ill-planned and ill-directed attacks on foreigners. Most notable of these was the Boxer Rebellion in 1900, which the Western powers crushed with singular brutality.

Realizing the futility of such tactics, a new reform group sought to rid China of the Manchus. This is the group, led by Dr. Sun Yat-sen, which later came to be called the Kuomintang. In 1911, Sun succeeded in overthrowing the Manchus and establishing the Republic of China. Before World War I, Sun had been convinced that a Western-style democracy could modernize China and eliminate foreign influence. He won the sup-

Mao Tse-tung (dark clothing) chatting with peasants in Yenan, China, in the late 1930s. Peasant support was crucial in the later success of Mao's forces. (East-foto—Sovfoto)

port of the growing Chinese business class, which wanted a stronger government to protect it against foreign competition.

By 1919, Sun no longer believed that a narrowly based liberal government could counter Western influence. Adopting passive resistance and the boycott of foreign goods, Sun began the transition to the third stage of nationalism. This transition was completed when he reorganized the Kuomintang as a mass party with an army aimed at revolution and aligned the Kuomintang with the Communist party led by Mao Tse-tung.

When Sun died in 1925, the Nationalist movement split between the followers of Mao and the more conservative followers of Sun's successor, Chiang Kai-shek. Chiang rejected social reform, whereas Mao proclaimed an Agrarian Revolution in 1927. Now Chiang, leading the Kuomintang forces and supported by businessmen, financiers, and landlords, attacked Mao's Communist forces, pushing them back into the far north of China. While Mao built up Communist strength in Shensi province in the 1930s, the corruption-riddled Kuomintang split into factions as the Japanese took over control of most of the heavily populated areas of China.

During World War II, a three-cornered war broke out between Mao, the Kuomintang, and the Japanese. When the Japanese Empire collapsed in 1945, the United States tried to arrange a coalition between the Communists and the Kuomintang. Neither side was willing to cooperate, and civil war broke out again in 1946. Although Chiang's forces controlled most of the cities, they could not subdue the countryside. Despite more than $2 billion in American aid, Mao's forces gradually pushed southward, gaining the support of China's peasants with their policy of land reform.

Mao said, "Whoever wins the support of the peasants will win China; whoever solves the land question will win the peasants." Now his prophecy was borne out. Winning the support of the peasantry as they advanced, the Communists took control of Peking in January 1949 and proclaimed the Chinese People's Republic in October. By 1950, the Kuomintang was driven off the Chinese mainland onto the island of Formosa, now called Taiwan. Mao's organization of the peasantry and guerrilla warfare tactics were to provide the theories and techniques for the conquest of power in other underdeveloped countries.

Indochina's Independence Movement

The lesson of China was not lost on Ho Chi Minh, the Indochinese Nationalist. As early as 1925, he formed the Revolutionary League of the Youth of Vietnam to exploit popular discontent over French colonialism and to organize the peasantry and workers. Groups representing the first two Nationalist stages existed in Indochina but were never strong enough to challenge the revolutionaries. A proto-Nationalist Constitutional party, formed early in the century, opposed both social revolution and demands for independence, and it refused to support nationalistic uprisings in Tonkin and Annam in 1930 and 1931. No democratic-liberal group could gain major support. French colonial policy restricted business activity to French and Chinese entrepreneurs, thus thwarting the development of an indigenous middle class that might have favored a moderate Nationalist course.

The Vietnamese National party (VNQDD), a liberal Nationalist group formed in 1927, gained the support of only a small group of intellectuals. Denied legal existence by the French and ideologically incapable of appealing to the peasantry or workers, it joined Ho Chi Minh's Communists in the abortive revolts in Tonkin and Annam. Remnants of the VNQDD fled to the Kuomintang in China and did not return to Indochina until World War II.

The Communist party, which Ho had formed in 1930, also suffered severely when the French crushed the Communist-led Annam Revolt in 1930 and 1931. French governor-general Pasquier declared, "As a force capable of acting against public order, Communism has disappeared." Ho Chi Minh fled to Moscow, where he remained until 1941. The Indochinese Communists were permitted a legal existence between 1933 and 1939, but a three-way division into Trotskyites, Stalinists, and followers of Ho, together with close French scrutiny, prevented a serious challenge to French rule.

The Communists were forced into hiding again in 1939 after the signing of the Stalin-Hitler Pact led to the outlawing of the Communist party in France. But, as in China, the outbreak of World War II was to have a major impact on the liberation struggle. After an initial abortive Nationalist-Communist attempt to overthrow the French, the Communists and many VNQDD supporters united under the banner of the League for the Independence of Vietnam, or Vietminh, to resist the Japanese invaders. Hitler's invasion of the Soviet Union and Japan's attack on Pearl Harbor propelled the Vietminh into a new role as opponents of fascism.

During the war the Japanese permitted France's Vichy government to continue the administration of Indochina. Ho and the Vietminh, supported by Chiang Kai-shek after 1942, refused to make an all-out effort against the Japanese because they feared that Japan might destroy them; they chose instead to wait for the expected defeat of the Japanese, which would give them the opportunity to assume power. The Japanese paved the way for the Vietminh by disarming and imprisoning the French, who were supplied by the Free French forces of Charles de Gaulle and were planning an attack on the Japanese. When Japan capitulated on August 15, 1945, the Vietminh assumed power under the banner of the hastily organized National Liberation Committee of Vietnam. Ho Chi Minh proclaimed the independence of the Democratic Republic of Vietnam in September 1945. Ho's leadership was acknowledged by Bao Dai, the former emperor of Annam under the French.

Distrusting Ho Chi Minh, the Western Allies had other plans. They assigned administration of the area north of the sixteenth parallel to the Chinese Nationalists and the area south of the sixteenth parallel to the British. The British immediately released the French soldiers and administrators from prison and helped them reestablish their control over the Saigon area. Fearing Chiang Kai-shek, the Vietminh wanted a close association with the French. The left-dominated government in Paris reached an agreement with Ho Chi Minh in March 1946 that recognized his government as a free state within a French Federation in Indochina.

But the French administrators and military in Saigon sabotaged the agreement by setting up the free state of Cochin China in the south. In response, the Vietminh established a dictatorship in the north. In December 1946, war broke out, and the French drove the Vietminh back to their guerrilla bases in the mountains. The military justified the attack by reporting that the Vietminh had tried to kill all the Europeans in Hanoi. What Paris was not told was that the Vietminh action followed on the heels of a French naval attack on the Vietminh quarter of Hanoi that killed 6,000 Vietnamese. The French now set up Bao Dai as the puppet ruler of all Vietnam and granted Cambodia and Laos independence in internal affairs. France hoped it would later be able to set up a federation of states under French hegemony in Indochina.

French attempts to wipe out the Vietminh were frustrated by Vo

Nguyen Giap, who had mastered guerrilla warfare tactics while fighting with Mao's Communist forces in China. Guerrilla warfare continued until 1949, when Mao's victory in China permitted him to start supplying the Vietminh. As the fighting shifted to more conventional warfare after 1950, the United States began to supply the French. Viewed as a part of the worldwide Communist expansion, the Truman administration considered Ho Chi Minh and the Vietminh to be puppets of the Chinese and the Soviet Union.

American financial aid increased from $150 million in 1950 to $1.3 billion by 1953. In spite of this aid, the French attempt to challenge the Vietminh in their mountain strongholds failed in 1954. At the battle of Dien Bien Phu, a French force of 16,000 had to capitulate to the Vietminh after an eight-week siege. The United States provided no military aid at this time because it had just negotiated an end to the war in Korea and President Eisenhower was opposed to another land war in Asia.

The Geneva Conference, called before the battle of Dien Bien Phu, was meeting to bring the war in Indochina to an end when news of the defeat came. The announcement put France in a very weak negotiating position. The French agreed to withdraw from north of the seventeenth parallel, and the Vietminh agreed to pull their troops out of the south. Elections were to be held in 1956 to decide on a government for all of Vietnam. The United States representative at Geneva, John Foster Dulles, refused

Nikita Khrushchev, Mao Tse-tung, and Ho Chi Minh at a banquet in Peking marking the 10th anniversary of the founding of the People's Republic of China, September 30, 1959. (The Bettman Archive)

to take part in the agreement. Following Geneva, the United States pushed aside the French and assumed a preponderant influence in South Vietnam. In 1956, when South Vietnam refused to hold elections, the move had the United States' support.

The second stage of the struggle to liberate all of Vietnam began after 1956, with the United States protecting South Vietnam against the Vietcong Nationalists in the south and against North Vietnam. Another long war ensued. The Vietcong and North Vietnamese resorted to guerrilla warfare against vastly superior American military power. And, despite U.S. efforts to set up a stable government in South Vietnam, a succession of incompetent, corrupt administrations could not win the support of the South Vietnamese. Eventually, international and domestic criticism of the American role in Vietnam forced the United States to withdraw in 1973.

Indonesia's Independence Movement

The impact of World War II was even more decisive in Indonesia, where the Nationalist movement never completely reached the third stage. Neither the Sarekat Islam movement, led by Tjokro Aminoto, nor the *Partai Nasional Indonesia* (PNI), formed by Achmed Sukarno in 1927, made a successful appeal to the peasantry. Led by students and members of the professions, the PNI could not withstand the Dutch military attacks.

But the power of the Dutch was broken by the German conquest of the Netherlands during World War II and the Japanese occupation of the East Indies. When Japan was defeated and World War II came to a close, before the Japanese pulled out of Indonesia they encouraged Sukarno, who had cooperated with them, to set up an independent state. The Dutch, weakened by war, had no choice but to acquiesce when Sukarno proclaimed Indonesia a republic in August 1945. When the Dutch regained their strength, they tried to divide the Nationalists and destroy the independence movement by occupying the cities and imposing an economic blockade. Although they managed to capture Sukarno and other Nationalist leaders in 1948, the United States exerted overwhelming diplomatic and economic pressures on the Dutch to relinquish their East Indies Empire. Since Sukarno and other Nationalists had crushed a Communist regime set up in Maduim in September 1948, the United States evidently hoped it would obtain a strong anti-Communist ally by supporting an independent Indonesia under Sukarno.

In August 1949, the Dutch, realizing that they lacked the military strength to defeat the rebels, agreed to the establishment of the United States of Indonesia within a larger Netherlands-Indonesian Union. However, Sukarno was unhappy with this federalized solution and the continuing ties to the Netherlands, and in 1950 he set up the unitary Republic of Indonesia. Since the Nationalists were divided when independence came and the masses had not been included in the Nationalist movements, a long struggle then ensued to destroy regional loyalties and weld Indonesia's masses into a modern nation state.

Arab Independence Movements

Most of the Arab states in the Middle East and north Africa had gained a measure of independence long before nationalism had developed into a third stage. As a result of the collapse of the Ottoman Empire during World War I and the increased influence of Great Britain and France throughout the Arab world, these new states emerged under native dynasties or aristocratic oligarchies but with special ties to the British or French. Iraq, Palestine, and Transjordan were under a British mandate, and Syria and Lebanon under a French mandate from the League of Nations. Morocco and Tunisia were French protectorates. The other areas were directly controlled (French Algeria and Italian Libya), dominated (British Egypt), or independent (Saudi Arabia and Yemen).

During the interwar years, Britain and France employed several methods to head off middle-class nationalism: propping up existing dynasties, granting quasi-independence, or creating territorial divisions. Britain preferred to support existing dynasties or grant quasi-independence. Immediately after World War I, it supported Reza Khan in Iran and King Farouk in Egypt, and it installed Faisal as king in Iraq. France used the territorial-division method in Syria when it destroyed the unity the Syrians had achieved under the Ottoman Empire by dividing the country into six administrative zones. One of these later became the present state of Lebanon. These divisions created a heated Syrian nationalism that was suppressed only through large-scale imprisonment and exile of Syrian leaders. To this day Syria remains a principal center of Arab nationalism and opponent of Western imperialism.

Three Syrian political groups—the Muslim Brotherhood, the League of National Action, and the Baath party—led the struggle for a united Arab Islamic Empire and emancipation from colonial rule. However, by remaining narrowly intellectual and pan-Arab, these parties were unable to tap the energies of the masses. As a result, France had little difficulty in overcoming the nationalistic movement in the interwar years.

Despite British and French opposition, middle-class nationalism grew. In Tunisia, Habib Bourguiba's middle-class, Nationalist Neo-Destour party replaced the Islamic-inspired Destour party that desired reforms within a French-dominated Tunisia. By 1943, the Nationalist Moroccan Istiqlal party, based on the middle class, rose to prominence. In Iraq and Egypt, middle-class opposition came primarily from the military; many educated Arabs joined the military because they found little opportunity to use their talents elsewhere in their underdeveloped traditional societies.

Reforms in Iraq, Egypt, and Syria were begun by military leaders after successful revolts against traditional rulers.

The First Arab-Israeli War   Immediately after World War II, British and French influence began to crumble in the Arab world. With de Gaulle cynically remarking that their actions "stank of oil," Britain and the United States forced the French out of Syria in 1946. But the event that led to a general attack on Western colonialism by shocking much of the Arab world into the third stage of nationalism was the Arab-Israeli War in 1948–1949.

The war was partially a result of British policies that stretched back to World War I. In order to obtain Jewish and Arab support against the Central Powers, Britain had made promises to both. The Balfour Declaration of 1917 promised the Jews a national homeland in Palestine, yet the Arabs believed all of Palestine had been promised to them by Sir Henry McMahon, British high commissioner for Egypt during World War I. The British mandate over Palestine, granted by the League of Nations in 1923, instructed the British to establish a Jewish national home in Palestine and facilitate immigration. The mandate promised a home, not a state. The Arabs began to protest the influx of thousands of Jews into their midst.

As anti-Semitic policies in Europe increased the flow of Jewish immigrants in the interwar period, Britain reacted to the Arab opposition by trying periodically to curtail Jewish settlement. Despite British actions, the Jewish population of Palestine increased by about 350,000 during the interwar period. When Britain put limits on the number of immigrants permitted during World War II, Jewish terrorist groups resorted to violence in order to force the British to accept more of the Jewish refugees fleeing persecution in Europe. Caught between Arab demands to limit Jewish immigration to Palestine and Jewish violence to prevent any such limitation, in 1947 Britain asked the United Nations to resolve the dilemma.

The United Nations decided to partition Palestine into a Jewish state and an Arab state and to internationalize Jerusalem. In May 1948, when Britain pulled out its troops, war broke out between the new state of Israel and the neighboring Arab states. Although vastly outnumbered, Israel relied on superior organization to achieve victory in February 1949. Now Israel encompassed not only the area assigned to it by the United Nations but the city of Jerusalem, a corridor to the coast, and the remainder of Galilee as well. Nearly a million Arabs fled Israel in the wake of rumors of impending massacres and orders by their leaders to leave. The Palestinians established no permanent settlements elsewhere; to this day they remain refugees, symbols of Arab humiliation and a permanent irredentist force that has never accepted the new Israeli state.

The Arab defeat, blamed on the traditionalist regimes in the Arab world, generated military revolts in Syria, Jordan, and Egypt. The Syrian and Jordanian revolts failed initially to replace the existing regimes with a modernizing leadership. But in Egypt the corrupt, British-supported regime of King Farouk was overthrown by General Mohammed Naguib and Colonel Gamal Abdel Nasser, an act that was to have a far-reaching impact in the Arab world. Naguib abolished the monarchy and began the modernization of Egypt by replacing the old elite with fellow officers. He was supplanted by the more energetic Nasser, whose interests focused on more revolutionary changes in society and the ouster of the British from the Suez Canal.

Nasser eliminated all opponents, put an end to parliamentary government, and adopted a single mass organization to arouse and channel political consciousness. With these measures he set a pattern for many of the one-party governments that followed political liberation throughout Africa. Nasser's ultra-Nationalist dictatorship and those that followed were grounded on the premise that political democracy without social democracy is meaningless.

The Suez Crisis One of Nasser's ways of providing more social democracy was to improve the lot of the peasantry by building the Aswan High Dam, which regulated the flow of the Nile River. This led him into conflict with Britain and France over the Suez Canal.

Nasser expected aid from Britain and the United States for building the Aswan Dam. When aid was refused, Nasser responded by nationalizing the Suez Canal on July 26, 1956. Nasser had purchased arms from Czechoslovakia because the West would not provide him with the type or quantity of weapons he wanted. Also, he had recognized Communist China in 1955. Now the United States denied him aid because of what it considered to be his anti-Western attitude. In the Cold War milieu of the 1950s, the United States equated neutralism with opposition and viewed Nasser's actions as setting a dangerous precedent of playing off West against East. Britain, angry at Nasser's seizure of the canal, sought to punish him and give a warning to other Arab Nationalists. The French were happy to join with Britain because they hoped to cut off the material support being provided by Nassar to the Algerian rebels.

England and France decided on joint action to capture the Canal Zone, coordinated with an Israeli attack ostensibly to destroy guerrilla bases in the Sinai Peninsula. The effort was a dismal failure. Israel captured a large part of the Sinai and Anglo-French forces captured Port Said, but United States and international pressure forced a halt to the attempted seizure of the Canal Zone. (The United States feared that the Anglo-French invasion would have a deleterious effect on Western popularity and influence in the Middle East. Furthermore, because the United States was leading the attack in the U.N. against the Soviet Union's invasion of Hungary, it could not at the same time approve the invasion of Egypt.)

The subsequent withdrawal of Anglo-French forces rid Egypt of all foreign influence, left it in control of the canal, and greatly enhanced

Nasser's reputation, especially among Third World countries. It now seemed possible to oppose the militarily superior colonial powers by appealing to the United Nations and world opinion. The Suez fiasco provided a major impetus to national liberation movements in sub-Saharan Africa. In the Middle East, Nasser's military junta served as a model for similar governments in Syria and Iraq.

Africa's Independence Movements

The weakened international position of Britain and France after 1956 accelerated the process of national liberation in Africa. Indochinese and Algerian pressures on France and a national Resistance movement centering around the traditional sultan brought independence to Morocco before the three stages of nationalism had fully developed. The middle-class Istiqlal party had led a national Resistance movement against the French since 1943. But it was the exile of the sultan in 1953, inspired by French *colons*, that promoted mass resistance of the kind usually associated only with ultra-Nationalists, in support of the sultan's traditional regime. The sultan, Mohammed V, had the support of his people not only because of his reform program but also because the sultan was by tradition the country's Islamic leader. The French *colons* set up a puppet government, but the populace demanded the return of the legitimate ruler. When the traditionally antisultan Berber tribes transferred their support from the puppet government to the exiled sultan and began to attack European settlers, France reinstated the sultan in November 1955 to end the growing anarchy. In March 1956, France granted Morocco full independence. Faced with a *fait accompli*, the other protecting power, Spain, was forced to acquiesce.

During the next five years, Mohammed V tried to change Morocco to a modern constitutional monarchy. But the challenge of the ultra-Nationalist Neo-Istiqlal party headed by Ben Barka led Mohammed and his son, Hassan II, to depose the left-leaning government of Premier Abdallah Ibrahim and slow Morocco's progress toward genuine constitutional government. A struggle ensued in the 1960s between the more conservative middle-class Istiqlal party and the social revolutionary Neo-Istiqlal party under the watchful eye of the kings.

Again, in Tunisia, independence came before the Nationalist movement reached the ultra-Nationalist stage. The bourgeois Destour party had led a movement for greater independence from France since 1919. Although led by the middle class, it differed from the bourgeois second stage in that it was willing to accept administrative reforms and greater middle-class participation under French auspices and Islamic influences. The secular Neo-Destour party, formed in 1934 under Habib Bourguiba's leadership, adopted a mixture of bourgeois and ultrarevolutionary aims. Bourguiba's party appealed to the masses through a revolutionary reform program but stopped short of the ultra-Nationalist, anti-Western aspects of the typical third-stage Nationalists. This pattern also characterized the independence movements in the Gold Coast, Nigeria, and Tanganyika.

Bourguiba was often hard-pressed by more radical Arab and African Nationalists, especially in neighboring Algeria, to justify his pro-Western stance. Nevertheless, his program led to national independence in 1956 because the masses identified with his leadership and because France's position weakened after 1956. The French settlers feared they would lose their privileged economic status if Tunisia gained independence. The punitive actions they instituted, which included the exile and imprisonment of Bourguiba, instigated a mass reaction among the Tunisian populace in 1954. Alarmed by the outbreak of partisan warfare, Premier Mendès-France promised Tunisia internal autonomy only one week after he negotiated an end to French involvement in Indochina. Bourguiba was returned to Tunisia and independence was proclaimed on March 20, 1956. Because Tunisia achieved its independence under what was essentially second-stage leadership, it has retained a parliamentary, democratic form of government and a pro-Western political orientation. Revolutionary Neutralist groups have not been able to change Tunisia's moderate pro-Western policies.

The stampede to independence of sub-Saharan African states after 1956 was the result of many factors that instilled a new confidence in African Nationalists. Independence for Morocco and Tunisia in 1956, the successes of the Algerian rebels, and the Suez debacle were obvious immediate factors. While these events speeded up the liberation process, the independence movements had already reached the ultra-Nationalist stage in Ghana and the bourgeois stage in several colonial areas.

World War II had already seriously weakened the control of Europeans over their colonies. Africans came into contact with Nationalists in India and with African Nationalists serving in the British and French military during the war. The defeat and occupation of France convinced many Africans that their European overlords were not invincible.

At home, increased economic activity in support of the Western war effort increased the size of the native lower-middle-class—nurses, teachers, mechanics, artisans, and so on. After the war, these people were frustrated by their inability to find jobs and by the Europeans' monopoly of the top administrative positions. In addition, the Cold War led the united States and the Soviet Union to seek support among Third World countries by encouraging independence movements.

The events of 1956 were instrumental in ending France's dream of assimilating French colonial areas within a greater France and in convincing the British that granting independence was the only alternative. Before the war, assimilation into a greater French Union had been accepted by many African Nationalists. In 1936, an Algerian Nationalist, Ferhat Abbas, asserted:

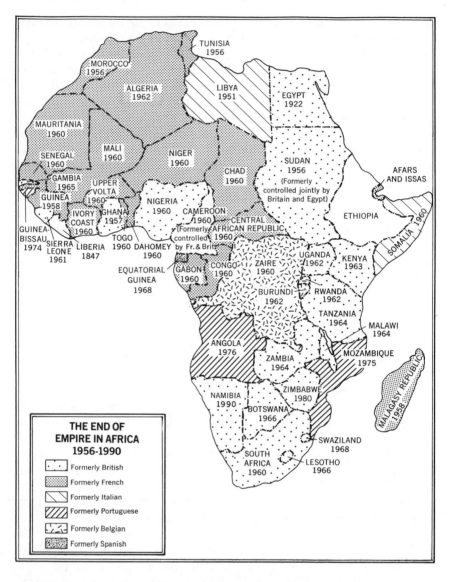

THE END OF
EMPIRE IN AFRICA
1956-1990

Formerly British
Formerly French
Formerly Italian
Formerly Portuguese
Formerly Belgian
Formerly Spanish

> Six million Moslems live on this soil which has been French for a hundred years; they live in hovels, go barefoot, without clothing and often without bread. Out of this hungry mass we shall make a modern society . . . elevate them to human dignity so that they may be worthy of the name of Frenchmen.

By the time Ferhat Abbas became premier of the provisional government of the Algerian Republic in 1958, he had become a staunch advocate of Algerian independence.

Britain's system of local administration permitted its colonies to make a smoother transition to independence. Having been brought into colonial administrations in the nineteenth century, many Africans had become capable administrators. When Britain's Asian Empire was lost in the late 1940s, most British leaders recognized that African independence was inevitable. As British administrators gradually relinquished their control, well-trained Africans easily picked up the reins of government.

In late 1956, most French colonies demanded and received the *loi-cadre* (semiautonomy) from a weakened France. Because of the weakness of the European powers, independence often came to sub-Saharan Africa when the ultra-Nationalist groups were just forming. In cases where the Nationalist movement had reached the third ultra-Nationalist stage, the transition from the second to third stage may have taken only a few years. The Belgian Congo provides a perfect example of this telescoping of the Nationalist movements. In 1956, Patrice Lumumba's demands were for more liberal measures for the educated Congolese; two years later he formed the *Mouvement National Congolais*, a mass ultra-Nationalist party.

Unfortunately, the independence movements often were splintered by regional and tribal differences that were overcome only through civil war. These divisions encouraged and in some cases forced the new states to set up one-party governments or military regimes in order to overcome the opposition.

In Ghana (Gold Coast), ultra-Nationalists had gained control of the independence movement before independence came in 1957. Ghana provides the best example of the three-stage Nationalist transition, with the Aborigines' Rights Protection Society, the Gold Coast Convention (GCC), and the Convention People's party (CPP) representing the three stages. Typically, the CPP, headed by Kwame Nkrumah, became dissatisfied with the moderate leadership of the GCC and formed its own mass-based political party. Nkrumah claimed that "a middle-class elite, without the battering-ram of the illiterate masses" would never be able to "smash the forces of colonialism." His "positive action" campaign of strikes and boycotts was deeply influenced by his training in Marxian economics in the West and by Gandhi's tactics in India.

Finding Nkrumah's policies too revolutionary, Britain imprisoned him in 1950. A British Commission report in 1948 said: "We have no reason to suppose that power in the hands of a small literate minority would not tend to be used to exploit the illiterate majority." It recommended that Britain retain control over Ghana until literacy and political experience had reached a stage whereby the masses could not be exploited. However, when the CPP won an overwhelming victory in the 1951 elections, Britain decided that it was politically expedient to release Nkrumah from prison and include him in the government.

Granted self-government in 1951, Ghana's leaders had considerable experience when full independence came in 1957. Despite this advantage, Ghana has suffered from regional and tribal opposition to the central government since independence. Nkrumah's attempt to build up support among his countrymen, including assuming adulatory titles such as savior, increased middle-class opposition to his government. In order to curb the opposition, he became president in 1960 under a new CPP constitution that permitted him to rule without Parliament. Several years after he forbade the existence of other political parties, Nkrumah was overthrown by a military coup that was supported by his middle-class opponents and the powerful Ashanti tribe. The Ashantis had gained important positions in the military and among Nkrumah's political opponents.

The Nigerian Nationalist movement, split among strong tribal lines, was a more complicated but perhaps more typical example than Ghana of the African independence struggles. Not one but two proto-Nationalist groups emerged: the Nigerian National Democratic party, led by Herbert Macauly, and the Traditionalist Muslim Northern People's Congress (NPC), based on the Fulani-Hausa tribe in the predominantly Muslim north. At first the NPC opposed independence since the powerful Muslim leaders did not desire integration with the more Westernized non-Muslim south and west.

Among the Ibo tribes in the east, a Westernized group, the National Council of Nigeria and the Cameroons (NCNC), was set up by a newspaper publisher, Dr. Nnamdi Azikiwe, in 1944. Azikiwe had gained popularity before the war when he spoke out against British control and for independence.

In the more urban west, dominated by the Yoruba tribe, Chief Obafemi Awolowo put together the Action party. Basically a middle-class-led group, the Action party at first followed a pro-Western moderate course toward independence. After gaining independence, Awolowo switched to a neutralist and more radical program of Nigerianization. But he stopped short of any Nkrumah-style ultra-Africanism with its strong appeal to the urban and peasant masses.

Independence necessitated bringing these disparate groups together by satisfying regional and tribal differences. Britain, fearful that it might alienate the Muslim north by granting autonomy prematurely, encountered increasing resistance from Azikiwe and Awolowo. NPC resistance was overcome when younger NPC members persuaded their colleagues to form an NCNC-NCP coalition, which chose NPC leader Abubaker Tafawa Balewa to be the first prime minister of Nigeria. The organization of Nigeria on a federal basis permits considerable local autonomy; for example, the Muslim leader in the northern province, Sir Ahmadu Bello, was able to retain much of his local authority. Azikiwe, who at first favored a coalition with the Action party, accepted the NPC coalition because of pressure from within his own group. This compromise permitted Azikiwe to become governor-general of independent Nigeria in 1960. Awolowo, as a member of the opposition in the new government, resorted to more radical policies and was imprisoned in 1963. After independence, a genuine ultra-Nationalist Nigerian Socialist party formed.

Nigeria is one of the few African states to retain a Western-style parliamentary system that permits political opposition. Most African leaders believe that political power has to be centered in one group or party that can bring about the needed modernization without having to deal with crippling parliamentary opposition.

In British East Africa, Tanganyika obtained independence in 1961 under the leadership of the Tanganyika African National Union (TANU) headed by Julius Nyerere. When independence came, TANU stood somewhere between the bourgeois and ultra-Nationalist stages of nationalism. It was organized on a mass basis, but it lacked the social revolutionary and anti-Western aspects of a genuine ultra-Nationalist program.

Not until 1966, after Tanganyika had merged with Zanzibar to form the new state of Tanzania, did Nyerere adopt a revolutionary program that included nationalization of banks and industry and a cooperative agricultural program. Tanganyika was spared the divisive tribal rivalries characteristic of most African states because none of its 120 tribes was large enough to challenge the government.

Nyerere's government was similar to many others in Africa in that no organized opposition was permitted. However, considerable differences were to be found within TANU. Before 1966, a strong left wing, composed of the trade union and cooperative movements, was critical of Nyerere's moderate social policies. This group was instrumental in swinging Nyerere's policies to the left in 1966. Differences such as this, which exist in many one-party governments in Africa, have led political observers to conclude that the decision-making process is often as democratic in these states as it is in some multiparty systems. In foreign affairs, Nyerere chose to keep his country in the British Commonwealth along with the other seven former British colonies and protectorates in east and west Africa.

With the exception of Guinea, the French territories in Africa followed a similar path to independence. All had experienced a common French policy of assimilation before 1956 that reduced tribal authority and concentrated administration of the eight colonies of French West Africa and the four in equatorial Africa and Madagascar from the administrative centers at Dakar and Brazzaville. France hoped, thereby, to prevent the emergence of native elites that would challenge French rule.

But the events of the mid-1950s crushed French hopes that these territories could ultimately be incorporated into a greater France as Guadeloupe, Martinique, French Guiana, and Réunion already were. With the granting of the *loi-cadre* in 1956, the colonies were given the right to exercise full executive power through their local assemblies and cabinets. In 1958, de Gaulle gave the colonies a choice: autonomy within a community of French nations, complete independence, a continuation of their present status, or incorporation within France as a department. Twelve of the colonies chose autonomy within the French community, and Guinea opted for complete independence. Beginning in 1960, the twelve colonies that had chosen autonomy were granted their independence as de Gaulle recognized the futility of trying to keep them in a larger French community. Nevertheless, most of them retained close economic and cultural ties with France after independence.

Only Guinea, under the ultra-African leadership of Sékou Touré, deviated from an essentially moderate Westernized leadership common to all the French territories. Most leaders in French Africa had acquired their political education in the *Rassemblement Démocratique Africain* (RDA), the strongest of the African political parties represented in the Chamber of Deputies in Paris. Except for a period of Communist influence from 1948 to 1954, the RDA remained in the hands of moderate Francophile leaders such as Félix Houphouët-Boigny from the Ivory Coast. Houphouët-Boigny, a member of the Mollet cabinet and leader of the RDA, was the main author of the *loi-cadre*. Once the colonies received autonomy, the RDA often became the leading party in the individual states.

Only in Guinea and Senegal did the RDA lose out to more Socialist, Africanist parties. After independence, power fell to a Westernized elite that normally set up the one-party state dominated by a strong personality, such as Houphouët-Boigny in the Ivory Coast or Léopold Sedar-Senghor in Senegal.

The Pattern of Nationalism

What we have seen in Asia, the Middle East, and Africa is a three-stage pattern of nationalism that emerged as a result of Western modernization and domination along with traditional feelings of uniqueness and pride. The occasional failure of the third ultra-Nationalist stage to develop before independence can be attributed to the weakness of the colonial powers and their realization that continued domination might drive their colonies into savage resistance. With Portugal's loss of its colonial empire in the 1970s, and the fall of the white minority government in Rhodesia in 1980 (now called Zimbabwe), only South Africa has managed to suppress its Nationalist movement.

FURTHER READING

For an outstanding concise interpretation of the politics of national liberation, see the chapter on decolonization in Geoffrey Barraclough, *An Introduction to Contemporary History* (1967). For a more detailed description, see F. Mansur, *Process of Independence* (1962). R. F. Holland's

European Decolonization 1918–1981. An Introductory Survey (1985) challenges the interpretation of Barraclough and Mansur. Holland argues that the colonized areas were not liberated by disinterested modernizing elites but by small urban elites hungry for power and wealth. The timing of decolonization resulted from the actions of these urban elites and the colonizing powers' more beneficial returns from cooperating among themselves in such organizations as the Common Market.

The decline of the British Empire is described in Rupert Emerson, *From Empire to Nation* (1960); Eric Estoric, *Changing Empire: Churchill to Nehru* (1950); and John Strachey, *The End of Empire* (1960). John Gallagher's *The Decline, Revival, and Fall of the British Empire* (1982) argues that World War I permitted the victorious powers to absorb vast new overseas territories and that any retreat from empire in the interwar years resulted from lack of resources rather than lack of will. French colonialism and its decline is described in Guy De Carmoy, *The Foreign Policies of France 1944–1968* (1970). The role of the French Army in the colonial territories is covered in John Ambler, *The French Army in Politics, 1945–1962* (1966). France's Algerian policy is excellently treated in Alistair Horne, *A Savage War of Peace: Algeria, 1954–62*, and Tony Smith, *The French Stake in Algeria, 1945–1962* (1978). Smith contends that the collapse of the French Fourth Republic was more the result of its efforts to keep Algeria French than its internal institutional defects. Horne's work provides a comprehensive history of the conflict itself, but needs to be supplemented with a fuller historical background.

For the collapse of colonialism in Asia, see K. M. Pannikar, *Asia and Western Dominance* (1953); J. Romein, *The Asian Century: A History of Modern Nationalism in Asia* (1962); Truong Buu Lam, *Patterns of Vietnamese Response to Foreign Intervention; 1858–1900* (1967); P. Spear, *India, Pakistan and the West* (1961); Gowher Rizui, *Linlithgow and India: A Study of British Policy and the Political Impasse in India, 1936–43* (1978); B. R. Tomlinson, *The Political Economy of the Raj, 1914–1947: The Economics of Decolonization in India* (1979); Ellen Hammer, *The Struggle for Indochina, 1940–54* (1955); and G. M. Ziadeh, *Nationalism and Revolution in Indonesia* (1952).

The course of national liberation in the Middle East is described in M. Rowlatt, *Founders of Modern Egypt* (1962); Philip K. Hitti, *Islam and the West* (1962); and John Campbell, *Defense of the Middle East* (1960).

Nationalism and the stages of the independence movements in Africa are analyzed in Immanuel Wallerstein, *Africa: The Politics of Independence* (1961); George W. Shepherd, *The Politics of African Independence* (1962); and Thomas Hodgkin, *Nationalism in Colonial Africa* (sixth impression, 1968). For a comparative study of European rule in Africa, see A. J. Hanna, *European Rule in Africa* (1961). Two studies that describe the three-stage pattern of nationalism in Africa are D. E. Apter, *The Gold Coast in Transition* (1955), and J. S. Coleman, *Nigeria: Back-*

ground to Nationalism (1958). Political decolonization in west Africa has been treated recently by John D. Hargreaves, *The End of Colonial Rule in West Africa: Essays in Contemporary History* (1979). Hargreaves shows how the British retained much of their former political initiative by collaborating with the new urban national movements. British policy in east Africa has recently been examined in Cranford Pratt's, *The Critical Phase in Tanzania 1945–1968: Nyerere and the Emergence of a Socialist Strategy* (1976).

Decolonization's impact on internal affairs in Britain and France (discussed in chapter 5) is expertly described in Miles Kahler's *Decolonization in Britain and France: The Domestic Consequences of International Relations* (1984). Kahler explains both how external relations affect domestic politics and how internal politics influence foreign policy. He argues that the British liquidated their colonial empire with less internal disruption than the French because the French right had still not accepted defeat at the hands of Nazi Germany and hoped to redeem French honor by retaining her colonies. Kahler also points out that the more heated settler resistance in the French colonies resulted in greater French domestic turmoil.

7 The Soviet Union and Eastern Europe in the 1950s and 1960s: The New Course and Polycentrism

> The heart of Lenin's comrade-in-arms and the inspired continuer of Lenin's cause, the wise teacher and leader of the party and the people, has stopped beating. Stalin's name is boundlessly dear to our party, to the Soviet people, to the working people of the world.
>
> *Pravda*, March 5, 1953

The above announcement signaled the end of an era, but several years were to elapse before the nature of the new era became clear. Between Stalin's death and the denunciation of his so-called cult of personality that Nikita Khrushchev made at the Twentieth Party Congress in 1956, a struggle for power raged between the Stalinists and the proponents of a new course.

The Stalinists continued to support heavy industry, the collectivization of agriculture, the extreme centralization of economic planning, and, in foreign policy, continued hostility toward the West. The followers of the so-called new course stressed increased production of consumer goods, light industry, decentralization of economic decision making, relaxation of internal political controls, and the achievement of an understanding with the West.

This internal Soviet division, combined with National Communist movements (domesticism) and what the Soviet Union classified as "revisionism," was to lead to a weakening of Soviet hegemony in Eastern Europe. Although the Soviet Union still had military control over most of Eastern Europe in the 1960s, the Soviet satellites had gained a large measure of independence. Furthermore, where only one leader of world communism had been acknowledged before 1948, at least three centers existed by the 1960s: the Soviet Union, Communist China, and Yugoslavia.

Postwar Society under Stalin

During World War II, Stalin relaxed his dictatorship in order to rally popular support for the war. After the massive purges of the 1930s when almost all the old Bolshevik leaders had been wiped out, the war years brought a partial reprieve from fear and insecurity. Loyalty to the state rather than loyalty to Stalin became the major criterion for social acceptance. Emphasis was placed on the fatherland and past Russian heroes. The Russian Orthodox church escaped persecution for the duration of the war. When the Communist party relaxed its admittance requirements in 1943, party membership swelled from 3.4 to 6 million. The army experienced a similar relaxation when the Communist party commissars, who had formerly shared command with the army officers, were limited to an advisory role.

Such relative freedom led many Soviet citizens to expect that the quality of life would improve in the postwar period. They were in for a rude shock.

Soviet society grew more repressive after the war. Instead of relaxation, citizens were faced with a conservative restoration, a return to total orthodoxy. The immediate postwar period has become known as the Zhdanov era, after anti-intellectual party bureaucrat Andrei Zhdanov, who reimposed the ideological uniformity that had existed before the war. The secret police (NKVD), headed by Lavrenty Beria, rounded up all people classified as enemies of the state and exiled them to Siberian labor camps run by the NKVD. War heroes such as Kliment Voroshilov and Georgy Zhukov were demoted to minor posts, and party control over the military was reestablished.

These acts reflected Stalin's apparent fear that a complex society with many centers of authority would threaten his authoritarian control. He considered himself responsible for the Soviet victory over Germany and particularly resented the praise heaped upon the Soviet generals. By humbling these generals—he made Voroshilov ask permission to come to each Politburo meeting—he could enhance his own feeling of importance.

In the arts, the postwar period was marked by a return to Socialist realism. Creativity was sacrificed to a pervasive uniformity. Writing had to sing the praises of Soviet society and the Communist party. Writers, social scientists, even natural scientists had to follow the party line. One of the greatest sins was cosmopolitanism; composers Dimitry Shostakovich and Sergey Prokofiev and film director Sergey Eisenstein were adjudged guilty of this sin. In all fields, particular emphasis was placed on Stalin's role as the savior of the Soviet Union. It was this Caesarian worship that Khrushchev denounced as the cult of personality.

When Stalin died in 1953, he apparently had been planning another major purge. The arrest of some prominent doctors, most of them Jewish, for plotting to kill government officials seems to have been the opening move in a much broader purge. Stalin is reported to have told Minister of State Security E. Ignatiev, "If you do not obtain confessions from the victims, we will shorten you by a head." Khrushchev charged that among the intended victims were some of the top members of the party: Anastas Mikoyan, Voroshilov, and Vyacheslav Molotov.

The Postwar Economy under Stalin

The Soviet Union experienced a postwar economic restoration of Stalinism similar to the social one. As in the 1930s, supply, demand, and investment were directed by an extensive bureaucracy with headquarters in Moscow. Stalin again stressed heavy industry at the expense of agriculture and consumer goods. Agriculture was to provide the necessary capital for industry; it contributed one-third of the gross national product but received only 15 percent of total investments.

Soviet production figures, which were always inflated until the late 1950s, reported that industrial output had reached the 1940 level by 1953. Despite this growth, the standard of living remained among the lowest in Europe. Real wages rose 83 percent in the Soviet Union (according to inflated Soviet statistics), but doubled in Western Europe between 1950 and 1966. Moreover, the concentration on producer goods caused serious shortages of consumer goods. Bread rationing, for example, continued through the 1950s.

Most industrial products were either of poor quality or outdated. In part this was because there was no competition and no need to please the customer. And in part it was because some of the quotas set by the central planners left factory managers no choice but to turn out inferior products. According to Khrushchev, most Soviet leaders were aware of these problems but were afraid to go counter to Stalin's view that only centralized control could make things work. As a result, local factory managers were deprived of all decision-making power.

The Choice of Stalin's Successor

At the time of Stalin's death, no one had sufficient support to fill his dictatorial shoes. When Soviet leaders asked the citizenry not to panic, they revealed their own fears. As Nikita Khrushchev remarked later, "If you put fifteen of us [in the Presidium] end to end, it would not make a Stalin." It was not clear at this point whether the next leader or leaders would come from the Communist party organization or the state organization, since Stalin's dictatorial regime had severely curtailed the authority of the party.

It soon became apparent that the supporters of the new course were in the majority. The closest followers of Stalin soon lost out in the power struggle. Beria, who was head of the secret police and best qualified to assume Stalin's position, was liquidated on both real and trumped-up charges. But another close follower, Molotov, was to remain as one of the top policymakers until 1955, when his hard-line foreign policy objectives were defeated.

Soviet leaders soon began to stress the collective nature of leadership. Georgy Malenkov succeeded Stalin as both party secretary and chairman of the council of ministers, but he was removed as party secretary after only a few weeks by the Central Committee. This move heralded the greater diffusion of power and the revival of the Communist party's role as the major decision-making body. Stalin, with the aid of the secret police, had limited the party's power to merely rubber-stamping all of his decisions. Now, after Beria was liquidated, it was the power of the secret police that was severely circumscribed.

Until Khrushchev became dominant, the party Presidium made all policy decisions. Throughout the 1950s, party organs made major decisions on leadership and policy changes. Khrushchev realized the importance of the party; in 1957, he defeated his opponents by appealing a Presidium decision against him to a meeting of the party's Central Committee. The decision to remove Khrushchev from power seven years later was made by a majority of the Presidium and the Central Committee. True, some decisions had already been reached before the meetings of the government organs, but they were not always final, as the reversal of the 1957 Presidium decision attests.

Nikita Khrushchev's rise to power corresponded to Georgy Malenkov's fall. The battle was waged over Malenkov's advocacy of the new course and Khrushchev's support of heavy industry and agriculture. In stressing improvement in the standard of living through concentration on light industry, housing, and consumer goods, Malenkov promised "an abundance of food for the people and of raw materials for consumer goods industries in the next two or three years." A struggle then ensued between Khrushchev and Malenkov over the economy and ultimately over party leadership.

Malenkov's program would have required a massive shift in economic priorities, thus reducing investment in heavy industry and armaments. Khrushchev was able to convince most of the party members that such a course would imperil Soviet security since there was not enough money for heavy industry and armaments as well as for agriculture and consumer goods. And, Khrushchev argued, huge investments in machinery were needed so that enormous new territories in Kazakhstan and western Siberia (virgin lands) could be opened up to agriculture. Although this virgin lands project was ultimately to fail, it provided Khrushchev with a means to defeat Malenkov (see below).

With the majority of the party behind him, Khrushchev became first secretary of the party in September 1953 and finally forced Malenkov to resign as chairman of the Council of Ministers in February 1955. With the appointment of Nikolai Bulganin as Malenkov's successor, Khrush-chev had established his ascendancy.

Struggles for leadership followed Stalin's death in many East European countries as well. The initial division of party and government leadership that had ensued in the Soviet Union occurred in Czechoslovakia and Hungary in 1953 and in Bulgaria and Poland in 1954 at Soviet insistence. The Hungarian division left Matyas Rakosi as party secretary and brought the "new course" reformer Imre Nagy to the premiership. Such seeming indecision in the Soviet Union and elsewhere left a public impression of weakness among the leadership. This division among party officials con-tributed to labor unrest in Czechoslovakia, East Germany, and Bulgaria in 1953. Instructed by Soviet leaders to institute a new course in East Germany, the East German leadership divided over the extent of the reforms. They failed to rescind increased work demands on East German workers decreed in May. When the government, led by Stalinists such as Walter Ulbricht, the secretary-general of the party, resisted worker demands, the strikers increased their demands from a rescinding of the increased work norms to include free elections, parliamentary democracy, and reunion with West Germany. When the police failed to quell the rioting, the Soviet military stepped in to crush the uprising.

Khrushchev's Leadership

Once Khrushchev gained the upper hand in the Soviet Union, he tried to find a new way to establish Soviet hegemony in Eastern Europe. It had become clear to Khrushchev that some relaxation of Stalinist orthodoxy was necessary to prevent massive upheaval in Eastern Europe. Therefore, in 1955 and 1956, he launched a campaign to put the Soviet Union in the forefront of this relaxation. As a first step he had to counteract Tito's influence in Eastern Europe, for Yugoslavia had taken the lead by aban-doning collectivization in 1953, initiating worker self-management in in-dustry, and turning the Communist party into a broader, more popular organization called the League of Communists.

The Khrushchev offensive began with a 20,000-word denunciation of Stalin at the Twentieth Party Congress of the Soviet Union in February 1956. The official reports from the congress contained little surprising information. His acceptance of Yugoslavia's different "forms of transi-tion" to socialism was expected. But in a secret speech to a closed session of the congress, Khrushchev charged Stalin with the murder of loyal party leaders and with alienating Tito. By making Stalin the scapegoat for all the evils in Eastern Europe, Khrushchev hoped to take the onus off the present Soviet leadership and discredit his internal opponents. This policy was, of course, dangerous since any criticism of former leaders could reflect on him and on the party as well. Even some West European Com-munists, such as Togliatti, expressed alarm at the harshness of the criticism. Fearing that the criticism had gotten out of hand, the Soviet Central Committee on June 30 partially exonerated Stalin by claiming that strict discipline and centralization were needed during his time in office.

Khrushchev's dissolution of the Cominform in April 1956 confirmed his earlier promise to Tito that ideological uniformity would not be imposed on the East European countries. Finally, his announcement of the doctrine of diversity at a meeting with Tito on June 20 seemed to put the Soviet stamp of approval on different roads to socialism. It was not long before Khrushchev's new policy was to be put to the test.

The Polish October

Only eight days after Khrushchev's meeting with Tito, riots erupted in Poznan, Poland. These riots were not solely the result of Khrushchev's policies; primarily, the workers were protesting their low standard of living, which had its roots in earlier Soviet pressure to concentrate on heavy industry. Malenkov's new course, which was urged on Polish leaders to improve relations with the masses, actually divided the leadership into Stalinists and followers of the new course; and at the same time, it accelerated worker demands for economic improvement. Revelations by Khrushchev and the Polish Secret Police further undermined the credibility of Polish Stalinists: Khrushchev reported at the Twentieth Party Congress that Soviet agents had destroyed the Polish Communist party leadership in 1938 and remade the party to conform to Soviet desires. These revelations followed those of a Polish Secret Service agent who had escaped to the West in 1954 and revealed extensive corruption, terror, and favoritism among the Polish leadership. The 1954 revelations led to a purge of the secret police and the release of the previously discredited Władysław Gomułka from detention.

Even before Khrushchev's 1956 offensive, Polish intellectuals had become increasingly critical of the hard-line Polish leadership. Following the onset of the new course, they had discussed the inappropriateness of agricultural collectivization in Poland and the lack of worker participation in industrial management. Undoubtedly, Yugoslav "deviationism" in agrarian and industrial policies had a further impact upon the Polish debate.

Among the noteworthy consequences of the Polish revolt were the ending of collectivization in Polish agriculture and the establishment of workers' councils in Polish industry.

The workers' revolt for bread and freedom and the refusal of the police and army to fire on them left the Polish leadership with two options: to comply with popular demands or depend on Soviet troops to put down the rioters.

The reform movement had had its effect. Polish leaders, in an unprecedented move, apologized to the workers for their poor conditions and promised reforms. At a meeting of the Central Committee between July 18 and 28, attended by Soviet leaders Nikolay Bulganin and Georgy Zhukov, Polish leaders tried to pick their way between two equally undesirable extremes: an anti-Communist revolution or Soviet intervention. Bulganin told the Poles, "Every country can go a different way to socialism"—as long as it did not break up the Soviet bloc. This was rejected at the meeting, but it became the basis for the final settlement.

During the next three months, the Polish leadership came to the conclusion that only the return of the recently discredited National Communist leader Gomułka could resolve the crisis. While the Stalinists wished to use Gomułka merely to quiet revolutionary ferment, Gomułka said he would return to the Polish leadership only if he were empowered to implement his program. During these three months, Poland had obtained the support of Communist China for its National Communist course by convincing the Chinese that the Polish national road was not to be similar to the Yugoslav one. The Soviets also had to consider the masses' growing identification with Catholicism after the massive pilgrimage to the Jasna Gora monastery to commemorate Poland's delivery from another foreign army's siege three hundred years before. Early in October, worker intervention helped the Polish leaders survive an attempted coup by Stalinists. With the Polish Stalinists defeated, Soviet leaders decided it was time to come to an understanding with the reformist forces.

On October 19, Khrushchev, Lazar Kaganovitch, Anastas Mikoyan, and Vyacheslav Molotov flew unannounced to Warsaw. Before the Soviet delegation arrived, the Polish leadership chose Gomułka as first secretary in order to satisfy the masses and save Polish communism. Khrushchev accused the Polish leaders of misleading him about the internal situation, but the recently rehabilitated Gomułka convinced the Soviet leaders that Poland was going to remain within the Soviet bloc and that Poland's anti-Stalinist views were no more radical than those of the Soviet Union. Moreover, he convinced Khrushchev that only a somewhat revisionist course would be acceptable to the Polish masses. Khrushchev accepted Polish assurances since he did not want to intervene in Poland at the same time that he was dealing with Hungarian revolutionaries, he did not wish to sacrifice his recent understanding with Tito, and he could find no other Polish leader who could preserve Polish communism without a civil war or Soviet intervention. The Polish masses were convinced not to push their demands beyond what Gomułka had obtained by the Soviet crushing of the Hungarian Revolution in November 1956. Gomułka released the Catholic primate Stefan Cardinal Wyszynski from monastic internment to help convince the Polish masses to accept the compromise.

The Soviet visit was not altogether in vain. Since Khrushchev had previously enunciated a policy of diversity and had accepted the Yugoslav revisionists, the Polish promises of support for Soviet foreign policy and continued control of the Communist party in Poland were sufficient to allay Soviet fears.

Despite Soviet acquiescence on the Polish demand for decollectivization of agriculture and de-emphasis of heavy industry, there was little else about the Polish policy that was revisionist from a Soviet perspective. Until Gomułka fell from power in 1970, he followed a pro-Soviet course, in part because he realized that Poland's geographic position demanded a close working relationship with the Soviet Union and in part because he disliked radical revisionism.

Gomułka continued to oppose Titoism and a liberalization of the press in Poland. Eventually, he stilled most of the voices that had demanded greater liberalization, or the so-called "Polish spring" in October. His orthodoxy extended even outside his own country. He joined in the denunciation of the 1956 Hungarian Revolution that followed on the heels of the Polish revolt and ironically was inspired, at least to some extent, by Poland's defiance of the Soviet Union; and he also helped crush the 1968 Czech Revolution.

The Hungarian Revolution

The Hungarian Revolution presented a much more serious challenge to the Soviet Union than the Polish uprising had done. While Poland threatened to establish its own brand of national communism, the Hungarian Revolution ultimately threatened the very existence of the Communist party. Poland continued to acknowledge the supremacy of the Soviet Union in Eastern Europe, but Hungary aimed to chart a neutral course by severing its ties with the Soviet Union. If this uprising had been allowed to succeed it might have engendered similar revolutions throughout Eastern Europe.

Hungarian political and economic developments prior to the 1956 revolt mirrored those of the Soviet Union. Malenkov's new course was followed in Hungary by Imre Nagy's new course. Appointed premier in July 1953 at Soviet insistence to correct the worst aspects of Stalinism, Nagy saw as his task the restoration of economic stability and confidence in the Communist regime. His predecessor as premier, Matyas Rakosi, who retained his position as leader of the Communist party, had brought Hungary to the brink of economic catastrophe by his Stalinist emphasis on the buildup of Hungarian heavy industry at the expense of the rest of the economy. Nagy began to divert the country's resources to light industry and stopped the forced collectivization of agriculture.

The economic relaxation led to a corresponding intellectual relaxation. Intellectuals began to discuss not only the nature of the changes in Hungarian communism but also the value of a Communist system. A group of intellectuals gathered in the Petöfi Circle—named after a nineteenth-century Nationalist poet and established by the Communist party in March

1956 as what the party hoped would be a harmless escape valve—and debated the possibility of achieving democracy in a Communist state. Nagy and the intellectuals appear to have been influenced by the independent course in Yugoslavia, believing it possible for Hungary to achieve the same independent position.

Nagy's plans were cut short by the fall of his Soviet protector, Malenkov, in February 1955. Rakosi now seized the opportunity to regain leadership over both the state and the party, reinstituting a Stalinist hard line. Nagy gave in without a fight, perhaps because he expected Rakosi would fail in his attempt to reimpose ideological conformity.

Yet Nagy could hardly have expected the shake-up in the Soviet bloc that was to result from Khrushchev's denunciation of Stalin at the Twentieth Party Congress in February 1956. While Rakosi tried to reestablish his authority, Khrushchev was exonerating Béla Kun, a discredited former Rakosi rival and a National Communist. Buoyed up by Khrushchev's action, Hungarian intellectuals demanded an investigation of Rakosi's past, especially the part he had played in the liquidation of the National Communist Láslo Rajk. Rajk had been accused of Titoist deviationism and had been executed during the Stalinist purges in 1949. In March 1956, Rakosi conceded Rajk's innocence.

Three months later, the Hungarian Writers Union and the Petöfi Circle, inspired by Gomulka's successful stand in Poland, openly opposed Rakosi in the columns of the party newspaper *Szabad Nep*. The Soviet Union opposed Rakosi's plan to silence his opposition by arresting Nagy and four hundred intellectuals, both because the plan might fail and because it certainly would not endear the Communist party to the Hungarian population. Rakosi was handcuffed by the Soviet directive to reintroduce Stalinist economic priorities without the Stalinist terrorist methods that would have made such changes a possibility.

Wanting a more popular leader for the Hungarian Communist party (CPH), the Soviet leaders chose Ernö Gerö as Rakosi's successor, but he was not acceptable to the majority of the anti-Stalinist intellectuals. According to Tito, distrust of Nagy led the Soviet leaders to make it "a condition that Rakosi would go only if Gerö remained. And this was a mistake, because Gerö differed in no way from Rakosi." Had the Soviet leaders supported Nagy at this point when he still had a chance to put himself at the head of the reforming forces, they might have prevented the more radical revolution that was to follow.

The first stage of the revolution was touched off when a group demonstrating in support of the Polish insurrection was fired upon by the Hungarian police on October 23, 1956. Several mass demonstrations had already been held by the Petöfi Circle to demand a new party congress and the reinstatement of Nagy. For example, three days earlier, 200,000 people marched in Budapest, chanting the Petöfi verse, "We will never again be slaves." Hungarian revolutionaries had mistakenly viewed the reinstatement of Gomułka in Poland as a Soviet surrender to the forces of change in Eastern Europe.

Gerö made his most serious mistake on that fateful day when he called on the Soviet army to put down the demonstration. In the minds of most Hungarians this act completely discredited the party and increased their desire for a non-Communist Hungary. Although Soviet troops halted their intervention once they realized that workers had joined the student demonstrators, their presence stimulated a violent reaction. Workers set up anti-Soviet, anti-Communist workers' councils throughout Hungary. In the countryside student parliaments and Socialist revolutionary councils arose spontaneously, demanding free elections, the withdrawal of Soviet troops, and the dissolution of the security police.

When segments of the Hungarian army joined the revolt, Soviet leaders decided that only a Communist government headed by Nagy as premier and János Kádár as first secretary could survive without Soviet support. The Soviets expected that Kádár would satisfy the more orthodox Communists as well as moderate Nagy's more radical objectives. On October 28, Soviet troops began to withdraw from Budapest, and Nagy set up a new government.

By now, hatred of the Soviet Union and the Hungarian Communist party had reached such intensity that even Nagy would have found it difficult to install a solely Communist government, had he wanted to do so. Nagy not only permitted the reestablishment of opposition parties but also set up a coalition government with Social Democratic, Smallholder, and National Peasant party participation. By October 31, he had withdrawn Hungary from the Warsaw Treaty Organization, proclaimed Hungarian neutrality, and requested United Nations protection.

These acts confirmed Khrushchev's fears about Nagy. Hungary had presented the Soviet Union with a challenge to its authority that it could not ignore. If the Hungarians were permitted to continue, the Soviets faced the prospect of more anti-Communist revolts in Eastern Europe and an end to Soviet hegemony in Eastern Europe. Even Tito approved the crushing of the "fascist counter-revolution" in November since Nagy's program threatened the very existence of the Communist party. Despite the valiant opposition of most of Hungary's population, the Soviet army soon smashed all resistance. Before being hanged for his part in the revolution, Nagy prophetically remarked, "If my life is needed to prove that not all Communists are enemies of the people, I gladly make the sacrifice. I know that one day there will be another Nagy trial that will rehabilitate me. I also know I will have a reburial. I only fear that the future oration will be delivered by those who betrayed me." His reburial came on June 16, 1989, but those responsible were not his betrayers but a Committee for Historical Justice that was seeking his exoneration.

Because the next Hungarian Communist party and government leader János Kádár called on the Soviet Union to put down the revolution, he

The aftermath of an anti-Soviet demonstration in Budapest, Hungary, on October 31, 1956. A huge statue of Soviet premier Joseph Stalin was toppled by demonstrators and dragged two miles to the center of the city, where it was broken apart by souvenir hunters. The broken head remains at an intersection. (Keystone Press Agency, Inc.)

was termed "a standing affront to national memory and pride." But after the revolution, he led Hungary to its own form of national communism. Having been imprisoned by Rakosi for his nationalism, Kádár was not unaware of the desires of his countrymen. If we compare conditions since the early 1960s in Hungary and Poland, where Gomułka instituted a more orthodox regime, we might wonder whether it was the Hungarians or the Poles who won in 1956. Kádár removed the Stalinists from the party and concentrated on promoting economic development and raising the standard of living. The Hungarian people eventually came to accept Kádár as the result of improved economic conditions in the sixties and seventies, but an economic downturn in the eighties forced him from power (see chapter 11).

The Hungarian Revolution seriously eroded Khrushchev's support in the Soviet Union. The cost of putting down the revolt and financing the recovery of Hungary put the brake on Soviet economic growth. Certain of Khrushchev's enemies, Bulganin among them, used the financial crisis and the Hungarian debacle as grounds for challenging Khrushchev's position. In defense, Khrushchev tried to blame the highly centralized government agencies for the economic failures. His proposal for lodging economic decision making in regional economic commissions, called *Sovnarkhozy*, gained the support of a majority of the Central Committee in May 1957.

Since local party officials then were given more say in local economic affairs, support for Khrushchev increased among party members. But in June 1957, while he was on a trip to Finland, his opponents managed to gain a majority in the Presidium. When he returned, he was vigorously attacked by Malenkov, Molotov, and Bulganin for creating economic problems and violating the principle of collective leadership. Undaunted, Khrushchev had the entire Central Committee called together in June 1957 and gained a majority over his opponents. As a result, a so-called antiparty group, including Malenkov, Kaganovitch, and Molotov, were expelled from the Presidium of the party. Such an exercise of party democracy, not used since Lenin, indicated the changed nature of party leadership.

Polycentrism

Khrushchev faced an equally serious challenge to Soviet leadership of international communism. The revolts in Hungary and Poland as well as Yugoslav "deviationism" threatened Soviet domination in Eastern Europe. In fact, international communism underwent a three-way division in the 1950s among revisionists, dogmatists (Stalinists), and National Communists. The split left the Communist world with several centers of power, a state of affairs known as *polycentrism*.

The *revisionists*, mainly Yugoslavia, rejected the Soviet model in its entirety, contending that it was the Soviet Union—not Yugoslavia—that had strayed from the path of Marxism-Leninism. They began to decentralize economic and political decision making to prove that they were closer to the Communist society envisioned by Marx than the highly centralized dictatorial government in the Soviet Union.

The Yugoslav revisionists were labeled deviationists and were vehemently opposed by the *dogmatists*, especially Communist China and Albania. In international affairs the dogmatists supported a continuation of the struggle with capitalism and violently rejected peaceful coexistence. At home they opposed a relaxation of Stalinist principles. Therefore, they viewed Khrushchev's destalinization efforts as revisionist.

The *National Communists*, led by Gomułka, stressed Communist solidarity in foreign affairs but insisted that each state be permitted to achieve communism in its own way. They held that local conditions were sufficiently different to preclude adoption of the Soviet economic and social model without adjusting it as needed. In practice, most of the states led by National Communists retained much of the Soviet model.

Revisionism in Yugoslavia It was the revisionist Yugoslavs who offered the most serious challenge to the Soviet model. There the establishment of the League of Communists reduced the strong centralized control of the party. Economically, many capitalist practices were adopted to stimulate the economy (see chapter 11). Some Communist critics, in fact, viewed Titoism as nothing more than Western European social democracy. Much of Yugoslavia's unorthodox mixture of Communist and Capitalist practice has grown out of an ideological need to defend itself against charges of deviationism and a fundamentally pragmatic approach to Communist economic practices.

Khrushchev's denunciation of Stalinism and confirmation of separate paths to socialism in 1956 seemed to clear the way for a rapprochement between the Soviet Union and Yugoslavia. However, the Soviet's crushing of the Hungarian Revolution, which each blamed the other for causing, and subsequent efforts to achieve greater unity among Communist bloc countries encouraged Tito to maintain more stoutly the principle of national independence. Khrushchev ignored Tito's demand that the Soviet Union act against Stalinist leaders throughout Eastern Europe. In fact, Stalinism became more rigid in Eastern Europe after the Hungarian uprising. Led by Walter Ulbricht in East Germany and Antonin Novotny in Czechoslovakia, Eastern Europe became more dogmatic than the Soviet Union. Attacks on Yugoslavia in the Soviet and East European press and accelerated economic pressures led Tito to take a much more militant ideological position.

The 1958 draft program of the Yugoslav Party Congress asserted that Yugoslavia was closer to Marxism-Leninism than the Soviet Union was. With worker self-management and the diffusion of political power to local communes, the 1958 program stated, the League of Communists "will gradually, in the long run, disappear with the developing and strengthening of ever more inclusive forms of immediate socialist democracy."

Furthermore, the program asserted Communist parties were not the only creators of socialism. This was an apparent attempt to solidify Yugoslavia's position as a bridge between East and West by implying that Western European welfare states were also finding their way toward socialism. Although the program suggested no major change in Yugoslav policy, it was anathema in China, Albania, and Romania.

Dogmatism in China   What China considered to be Khrushchev's coddling of deviationism became the immediate cause for the division of the Communist world into three major centers—the Soviet Union, China, and Yugoslavia—and many minor centers.

However, the development of the Sino-Soviet-Yugoslav split had long been evident. The Chinese had been disenchanted with Khrushchev's leadership since his denunciation of Stalin in 1956 and had long been opposed to the Soviet Union's territorial acquisitions in Asia, its monopoly of economic power within the Communist bloc, and its policy of peaceful coexistence. Mao Tse-tung was, in fact, always independent of the

Soviet Union but had adopted Stalinist totalitarian methods to maintain his authoritarian government. Therefore, any denunciation of Stalin was a condemnation of Mao's rule as well.

China especially resented the favored economic position of the Soviet Union among the other Communist countries. Stalin had treated China the way he had treated the East European countries: as economic dependencies of the Soviet Union. In his view, China's function was to provide cheap raw materials to the Soviet Union and to serve as a buyer of Soviet manufactured goods. Stalin had also refused to help the Chinese develop nuclear weapons. Rejecting a subordinate role, China propagandized that the Soviet Union should have raised all other Communist states to the Soviet Union's economic level.

Since Stalin and Khrushchev were more interested in developing the Soviet Union than in fomenting world revolution, they were not interested in building up China. In fact, Stalin and Khrushchev were more afraid of China than of the West. Soviet propaganda against the Chinese smacked of the late nineteenth century, when Westerners were warning of the "yellow peril."

Chinese and Soviet claims to the same territory—Sinkiang, Amur, Sakhalin, Transbaikalia—were much more immediate than Western threats. The failure of the Soviet Union to back China against India in 1962 was seen by Chinese leaders as further evidence of Soviet revisionism. However, to say, as some have done, that the Sino-Soviet rift is national and not ideological is to overlook a major element in the conflict.

The Chinese tolerated Khrushchev's denunciation of Stalin only because they thought the World Communist movement should be unified around the Soviet Union. From 1956 to 1958, they tolerated Soviet revisionism because they were much more afraid of polycentrism. In 1957 and 1958, as Khrushchev implemented his own pragmatic brand of communism in the Soviet Union, China attempted the Great Leap Forward to collectivize and communize China completely. When this experiment failed, even greater emphasis was placed on Stalinist orthodoxy (except for the Stalinist emphasis on industry at the expense of agriculture) in order to assure unity at home and save face abroad. Khrushchev's unsuccessful attempt to unseat Mao in 1959 by instigating a party revolt exacerbated relations.

At a series of conferences and party congresses from 1960 until Khrushchev's fall from power four years later, the Soviet Union tried to discredit China. At the Twenty-second Party Congress in Bucharest during June of 1960, Khrushchev succeeded in obtaining majority support for his condemnation of Chinese factionalism. Unsubdued, the Chinese continued to charge that the World Communist movement was threatened by compromise with the enemy. Khrushchev's attempt to obtain "peaceful coexistence" with the United States at the summit conferences at Camp David (1959) and Paris (1960) were vehemently denounced in Peking.

The Soviet decisions to remove Stalin's body from the Kremlin, where it had rested in state next to Lenin's body, and to expel the pro-Chinese Albanians from the World Communist movement at the Twenty-second Congress of the CPSU in 1961 were indirect slaps at the Chinese. The gap became virtually unbridgeable with the withdrawal of Soviet forces from Cuba in 1962 and the signing of the Nuclear Test Ban Treaty a year later. The Chinese saw these actions as final proof that the Soviet Union would use nuclear weapons only to further its own interests and not to achieve world revolutionary aims.

National Communism in Romania   The establishment of a form of national communism in Romania in 1963 and 1964, influenced by the growing divisions in world communism, was even more clearly the outcome of Soviet economic policies and Khrushchev's anti-Stalinist offensive. In response to Soviet destalinization in 1953, Gheorghe Gheorghiu-Dej set Romania on a new course by instituting collective leadership and, with Soviet permission, abolishing the hated Soviet-Romanian joint companies (*sovroms*). Inspired by Malenkov's new course in the Soviet Union, Romania also sought to obtain a more diversified economy by increasing expenditures on the production of consumer goods and on agriculture.

Responsibility for Romania's decision to follow an independent course can be laid at the feet of Khrushchev, whose drive to obtain economic and diplomatic unity in Eastern Europe after the Hungarian Revolution provided a major impetus to Romanian national communism.

Throughout the 1950s, Romania drew closer to China as both nations resisted Khrushchev's policy of de-Stalinization within the Communist world. Gheorghiu-Dej and Mao resented Khrushchev's continuing denunciations of Stalin and his pressure on them to follow suit. The Stalinist line in Romania hardened, and the likelihood of integration within the Soviet bloc dwindled.

When a pro-Khrushchev force in Romania allegedly challenged Gheorghiu-Dej's leadership in 1957, a campaign ensued to remove all revisionists—that is, Khrushchevites—from power. In order to strengthen the regime at home and continue Romania's drive toward economic independence from Moscow, Gheorghiu-Dej stepped up his efforts to obtain aid from the West. Trade with the West reached 25 percent of Romania's total foreign trade in 1960, by which time, Gheorghiu-Dej had strong support from the Romanian masses for his independent course. His death in March 1965 brought little change to Romania policies since his successor, Nicolae Ceauşescu, had been groomed to fill his shoes.

Council for Mutual Economic Assistance (Comecon) and Economic Nationalism   The final shaping of Romanian national communism stemmed from Khrushchev's attempt to make Comecon a supranational economic agency with jurisdiction over the economies of each member state. Khrushchev saw Comecon as an answer to the growing economic division of labor in the European Economic Community. Only by achieving a similar division of labor in Comecon could the Communist countries keep pace with economic growth in the West. Romanian fears that the Comecon envisioned by Khrushchev would frustrate its own industrialization were well founded. Khrushchev planned to have Romania continue as a supplier of raw materials to the more developed Comecon countries—Czechoslovakia, East Germany, and the Soviet Union.

Khrushchev's determined drive in 1962 and 1963 to integrate all the East European economies was to founder on the rocks of economic nationalism. In advance of a meeting in July 1963 to determine whether Comecon was to be a supranational body, Romania got the support of both China and Yugoslavia to keep it international—and also received promises of financial support from the West. As an international agency, Comecon can suggest integrative measures but cannot enforce them, as a supranational body could do. At the meeting, not only was supranationalism defeated but the right of member states to develop independently was upheld.

Now embroiled in his dispute with China and Albania, Khrushchev could not force the majority of East European states to accept a reinvigorated Comecon. Because of a continued friendship with China as well as with the Soviet Union, Romania attempted in 1963 to mediate the differences between the two. Romania's independent stand reached its apogee in 1968 when Ceauşescu, not only refused to join other Warsaw Pact states in the invasion of Czechoslovakia but also publicly denounced the invasion.

Strong support of Soviet foreign policy in recent years has taken the sting out of Romania's earlier rejection of economic cooperation: it subscribed to Khrushchev's policy of peaceful coexistence and backed the Nuclear Test Ban Treaty. Coexistence suited Romania's goal of developing trade with the West in order to promote economic independence. Yet the Romanians may in fact have been saved by a more fundamental change—the unexpected fall of Khrushchev in October 1964.

Khrushchev's Fall from Power

Failures in both domestic and foreign policy led to Khrushchev's fall. The weakening of Soviet hegemony in Eastern Europe, the growing disagreement with China, and the Cuban fiasco had undermined Khrushchev's position. His opponents were especially upset by his hasty decision to set up missile sites in Cuba and the humiliation of having to dismantle them.

Added to his foreign policy debacles were a number of economic failures. Especially harmful was the failure of Khrushchev's agricultural Virgin Lands Project, which did not provide the promised amount of food. Despite a 17 percent increase in the acreage sown to crops from 1960 to 1963, massive imports of Canadian wheat and rationing of bread were necessary in 1963. Rather than increasing the acreage, Khrushchev should have concentrated machinery and fertilizer on the existing arable land.

The failure of the sixth Five-Year Plan added to Khrushchev's woes. The attempt to keep the Soviet Union's space program ahead of the United States while investing heavily in new plants and equipment overtaxed Soviet resources. As defense spending rose by one-third between 1959 and 1963, the rate of industrial growth declined. The GNP growth rate declined from 10 percent in 1958 to about 3 percent in 1962 and 1963. Khrushchev also lost the support of the military and the heavy industry advocates in 1964 when he began to emphasize the production of consumer goods.

But it may have been Khrushchev's political reforms that were decisive in his fall, since they stripped even Central Committee members of their security. Khrushchev's proposed reforms would have forced a turnover of one-third of the governing party bodies at every election. As a result, party functionaries (*apparatchiki*) would suddenly be deprived of lifetime bureaucratic posts. Another unpopular innovation, the 1962 division of regional party administration into industrial and agricultural sectors, cut local party functionaries' authority in half. Such tampering with party functionaries' livelihoods cost Khrushchev much of the support he had previously had in the Central Committee. Party faithfuls were no longer assured continuing local political office and, if they became a local party secretary, national political office and economic security. A local party secretary now had to compete with his industrial or agricultural counterpart for a seat in the Central Committee and with his counterpart and local government (Soviet) officials for a seat in the Supreme Soviet of the USSR. The result of this local division of authority was not greater efficiency through new leadership but confusion and economic decline.

Despite these setbacks, Khrushchev's opponents had to maneuver his fall while he was vacationing in the Crimea. Called back by the Presidium, he was unable to turn the table on his opponents by appealing to the Central Committee, as he had done in 1957, because his supporters were now in the minority there.

Two days after his removal from office, *Pravda*, the Soviet newspaper, denounced his "hare-brained scheming, immature conclusions, hasty decisions, and actions divorced from reality."

Although the post-Khrushchev period is often called the Brezhnev era, the policies pursued until Brezhnev's death in November 1982 were normally the result of collective decisions of the fourteen-member Politburo of the Communist party. In order to prevent any one person from monopolizing power as Stalin and Khrushchev had done, the Politburo reduced the Central Committee of the party and the Party Congress to a mere rubber-stamping of decisions already reached in the Politburo. Brezhnev's position as party secretary did not permit him to pack the Politburo with his supporters; after eighteen years as party secretary, only five members of the Politburo were indisputably his political protégés and they were not the more powerful members. As a result, Brezhnev had to put together a majority in the Politburo for any decision or policy.

During Brezhnev's early years as party secretary, the Soviet Union achieved internal stability, military parity with the United States, and international recognition as a true superpower. Domestic stability was obtained by scrapping Khruschchev's administrative reforms: his decentralization of authority, his division of regional party administration into agricultural and industrial sectors, and his rejection of seniority as the primary means for advancement. With local Communist party officials regaining full authority, local administrative conflicts were reduced. Also, de-Stalinization ended with Khrushchev since the Politburo apparently determined that a continuing public criticism of former leaders was undermining the present leadership. This newly found order was obviously comforting to the leadership, but it reduced local initiative and added to the enormous bureaucratic machine at the center. As will be discussed in chapter 10, the economy suffered from this excessive centralization of authority.

Although Khrushchev fell from power in 1964, the consequences of his rule were to play an immediate role in the Czech uprising in 1968 and a long-term role in the undermining of totalitarianism within the Soviet Union. His attempts to reform the ossified party cadres in the Soviet Union set in motion a similar questioning of bureaucratic party structures and centralized decision making in Czechoslovakia (chapter 12). His efforts also stimulated national Stalinist movements in Romania and Albania that were further aided by the great schism between China and the Soviet Union. The 1968 revolt in Czechoslovakia also gained momentum as a result of Soviet concentration on its own domestic problems after 1964 and its indecisiveness once the Czech unrest began in 1968.

FURTHER READING

Soviet internal affairs are analyzed in Merle Fainsod, *How Russia Is Ruled* (2d ed. 1963); Leonard Schapiro, *The Communist Party of the Soviet Union* (1964); Robert Conquest, *Power and Policy in the U.S.S.R.* (1961); Adam B. Ulam, *The New Face of Soviet Totalitarianism* (1963); and John Reshetar, *The Soviet Polity* (1971). For more recent events and policies, see Donald D. Barry and Carol Barner-Barry, *Contemporary Soviet Politics* (2nd ed. 1982), and Jerry Hough's enlarged and revised edition of Fainsod, *How the Soviet Union Is Governed* (1979).

For the Soviet role in world affairs, see Alvin Z. Rubinstein, ed., *The Foreign Policy of the Soviet Union* (1960); Louis Fischer, *The Soviets in World Affairs* (1960); David Dallin, *Soviet Foreign Policy after Stalin*

(1961); Philip Mosely, *The Kremlin and World Politics* (1960); and Adam Ulam's *Dangerous Relations: The Soviet Union in World Politics, 1970–1982* (1983).

The best studies of the changing nature of the Soviet bloc in the fifties and sixties are Zbigniew Brzezinski, *The Soviet Bloc, Unity and Conflict* (rev. ed. 1967), and Ghita Ionescu, *The Break-up of the Soviet Empire in Eastern Europe* (1965). Some perceptive short studies of polycentrism are in Kurt London, ed., *Eastern Europe in Transition* (1966); Alexander Dallin, ed., *Diversity in International Communism* (1963); Paul Zinner, ed., *National Communism and Popular Revolt in Eastern Europe* (1956); and Stephen Fischer-Galati, ed., *Eastern Europe in the 1980's* (1981).

Scholarly treatments of Khrushchev can be found in Edward Crankshaw, *Khrushchev: A Career* (1966); Carl A. Linden, *Khrushchev and the Soviet Leadership* (1966); Abraham Blumberg, ed., *Russia under Khrushchev* (1962); and Roy A. Medvedev and Zhores A. Medvedev, *Khrushchev: The Years in Power* (1976).

For the period after Khrushchev, see Seweryn Bialer, *Stalin's Successors: Leadership, Stability and Change in the Soviet Union* (1980) and *The Soviet Paradox: External Expansion, Internal Decline* (1987).

Competent studies of the Romanian separate road and Romanian communism are Ghita Ionescu, *Communism in Rumania, 1944–1962* (1964); Stephen Fischer-Galati, *The Socialist Republic of Rumania* (1969); and David Floyd, *Rumania: Russia's Dissident Ally* (1965).

For Poland, see Hansjakob Stehle, *The Independent Satellite: Society and Politics in Poland Since 1945* (1965); James F. Morrison, *The Polish People's Republic* (1969); Richard Hiscocks, *Poland, Bridge for the Abyss* (1963); and Nicholas Bethell, *Gomulka: His Poland, His Communism* (1969). For a thorough historical background, see Norman Davies, *God's Playground: A History of Poland, Vol. II: 1795 to the Present* (1982).

The Hungarian Revolution is detailed further in Paul Kecskemeti, *The Unexpected Revolution* (1961); Ference A. Vali, *Rift and Revolt in Hungary* (1961); Paul E. Zinner, *Revolution in Hungary* (1962); Bennet Kovrig, *The Hungarian People's Republic* (1970); and Tamas Ceczel, *Ten Years After: The Hungarian Revolution in the Perspective of History* (1967).

For studies of recent events and recent studies of the fifties and sixties, see the Further Reading section following chapter 13.

8 European Unity

The creation of a large internal market is indispensable to make it possible for Europeans to take their place in the world again.

Jean Monnet *Les États-Unis d'Europe Ont Commencé: Discours et Allocutions, 1952–1954*

Why should we have recourse to this idea, to this new-fangled supranational institution [European Coal and Steel Community]? To enable Germany to accept restrictions on her own sovereignty which is being gradually and irrevocably restored to her. And if we wish to make Germany accept these restrictions, we must set her an example. . . . It will mean identical renunciation on both sides and in the most delicate matters, such as the army and the production of coal and steel, products essential to the preparation of war and for the formation of policy.

Robert Schuman, *French Policy Towards Germany since the War*

The omnipresent fear and impotence of small nations in a world dominated by superpowers, the desire to incorporate Germany into a federated Europe so as to prevent a recurrence of war and its attendant devastation, the longing for the economic advantages thought to be inherent in a larger economic unit—together, these provided the initial impetus for European integration. The unification movement had slowed by the 1950s, but then the Soviet Union crushed the Hungarian Revolution, the British and French failed at Suez, and Europe lost its colonial empire. All these now convinced a growing number of Europeans who had originally opposed union that closer cooperation might be their only salvation. Externally, the United States pressured Europe to cooperate so that it could pay for more of its own reconstruction, restore its markets for American goods, and prevent calamitous political developments similar to those that followed World War I.

As French author and critic André Malraux noted, Europe was united only under Rome and under Christianity in the medieval period. By the end of World War I, the triumph of the national state was complete. Few questioned the right of the national state to command the obedience of the people living within its borders. Nineteenth-century philosophers such as Hegel justified the carving up of Europe into smaller national states that began in earnest with the French Revolution. The French Revolution had shown how brittle empires were and how powerful a political entity could be when supported by its citizenry.

Hegel and the romantics found in the national state the proper vehicle for the full development of a people's genius. In their view, the empires and Christian Europe had impeded the full development of this genius. To them, true creativity in literature, music, and the other arts was no more than the ability to express this folk genius embodied in the national state. Nationalism became one of the major forces in the disruption of the Ottoman and Hapsburg empires before and during World War I.

The Beginnings of Unity

Until after World War I, few questioned the legitimacy of the national state. Count Richard Coudenhove-Kalergi, an aristocrat brought up in the Hapsburg monarchy, was the strongest advocate of European unification in the interwar years. Others, such as French foreign minister Aristide Briand, had prepared a memorandum for a united Europe in 1930, but Europe was already on its way to an unlooked-for union under the jack-boots of Adolf Hitler's Third Reich.

From the sufferings of World War II emerged a much more broadly based desire for some form of European union. Countless wartime Resistance fighters decided that the Europe of nation states should be replaced by a unified and therefore less warlike Europe. A Dutch Resistance publication of 1944, *De Ploeg*, visualizing a divided postwar Europe under the influence of either the United States or the Soviet Union, had this to say: "We Dutch are Europeans and we believe in a future for Europe. We do not belong to the Americans, who see Europe as senile and who from the outset are dividing it up into an Asiatic and an American sphere of interest."

European leaders of the stature of Winston Churchill, Pope Pius XII, Paul-Henri Spaak, Alcide de Gasperi, Robert Schuman, and Konrad Adenauer added their voices to the outpouring of support for a united Europe. Numerous organizations, Britain's United Europe Movement and Coudenhove-Kalergi's European Parliamentary Union among them, sprang up in support of European union.

In addition to the desire of Europeanists to avoid wars, the economic arguments for European union were compelling. Integration of the European economy would promote large-scale, low-cost production that would lead to greater economic output and an improved competitive position in the world market. Moreover, a customs union would enlarge the European market for member countries by bringing down the high tariff walls that separated them. Europeanists were convinced that a primary factor in American productivity and competitiveness was the huge American common market of 160 million people. Despite these advantages, many Europeans were unwilling to relinquish a measure of national sovereignty in order to attain economic integration. Two outside influences were dominant in breaking down resistance to European economic integration: the Cold War and American pressure in support of European integration to block possible Soviet expansion into Western Europe.

The first major step toward integration was taken in 1947 when the United States asked for the establishment of a common European organization to plan the distribution of American aid under the European Recovery Program, known more familiarly as the Marshall Plan. Presented with the possibility of forestalling a severe postwar economic crisis, seventeen European nations, acting in concert, set up the Organization for European Economic Cooperation (OEEC) to distribute the funds and promote trade among the member nations. Only the East European countries, pressured by Stalin, refused to take part. Since the OEEC was to remain an international rather than a supranational organization—the United States eventually became a full member—there was never any possibility that a participant would have to sacrifice its national sovereignty.

The rapid expansion of trade across European borders—it doubled between 1948 and 1955—convinced many Europeans of the OEEC's value. But attempts to expand it into a European customs union, with common external tariffs against nonmembers, encountered the resistance of Britain, which did not want to jeopardize its own economic ties with its Commonwealth partners. To those who wanted further European unification, it became clear that the OEEC was incapable of achieving this. Still, it had brought Europeans together to discuss their economic needs and had in this way helped break down some opposition to integration.

The Council of Europe

The second major step toward integration was taken with the establishment of the Council of Europe. In May 1948, European federalists convoked a Congress of Europe that was attended by 750 delegates, including some of Europe's leading statesmen: Churchill, Spaak, de Gasperi, Schuman, and Leon Blum. This body's proposal for the political and economic unification of the Continent led a year later to the establishment of the Council of Europe, a permanent European assembly that was to plan some form of European integration.

The Council's attempts to put together some form of union encountered serious resistance. Once again, none of the Eastern European states joined in the deliberations. Britain signed the agreement reluctantly because of the governing Labour party's concern for Britain's Commonwealth partners and its disapproval of what it considered to be the anti-Soviet orientation of the Council. Beneath the surface was Britain's feeling that it really did not belong to Europe and that its interests would be best served by acting as a middleman between Europe and the United States.

As a result of British opposition, the Consultative Assembly of the Council of Europe was limited to the right of recommendation and had no true deliberative power. A Committee of Ministers, comprising the foreign ministers of the member states, was the sole decision-making body. Obviously, the foreign ministers would act as representatives of their individual states rather than as spokesmen for a new sovereign body. Thus, the Council was reduced to making recommendations and offering advice rather than moving toward any real supranational integration of the European states.

The first president of the Council of Europe, the Belgian prime minister and foreign minister from 1948 to 1951 Paul-Henri Spaak, angrily denounced those who thwarted the establishment of a meaningful supranational body when he resigned his office in 1951. In his words, "If a quarter of the energy spent here in saying no were used to say yes to something positive, we should not be in the state we are in today."

Had the movement for European integration stopped with only the OEEC and Council of Europe to its credit, there would be little need today to speak of a possible united Europe. However, there were strong pressures for decisive action. Especially instrumental in promoting tighter bonds was the unstable international situation and the reemergence of a German state. The 1948 Communist coup in Czechoslovakia convinced many opponents of integration that a larger European community was necessary to forestall Communist thrusts into Central and Western Europe. The United States, searching for support in the Cold War with the Soviet Union, encouraged a stronger economic and military organization.

When the Soviet Union exploded its first atomic bomb in 1949, the general sense of insecurity increased. The outbreak of the Korean War lent new urgency to pan-European deliberations because it seemed to some a clear indication of the Communist world's intentions, and to many more it imparted fears for German security. While the United States was tied down in Asia, the reasoning went, American troops would be in short supply in Germany, and that would make Germany a tempting target for Soviet aggression. Europeans were, of course, aware that the United States wanted to rearm Germany in order to steel her defenses against the Soviet Union. This step the other European countries did not favor unless there was some larger European organization to control a rearmed Germany.

The European Coal and Steel Community

France took the lead in the negotiations for a genuine supranational body. Led by two of its greatest statesmen, Commissioner of Planning Jean Monnet and Foreign Minister Robert Schuman, France proposed in 1950 the Schuman Plan, a pooling of Europe's coal and steel resources that would, in Monnet's words, make war between France and Germany "not only unthinkable but materially impossible." France's desire to gain security against Germany provided the major impetus for European integration. Once France realized that Germany would not remain a weak, fragmented entity as it had hoped and Britain would not remain on the Continent as a counterweight to a revived Germany, France had no alternative but to seek some form of French-German association. British failure to cooperate in the European Payments Union (EPU), set up in 1950 to handle financial transactions between states, pointed toward the "little European" (France, Germany, Italy, and the Benelux countries) solution to economic reconstruction. Britain feared the impact any common financial arrangements would have on its sterling trade area.

In the summer of 1952, Monnet's proposal for a pooling of coal and steel resources came to fruition when France, Germany, Italy, and the Benelux countries put into force the agreement setting up the European Coal and Steel Community (ECSC). Britain refused to join because of what it considered to be the excessive power given the six-member High Authority of the ECSC, whose decisions were binding on all members. Britain, with fewer economic problems at the time and with important ties to the United States and to its Commonwealth associates, was not prepared to sacrifice its national sovereignty. Had Britain joined the ECSC, the integration of its coal, steel, and iron industry with the six would have made avoidance of the next step, the European Economic Community, almost impossible. Many British Labour leaders continued to see such supranational organizations as a conspiracy of big business to circumvent the demands of national labor movements.

The European Defense Community

Strangely enough, attempts to form a common European military force encountered opposition not only from the British but ultimately from the very country that had initially proposed it: France. In October 1950, French prime minister René Pleven proposed, as a military counterpart to the ECSC, a unified European army made up of small national contingents from each member nation. France was under pressure from the United States to agree to the rearmament of Germany because of U.S. fears that the Soviet Union might put pressure on or even attack in Europe to help North Korea by diverting U.S. troops from Asia. France therefore offered the Pleven Plan to avoid the establishment of an independent

German military force. Even in Germany there was support for the proposal, because German leaders hoped a common European military might bring an end to Allied occupation.

Perhaps a new supranational army with recruits from all states could have been realized if the former national contingents had been left intact. Yet it is difficult to see how even that proposal could have succeeded without a supranational political organization, and that was never a possibility.

In any case, the Pleven Plan for a European Defense Community (EDC) became the victim of events. The need for a European army diminished with Stalin's death and the thaw in Soviet-Western foreign relations. Although U.S. secretary of state John Foster Dulles continued to threaten to cut military aid to Europe if the EDC was not accepted, United States demands for a European force became less insistent with the end of the Korean War. As for the French change of heart, there were several motivations for it. After France's defeat by the Vietminh at Dien Bien Phu in May 1954 and the subsequent withdrawal of all French forces from Southeast Asia, many French leaders saw surrender of jurisdiction over its army as yet another disgrace. The French premier at this time, Pierre Mendès-France, was not a strong supporter of the EDC. He found it too anti-Soviet and too drastic a move toward supranationalism.

The English refusal to cooperate in the EDC was the final blow, because France feared an EDC that did not have the participation of British forces to offset those of Germany. On August 30, 1954, the French National Assembly rejected the EDC by 319 to 264 votes. With the EDC defeated, the only way to deal with a German military force was to integrate it into the North Atlantic Treaty Organization (NATO) forces. This integration was brought about through the Western European Union (WEU), a body that provided for the stationing of British troops on the continent. Since all the signatories were members of NATO, it was agreed to incorporate the WEU into NATO. As a condition of its membership within the WEU, West Germany agreed to limit its military forces and armaments to levels determined by WEU members. Once French fears of a rearmed Germany were allayed by Britain's promise to keep its forces on German soil indefinitely, German military contingents joined NATO in 1955.

The European Economic Community

Fortunately for the Europeanists, economic integration was not stymied by the failure to reach a military agreement; the apparent success of the Coal and Steel Community in promoting production and trade was a persuasive argument for those advocating further economic integration, even though the ECSC had encouraged overproduction of steel and had thereby lost the support of some industrialists. With production increasing twice as fast among the six as in Great Britain from 1950 to 1955, many former opponents of European economic cooperation became ardent supporters of further economic unification.

Foreign affairs were again significant in marshaling support for closer economic cooperation. The extent of the decline in France's importance was made abundantly clear by Nasser's nationalization of the Suez Canal in 1956. This action triggered speculation as to whether Europe would be cut off from its supplies of fuel. Monnet's new Action Committee for the United States of Europe said that Europe's life might "in the near future, . . . be paralyzed by the cutting off of its oil imports from the Middle East." British and French attempts to make Nasser return ownership of the canal to the original stockholders met resistance not only from Egypt but also from the United States, which sought to prevent war in Egypt. Even French and British bombardment of Egypt, coordinated with an Israeli attack into the Sinai desert, failed to produce the desired results.

The cutting off of oil imports to France led to a winter of unheated homes and immobilized automobiles and made French leaders starkly aware that France could not act alone and that its alliance with the United States did not guarantee unconditional support for any French action. Britain attempted to obtain U.S. financial support so as to stabilize its finances after its military action had caused a worldwide run on the pound, but it was turned down. That the Soviet Union was unhampered in crushing the Hungarian Revolution was further proof that, individually, Europe's nations were helpless in the world of superpowers.

Recognizing the weakness of the individual nations of Europe, the French now threw their support to plans for expanding the ECSC into a common market that would include all industrial and agricultural production.

The Council of Ministers of the ECSC had already begun negotiations for a further integration of Europe's economy. Led by Paul-Henri Spaak, the Benelux countries took the initiative in these discussions. Belgium, the Netherlands, and Luxembourg had already been brought together in a customs union in 1948; now the objective was to establish an area free of internal tariffs similar to that in the Benelux countries and the United States. At a meeting in Messina in 1955, the council decided to discuss the possibility of a common tariff among the ECSC member states. This was the initial step toward economic unity. The organization it led to was the European Economic Community (EEC) or Common Market. The Rome Treaties of 1957, the founding treaties of the EEC, envisioned the elimination of customs barriers by 1967 and the development of an economic unit that could compete with the United States.

Authority in the EEC was lodged in four bodies—a Council of Ministers, representing the interests of each member state; an elected Commission, representing the supranational interest; a Court of Justice; and a European Parliament. The founders realized that the members would not be willing initially to sacrifice all their national jurisdiction over their separate economies.

The Council of Ministers, made up of the foreign ministers (or their representatives) from each member state, considered and voted on proposals from the Commission. The size of each member's vote was determined by the size of the state. France, Germany, and Italy had four votes each, Belgium and the Netherlands two, and Luxembourg one.

The Court of Justice was comprised of seven judges appointed by the separate governments for a maximum term of six years. The court settled disputes among the member nations.

The European Parliament, to which delegates from national Parliaments are sent, and which Europeanists hoped would soon blossom into a genuine supranational assembly, could question the Commission members and force the resignation of the Commission by a two-thirds vote. Normally, decisions were reached through a rather exhausting process of having the Commission submit and resubmit proposals before they were accepted by the Council. In the 1950s this system provided a good balance between national and supranational interests; but in the 1960s, de Gaulle's narrow view of EEC duties and authority severely reduced the power of the Commission and thus the hopes for a united Europe.

In 1960, Europe was far from the unity envisioned by many EEC founders. In fact, it was divided into three economic areas: the EEC; the Eastern European Comecon countries; and a new British-led European Free Trade Association (EFTA), consisting of Britain, Sweden, Denmark, Norway, Portugal, Switzerland, and Austria. EFTA's primary aim was to remove trade barriers between member countries. Before the formation of EFTA in 1959, Britain had tried to set up a larger free-trade area that included the EEC. But EEC members were fearful that it would keep them from their goal of making the EEC a fully integrated economic area. EFTA did not, for example, include a common external tariff.

In practice, EFTA had a very limited impact on the redirection of trade in Europe. Austria, Sweden, and even Great Britain traded more with EEC members than with members of EFTA. Richard Mayne, an EEC official, correctly perceived it as "partly a salvage operation, to secure whatever benefits were possible on a smaller and more scattered basis" than the EEC envisioned. Given Britain's close ties to the United States and the Commonwealth and rather ambivalent feelings about its Europeanness, in 1959 an organization such as EFTA seemed the only possibility.

Only two years later, convinced by the EEC's economic success and discouraged by its own economic problems and declining role in the world, Great Britain decided to seek admittance to the EEC. The British were especially concerned with reports that the EEC had decided to institute political as well as economic cooperation, which would exclude Great Britain from any possibility of future integration with the six. A communiqué from a meeting of the six in July 1961, setting up a committee to draft a political treaty, announced that the EEC sought "to give shape to the will for political union already implicit in the Treaties establishing the European Communities." The British need not have worried. This statement was issued by the Fouchet Committee, which later failed to reach an agreement on political cooperation.

Britain's conception of itself as an intermediary between the United States and Europe was undermined by President John F. Kennedy's grand design to bring Europe and the United States closer together and prevent the imposition of high tariffs between the United States and the EEC. The so-called Kennedy Round of tariff negotiations, which resulted in the U.S. Trade Expansion Act of 1961, did reduce tariffs 30 to 50 percent (depending on the commodity) on trade between Europe and the United States. Included in the Trade Expansion Act was a clause that would have permitted President Kennedy to cut tariffs even further if Great Britain had been an EEC member.

President Kennedy, as well as his predecessors, hoped to see Great Britain join the EEC. In March 1961, George Ball, U.S. under secretary of state for economic affairs, told Edward Heath, later to be prime minister, "So long as Britain remains outside the European Community, she is a force for division rather than cohesion, since she is like a giant lodestone drawing with unequal degrees of force on each member state." He went on to say that British membership in the EEC would lead to "a unity that can transform the Western world." So with a mixture of anxiety over its economic and political position, fear that Europe would go it alone, and assurance that the United States approved, on August 10, 1961, Great Britain asked to negotiate with the EEC.

Fourteen months later, with the basis for British entry not yet completely settled, de Gaulle intervened. On January 14, 1963, he informed the world:

> England in fact is insular, maritime, bound by her trade, her markets, her supplies to countries that are very diverse and often far away . . . The nature, the structure, the situation that are peculiar to England are very different from those of the continental countries. How can England, as she lives, as she produces, as she trades, be incorporated into the Common Market as it was conceived and as it works?

Fifteen days later the negotiations were brought to a close by a French veto of the British application.

De Gaulle disapproved of British entry into the EEC for a variety of reasons. Perhaps most important was the likelihood that it would destroy France's domination of the organization. The EEC had made it possible for France to play a much larger role in the world than its own resources warranted. After the loss of its colonial empire, de Gaulle hoped to regain in Europe what France had lost in the world. Furthermore, de Gaulle

EUROPEAN ECONOMIC ALLIANCES, 1990

European Economic Community (Common Market)   founded 1957

European Free Trade Association (EFTA)   founded 1960

Council for Mutual Economic Assistance (COMECON)   founded 1949

resented Britain's close relationship with the United States. He resented Britain's refusal to cooperate with France in developing nuclear weapons and her acceptance of American weapons. De Gaulle could not say in so many words that France did not want to share its leadership of the EEC, but he could say the British were acting as a "Trojan horse" for the Americans.

A final roadblock to British entry was a number of conditions that Britain wanted taken into consideration, including protection for its agriculture and special consideration for the interests of its Commonwealth and EFTA partners. De Gaulle was not alone in opposing the special conditions, for if every member had been given such consideration, there would have been no EEC. Still, it was the brusque manner of de Gaulle's rejection, without warning, that so embittered the British and impaired EEC operations in the mid-1960s.

The difference between de Gaulle's conception of Europe—as a springboard for French designs—and that of the European federalists became the subject of a 1965 struggle to decide which of the EEC governing bodies should have precedence. The focus of the conflict was a clash between de Gaulle and the German head of the EEC Commission, Walter Hallstein. De Gaulle needed EEC support for his policy of grandeur (see chapter 3), but he did not want to have any economic decision making taken out of French hands. Therefore, he refused to give the Commission and its chairman, Hallstein, the authority they desired.

Hallstein, in turn, tried to move toward a federal Europe by lodging the authority to debate and reject the Community's budget in the EEC's legislative body, the European Parliament. This de Gaulle opposed as an infringement on the rights of national government. In his turn, he prevented the establishment of a truly federal parliament of the kind favored by the EEC founders by keeping decision making primarily in the hands of the Council of Ministers.

Although the other EEC members stood firm against de Gaulle, they could not compel the French to accept an increase in the authority of the Commission. The crisis was resolved in 1966 when the six governments signed the Luxembourg Agreement stipulating that the EEC Commission consult the individual states before making major proposals. Further, the agreement provided that no member nation could be overruled in the Council of Ministers on an issue that that nation saw as affecting its vital interests.

In July 1967, a new European Commission replaced the institutions of the EEC, Euratom, and ECSC's High Authority. But real authority remained in the hands of a new single Council of Ministers, which appointed the Commission members and took its orders from the member governments. The conflict between de Gaulle and the federalists proved a serious setback to the supranational concept of Europe from which the EEC has never fully recovered.

The period from 1967 to 1971 was dominated by new British attempts to enter the Common Market. Prime Minister Harold Wilson tried to reopen negotiations in 1967 and was again turned back by de Gaulle, but a series of later events combined to make British entry possible. Foremost among these events was the change of government in France when de Gaulle retired in 1969. His successor was Georges Pompidou, a supporter of a confederated Europe who was not as firmly opposed to British membership since his goals for France were not as exaggerated as those of de Gaulle.

Equally persuasive in shaping the new French attitude was the growing power and independence of West Germany. When de Gaulle and the Francophile Konrad Adenauer were in power, France had little difficulty in dominating the EEC. But after forced wage increases in 1968 and a growing trade deficit, French financial reserves, once a threat to the

United States, began to dwindle. De Gaulle tried to get Germany to re-value its currency higher so as to keep France from having to devalue. That he failed was a severe blow to his prestige and the first indication that West Germany's politics would no longer be tied to French coattails.

When the Social Democrat Willy Brandt came to power, the change became even more apparent. Brandt's *Ostpolitik*, or Eastern policy, pointed to an independence in foreign affairs that could unify Germany and make it an even stronger economic and political entity. In addition, Brandt's attempts to resolve difficulties with the Soviet Union and Eastern Europe stole the thunder from de Gaulle's attempts at détente.

The French reaction to Brandt's designs reflected growing fears with regard to Germany. A final blow to French pride was a German unilateral decision to let the strong German mark float against other currencies in May 1971. One Gaullist deputy was quoted as saying, "The importance of the power of Germany now makes the French people think that Great Britain will be very, very useful in the Common Market."

Britain's economic woes made entry into the Common Market seem daily more desirable. The hope was widespread that EEC membership could step up Britain's economic pace and cut its persistent trade deficits. Politically, Prime Minister Edward Heath realized that the EEC concept of confederation would mean no significant sacrifice of Britain's sovereignty. Now Britain's view was that the EEC, stripped of its supranational tendencies, could strengthen Britain's economy and restore a measure of its dwindling stature.

The negotiations for British membership, which began in July 1970, were concluded within one year. The British were now willing to forgo some special privileges; for example, instead of a six-year transition period before its agriculture had to meet all the requirements of membership, Britain now agreed to a three-year transition. It also accepted a diminished world role for sterling in order to insure the equality of all EEC currencies. In 1972, the remaining obstacles to entry were cleared up, and Britain joined two other nations, Ireland and Denmark, in assuming membership in the EEC.

After the acceptance of Britain, Ireland, and Denmark in 1972, the economic crisis brought on by the cutbacks in Arab oil production temporarily brought any further integration to a standstill. The 1980 deadline for European union that was agreed to at the Paris Summit Conference of the nine heads of state in 1972 had become a laughing matter only a year later as each country tried to find its own way out of the economic recession that began in that year. The common energy policy that was proposed at the Copenhagen Summit by the nine heads of state in 1972 had also failed to materialize.

Perhaps most disheartening for those Europeanists who had fought so hard for unification was the refusal of members to act like genuine economic partners. During the fuel crisis that was an aftermath of the Arab-

Israeli War in 1973, the nine went their separate ways, trying to make unilateral deals for oil and refusing to stand behind the Netherlands, which was denied Arab oil because of its support of Israel. Nor did the EEC countries seek a common solution to the economic recession that began in the late seventies. One European diplomat's remark, "These countries are so different that it's very hard to put the same saddle on all ten horses," pointed out the great differences between member countries.

Their initial inability to overcome the disagreements over agricultural policies further illustrated the disunity. Most members wanted to scale down the excessively high farm subsidies that inflated food costs. But the French, who benefited most from the subsidies due to their larger agricultural areas, opposed any meaningful reduction. Discussion of Spanish and Portuguese entry to the EEC (1986) further exacerbated the agricultural problem since their lower priced grain and produce caused some existing EEC farmers to panic. In 1982, French farmers were destroying Spanish shipments of produce entering France. Only after eight years of debate and compromise were Spain and Portugal brought into the EEC in 1986. But they are merging over a seven-year period through the Integrated Mediterranean Programs adopted in 1985.

Nor did the British entry promote European unity; instead, it actually retarded integration. Britain dragged its feet on full economic integration because the newly elected Labour government of 1974 was dissatisfied with the terms of entry into the Community and because British leaders feared that the EEC wanted a share of the oil discovered in the North Sea. Although a British referendum favoring participation in the EEC passed by a two-to-one majority in 1975, later opinion polls swung decisively against participation. The British blamed increasing food prices on the high EEC farm subsidies that artificially created high prices. They were also the largest net contributor to the ECC's budget. Perhaps most important, the EEC had not been the economic panacea for Britain's economic woes that many British expected. If Labour had won the British elections in 1979, they would have had popular support for their threat to pull Britain out of the EEC. Greece also proved disruptive when it sought to renegotiate the terms of its entry in 1981.

A special fifteen-member EEC committee set up to investigate the outlook for economic and monetary union reported in April 1975: "Europe is no nearer to economic and monetary union today than when it was proposed six years ago, largely because of lack of political will." The report attributed this to the international monetary crisis that began in the late 1960s, the financial problems caused by the sharp rise in oil prices in 1973, and the tendency of each government to search for its own way out of the crisis. A high-ranking EEC official expressed similar pessimism in 1981 when he remarked, "People in general just don't believe anymore that the Community can deal with their real problems."

If economic integration seemed to be threatened, some Europeanists'

**EUROPEAN
ECONOMIC COMMUNITY**

Original EEC members
Joined 1973
Joined in 1981
Joined in 1986

ATLANTIC OCEAN

FINLAND

NORWAY

SWEDEN

Baltic Sea

SOVIET
UNION

North
Sea

DENMARK

POLAND

IRELAND

GREAT
BRITAIN

NETH.

BELG.

LUX.

EAST
GERMANY

WEST
GERMANY

CZECHOSLOVAKIA

AUSTRIA

HUNGARY

FRANCE

SWITZ.

ITALY

YUGOSLAVIA

ROMANIA

BULGARIA

PORTUGAL

SPAIN

ALBANIA

GREECE

TURKEY

MEDITERRANEAN   SEA

aim of political unity appeared even more farfetched in the late seventies. If the members' economies had been fully integrated as the federalists desired, further unification might have been a possibility. The weakness of the EEC Commission and the European Parliament vis-à-vis the Council of Ministers pointed out the failure of political unity. The Commission, an elected body that has some independence from member governments, has almost no power to initiate policy. It acts as a broker between governments, while the Council of Ministers, whose members are appointed by the individual governments, initiates policy. Decisions are, therefore, still being made at the national level. The European Parliament seemed to offer some hope for greater unity when it was decided to elect members directly rather than continuing to send delegates from national legislatures and it was given the right to reject the EEC budget. After the first direct election in 1979, the Parliament did indeed reject the Commission's 1980 budget proposals. Since then, however, it has taken a back seat to the Council of Ministers and the Commission.

The EEC's dilemma was complicated by the international integration of economies through vast corporations, advisory organizations such as the Organization for Economic Cooperation and Development (OECD), and the many economic and political ties with the United States. International corporations, many based in the United States, dominated various branches of trade and industry in Europe. There seemed to be as good a chance of integrating Europe into a larger Atlantic unit as into a European Community. One West German official maintained that if Chancellor Helmut Schmidt were forced to choose between Europe and Washington, he would choose Washington. The Labour government in Britain warned its EEC Partners in March 1974 that Britain's ties with the United States were as important as those with Europe. As Labour foreign secretary James Callaghan put it then, "My country wishes to remain a member of an effective Atlantic Alliance and there is therefore concern about the degree of disagreement between the Community and the United States." The Conservative government under Thatcher maintained, if not strengthened, the close economic and political ties with the United States. That this relationship could change, however, was indicated by the European disenchantment with the Reagan administration over its opposition to a Soviet oil pipeline to Europe and détente.

One factor that preserved economic cooperation among EEC members during this time of trouble was the network of economic ties that had developed over the past two decades and the fact that extensive trade cooperation did indeed exist. Between 1958 and 1968, trade quadrupled among the six original members of the EEC. By 1968, 61 percent of the EEC's manufactured goods were sold within the Community. Even with the European Community's increasing trade with the Third World and developed Asian countries, 51 percent of the Community's trade was with other members in 1979. The Italians would be as reluctant to give up the huge tariff-free zone for their refrigerators and wine as the other members would be to lose this advantage for their own national specialties.

Not only had the two oil crises of 1973 and 1979 hindered further cooperation in the seventies, but unrealistic plans for greater political union went far beyond the vision of most EEC members. The EEC had gotten away from the earlier directives of Robert Schuman and Jean Monnet that Europe had to be built on concrete agreements and timetables that were more limited in their goals. The Fouchet Plan of 1961 that envisioned a joint European foreign policy struck too deeply at the sovereignty of members. A plan for Economic and Monetary Unity (EMU) of 1970 also frightened those countries wishing to maintain financial independence. The British could not accept the disappearance of the pound nor the French the franc. What the EEC needed was more clearly designed plans for further economic cooperation that would move the countries closer together without compromising their political independence.

This impetus came with the appointment of Jacques Delors as president of the EEC in 1985. Delors had already brought about major economic improvement in the French economy as finance minister by reducing inflation and cutting foreign dept. By presenting the member states with a more limited program for developing internal trade further, Delors began to move the EEC forward. Delors was aided by a general European feeling that they were falling behind Japan and the United States in the important areas of computer technology and behind the United States in space-related technology and that greater European cooperation was needed to meet the challenge. Delors had a white paper prepared that listed three hundred measures that were necessary to achieve a true customs union such as that in the United States He and his vice-minister Lord Cockfield set 1992 as a reasonable timetable for implementing these measures. Although the total number of measures declined during discussions, the more precise goal of ridding the EEC of internal obstacles to trade seemed achievable and did not violate the individual member countries of a sense of sovereignty as much as the political goals had done. Delors' initiative resulted in the passing of the Single European Act (SEA) of 1987 that bound member countries to the goal of a single EEC market by 1992. While the original goal of the SEA to obtain a working European Parliament had to be sacrificed on the altar of national sovereignties, the single-market goal was accepted. One aspect of the SEA that is causing a great deal of foot dragging is financial unity and a common European currency. While the creation of a European supereconomy will undoubtedly require financial unity, member countries such as Britain will not easily discard their own currency. The move toward a barrier-free internal market has been aided by European Court of Justice decisions that have struck down national decisions restricting trade between EEC members. Essentially, the court decided that the movement of goods and services cannot be blocked except for reasons of health, fiscal supervision, fair trade, or consumer protection. Even a German demand to maintain high-purity standards for its sausages (wurst) was struck down by the court.

As the EEC moves closer to a single market on the order of the United States, speculation about more political unity will undoubtedly continue. Such speculation hinders legally neutral countries such as Austria from entering the EEC and spreads suspicion among existing members such as Britain that some EEC members want more than mere economic unity. Delors' speculation in 1988 that "in ten years' time 80 percent of economic, and perhaps social and tax, legislation will be of Community origin" indicates that he sees a great deal of Community involvement in what formerly were national matters. What the EEC will probably achieve in those ten years is a frontierless market but not a common currency or a common Parliament. Decisions will continue to be made by the Council of Ministers with its nationally appointed members. But the frontierless market will continue to prod the EEC toward further economic integration and greater cooperation. The business community will continue to push for greater integration since they see the benefits of a larger market for their products and cheaper labor costs with the free movements of member populations. Businesses may also move production to the cheaper labor areas such as Greece, Spain, and Portugal, a prospect alarming to northern laborers unless safeguards can be achieved. On the other hand, labor is excited by the possibility of many new jobs as a result of business expansion in the EEC.

Enthusiasm for the European Community, which it is increasingly being called, continues to grow in Europe. An official EC opinion survey in 1986 found that over 60 percent of the French, Germans, Italians, and Dutch thought membership in the EC was good for their country. Only British citizens with their strong ties to the United States and their strong independent tendencies thought that membership was bad (34 percent) rather than good (31 percent) for their country. This could change rapidly if British industry profits from the closer economic association that will come.

There are still major obstacles to overcome before the EC obtains a common internal market. Common tax rates, product standardization, and the free movement of labor are all difficult problems that have yet to be resolved. France, West Germany, and the Benelux countries took a giant step toward the free movement of labor in June 1990 when they agreed at Schengen, Luxembourg, to permit the free movement of people across their borders sometime in 1992 after each state ratifies the agreement and German unification is completed. But the enthusiasm in Europe in 1990 for a barrier-free internal market is overwhelming. Although the EC will not achieve its goal of a full economic union by 1992, it will be well on its way to one internal market. In addition to these economic achievements, the EC has contributed to the reduction of cultural isolation in Europe and has helped make friends out of former enemies. One of the major original purposes of the European Community, the avoidance of war in Europe through economic integration, has been achieved. Much of the unity achieved within the Community has been built on the co-operation between the two long-standing rivals, France and Germany.

FURTHER READING

For standard thorough accounts of the early stages of European integration, see Hans Schmitt, *The Path to European Union: From the Mar-*

Table 9-2   1987 GDP per Person (in 1988 dollars)

	At Market Exchange Rates	Purchasing Power Parities
Australia	15,470	11,664
Belgium	14,071	11,802
Denmark	19,730	13,241
France	15,818	12,803
Germany	18,280	13,323
Greece	4,719	6,363
Ireland	8,297	7,541
Italy	13,224	12,254
Luxembourg	16,138	14,705
Netherlands	14,530	12,252
Norway	19,756	15,405
Portugal	3,761	6,297
Spain	7,449	8,681
Sweden	18,876	13,771
Switzerland	25,848	15,838
United Kingdom	11,765	12,340
United States	18,338	18,338

Source: *OECD in figures, OECD* Observer *158, supplement (June–July 1989).*

Wages and Fringe Benefits

While the gap between rich and poor has remained wide (see chapter 10), few would dispute that wages have increased more than costs since World War II. In most European countries, government and industrial leaders have adopted a new attitude toward labor because of their acceptance of the welfare state. They now promote higher wages for laborers, in line with the conviction that this will increase the demand for consumer goods and avoid industrial conflict. This new attitude is often reflected in the guidelines set by the government to guarantee wage increments. In Sweden, labor leaders, employers, and government officials negotiate annual contracts for the work force. This so-called incomes policy assures labor of annual increases to meet rising costs. The 1963 labor contracts included an increase of 7.5 percent in the annual wage bill even though the gross national product (GNP) rose by only 3.3 percent.

European wages increased most during periods of rapid economic growth and low inflation. Between 1953 and 1965, real wages rose 36 percent in the United Kingdom, 58 percent in France, 80 percent in Italy, and 100 percent in Germany. Despite these increases, wages remained comparatively low in France, the United Kingdom, and Italy. Although Table 9-3 gives the average wage in manufacturing for each country, it

Table 9-3   Average Hourly Wages in Manufacturing (in current U.S. dollars)

	1960	1971	1974	1980	1988
United States	2.28	3.57	4.40	7.27	10.30
Sweden	1.14	2.88	4.02	7.72	10.00
Belgium	1.00	2.34	N.A.	7.45	8.50
Norway	0.90	2.29	3.50	7.84	13.00
West Germany	0.82	2.49	3.44	7.25	10.60
Great Britain	0.82	2.14	2.66	5.62	6.89
France	0.51	1.24	1.86	4.37	6.75
Italy	—	1.10	1.87	5.57	6.60

Source: Bulletin of Labor Statistics *(Geneva: International Labor Office, 3rd quarter, 1975),* 57–62. Worldwide Economic Indicators: Comparitive Summary for 131 Countries *(Business International Corporation, 1982 Annual).* Bulletin of Labor Statistics *(1989-2): 100–105.*

does not include expenditures for social services or benefits received by workers, both of which are higher in European countries than in the United States. In Scandinavia, the Benelux countries, and West Germany, where workers receive high fringe benefits along with high wages, workers' living standards have reached or surpassed those of laborers in the United States.

The gap between the upper-income groups and manual and service-class workers is narrowed somewhat by state benefits—tax rebates, pensions, family allowances, rent assistance, and so on—that go primarily to low-income groups. Although still a major portion of a worker's income, they have diminished since the early seventies. Using data for 1972, the Organization for Economic Cooperation and Development calculated that state benefits increased the disposable income of a worker with two children and a nonworking wife to 106 percent of gross pay in France, 102 percent in Spain, and 96 percent in Italy. In 1983, workers in Austria, France, and Luxembourg received more than 90 percent of their gross earnings, compared to between 70 and 80 percent in Finland, Germany, Italy, the Netherlands, Sweden, and the United States.

Status of Working Women

While women's status has improved since 1945, they are still treated as second-class citizens in many European countries. Compared to the nineteenth century, when women were employed primarily in domestic service, they now make up a large segment of those employed in white-collar occupations and an increasing number of those in blue-collar occupations.

Table 9-4 shows that both the present participation rate of women in the labor force and the female share of the labor force has increased since

Time seems to have stood still in this poverty-stricken village in Sicily as hens scratch in the street and an old woman hides her face from the photographer. (Alfred Gregory—Camera Press London)

1950, except in countries where it was already high and in the less-developed countries where it remains low. Women comprised from 35 to 47 percent of the labor force in the developed European states in 1986. As John Ardagh states, "To have a wife who does not work is often a status symbol" among the poorer classes.

Women's unemployment rates are invariably higher than those of men since they lack job seniority and are more involved in part-time work. When economic difficulties occur, women are the first to lose their jobs.

But recent investigations make it apparent, as shown in Table 9-5, that gender differences in pay within the EEC have narrowed substantially since 1970. In 1974, the EEC rebuked Britain, Ireland, and Denmark for their unequal treatment of women. The other EEC states had established equal-pay-for-equal-work guidelines, although in practice the gaps had not been completely closed. By 1986, women's earnings in Denmark, France, Norway, Italy, and the Netherlands reached over 80 percent and in Sweden over 90 percent of those of men; but those in Germany and Belgium were only about 70 percent; and in Greece, Ireland, Luxembourg, the United Kingdom, and the United States less than 70 percent of men's wages.

Table 9-4 Labor Force Participation Rates and Female Share of Labor Force

	1950		1986	
	PARTICIPATION RATE	SHARE OF LABOR FORCE	PARTICIPATION RATE	SHARE OF LABOR FORCE
Austria	51.0	38.5	51.7	39.6
Belgium	32.8	27.9	51.3	40.3
Denmark	49.6	33.6	76.5	45.8
France	49.5	35.9	55.3	42.1
Germany	44.3	35.1	50.4[a]	38.9[a]
Greece	41.4	32.1	41.8[a]	35.6[a]
Ireland	36.9	25.5	37.2	30.0
Italy	32.0	25.4	42.3	35.5
Netherlands	28.5	23.4	41.1	34.8
Portugal	26.3	22.4	56.2	40.7
Spain	17.6	15.4	34.1	30.4
Sweden	35.1	26.3	78.3	47.6
United Kingdom	40.7	30.7	61.0	40.9

Source: *Figures for 1950 are from the OECD* Observer *104 (May 1980); figures for 1986 are from the OECD* Observer *152, supplement (June–July 1988): 10–11.*
[a] *Figures for 1985.*

Table 9-5 Women's Earnings as a Percentage of Men's (1986 average hourly earnings)

Country	1970	1975	1986
Belgium	66.7	69.7 (1979)	73
Denmark	72.4	83.2	82.2
Germany (FRG)	69.2	—	73
France	78.8 (1973)	79.2 (1979)	82.2
Greece	—	—	67.2
Ireland	56.2	60.9	67.6 (1981)
Italy	74.2	78.7	83.2 (1980)
Luxembourg	57	63.3	64.7 (1980)
Netherlands	73.3	79.5	77.9 (1980)
Norway	75.1	78	81.9 (1980)
Sweden	—	—	91 (1985)
United Kingdom	—	72.1	74 (1985)
United States	—	58.9 (1977)	64.3

Source: *"Closing the Wage Gap: An International Perspective," National Committee on Pay Equity, Washington, D.C.*

Status of Immigrant Laborers

Only partially profiting from the new affluence are the thousands of immigrant laborers who flocked to northern Europe's factories in the 1960s (see chapter 4 for details). When the employment of foreign workers reached its peak of about 10 million in Western Europe, before the recession following the 1973 Arab oil embargo led to mass firings, over one-third of the Swiss labor force consisted of foreign workers. Filling initially the least desirable jobs in municipalities and on assembly lines, they constituted an underpaid, neglected segment of the working class; they swept streets, collected garbage, cleaned rest rooms, and did unskilled work in factories. But they gradually came to fill many of the semi-skilled jobs in manufacturing: about 80 percent of the assembly-line tasks at the Renault factory near Paris were performed by foreign laborers in the seventies.

When their labor was essential during the economic boom years and their numbers were relatively small, they were accepted by Europeans with only the occasional protests. But the economic slowdown that began in the seventies combined with the sizable numbers of immigrant workers spread resentment of the foreign workers. The growing unemployment and the willingness of foreign workers to accept lower wages than northern European workers led to popular agitation to limit their numbers. To prevent a further influx of Italian workers in the seventies, some Swiss resorted to fear tactics and hate slogans: "Would you like to share a hospital room with a Sicilian?" Governments began to reduce the number of foreign workers in the seventies by offering them departure payments and reducing the inflow of immigrants. But the number of foreigners continued to increase since many families stayed on, some even starting small businesses, and their families increased in size. While Germany was able to decrease the number of foreign workers from 2.6 to 1.9 million between 1973 and 1983, the total number of foreigners rose from below 4 million to 4.4 million in 1986 or 7.4 percent of Germany's population. OECD figures show that immigrants and their families comprised 6.8, 9.1, 26.2, and 14.7 percent of the French, Belgian, Luxembourg, and Swiss populations, respectively, in 1986. Many nursery and elementary schools are now filled with immigrant's children because of their large families and the exceedingly low northern European birthrates.

Some rightist political groups have sprung up with the reduction of immigrants a major aspect of their appeal. Much of Jean-Marie Le Pen and his National Front's appeal in France, "Send them back home," has come at the expense of the foreign workers. The unexpected success of Norway's rightist Progress party in the 1989 elections can be mainly attributed to the resentment of foreign workers.

In order to save money to buy a car, support their families, and set themselves up when they return home, many of the immigrants were willing to live in slums. In France, shantytowns (called *Bidonvilles*) sprang up on the outskirts of the major cities in the sixties to house most of the foreign workers. Many moved into more permanent residences after bringing their families to their place of work. But this often created ghettos since the previous residents moved out and left only the immigrants. While many of the Italian and Greek workers have obtained acceptance in northern Europe, the Turks, who remain rather exclusive, and the Arabs have not gained acceptance. Recently Arab immigrants have suffered most severely due to the fear of terrorism and the dislike of Muslim fundamentalism. For the most part, northern European workers show little concern for this "subproletariat." A semiskilled worker in West Germany rationalized his renting a small house to several families of these foreign workers with the excuse that they were accustomed to such overcrowding in their home countries.

Governments, on the other hand, have instituted many programs to speed the integration of foreign workers who wish to stay in northern Europe. They have allocated funds for language instruction, for improved housing, and for cultural adaptation. Germany abolished rules that had set quotas on foreign habitation of urban areas and reduced the time needed for a foreigner to gain permanent residence from ten to eight years. Sweden gave foreigners the right to vote and stand for election at the local and regional level in 1978.

The Standard of Living

Although Europe still trails the United States in level of consumer goods used, the more industrialized European states now enjoy an affluence near that of the United States. As smaller percentages of their wages have been used up on clothing, food, and rent, workers have had considerably more money to spend on the kind of consumer goods known as durables because they are longer lasting. Ownership of telephones, refrigerators, television sets, and cars began to reach levels near that of the United States in the more developed countries. Not that the different nations had the same priorities for consumer goods. As a case in point, the Scandinavian countries, with a standard of living near that of West Germany, have about twice as many telephones per capita. The ownership of passenger cars is perhaps more reliable, although not conclusive, as an indicator of standard of living. Both per-capita gross domestic product (Table 9-2) and automobile ownership (Table 9-6) place Britain, France, and Italy below West Germany, Switzerland, and Luxembourg. Automobile expenditures consumed 4 to 6 percent of family income among European countries during the 1980–1985 period.

Before World War II, workers tended to spend about half their income on food. By 1980–1985, food and clothing expenditures in the developed European countries reached only between 20 to 24 percent of total household consumption, according to the World Bank. As Table 9-7 shows, the

Table 9-6 Ownership of Consumer Durables (number per 1,000 inhabitants)

	Telephones			Passenger Cars			Television Sets		
	1969	1980	1985	1969	1980	1985	1969	1980	1985
United States	567	789	800	427	536	710[a]	399	635	798
Sweden	515	796	890	275	345	377	300	374	390
United Kingdom	253	477	521	205	256	312	284	394	333
Luxembourg	314	547	590	251	423	414	183	245	252
Switzerland	457	727	832	206	324	402	184	312	400
West Germany	212	464	621	208	346	424	262	337	372
France	161	459	608	238	327	380	201	292	394
Italy	160	337	448	170	300	390	170	231	253

Source: *OECD* Economic Surveys *(1976, 1981–82); OECD* Observer *74 (March–April)* 75; *OECD* Observer *56 (February 1972); OECD* Observer *115 (March 1982); eurostat, Basic Statistics of the Community, 1988.*
[a] 1984

amount of work time needed to purchase food and clothing had declined markedly since 1950 in Germany.

Nevertheless, it is important to remember that countries differ markedly in enjoying this new affluence. While unskilled workers and low-paid white-collar workers in northern Europe can now afford to spend more of their income on consumer goods, those in Greece and Portugal still spend a large portion of their income on food and drink. Food and clothing consumed 38 percent of total Greek consumption and 44 percent of Portuguese consumption between 1980 and 1985, according to the World Bank. Workers in these countries have had to migrate to the richer northern countries. With increasing subsidies by the European Community and the common internal market sometime after 1992, these inequities should diminish in the next decade.

Table 9-7 Work Time Needed to Buy Commodities in Germany

	1950		1960		1985	
	HOURS	MINUTES	HOURS	MINUTES	HOURS	MINUTES
Sugar (1 kg)		56		30		10
Butter (1 kg)	4	24	2	40		49
Coffee (1 kg)	23	02	7	12	2	06
Man's shoe	19	36	12	29	8	09
Man's bicycle	121	36	69	48	30	53

Source: Tatsachen über Deutschland (Facts about Germany), *Lexikon Institut Bertelsmann (Munich, West Germany), 1988, 173.*

Table 9-8   Per-Capita Private Expenditure
(in current U.S. dollars)

	1973	1980
Denmark	$3,050	$ 7,270
Switzerland	3,640	10,128
Sweden	3,240	7,630
France	2,913	7,690
Belgium	2,810	7,540
West Germany	3,000	7,340
Netherlands	2,430	7,200
United Kingdom	1,960	5,581
Norway	2,530	6,600
Austria	1,870	5,650
Italy	1,620	4,270
Ireland	1,370	3,310
United States	3,840	7,370

Source: *OECD* Economic Survey: Germany *(Paris: 1975)*,
International Comparisons. *OECD* Economic Surveys,
1981–1982: Germany Statistical Annex: *(June, 1982)*.

Both the improvement in the standard of living and the wide gap between northern and southern Europe are revealed in the rise in per-capita
private consumption since 1955. Table 9-8 shows the countries' rankings
according to private consumption in 1973 and 1980; the figures agree fairly
closely with previous figures on income and the ownership of consumer
goods. However, if the higher prices in the top-ranked countries are taken
into consideration (PPPs), the differences between consumers in the countries at the top and the bottom of the ranking are reduced somewhat.
Table 9-9 measures disparities for 1987 in private consumption per capita
in PPPs. Some of the disparity between the United States and Europe

Table 9-9   Private Consumption per Capita Using Current PPPs (1987)

United States	12,232	Netherlands	7,461
Switzerland	9,349	Germany	7,374
Luxembourg	8,694	Sweden	7,273
Norway	8,145	Denmark	7,236
France	7,796	Spain	5,521
United Kingdom	7,731	Ireland	4,378
Belgium	7,593	Greece	4,273
Italy	7,543	Portugal	4,167

Source: *OECD* Economic Surveys: Switzerland, 1988/1989 *(Paris, 1989)*, *Basic Statistics: international comparisons.*

results from the higher savings rate in Europe compared to the United States.

The Work Week and Vacation

For most workers, reduced working hours and paid holidays and vacations have relieved the boredom of the factory. The working week has declined from forty-eight hours in the prewar period to less than forty hours throughout Europe. The Bulletin of Labor Statistics of the International Labor Office (1989-2) reports that the hours of work per week in manufacturing declined to forty or below in 1988 in the following countries: Norway (31.2), Belgium (32.6), Austria (35), Spain (37.5), France (38.7), Italy (38.9), and Germany (40).

Even more responsible for reduced work time has been the extension of paid vacations to four and often five weeks a year. Since vacations are seldom based upon seniority, laborers can expect these long vacations during their first years of work. French workers get two days' vacation for every month on the job or about five weeks' vacation a year. In West Germany, where two-thirds of the work force gets six weeks of paid leave annually, workers prize leisure time as much as advancement. In a recent opinion poll, family, time off, and friends ranked ahead of their job. In the United States, where vacation time depends on the time of service with a company, most workers receive only two weeks' paid vacation a year. European governments and businesses also provide extra vacation bonuses and low-cost holiday excursions for workers. Austrian workers receive two extra months' pay as bonuses each year. France's state-owned Renault automobile firm provides support for thirty vacation villages. Employees paid as little as $51 a week in the seventies to stay at these resorts. Most companies throughout Europe now provide additional vacation bonuses for their workers.

Because of higher incomes and paid vacations, entire countries come almost to a standstill at certain times of the year. In one of the richest countries in Europe, Sweden, three out of four residents take a vacation outside their place of residence each year. In August, the only people left in Paris are the poorer workers, tourists, and those few unfortunates who are left behind to serve the tourists. Vienna has now worked out a staggered vacation plan so that the tourist trade will not be adversely affected by the massive departure of the populace, and the windows of closed restaurants display signs directing tourists to nearby restaurants that have remained open.

The Voices of Labor

Affluence, full employment, and diminished economic crises in the most developed European countries have changed the goals of labor unions and labor parties from revolutionary to reformist. Some unionists still pay lip service to Marxism, but unions and labor-oriented parties now concentrate their demands on higher wages, full employment, fringe benefits, and price stability. French and Italian unions have changed their goals as reform-oriented German and Scandinavian unions have succeeded in improving the position of the workers in their societies.

Swedish and German labor unions work closely with business leaders and government officials in negotiating working conditions, wages, and fringe benefits. Swedish unions, which represent 95 percent of the workers, have become a powerful interest group. German labor leaders sit on the boards of directors of the top German industrial enterprises. The Confederation of German Trade Unions (DGB), which speaks for about 38 percent of German workers, operates schools, banks, and insurance companies. The head of the DGB maintains, "You can't stop progress—our job is to see that workers get the benefit of it." Since the DGB is not affiliated with any political party, it is a strong, independent political force. German labor leaders stoutly defend their gradualism against more militant French and Italian unionists by pointing to the much larger number of workers organized in Germany, the much lower wages of workers in France and Italy, and the near absence of unemployment in Germany.

Swedish and German labor leaders believe profits must be high so that they can negotiate for higher wages. They also do not try to keep workers on the job in obsolete industries. Workers who become unemployed because their jobs are mechanized or because their industries are in a decline are immediately retrained at union expense. Militant unionists fear that close integration with big business and government means labor can offer no democratic counterweight to the ruling groups and will eventually be controlled and emasculated by the state.

Labor unions that cling to revolutionary goals have lost their effectiveness. In France, where unionism is divided among the Communist *Confédération Générale du Travail* (CGT), the Socialist CFDT, and a Moderate *Force Ouvrière*, only about 15 percent of the workers are organized. Moreover, the CGT continues to lose members while the more moderate *Force Ouvrière* has gained members. Despite considerable theoretical militancy, in practice French labor unions have been much less militant than their rhetoric would indicate. In fact, the CGT actually restrained workers during the 1968 national strikes. The average workdays lost annually for the ten-year period between 1977 and 1988 dropped below one hundred per year per thousand French workers. Only traditionally less strike-prone countries such as Austria, Switzerland, Holland, and West Germany had fewer days lost. Those countries with more than two hundred lost days have either been traditionally strike prone (Italy, Spain, Great Britain) or experienced unsettling economic growth or stagnation during this period (Ireland, Greece). In Italy, where unions are split among Communist, Socialist, and Christian federations, the number of days lost per thousand workers was about thirty times higher than in France in 1987, according to the International Labor Organization. Yet Italy has the lowest wages among the original six Common Market countries. In 1987, British unions, traditionally suspicious of management and unwilling to cooperate with industrialists or to amalgamate in a few strong unions, have become much less strike prone in the eighties. The 163 unions in the Trades Union Congress that frequently struck separately, often with little warning, sometimes minor issues, have become much less militant under the Thatcher government. Thatcher's breaking of the British miners' strike in the early eighties and the favorable response her actions received from the British public have seriously weakened the unions.

Although the more militant unions have lost support during the last decade, predictions that unionization will decline further as the various interests in society are fully integrated in the new Europe have not materialized. In fact, the influence of labor unions may grow as they become an integral part of the governmental price and wage mechanism, as in Germany and Sweden, and as workers defend their interests against proliferating organizations of teachers, renters, white-collar workers, students, and so on. In Sweden, not to be a member of an occupational organization is highly unusual. Organized labor may be hard put to justify its demands if it should be confronted by organized and lower paid clerks. The militancy of white-collar workers and professionals can be expected to increase if the high inflation rate—averaging more than 10 percent throughout much of Europe since 1974—is not reduced significantly. In most countries, even the organized laborers have not been keeping up with inflation since 1968.

Social Leveling

Much has been written on the blurring of class lines brought about by the improved standard of living of the working class and the growth of the service class. It is said that European society is undergoing an *embourgeoisement*—the word used for the drift of the working class into the middle class—and that classes as we know them now will cease to exist.

Service-class workers are salaried (a traditional status symbol) and usually have more education than blue-collar workers, but they often live in the same neighborhoods and acquire the same status symbols that have traditionally divided the middle and working classes.

Because of the continuing expansion of the service class and the declining proportion of manual laborers in the working populations, blue-collar workers and their offspring are moving into white-collar work. Approximately one-third of the offspring of industrial workers in Western Europe in the seventies rose into nonmanual categories, predominantly the service and professional classes. At the same time, a smaller but not

Table 9-10   Social Mobility of the Population 35–64 Years by Father's Socioeconomic Group (Percentages)

| | Father's Socioeconomic Group | | | | | | | | | | | |
| Own Socioeconomic Group | WORKERS | | | SALARIED EMPLOYEES | | | FARMERS | | | ENTREPRENEURS | | |
	De	Fi	Sw	De	Fi	Sw	De	Fi	Sw	De	Fi	Sw
Workers	38	41	35	19	20	15	32	26	29	24	24	21
Total salaried employees	23	18	34	50	53	58	18	16	27	37	31	29
Senior salaried employees	5	4	6	24	34	21	5	5	5	15	20	11
Farmers	2	5	1	1	2	1	18	23	14	1	3	2
Entrepreneurs	8	4	7	7	2	9	7	6	8	14	10	10
Other	29	32	22	24	23	17	26	29	23	24	36	19
Number	617	535	1269	238	195	446	469	718	636	233	140	402

Note: *De = Denmark, Fi = Finland, Sw = Sweden.*
Source: *Nordic Council/Nordic Statistical Secretariat, "Level of Living and Inequality in the Nordic Countries" (Stockholm, 1984), 197.*

insignificant group of white-collar workers moved down into working-class occupations. The results of surveys taken between 1976 and 1979 in Scandinavia (see Table 9-10) show that the children of manual laborers have the best chance in Sweden to move to a salaried white-collar position: 34 percent compared to Denmark's 23 percent and Finland's 18 percent. But it also indicates that it is difficult for the offspring of a manual laborer to move to a senior salaried position even in socially advanced countries such as Sweden (6 percent), Denmark (5 percent) and Finland (4 percent). Table 9-10 also shows that the children of salaried employees occupy a high percentage of the salaried and senior salaried positions. But the continued growth of the service class and the relative decline of manual laborers in the total work force will result in a rise in the number of workers who move into the service class.

New housing and intermarriage have also brought the service and working classes closer together. Living in the same areas and no longer divided by dress as they were in the nineteenth century, youth ignore social-class differences. Many new towns and suburbs are not socially segregated, as the major cities still tend to be. This is especially true in the more developed countries. In the new model-housing areas in Sweden, middle- and lower-class families are deliberately mixed by providing the poor with rent supports. The pervasiveness of modern advertising and cheaper mass-produced goods have also reduced the differences between working-class and middle-class homes and furnishings. And the behavioral pattern of manual workers in their new surroundings has changed as well. They

New housing projects with apartments affordable to the average citizen sprang up in Europe during the postwar economic resurgence. This building, located in a suburb of Paris, France, has 450 apartments and houses 1,500 tenants. In 1959, when it was built, it was the longest building in France. (Keystone Press Agency, Inc.)

tend to spend less time in pubs and more time at home watching television. The fact that working-class children in socially integrated neighborhoods attend the same schools as middle-class children has had a further leveling effect.

Despite this social leveling, class distinctions remain very much a part of European society, especially in Great Britain, France, and southern Europe. There has been little mingling of working class and middle class in the south. Even within social classes in Europe, divisions continue to exist. Divisions between skilled and unskilled laborers are often greater than those between the working and the middle class.

This is similar to the split found between the upper levels of the service class (administrators) and lower-level clerks. Most of the service-class workers consider themselves members of the middle class and pursue practices common to the middle class. In a recent French random survey,

51 percent of the respondents rated a lower paid clerical worker higher than a foundry worker. Based upon income, lower paid clerical workers do comprise a "white-collar proletariat," according to Rosemary Crompton and Gareth Jones, but their own perceptions of their status, their extended paid vacations, and the wide social net common to all developed European countries separate them from the misery associated with a true proletariat. Also, about half of the low paid women clerical workers are married and with their spouses' income enjoy a middle-class standard of living.

In 1969, Cambridge University sponsored a sociological study of seventy British working-class families. The report, titled *The Affluent Worker in the Class Structure*, revealed that "no more than one or two of the seventy couples in question here could be realistically represented as being even on the road to a middle-class pattern of social life." This study, drawn from a relatively affluent working-class area, concluded that the *embourgeoisement* thesis had limited validity in Great Britain in the sixties. The researchers found that only seven couples followed middle-class life-styles and had middle-class friends from other than family or work associations. The same author's study of British social mobility in the eighties contends that "the class position of individuals in the present-day population and their class origins remains essentially the same in its extent and pattern as that which existed in the inter-war period . . ." (Goldthorpe). So, although the relative size of the service class and laboring class has changed, the distance between them changed little.

Political Attitudes and Social Class

Although there have been some changes, the political attitudes of the working class and the service class continue to differ. The service class tends to support Moderate or Conservative parties, whereas the working class gives most of its vote to the political left. However, these voting patterns are beginning to change. Only in Italy does working-class support go overwhelmingly to left-wing parties. In Germany, half the working-class vote goes to the moderate Christian Democrats rather than to the Social Democrats. In the 1979 British parliamentary elections, 36 percent of labor voted for the Conservative party and another 14 percent for the Liberals. Even in France, support for the Communist party has declined among workers; the labor vote for the Communists dropped from 49 percent of the total labor vote in 1951 to 20 percent in the 1986 parliamentary elections. In those same elections, 34 percent of the workers voted for the moderate Socialists and 29 percent for the middle-of-the-road RPR-UDF coalition.

Of course, to some extent the shift in the labor vote can be attributed to changes in formerly conservative parties. In most European countries, the traditional laissez-faire parties have disappeared; in Sweden all parties accept the welfare state and Swedish socialism. Although the British Conservative party is now attempting to privatize many nationalized firms, it previously accepted the welfare state and the nationalization of much of British industry. Workers in an inflationary period may support a more conservative party because it promises to fight inflation while still supporting the welfare state.

Among the unskilled and semiskilled, working-class attitudes have changed very slowly. People at this level still believe that society is divided between those with and those without power, and that for the have-nots there is little chance of escape. In a 1976 poll of French workers, 44 percent of those questioned believed that class struggle was still a reality. Members of the working class still tend to think more collectively than members of the service class. The latter, thoroughly imbued with middle-class values, think in terms of individual rather than group achievement.

Compared to manual laborers, white-collar workers are much less satisfied with their occupations and put considerably more money into education so as to prepare their children for jobs that "lead somewhere." These service-class attitudes have now been adopted by many skilled and semiskilled workers in Western Europe, who hope to see their children rise into lower-middle-class or professional positions. These members of the working class now tend to think in terms of personal betterment rather than improvement of one's class.

Labor Dissatisfactions

That the worker is not at peace with society has been amply demonstrated by challenges to authority in factories even in the advanced societies of northern Europe. In Holland, workers drew a chalk line around a corner of their factory and forbade entry to anyone would could not give a satisfactory explanation of his or her mission. Swiss and Swedish workers are demanding—and getting—joint participation with management in the determination of work schedules, duties, and salaries.

Paradoxically, the Swedes, among the highest paid workers in Europe, have one of the highest industrial absentee and turnover rates in Europe. An enterprise with plants in Sweden and Germany reported a 1969 labor turnover of about 14 percent for the Swedish plant as against 4.8 percent for the German plant. The Volvo automobile factory in Torslanda reported a 1969 turnover rate of about 40 percent in its plant, compared to 16 percent for Daimler-Benz in Germany. Absenteeism and turnover are lower in German factories primarily because the affluent society developed later in Germany. In Sweden, labor absenteeism seems to be an outgrowth of the contrast between the high standard of living and assembly-line work in the factories, very liberal sick leaves, and high income taxes that led workers to reduce their income by staying home.

A French sociologist explains, "The threshold of tolerance is dropping" and "What was accepted years earlier, like physical discomfort on the job, has now become unbearable because workers have seen for too long the way others in society are living."

In an attempt to come to grips with the so-called new worker, the Organization for Economic Cooperation and Development (OECD), to which all developed Western countries belong, has conducted seminars for personnel directors and management officials to devise solutions for what has been described as worker alienation. In most northern European countries, management began to make workers a more integral part of the factory in the seventies by giving them a say in management decisions and by eliminating the routine in their work. At the Volvo plants, workers now change their places of work six times a day in order to relieve the boredom of the production line. At the Lunby truck factory, workers decide at the beginning of the week how the work is to be apportioned, when duties are to change, and when rest periods are to be taken. They have also done away with the traditional assembly line by assigning to groups of workers the responsibility for assembling sections of automobiles within their practically autonomous work area. Since these changes were instituted, worker absenteeism and turnover have declined markedly while production has improved.

The transformation in French workers' attitudes is perhaps most indicative of the changes in European labor attitudes since a large gap separated labor and management well into the sixties. The French student and worker riots in 1968 revealed the large gap that still separated labor and management and labor and government. French workers, primarily the young, joined the student rioters to protest low wages, poor working conditions, authoritarian factory managers, and a spiraling inflation that ate into their wages.

The protest began with a strike at the Renault plant at Boulogne-Billancourt, where one-third of the workers were migrant laborers. As a consequence of the disturbances, the minimum hourly wage was raised from 2.22 francs to 4.64 francs in 1973, more workers were paid by the month rather than by the hour (a prestige factor), and automatic pay increases were promised whenever prices rose. These automatic pay increases were ended only in the 1980s under the Mitterrand government. In effect, the unskilled workers were given what the skilled laborers were already receiving. But an even more important result of the 1968 events has been a lessening of management's autocratic attitudes toward labor. While French management has stopped short at comanagement, it has now instituted flexible work hours, group work, and a reduction in boring mass-production assembly-line work.

In Sum . . .

It is difficult to generalize about the thesis of a new European society throughout Western Europe because of the wide variety of conditions and attitudes. However, one can draw certain conclusions. In Scandinavia, West Germany, the Benelux countries, and France a new society has emerged. The standard of living bears little resemblance to the prewar period. Most workers are no longer underpaid, overworked, and without voice in the determination of their working conditions or wages.

A Swedish worker's income is now comparable to that of a laborer in the United States. Perhaps more important, workers in Sweden, West Germany, and France have more autonomy and a greater share in management decisions than workers in the United States; and workers' representatives already sit on all companies' boards in Sweden. One observer's assertion that Sweden is becoming a trade-union state may be an exaggeration, but there is no denying that labor and capital now deal with one another as near equals. Trade-union officials in Sweden are quick to point out that they do indeed have more power than industrialists when deciding wages, but industrialists are dominant in all other matters pertaining to business.

The concept of a new Europe is less applicable to a number of smaller developing states. Certainly, a much larger section of the population is now upwardly mobile and is sharing in the new-found affluence. Yet with 20 to 25 percent of their populations living near the poverty level, it calls to mind images of the old Europe.

There is considerably less mixing of social classes in these countries than in Scandinavia or the United States. Nevertheless, remarkable progress has been made since the war. The majority of their populations now have vastly improved housing, more consumer goods and the money to buy them, more free time and income enough to enjoy *le weekend*, and annual vacations that amount to a month in most countries.

Southern Italy, Greece, Ireland, and Portugal have lagged far behind the rest of Western Europe. With a large segment of the population still at the poverty level, despite the emigration of thousands of workers, talk of an *embourgeoisement* of society has little justification. In Greece, Ireland, and Portugal, income and working conditions compare with those of northern Europe before World War II. It will be some time before these areas achieve the social transformation characteristic of northern Europe.

FURTHER READING

Recent studies of European society include Stanley Hoffman and George Ross, *The Mitterrand Experiment: Continuity and Change in France* (1987); John H. Goldthorpe, *Social Mobility and Class Structure in Modern Britain*, 2nd ed. (1987); Arthur Marwick, *Class: Image and Reality* (1980); and the works cited in chapter 10.

Two important surveys that contain extensive information on European society in the sixties are Stanley Rothman, *European Society and Politics* (1970), and Stephen Graubard, ed., *The New Europe?* (1963). Peter Flora and Arnold J. Heidenheimer, eds., *Development of Welfare States in Europe and America* (1981), provide a comparative look at different welfare states. Two studies of French social stratification are G. Dupeux, *French Society, 1789–1970* (1976), and Jane Marceau, *Class and Status in France* (1977). Dupeux provides a good historical introduction and Marceau's is a critical account from a leftist perspective. Good coverage of various aspects of the Mitterrand years can be found in Patrick McCarthy, *The French Socialists in Power, 1981–1986* (1987). William James Adams provides a thorough coverage of recent economic developments in his *Restructuring the French Economy* (1989). John Ardagh's *France Today* (1987) and *Germany and the Germans* (1988) provide suggestive theories about both societies. For information on British society, see Judith Ryder and Harold Silver, *Modern English Society: History and Structure, 1850–1970* (1977); Colin Bell, *Middle Class Families* (1969); George Bain, David Coates, and Valerie Ellis, *Social Stratification and Trade Unionism* (1973); and Philip Stanworth and Anthony Giddens, eds., *Elites and Power in British Society* (1974). Arthur Marwick's *British Society since 1945* (1982) provides a critical look at recent British society.

M. M. Postan, in *An Economic History of Western Europe, 1945–1964* (1967), believes the working class is gradually becoming middle class in the advanced Western European states and says the division between manual and nonmanual workers is decreasing as modern technology transforms skilled workers into technicians. Ralf Dahrendorf, in *Class and Class Conflict in Industrial Society* (1959), contends that industrial society has not evolved the way Marx believed it would. The development of an intermediate white-collar stratum has prevented the polarization of society between proletariat and bourgeoisie that Marx predicted. Moreover, Marx did not foresee the massive role of the state in modern capitalist society.

A number of works disagree with the *embourgeoisement* theory. André Gorz, in *Strategy for Labor* (1964), argues that capitalism alienates labor and molds workers into mass-production robots whose minds are diverted from the reality of their condition by mass consumerism. The theme of alienation is common to left criticism of modern industrialism. Herbert Marcuse, in *One-Dimensional Man* (1964), presents one of the clearest explanations of the alienation theme. Marcuse believes that the mass consumerism promoted by affluent societies satisfies only a few material needs while it destroys what should be humanity's ultimate objectives: the humanization of social, productive, and work relationships. Rosemary Crompton and Gareth Jones argue, in *White-Collar Proletariat: Deskilling and Gender in Clerical Work* (1984), that the degrading of much white-collar work, combined with low pay, has turned much of the work force into a new proletariat.

The disagreement concerning the impact of the modern industrial state is continued in some dated but classic studies. F. Zweig's *The Worker in an Affluent Society* (1961) and R. Miller's *The New Classes* (1966) agreed that the working class was moving toward middle-class values and existence in the sixties. Zweig argued that as the distinctive economic characteristics of the working class changed under neocapitalism, so did its cultural distinctiveness. Miller maintained that, in performing technically complicated tasks in modern industry, the skilled worker functioned as a technician rather than as the traditional industrial worker. Three studies edited by John Goldthorpe et al.—*The Affluent Worker: Industrial Attitudes and Behavior* (1968), *The Affluent Worker: Political Attitudes and Behavior* (1968), and *The Affluent Worker in the Class Structure* (1971)—reject the *embourgeoisement* thesis. These studies contend that the worker has generally not accepted middle-class cultural values and has not been accepted socially by white-collar employees. A classic study of the attitudes of the British white-collar worker was provided in David Lockwood's *The Blackcoated Worker* (1958).

Valuable studies of French labor are Val Lorwin's *The French Labor Movement* (1954) and Richard F. Hamilton's *Affluence and the French Worker in the Fourth Republic* (1967). Serge Mallet, in *La Nouvelle Classe Ouvrière* (1963), sees advanced technology leading to cooperation among workers, technicians, and managers against plant directors and executives that will, in turn, lead to worker control of factories, democratization of industry, and the decline of worker alienation. Alain Touraine, in "La Vie Ouvrière" in Alain Touraine, ed., *Histoire Général du Travail* (1961), criticized the *embourgeoisement* thesis. While he agreed that a certain segment of the working class was living a middle-class existence in an economic sense, he did not believe that the working class had adopted middle-class life-styles and attitudes. Guy Groux and Mark Kesselman's *The French Working Class: Economic Crisis and Political Change* (1984) provides a recent analysis of French labor. Michael Crozier, in *The Bureaucratic Phenomenon* (1964) and *The World of the Office Worker* (1971), provides excellent insights into the world of the white-collar worker and French society in the sixties. He argues that French society resists change until the last possible moment, when only a violent change will relieve the situation.

Another important study of European labor is Daniel Horowitz, *The Italian Labor Movement* (1963). Two important comparative studies are Richard Scane, *Social Democracy in Capitalist Society: Working-Class Politics in Britain and Sweden* (1977), and H. Hecho, *Modern Social Politics in Britain and Sweden* (1974).

Recent statistics and studies can be found in the OECD *Observer*, the OECD *Economic Surveys*, *International Labor Review*, the International Labor Office *Bulletin of Labor Statistics*, World Bank publications, and the many publications of the United Nations.

10 Postwar European Society: The Managers

> If property was the criterion of membership in the former dominant classes, the new dominant class is defined by knowledge and a certain level of education.
>
> Alain Touraine
> *The Post-Industrial Society*

Despite the spread of economic rewards and educational benefits in the postwar period, some people are, in George Orwell's words, more equal than others. Although government and administrative positions have increased, only in a few countries do those who occupy positions of power and influence in contemporary European society come from the lower-middle or working strata. Even among Socialist party leaders, the number coming from manual worker's homes has in fact decreased since the late 1940s. Government and industry were once viewed as providing a way for the lower classes to move up into positions of wealth and power. But top positions are now reserved, with some exceptions, for those whose power and authority are based on skill—called a *meritocracy*. And there is not an increased role for the lower classes primarily because the middle class has dominated the educational institutions where the people with the skill, called *technocrats*, are trained.

On the other hand, the emergence of the meritocracy has brought important social and political changes at the top. The increasing need for the highly skilled in government and politics has reduced even further the role of former elites. Parties with a traditionally conservative political program have ceased to exist in northern Europe; all political parties now reject a hierarchically organized society and are increasingly controlled by those with training in one of the professions.

The New Ruling Elite

The life-styles of this new privileged managerial stratum remain distinct from those of the lower strata. Although it is now difficult to distinguish social strata by traditional measures such as dress and ownership of con-

190

sumer goods, sizable differences remain in occupations, educational attainment, wealth, and housing, as well as in life-styles.

No single term can fully describe the ruling elites in Europe and the United States. Some observers still subscribe to the idea of a ruling class. Others have adopted one or another of the more sophisticated concepts: an establishment, a military-industrial complex, or a power elite. No matter which concept is used, most believe that European societies are ruled by a relatively small elite that preserves its position through various combinations of wealth, family eminence, and educational advantages.

However, the European countries are sufficiently different from the United States and from one another to warrant the use of several descriptions of their societies. For instance, one can speak of an establishment in Great Britain and France because of the continued influence of former elites and the similar training of government leaders. The leaders of British government and society have been trained primarily in the same schools—private secondary schools (referred to in Britain as "public" schools) such as Eton, then Oxford or Cambridge Universities—and retain their social ties (the old-boy network) long after their formal schooling ends.

In France, the ruling circles are trained in bourgeois-dominated secondary schools (*lycées*) and exclusive professional schools (*grandes écoles*). In both countries, individuals who follow the prescribed path to power may fill a diversity of government and economic positions merely because they have been initiated and accepted into the ruling circles.

None of the other developed nations in Europe has old-boy ties that bind the ruling circles together. For the remaining developed European countries, it seems best to adopt the theory of a more accessible but still rather exclusive ruling stratum. The more open German ruling elite is, according to Lewis J. Edinger, composed of "a few thousand elected and appointed, coopted and anointed leaders." But all ruling strata consist primarily of middle-aged, well-educated males from the highest social stratum as Table 10-1 shows is true in Germany.

Composition of the Elite

Although the composition of the ruling stratum has changed since 1945, power is still exercised by a small, privileged, slow-changing elite in most European societies. A French technocratic elite has maintained its monopoly of power in France since de Gaulle. This technocracy maintains its exclusivity through its monopoly of French technical education in the *grandes écoles* (see below) and the old-boy network. A 1961 study of 2,000 eminent people in France showed that 68 percent were recruited from the top 5 percent of the population and 81 percent from the top 15 percent of the population. This technocracy draws mainly from the upper bourgeoisie and seldom gets recruits from the lower middle class or the

Table 10-1 Profile of West Germans in Leading Positions of Public Life, 1981 (percent)

Organizational Sector of Leadership Position

	POLITICAL PARTIES			PUBLIC ADMINISTRATION	MILITARY	BUSINESS	TRADE UNIONS	MASS MEDIA	ALL
	SPD	CDU	FDP						
Age: Mean Age	49	50	51	53	55	54	54	52	53
% under 45	31	23	32	9	0	9	9	18	15
% 45–60	63	71	44	72	86	71	75	65	67
% over 60	6	6	24	19	14	21	16	17	18
University degree	55	74	68	94	33	75	8	47	69
Father with university degree	16	18	36	32	23	23	8	26	27
Father manual worker	36	14	4	7	0	8	51	6	11

SOURCE: *Lewis J. Edinger, West German Politics (1986), 128. Information taken from Rudolf Wildenmann, Max Kaase, Ursula Hoffman-Lange et al., "Deutsche Elite Studie, 1981," an unpublished survey of 1,744 persons in leadership positions.*

lower class. About two decades after the 1961 study, a survey of the 2,500 most famous or powerful French people showed that only 3 percent came from manual laborers' homes. Studies of German ruling circles have produced similar findings. Nearly one-third of all German higher civil servants are the children of higher civil servants. As Table 10-1 indicates, the leading positions in public life had little worker representation in 1981. As in France, the German elite is composed of technocrats recruited from a rather exclusive upper middle class. The German federal legislature elected in 1980 contained only 2.3 percent workers, down from 3 percent in 1966.

W. L. Guttsman's 1963 study, *The British Political Elite*, showed that about "two-thirds of the members of the highest occupational groups, comprising less than three percent of the population, are the sons of men who belonged to the same group." Arthur Marwick recently estimated that a British upper class comprising "two percent or so" of the population still dominates leadership positions in the mideighties. Moreover, in most European countries there has been a reversal of an immediate postwar trend to choose parliamentary members from the working class. Now more and more British Labour party leaders are chosen from the professions. In Germany, as Table 10-1 shows, only the German Social Democratic party and the labor unions have a large number of representatives from manual laborers' homes.

Only in Scandinavia, where the Social Democrats have long been in power and there are fewer educational and class obstacles to advancement, has there been a noticeable democratization of the elite. More than half the ministers serving in the Swedish Social Democratic cabinet from 1956 to 1968 had lower-class social origins.

Anthony Sampson's sixties' observation that "the chances of the son of a working man reaching a position of power are almost—but not quite—as remote as they were in 1789" seems to still be true for Europe in the eighties, with the exception of the Scandinavian states.

Women and Power

Women have also found it difficult to obtain positions of power and importance except in Scandinavia. In France, female deputies in the National Assembly dropped from a 1945 high of thirty to ten in 1977. Only the election victory of the feminist-oriented Socialist party in 1981 brought the number of women deputies back near the immediate postwar level of twenty-six, or 5.3 percent of all French deputies. Women have been more successful in obtaining cabinet posts in the last two presidencies: Giscard appointed five and Mitterrand six of forty-four. In Germany, women had only about half as many managerial positions as men but four times as many lower-level white-collar jobs in the mideighties. They also comprised only about 10 percent of the legislature (*Bundestag*) after the 1983 elections. Only in 1977 did German women gain the legal right to take a job without their husband's permission. Since 1945, only 2.7 percent of the British House of Commons has been female. Between 1964 and 1979, only four women, including Prime Minister Thatcher, have served in British cabinets. Women's minor elite representation is primarily due to their homemaking and child-rearing roles and the male perceptions that derive from them. While men are building their careers in their early years, women are starting a family. Even after they become available for political duties, parties are reluctant to nominate women for office since they fear they will not be elected. Also, once married the most highly educated women tend to give up their jobs more than others since their income is less needed in the family than that of lesser educated women.

But a hopeful sign has been the increasing political representation of women in northern European governments and legislatures. The Norwegian government of Mrs. Gro Harlem Brundtland contains seven other women cabinet members and women comprise 34 percent of the Norwegian legislature. Compared to the mere 5 percent of women in the United States Congress, northern Europe appears quite progressive. In 1988, women comprised 38, 30, and 29 percent of the legislators in Sweden, the Netherlands, and Denmark, respectively. Only Greece with 4.3 percent, France and Spain with 6.4 percent, the United Kingdom with 6.3 percent, and Portugal with 7.6 percent are near the low American portion of women legislators. The recent decisions among Socialist parties in Scandinavia and Germany to require that 40 percent of their legislative representives be women will soon bring even greater political equality in these areas.

Another important reason for women's limited role among the elite has been their underrepresentation in graduate and professional schools. While the proportion of women attending universities rose by the mid-eighties (to about half of the total students in Denmark and France and between 40 and 50 percent elsewhere), their underrepresentation in professional schools, and in mathematics and the physical sciences throughout their schooling, leaves them at a disadvantage. A recent OECD report shows that four successful candidates out of every five for the French humanities' baccalaureat in 1983 were women, compared to only one of three for the mathematics' and natural sciences' baccalaureats. These patterns then naturally continue into higher education. While a university degree alone would have provided a graduate with an excellent opportunity for a good position previously, the type of degree and school that issued it now conditions one's job possibilities. For example, the proportion of women studying at the French advanced professional schools has increased but still comprises only 15 percent of the students at the School of Administration (ENA) and 10 percent at the *École Polytechnique*. These percentages would, however, be large in comparison to women's participation in advanced professional education in southern Europe.

The New Managers

Liberal hopes that the new managers—also known as the meritocracy or technocracy—might form a separate elite distinct from the upper and middle bourgeoisie were soon disappointed. In France the new managers have not only merged with the *haute bourgeoisie* (upper middle class) but have also been drawn primarily from this class. A sixties' study of British top management personnel revealed that 43 percent came from the two highest occupational groups in the registrar-general's classification of society—groups that formed only 15 percent of the population. Marwick concludes that "in 1980 there still was a consolidated, coherent upper class, enjoying quite disproportionate wealth, power and life chances in Britain."

Such social exclusiveness has not been restricted to France and Great Britain. As Table 9-11 shows, the vast majority of Swedish senior white-collar employees came from the families of other senior white-collar employees in the late seventies; only 6 percent of the senior salaried employees came from manual laborers' homes.

Another factor that has prevented the establishment of a separate technocratic elite has been an extensive horizontal mobility between government and industrial managers. Many Frenchmen who have been trained for government service in the *grandes écoles* have received top industrial posts because of their old-boy connections with economic leaders.

Even within the ranks of the new managers the layers of authority and wealth are clear to see. Only the top managers wield significant economic and political power. As in the United States, the differences are reflected in the private possessions of the various strata. Middle-management officials buy less expensive automobiles—BMWs instead of Mercedes or Renaults instead of Citröens—and do not live in the same areas as their superiors. As Alain Touraine observed in *The Post-Industrial Society*: "A hierarchical continuity among bureaucrats and technocrats may appear to exist but it is a rare case when the members of a great organization cannot recognize the line that separates them." In Germany, the top government and management officials—ambassadors, generals, big business leaders—come predominantly from the upper middle class, whereas middle-management officials come primarily from the middle class.

Education of the Ruling Elite

Immediately after the war, a thorough democratization of Europe's ruling circles seemed imminent as more elite positions—especially those requiring advanced training—were filled by students from presumably more

Table 10-2 Access to Higher Education (percentage of relevant age group)

	1970	1985–1986		1970	1985–1986
Austria	15.6 (1972)	21.7	Norway	27.5	15.4
Belgium	28.5	39.3	Portugal	6.6	15.6
Denmark	34.3 (1973)	36	Spain	27.1 (1972)	30.5
France	30.0 (1971)	33	Sweden	31.1 (1972)	34 (84)
Germany	15.8	26.2	United Kingdom	21.3 (1971)	30.9
Italy	28.2	26.4	United States	43.8 (1972)	63.6
Netherlands	20.5 (1971)	38.3			

SOURCE: *OECD* Observer *74 (March–April 1975); OECD* Observer *158, supplement (June–July 1989); Swedish figures for 1984 taken from OECD* Observer *149 (December 1987–January 1988). These figures exclude the advanced professional schools.*

democratic educational systems. Confirming that the route to the top was indeed through higher education, a 1961 study showed that nearly 85 percent of a large sample of the French ruling stratum had received a university education (including *grandes écoles*) and that 63 percent of a smaller group from German ruling circles had had at least some university training. Still, postwar Europe lagged far behind the United States in access to higher education, and the number of lower-class children in the upper levels of European education increased only slightly by the early seventies. As Tables 10-2 and 10-3 show, some European countries permitted few to go on to higher education; and, with the exception of Great Britain, the increase in the number of manual workers' children attending the universities was minimal.

Advanced schooling continues to be the preserve of children of the

Table 10-3 Percentage of Manual Workers' Sons in University Student Bodies

	1960	1964	1980
Great Britain	25.0 (1961)		30
Sweden	14.0		2 (1979)
Italy	13.2	15.3	
Denmark	9.0 (1959)	10.0	5 (1976)
Holland	8.0 (1958)	6.0 (1961)	
Austria	6.0	5.0	
France	5.3	8.3	13
West Germany	5.2	5.3	18

SOURCE: *UNESCO,* Access to Higher Education *(Bucharest, 1968), 49. Nordic Statistical Secretariat, "Level of Living and Inequality in the Nordic countries," (1984).*

Uniformed and hatted students at Harrow, one of England's elite secondary schools, leaving chapel. (Keystone Press Agency, Inc.)

upper middle and middle classes. However, even in the most class-based educational system, the wall of social privilege started to break down in the late 1960s and early 1970s. Nevertheless, the various European countries differ sufficiently to necessitate the separate study of the major educational systems.

British Ruling-class Education   Success in British government has normally led through the exclusive private schools—Eton, Winchester, and so on—then Oxford or Cambridge universities. In 1964, slightly over one-third of the House of Commons members had attended Oxford or Cambridge—or Oxbridge, as they are referred to collectively. These schools are even more closely connected to the Conservative party. Four-fifths of the university-educated Conservative candidates for Parliament between 1950 and 1966 were Oxbridge graduates. A 1973 study by the National Foundation for Educational Research showed graduates of the twenty-six leading private secondary schools had as large a share of the elite positions in Britain as they had had in 1939. Edward Heath's 1971 cabinet of seventeen, for example, included fourteen members who had attended Oxbridge. Marwick argues that this private-school monopoly of leadership positions continued into the eighties.

Some Labour party leaders have concluded from such evidence that the only way to break the hold of the private schools is to abolish them. This view has, of course, raised howls of indignation from most Conservative party members and from the London *Times*.

Although Oxbridge graduates retain an inordinate share of the important positions of power in Britain, changes in education, even at Oxbridge, indicate that such a monopoly does not have the same social significance as it once did. For one thing, 30 percent of the university student body now come from working-class homes. For another thing, university education is becoming a decisive factor in the competition for positions of power and influence, except in France where the *grandes écoles* serve this purpose. So graduates who have working-class backgrounds will undoubtedly fill a greater share of the important positions in society.

Most working-class students attend the less prestigious universities, some of them not established until after the war, but Oxford and Cambridge have enrolled a larger number of students from working-class homes. Yet those colleges within Oxford University that have a large working-class enrollment, such as Wolfson College, lack the prestige of the older colleges, nor do the Wolfson graduates have the same occupational opportunities.

At the secondary level, comprehensive, or common secondary, schools are gradually increasing their share of students from that age group in Scandinavia and the Benelux countries. But the comprehensive schools have not achieved the academic excellence of the selective grammar schools. Labour's attempts to put all secondary students in comprehensive schools have encountered stiff opposition from the middle-class-dominated grammar and public schools. The opponents maintain that placing all students in comprehensive schools of the American type will mean the end of excellence in British education. The comprehensives have themselves promoted some of this opposition because of their diverse organization and often suspect pedagogy.

French Ruling-class Education   As in Great Britain, both France's top industrial positions and its government service have been dominated by the upper middle and middle classes. The *haute bourgeoisie* now dominates government service not merely because of social position but also because of their children's better education, which their wealth and social position make possible.

The persistence of social divisions in France has resulted from the ruling stratum's monopoly of an elite educational system. The domination begins in the state secondary schools, the *lycées*. In 1968, John Ardagh wrote, in *The New French Revolution*, "State *lycées*, though in theory free and open to all, are in practice still largely a preserve of the middle class, and they alone provide a passport to higher education and the best jobs." In his 1987 revised edition, *France Today*, Ardagh wrote that "social barriers and prejudices are such that the more prestigious of them [*lycées*]—such as Louis-Le-Grand in Paris—have in practice been almost as much the preserves of a certain class as the English £4,000-a-year public [private] schools; and even in the average *lycée* the children of workers were always much underrepresented." Bourgeois society itself has been divided between those who have obtained a *lycée* diploma (*le baccalauréat*) and those who have failed. With *le bac*, the student was prepared to attend the university or—for the fortunate few who proceed beyond *le bac*— one of the *grandes écoles*, where the future leaders of the nation are trained. Normally, two to three years of study beyond the *lycée* is needed in order to pass the rigorous entrance examination for the *grandes écoles*. Only about one of twenty students in higher education attends a *grande école*.

Leaders of business and government have long been recruited from these bastions of privilege, especially the *École Polytechnique*, the *École Normale Supérieure*, the school of civil engineering, and the newer national school of administration (ENA). Graduates of the *École Polytechnique*, affectionately called "X" because of its emblem of two crossed cannon, go on to more specialized postgraduate *grandes écoles* and from there to government posts. While the *grandes écoles* were first set up to provide government servants, many graduates are now buying themselves out of government service in order to take lucrative jobs in business.

Both the students' brilliance—the selection process is one of the most rigorous in the world—and their connections make such a choice possible for them. In fact, an old-boy network similar to the British one has existed for *grande école* graduates. In 1967, seven of the eleven top positions in the Ministry of Finance and sixteen of the twenty-nine cabinet minister positions were held by ENA graduates. In Mitterrand's first cabinet, eight of forty-four members were ENA graduates. Set up in the postwar period, ENA was intended to democratize recruitment to the higher administration. However, the competition for entry has restricted access to the elite. Only about one in ten graduates of the *lycée* make it into the prestigious *grandes écoles*. In the case of ENA, most recruits come from a few Parisian *lycées* that specialize in preparing persons for the entrance examinations. One must agree with Anthony Sampson that ENA has provided "an old-boy net or a 'Mafia' which makes others—the Harvard Business School, Balliol, or even the *Polytechnique*—seem amateurish." But ENA and other *grandes écoles* graduates are now receiving competition from French graduates of foreign business schools and administrators moving up through industry and business.

The majority of top business executives have continued to come from the *grandes écoles* as well. Table 10-4, based on a representative sample of 2,500 chairmen and chief executives of large companies who received university degrees, indicates how the *grandes écoles* dominated the business community in the sixties. More than 50 percent of the sample of university-educated businessmen came from the *grandes écoles*. Jane

Table 10-4 Educational Background of French Businessmen

Type of institution attending	Percentage of sample
École Polytechnique	21.4
Other engineering schools	34.5
Science faculties	3.8
Arts faculties	3.8
Law faculties	8.8
Political science faculties	9.6
Commercial schools	1.7
Military schools	2.6
Other schools	10.1
No answer	3.7

Source: *F. F. Ridley, "French Technocracy and Comparative Government," Political Studies (February 14, 1966), 499. © 1966 Oxford University Press, reprinted by permission of Oxford University Press.*

Marceau's recent study of the French business elite determined that "the top managers of major French companies are likely in the year 2000 and beyond to be chosen from milieux very similar to those of business's present leaders."

Of those entering the *grandes écoles* in 1967, only 2 percent came from the working class and 4 percent from the peasantry. In the same year, 57 percent of the students in higher education had professional parents while 17 percent came from the industrial and commercial bourgeoisie. In the mideighties, no *grande école* had more than 10 percent workers and peasants in the student body.

Beginning in the late fifties, reforms have reduced but not ended the middle-class domination of higher education. Examinations at the end of elementary school were abolished in 1957 as the sole criteria for entrance into the *lycée* and were replaced by school records and teacher evaluations. In 1963, an intermediate school—colleges for students aged 11–14 between the elementary school and the *lycée*—was begun in order to give children of working-class parents more time to catch up with their middle-class counterparts. Further reforms were added by Education minister René Haby after 1977. His reforms reduced tracking by intelligence, but did not totally abolish it as he desired. Many schools' reluctance to implement his reforms fully were supported by parents and teachers, who argued that they would destroy educational standards. Haby's master plan to reduce tracking in the *lycée* (ages 16–19) by making the first two years more general and the last year highly specialized also encountered stout resistance and was not implemented. Another plan to increase technical and practical education through *lycées techniques*, or technical schools, has gained only limited acceptance by the middle class. While these reforms resulted in increasing the percentage of working-class students from 3.8 to 9 percent of the total in higher education between 1959 and the early 1980s, they still leave France far behind its Scandinavian and British neighbors. Of course, many French prefer this more elitist system and will continue to place obstacles in the way of any more equalitarian reforms that the Socialist government has in mind. But the trend has been in the direction of greater equalization of opportunity.

German Ruling-class Education   In Germany no schools or families unite the ruling circles. Entry into the ruling stratum has come primarily through study at a university and, more specifically, through the study of law; Ralf Dahrendorf, in *Society and Democracy in Germany*, has calculated that in 1962, 85 percent of the civil servants in all government ministries had law degrees. Since university study has been restricted to the upper and middle classes in Germany even more than in France, a narrow social basis of the ruling stratum was assured.

Higher education was long considered appropriate for only the talented few; four-fifths of the students still left school at age fourteen in the early sixties. As in France, few children from working-class homes passed from the primary school (*grundschule*) into the select secondary school (*gymnasium*). But entry into German universities, and therefore German elite positions, has been opened up since the war. Nearly one-third of German youth now begin studies at the universities, compared to about 6 percent in the early fifties. Whereas only 4 percent of the university students came from wage-earner families in 1952–1953, 18 percent of those in 1977–1978 came from such families. This change has been brought about through government grants to students, the building of twenty additional universities since 1965, and increasing the number of *gymnasium* students. The number of *gymnasium* graduates increased from 48,000 in 1965 to 204,000 in 1978.

Scandinavian Ruling-class Education   The Scandinavian countries have the most socially progressive educational system in Western Europe. Modeled on that of the United States, Swedish education is free and open to all up to the university level. All students receive their primary and secondary education in the same common comprehensive schools, but here the similarity with the United States ends.

Despite thirty years of Social Democratic party equalization measures, the percentage of working-class children obtaining a university education has risen very little. The cultural deprivation of lower-class children has prevented them from performing as well as middle-class children in the common secondary schools. Children of a senior white-collar employee are still more than three times as likely to continue academic studies beyond age sixteen as the children of unskilled workers.

The Aristocracy

The *aristocracy*, defined here primarily as titled nobility, has received little attention thus far in this study, not because it has disappeared, but because it has become less important in the power structure of most European countries. It no longer rules as it did in most of Europe in the nineteenth century but has become a part, usually a minor one, of a new enlarged ruling stratum. With the exception of the southern European countries, nobles do not dominate the top military and diplomatic posts as they did before World War II. In most of the developed states the aristocracy no longer sets social standards for the bourgeoisie to emulate; instead, it has adopted a life-style much like that of the middle class. Many nobles can no longer live on the income from their estates and must take salaried positions in the senior civil service, in banks, sometimes even in industry.

In 1966, Britain's top hundred enterprises had ninety-one peers (members of the nobility) on their boards of directors, thirteen of them in the post of chairman. But because of their sizable landholdings and traditional flexibility, these aristocrats have preserved their social and political preeminence better in Britain than in any of the other highly industrialized countries. The peers and old established gentry remain among the largest landholders in Britain. Although some estates have been sold or diminished, increased land values—fourfold in the last twenty years—have raised the value of the remaining aristocratic holdings. Many of the wealthiest aristocrats own residential property. The Duke of Westminster owns most of Belgravia, in the middle of London, as well as estates in Canada, Australia, and South Africa. Included in the Duke of Hamilton's estates are the industrial towns of Motherwell and Cambusland, where development land was worth £3,000 an acre in the early sixties. In terms of political influence, the British nobility approaches the authority exercised by the aristocrats in southern Europe.

The aristocracy retains an elite forum in the House of Lords, which stands as convincing evidence that Britain still has a social and political hierarchy. Although the House of Lords has lost almost all its direct political power, it has retained indirect political influence and social preeminence. According to one peer, Lord Balniel, "Although the class has long ago shed the mantle of a ruling class, it has inherited a tradition of public service which gives it influence in the higher reaches of political and executive government." In the House of Lords, in exclusive social clubs, and to some degree in the Conservative party, the aristocracy exercises a degree of influence that it has lost in most of northern Europe.

French aristocrats, never as receptive to change as the English, have much less influence in society and politics than their English counterparts. They were never willing to engage in mundane occupations before World War II. As their financial position worsened after the war, they could no longer disdain to take positions in industry, banks, and the civil service. They have now merged with the *haute* (upper-middle) and *bonne* (middle-middle-class) bourgeoisie to form a new privileged elite, but socially they remain rather exclusive. The typical aristocratic child will live in exclusive neighborhoods, attend exclusive schools, be surrounded by servants, hobnob with the international aristocracy while growing up, and have a coming-out party at age nineteen. As an adult, a male aristocrat will serve in the diplomatic corps, in upper-level bureaucratic posts, and in municipal offices, especially as mayors; he will join exclusive social clubs such as the Jockey Club; and he will belong to philanthropic organizations.

The Plutocrats

In the prewar period, the upper middle class—numbering 2 to 3 percent of the population—was distinguished primarily by its dominance of political power, its wealth, and its life-style. Now it has to share power with a much broader segment of the middle class. This new ruling stratum, comprising at most 10 percent of the population of any Western European country, has at its disposal a major share of the wealth. Table 10-5 indicates that its share of total income declined between 1954 and 1981. In 1978, the upper 10 percent of French families received 26.4 percent of all take-home income, compared to only 5.5 percent for the lowest 20 percent. The Mitterrand government initially struck hard at this plutocracy with new income and luxury taxes. But there was much successful evasion of those taxes, as is typical in France, and the Conservative premier, Jacques Chirac, reversed many of these taxes during his premiership between 1986 and 1988. The Socialists' turn to modernization rather than equalization after 1983 has made them less interested in increasing taxes.

Other indicators of wealth, such as taxable income and possession of

Table 10-5 Portion of Total Income Received by the Top 10 Percent of Families before Taxes

	1938	1954	1964	1981
United Kingdom	38	30.4	29.3	23.4 (1979)
France	–	34.1	36.8[c]	26.4 (1975)
West Germany	39[a]	44.0[b]	41.4	24 (1978)
United States	36	30	28	23.3 (1980)
Sweden	–	–	–	28.1

[a] *Data for all Germany in 1936.*
[b] *French data for 1956, German for 1955.*
[c] *Data for 1962.*
SOURCE: *Stanley Rothman,* European Society and Politics *(New York: Bobbs-Merrill, 1970), 137. World Bank, World Development Report 1988, 273.*

private property, confirm the existence of a relatively small plutocracy in most European countries. According to the British Inland Revenue Board's estimate of ownership of wealth (based upon inheritance taxes) from 1960 to 1968, the number of those possessing over £50,000 had doubled while the number possessing less than £5,000 had declined by only 16 percent.

On the other hand, in Scandinavia and several smaller countries there has been a redistribution of income in favor of employees. Sweden, paradoxically, has the most egalitarian allocation of wealth and the smallest group of extremely wealthy families; Michael Jungblut calculated that fifteen families and two large banks controlled 90 percent of the country's private industrial capital in the early seventies. This situation came about primarily because high income taxes prevented the bulk of the population from investing in industry and because many Socialists wanted to keep the financial elite intact but small so that it would offer little resistance to Socialist programs. Sweden's taxes are so high that a jump in income from 20,000 to 40,000 kroner a year will produce a real income increase of only 3,000 kroner.

In Norway, even higher taxes on income and property forced about 2,000 wealthy Norwegians to pay taxes in excess of their 1973 incomes. Now, however, the Socialist majority in Parliament has apparently decided to return to an earlier law limiting taxes to a maximum of 80 percent of one's income.

In West Germany, where class lines are not as distinct as in France or Great Britain, there are reports of the beginnings of a service-class society. According to this view, all who hold service jobs—soon to be the majority of the employed—from the clerk to the top government minister, are involved in the exercise of power and can no longer be divided into distinct social classes. Yet service-class workers do not behave as a class or think as a class; they behave and think as individuals. Although the German class structure is certainly less distinct than those in France and Great Britain, the service-class thesis seems somewhat premature.

Class demarcations in wealth and the exercise of political power remain clear in West Germany. In a study of the "rich and superrich in Germany," Michael Jungblut singled out a new "oligarchy of wealth" numbering some 50,000 families. In 1960, each family had more than 10 million marks, and as a group they controlled 16 percent of the country's capital shares and 7 percent of the individual wealth. A slightly larger group, 1.7 percent of the population, possessed 35 percent of the country's wealth. But wealth is probably less necessary in West Germany to obtain power than it is in the United States. Many leaders of the Social Democratic party and the powerful labor unions came from humble beginnings, as Table 10-1 shows. Willy Brandt, for example, the illegitimate son of a shop clerk, rose to head the German government and the Social Democratic party.

Housing and Life-style of the Ruling Class

There are still immense gaps between the life-styles of the middle and working classes, as the differences in their housing make particularly evident. The bourgeoisie and aristocracy inhabit distinct bourgeois or aristocratic sections of the cities or suburbs as well as having villas in the countryside.

The Austrian government had to enact laws to prevent rich West Germans from buying up much of the Tyrol for vacation cottages. In Paris the aristocrats live primarily in the Saint-Germain district. For the bourgeoisie there is, according to John Ardagh, "a chic new town flat in Neuilly (Paris) at half a million francs, a modern 'maison de campagne, style anglais,' in the woods of the Ile-de-France." This housing pattern is similar for top French administrators, who are primarily drawn from the upper bourgeoisie. A study of 347 of them found that 103 lived in the middle-class district of Passy and 42 in the elegant suburb of Neuilly.

In London the expensive West End is far from the cramped quarters of the working-class section. Similarly, the housing of the Viennese bourgeoisie on the edges of the nineteenth district (Döbling) amid parks, vineyards, and portions of the Vienna Woods bears little resemblance to the crowded working-class housing in the tenth district (Favoriten). The life-style of the bourgeoisie—including smart new apartments or modernized villas and sleek new cars—is a constant reminder that class distinctions remain important in Europe.

The suburban areas that have been developed around Europe's major cities, like those in the United States, have catered to the bourgeoisie. West of Paris, American-style housing developments with tennis courts, boutiques, and *discothèques* are fast filling the landscape. Named *le Parc Montaigne* or *le Residence Vendôme*, the new homes feature sun terraces and built-in barbecues. The estate of 520 villas built by the American firm of Levitt and Sons southwest of Versailles was subscribed twice over in three weeks, primarily by engineers, doctors, and middle-management officials.

Housing developers are proving that the Parisian does not always prefer an apartment; indeed, many French feel that these new suburban homes enhance their social status. Now they can bring prospective clients or friends to their new villas, whereas before they may have been unable to accommodate guests in their crowded Paris apartments. Every morning they follow a routine much like that of an executive from New Jersey or Long Island who works in New York City as they climb into their new Citröens or Peugeots or crowd into the early morning trains for the trip to their Paris offices.

The differences in life-style extend to leisure activities as well. England's upper class prefers rugby and tennis; the lower class enjoys soccer. Certain ski resorts cater primarily to the middle class, providing expensive accommodations, *après ski* rituals, and smart shops. The wealthy often make two or three visits a year to Saint Moritz, Davos, or Kitzbühel.

As the lower middle class and even the working class began visiting the Spanish and Italian coasts, the wealthy sought more exotic retreats. German tourist agencies now offer safaris in Kenya, gold-digging holidays in Alaska, and camel caravans in the desert. One tourist organization, the Club Méditerranée, offers holiday camps where one can live in a well-organized "primitive" environment.

To cater to wealthy European travelers, expensive hotels have multiplied throughout Western and Eastern Europe. The Hotel Intercontinental chain now provides a luxurious home away from home throughout Europe, where the hotels dish out native culture in small, acceptable doses so that the wealthy guests, watching local folk dances and trying one meal of local delicacies in the security of their hotel, will have the impression that they are indeed in another country.

The Technocrats

Still, European society in the 1970s is not what it was in the prewar period. As more and more industrial ownership has passed into the hands of governments and corporations, a new technocratic elite has replaced the traditional industrialist as the manager of these transformed enterprises. The directors of Italy's two major public corporations exercise more authority than any industrialist, including the owner of Fiat.

Despite this change, the power structure has been transformed very little, since the vast majority of the new managers have come from the middle class. In addition, those few technocrats who rose from the lower middle class or lower class quickly adopted the life-style of the bourgeoisie and no longer considered themselves a part of their former social class.

Yet the possessors of economic power are not altogether free to use it for their own political and economic gain. On the contrary, they must contend with increased government intervention and the demands of other interest groups, especially labor. Although they have managed to maintain or even increase their share of national wealth, the members of this new ruling stratum no longer have the political authority previously exercised by the leaders of business and industry.

Of course, there are important differences from country to country. Technocrats and entrepreneurs have considerably more political influence in France and Great Britain than they do in the Scandinavian countries. Managers in Sweden must contend with a Social Democratic government that guarantees wage increases and similar benefits to the labor force. In France and Italy, on the other hand, management decisions are not so circumscribed.

With the exception of the Scandinavian states, postwar European society has experienced only a limited shift in educational opportunity, equalization of wealth, and access to positions of power and influence. However, there is strong pressure for a further democratization of education, and plans are being made. Since the important positions in business and industry are going to the well-trained managers, educational democratization could one day lead to greater social mobility. But the opposition of traditional interests will probably prevent full educational democratization of the kind that has been achieved in the United States. It appears that a greater equalization of wealth will be difficult to accomplish. The lower income groups have increased their incomes in the postwar period, as have the middle and upper classes. Nevertheless the income gap between the two groups has actually narrowed since the war. But because the lower classes own little property and do not invest their money, a large percentage of their income is taxed. The rich, on the other hand, have managed to avoid paying their proper share of the tax burden, since most of their income comes from property and investments, not from a salary. The statistics on income presented in this chapter cannot tell the whole story of the disparity in wealth between the two groups because a large portion of the wealth of upper income groups is not reported.

FURTHER READING

Informative general surveys of class are Arthur Marwick's *Class in the Twentieth Century* (1986) and *Class: Image and Reality* (1980). Two recent studies of the French elite are Jolyon Howorth and Philip G. Cerny, eds., *Elites in France* (1981), and Luc Boltranski, trans. Arthur Goldhammer, *The Making of a Class: Cadres in French Society* (1987).

Two interesting and informative surveys of Europe in the sixties are Anthony Sampson, *Anatomy of Europe* (1968), and Stanley Rothman, *European Society and Politics* (1971). Although acknowledging a general improvement in the standard of living, Sampson was critical of Europe's failure to institute more far-reaching educational and social reforms. Rothman's study—a competent survey of the relationship between politics and society in Britain, France, West Germany, and the Soviet Union—is especially valuable for its many excellent tables.

Two thorough studies of the relationship between social background and educational opportunities are Torsten Husen's *Social Background and Educational Opportunity* (1972) and *The School in Question* (1979). Stephen Graubard's *A New Europe?* (1963), cited earlier, is invaluable on many aspects of postwar society. Other examinations of European education are Fritz K. Ringer, *Education and Society in Modern France* (1979), and the two volumes edited by Lawrence Stone, *The University in Society* (1974) and *Schooling and Society* (1976). All these works, in seeking to compare educational systems, reveal wide cleavages among

American, British, and continental educational practices and social perspectives.

Two valuable comparative studies of women are Lynne B. Iglitzen and Ruth Ross, eds., *Women in the World: A Comparative Study* (1976), and Janet Zollinger Giele and Audrey Chapman Smock, eds., *Women, Roles and Status in Eight Countries* (1977).

Recent studies of British society are Arthur Marwick, *British Society since 1945* (1982), and John H. Goldthorpe, *Social Mobility and Class Structure in Modern Britain*, 2nd ed. (1987). Anthony Sampson's *Changing Anatomy of Britain* (1982) is a critical survey. E. A. Johns, *The Social Structure of Modern Britain* (1965), is a more thorough but narrower study. M. Young's *The Rise of the Meritocracy* (1958) found that education was replacing the family as the avenue to power. W. L. Guttsman, in *The British Political Elite* (1963), noted little change in the social background of British political leaders. A more up-to-date study, Richard Rose, *Politics in England*, 3rd ed. (1980), provides a valuable interpretive examination of present political and social trends. R. M. Punnett's, *British Government and Politics*, 4th ed. (1980), contains important information on the relationship between society and politics. Equally valuable is Samuel Beer, *Britain against Itself* (1982), and Trevor Noble, *Modern Britain: Structure and Change* (1975). Two highly critical studies are R. M. Titmuss, *The Irresponsible Society* (1960), and Michael Shanks, *The Stagnant Society* (1961). Aspects of the welfare state are explained in Pauline Gregg's *The Welfare State* (1969).

A sound and very readable survey of the impact of economic modernization on French society is John Ardagh's *France Today* (1987). Stanley Hoffman and his associates, *In Search of France* (1963), say the French Fourth Republic was characterized by a social stalemate that permitted only gradual change and thereby preserved the position of the dominant social groups in society. But they believed that the social stalemate was collapsing from the shock of World War II, the postwar economic modernization, and the strong Gaullist state. George Ross, Stanley Hoffmann, and Sylvia Malzacher, eds., *The Mitterrand Experiment: Continuity and Change in Modern France* (1987), provides excellent studies of the economy and society. Patrick McCarthy, ed., *The French Socialists in Power, 1981–1986* (1987), is a solid recent study of many aspects of French society.

More critical studies of French society are Michael Crozier, *The Stalled Society* (1973); M. Dogan, "Political Ascent in a Class Society: French Deputies 1870–1958," in D. Marvick, ed., *Political Decision-Makers* (1961); and Jane Marceau, *Class and Status in France: Economic Change and Social Immobility, 1945–1975* (1977). Crozier contends that France still suffers from a stalemate or a stalled society and discerns two opposing social forces: the desire for authority and an extreme individualism. The rigidity of society fosters periodic crises during which the French act collectively under dynamic leadership, but then they revert to rigidity. Dogan argues that little change has occurred in the social composition of those in positions of power and influence. Marceau grants that French living standards have vastly improved since 1945 but contends that social divisions have remained rigid, with the wealthy maintaining their economic, social, and educational advantages despite the growing wealth of French society. A competent study of French education is W. R. Fraser's *Reforms and Restraints in Modern French Education* (1971).

For good introductions to German politics and society, see Louis J. Edinger, *West German Politics* (1986); Arnold J. Heidenheimer and Donald Kommers, *The Governments of Germany*, 4th ed. (1975); David Conradt, *The German Polity* (1978); and Kendall L. Baker, Russell J. Dalton, and Kai Hildebrandt, *Germany Transformed: Political Culture and the New Politics* (1981). Edinger considers German interest groups and the persistence of a German political elite. Heidenheimer and Kommers compare East and West Germany and find greater social equalization in the East but greater political liberty in the West. The Baker et al. study contains important analyses of public opinion and voting patterns.

For a more critical study of modern German society, see Ralf Dahrendorf's *Society and Democracy in Germany* (1968). Dahrendorf believes that West Germany must institute a greater social equalization and political democratization. W. Zapf, in *Wandlungen der Deutschen Elite, 1919–1961* (1965) and *Beiträge zur Analyse der Deutschen Oberschicht*, 2d ed. (1965), finds a relatively rapid turnover of German political leaders in the postwar period but a low turnover for civil servants and business leaders.

Also highly critical is Michael Jungblut's *Die Reichen und die Superreichen in Deutschland* (1971). Similar to its American counterpart, *The Rich and the Superrich*, by Ferdinand Lundberg, Jungblut's study describes the monopoly of wealth and power exercised by a relatively small plutocracy.

Two valuable surveys of recent economic and social change are Donald Sassoon, *Contemporary Italy* (1986), and John Hooper, *The Spaniards: A Portrait of the New Spain* (1987).

A sound study of social and political change in postwar Sweden can be found in M. Donald Hancock's *Sweden: The Politics of Postindustrial Change* (1972). Insights into the distribution of wealth can be found in Michael Jungblut et al., *Schweden Report* (1974), and Per-Martin Meyerson, *Eurosclerosis—The Case of Sweden* (1985). For a severely critical, sometimes polemical study of postwar Sweden, see Roland Huntford, *The New Totalitarians* (1972). Much data is provided in the OECD survey, *Level of Living and Inequality in the Nordic Countries* (1981).

Recent statistics are available in publications of the OECD, United Nations, and UNESCO.

11 Economics and Society in the Communist World

> [In East Germany] the society of inherited status has largely given way to a society of achieved status.
>
> Ralf Dahrendorf
> *Society and Democracy in Germany*

While the East European countries and the Soviet Union made good on their promise to bring about a greater equalization of income immediately after the war, their economic policies ultimately lowered dramatically the standard of living for the vast mass of their populations and brought their countries near economic collapse. They achieved greater social equalization after the war through the abandonment of private ownership of property, the nationalization of industry, and a greater equalization of educational opportunity. But in place of an elite based upon private ownership, there emerged an elite based upon special privilege. Moreover, economic difficulties forced these countries to reintroduce income differentiation in order to bring about the economic reforms necessary to stimulate economic performance. While the income disparities are not as great as they are in the West, the higher income and greater privileges of the elite brought about social disparities and popular resentment in the East. This chapter will examine economic and social development within the Soviet bloc and Yugoslavia since 1945.

With the exception of Yugoslavia after 1952 and Albania and Romania after the early sixties, the East European states have generally followed, or been forced to follow, Soviet economic and social patterns. But the Soviet model has been difficult to follow since it has had three major transformations—associated with Stalin, Khrushchev, and Gorbachev—and many minor changes. Immediately after the war, government-imposed social-leveling measures brought about a much greater social egalitarianism than in the West. The expropriation of property from the landed classes (especially in Hungary and Poland) and the nationalization of industry eliminated the nobility and capitalist entrepreneurial classes. But a new elite of party bureaucrats and technocratic managers was soon to replace this former elite. A technocratic elite also arose as a result of the economic modernization that swept through Eastern Europe. The social disparities that reemerged in all countries, with the possible exception of economically underdeveloped Albania, were based less on income than on benefits received by this new elite. The privileged position of the party elite, known as the *Nomenklatura* in the Soviet Union and Poland, continued up to the present despite attempts to alter it.

The Soviet Economy

Although the Soviet Union had made considerable progress in the interwar years, World War II set back its industrialization temporarily. Much of the industry in the south and west and half of the total prewar railway network had been destroyed. The wartime deaths of millions had also reduced the skilled labor supply. Nevertheless, the war provided some lasting benefits to Soviet industrialization, for entire industries had been set up beyond the Urals to escape German destruction. With these industrial areas intact and the older ones rebuilt, the country's industrial potential was immensely increased. By 1953, the Soviet Union had surpassed its prewar levels of production in much of the heavy-industry sector. Production of steel rose from 18.3 million metric tons in 1940 to 38 million metric tons in 1953. Concentration on heavy industry put the nation in a position to challenge the United States in the production of raw materials and military equipment—though not consumer goods—by the 1970s. But growing economic problems in the late seventies and eighties severely limited any further Soviet economic advances and undermined both the whole course of Soviet economic development and leadership.

Khrushchev's Decentralization

Since Stalin's death, the Soviet economy has experienced three markedly different periods of development: the first under Khrushchev; the second under his successors, Brezhnev and Kosygin; and the third under Gorbachev. All three periods were reactions to Stalinist centralization and his concentration on heavy industry.

Beginning in 1958, Khrushchev instituted a major reorganization of the Soviet economy along regional lines. The rationale for this decentralization was sound. The extreme Stalinist centralization was adequate for a small developing economy but not for an increasingly complex developed one. The rigid centralized plans, longterm goals, and resource allocations led to wasted resources and shoddy manufactured goods.

However, because Khrushchev's decentralization was hastily instituted, it created new difficulties. Overall coordination and control of a hundred regional areas was extremely difficult. Local factory managers were hampered by greater interference than they had endured under Stalin since they now received endless directives, many of them conflicting, from the newly empowered local and state agencies. Nor was the factory manager freed from the exaggerated production goals typical of the Stalinist period since Khrushchev was equally determined to catch up with American industrial output. Because production goals were still couched in terms of volume or weight, managers went on meeting their quotas by hoarding materials, falsifying records, and turning out inferior products. The Soviet publication *Krokodil* once lampooned the system of output measurement and factory management by showing a nail factory that had met its quota by producing one giant nail. Since transport goals were expressed in ton-kilometers, transport firms made useless trips in order to fulfill their quotas.

Khrushchev's determination to raise agricultural production also misfired. The concentration on increasing corn and wheat production forced local officials to adopt monoculture. To raise production, fallowing was banned almost entirely. This led to weed infestation, wind erosion, and falling yields. And Khrushchev's emphasis on raising production in certain fertile areas left the land in less fertile areas with little fertilizer and little capital.

When Khrushchev realized that his policy of decentralization was failing, he resorted to further divisions of authority in order to stimulate competition among officials and thereby promote greater efficiency. As detailed in chapter 7, he divided the party into agricultural and industrial groups, thereby further complicating an already confused situation. Local Communist party officials were extremely resentful when the new division of responsibility deprived them of half their authority. Nor were things better at the national level, where both the Soviet *Sovnaskhov* (economic council) and the Supreme Council of National Economy were given the authority to issue directives in the same industrial sectors.

Khrushchev forced most of the East European countries into an economic division of labor with the establishment of Comecon. Under this plan, East Germany, Czechoslovakia, and the Soviet Union were to concentrate on heavy industrial production while the other countries would supply raw materials and light industrial products. The latter would, therefore, be permitted to develop only a portion of their economies. Naturally, this plan met much opposition from countries such as Romania that wished to develop their heavy industry but were not permitted to according to the new division of labor.

Economic Policy of Kosygin and Brezhnev

The second major shift in economic policy began after Kosygin and Brezhnev instituted reforms in 1965. They abolished regional administration and returned to centralized direction of the economy. But this was not a

Stalinist centralism with its complete control over all aspects of production, investment, and resource allocation. To be centrally determined were major investments, volume of sales, basic assortment of output, total wages fund, amount of profit and profit rate on capital, and payments to and allocations from the state budget. Local managers were to have the authority to handle most factory labor questions except gross wages and to authorize all minor investments out of their profit. Most important, volume of sales and profitability replaced gross output as indicators of the success of enterprises. Central controls now tended to be indirect rather than direct: taxes, subsidies, interest rates, rents, price ceilings, and profit rates.

The economic lag of the early 1960s came to a temporary end as a measure of order was restored in the economy. But growth rates turned down again after 1973 due to inefficiency, lack of technology, a too-rigid central allocation of materials and labor, and the concentration of investment on military spending. Khrushchev's boast that the Soviet Union would overtake the United States has not materialized economically; Soviet gross national product (GNP) per capita reached only about 41 percent of that of the United States in 1987, according to the U.S. Department of State. In fact much of the Soviet demand for consumer goods is met by the underground economy. Economists estimate that about 20 percent of all consumer purchases are made on the underground economy. Authorities permit this "second economy" to exist since it supplies scarce goods, reduces discontent, and even supplies goods needed by the official economy. Widespread pilfering from government-run industries is overlooked. There is a popular Soviet and East European view that those who are not cheating are cheating their own families. Soviet managers are hamstrung by the shortage of centrally allocated material if they wish to meet their production goals. Certainly, the sharp difference in the living standards of American and Soviet citizens has not been a good advertisement for the superiority of communism. Much of the support for Gorbachev's reforms has resulted from the failure of centralized economic planning.

Serious economic difficulties in the early eighties convinced Gorbachev and other reformers that economic reforms were absolutely essential to prevent a weakening of the Soviet Union. They believed that the free flow of information in a society was the basis for the economic, and ultimately political and military, strength of a country. Therefore, Gorbachev's efforts at restructuring, openness, and *Demokratia* were aimed at removing obstacles to reform, such as the ossified bureaucracy, and freeing up economic activity at the local level. His desire to increase local initiative and industrial output has encountered stubborn opposition from Communist party conservatives and the entrenched bureacracy, who fear a loss of local authority. As a result, Gorbachev has been driven to even greater demands for economic freedoms in order to achieve reforms. Gorbachev's drive to establish a strong economy through market socialism demands a destruction of the conservative Party forces that profited from the previous system. He needs to reform the Party with its gigantic officialdom in order to remove obstacles to his economic reforms. By encouraging popular involvement everywhere, he hopes to defeat the conservative forces and tap the energies of the masses. His dilemma is that he may not be able to achieve economic reforms in time to prevent a conservative counterrevolution against the reforms.

East European Economic Modernization

The basis for much of the transformation of Eastern Europe in the postwar years has been economic modernization. Most of the countries have made the transition from peasant societies to diversified economies. Having a good economic balance of agricultural and industrial output, East Germany made particularly rapid strides until the 1980s. With a population of only 17 million, East Germany became the tenth leading industrial country in the world in the seventies. Despite the loss of over a million skilled workers to the West, East Germany has maintained its reputation as one of the world's leading producers of optical and photographic equipment and has become a leading producer of chemicals and iron and steel products.

But East Germany exists in the shadow of the much more successful West German economy where consumer goods are abundant. A concentration on heavy industrial products has led to serious consumer-goods shortages. The immigrants who poured into West Germany after 1989 complained about inferior products and severe shortages, with delivery of automobiles taking about ten years. The loss of many skilled workers to the West further reduced industrial production and cut services. With the entire economy on the brink of collapse in early 1990, only massive aid from the West or unification with West Germany could prevent collapse.

Romania, with its important mineral resources, also made impressive economic gains until the seventies: its economic growth rate averaged 10 percent annually between 1950 and 1973. Romania's rejection of the role of mere raw materials supplier to the Soviet Union and the other members of Comecon led it to develop its own manufacturing industries. But raw-material, energy, and agricultural shortages, combined with a dogmatic insistence on developing heavy industry, led to a sharp economic downturn in the late seventies and eighties. Communist party leader Ceauşescu imposed a severe Stalinist centralization plan to overcome the economic problems. His attempt to export most of what Romania produced in order to obtain investment funds and cut the deficit, created extreme hardship, massive food and consumer-goods shortages, and mounting internal and foreign opposition. These economic problems helped undermine his leadership and contributed to his overthrow in December 1989. His successors will face a long and difficult task in restoring economic stability.

The economic development of the other Communist bloc countries has been more checkered. In the 1960s, their output fell far behind their goals. Czechoslovakia, with an advanced manufacturing sector, has suffered from overzealous planning, political turmoil, and a labor shortage. Although political stability between the Prague Spring (see chapter 12) and the overthrow of the Communist government in 1989 promoted economic improvement, highly planned resource allocation, worker apathy, and energy shortages severely inhibited economic growth.

Yugoslavia's self-management system, instituted by Tito to give workers a voice in industrial management and to win the ideological battle against Stalin, became increasingly ineffective in the seventies and eighties. Workers' councils in factories proved to be inept managers. Also, the necessity to treat each republic and autonomous area equally resulted in a ruinous duplication of production. Efforts to establish a free-market economy by the economically advanced republics of Slovenia and Croatia have encountered the opposition of most other areas, who fear the unemployment and greater inequality it will bring. As a result, all efforts to establish a free market have been stymied by central government intervention. Legislation passed in 1988 that was intended to move toward a free market and return management to factory managers attained only a portion of the economic freedoms demanded by free-market forces. The result has been a destructive mixture that has produced high inflation and worker unrest. Lack of capital and technological backwardness impede international competitiveness and industrial solvency. Efforts to resolve the conflict between the free-market north and the Serb-dominated south could well result in a further political fragmentation or a Serbian attempt to "unify" the country militarily.

As a whole, the Eastern bloc economies maintained a rapid economic advance in the early seventies; from 1971 to 1973, every country's industrial growth rate topped 6 percent. But higher energy costs, scarce raw materials, shortages of investment capital, and reduced exports curtailed economic growth after 1973. In addition, the East bloc countries have had to buy from the West much of the technologically advanced equipment they need to promote industrial expansion. The costs for countries attempting to establish competitive industries—East Germany, Romania, and Hungary—were enormous. By 1981, East Germany's debt to the West of $12.8 billion was second only to Poland's $22.6 billion debt that was brought about to a large extent by its internal political turmoil. Romania managed to retire most of its $10 billion debt to the West in 1989 but only by severe rationing measures that brought extreme hardship. Hungary avoided serious economic setbacks in the seventies by diverting some industrial endeavor from large state-owned enterprises to more efficient local and private companies and by introducing incentives and cost

Table 11-1   Per-Capita GNP (in 1977 U.S. dollars)

	1967	1977	1987
East Germany	3,093	4,363	11,860
Czechoslovakia	3,293	4,198	9,715
Soviet Union	1,554	3,976	8,363
Hungary	2,235	2.747	8,260
Bulgaria	1.795	2,511	7,222
Poland	1,917	2,888	6,890
Romania	1,787	2,766	6,358

SOURCE: *U.S. Department of Commerce,* Selected Trade and Economic Data of the Centrally Planned Economies *June 1979, 2, World Factbook 1989, Central Intelligence Agency. These estimates of per-capita GNP by the CIA are considered to be too high by many economists (Jan Wineicki,* The Distorted World of Soviet-type Economies*) and by the World Bank. The 1987 per-capita GNP is taken from United States Department of State, Bureau of Intelligence and Research,* Indicators of Comparative East-West Economic Strength 1987, *196 (December 30, 1988).*

accountability. But the eighties brought economic decline to Hungary as well. Efforts to reduce costs by allowing technology to replace labor encountered stiff resistance from more orthodox Communist officials who prized full employment more than profitability. Now, with new governments emerging throughout Eastern Europe, cost accountability and profitability will be necessary if East European companies wish to be competitive internationally. Western investors will also not invest unless they can expect a profit.

Per-capita gross national product rose steadily since the early 1960s. But as Table 11-1 shows, there was considerable variance from one country to another. Although Bulgaria has advanced rapidly in recent years, the latest data available indicate that only East Germany, the Soviet Union, and Czechoslovakia could be considered mature industrial societies. The World Bank report of 1988 classifies Poland and Hungary as intermediate-developed economies. A 1987 study, *Equality and Inequality in Eastern Europe,* found that two of the more advanced countries in Eastern Europe, Hungary and Czechoslovakia, had fallen far behind their next-door neighbor Austria since the interwar period: in 1938, per-capita income in Hungary and Czechoslovakia reached 66 and 118 percent that of Austria, repectively, compared to a 1978 GNP per capita of only 47 and 63 percent that of Austria. The economic dislocation after 1987 obviously produced an even greater disparity.

The economic reforms needed to make East European economies competitive in the world economy will require changes in previous economic practices that will not be popular with the masses. Previous economic practices have engendered a great deal of opposition to market principles and price reforms. Popular perceptions that the state is obligated to prevent inequalities of wealth and high prices for basic needs has and will produce extensive opposition to making industry profit oriented. Left Communists oppose market forces as leading to capitalism, while many workers oppose them because they have not had to work hard while receiving a government-supported wage. For example, economic reforms in 1987 that would have permitted higher incomes in the Soviet Union were thwarted by government bureaucrats who imposed exceedingly high taxes on private businesses and cooperative owners. Private tourist business on Romania's Black Sea coast vanished when government officials decided such ventures would produce some wealth among these small private owners. Many budding private entrepreneurs are afraid they will suffer if the reformers fall from power. Workers are also impatient with the pace of change. Many believe they must work more for less under Gorbachev and similar reformers. This attitude led to major coal miners' strikes in July 1989, which Gorbachev defused only by granting wage increases. The Soviet railway system, where many workers received only about $35 a month pay in 1989, is plagued by massive absenteeism (150,000 employees do not report for work each day). A railway worker commented in 1989 that Soviet leaders are oblivious to their suffering because "they don't taste the gravy of real life."

Agricultural Problems

Some of the Soviet Union's industrial progress, particularly in the Stalin period, has been at the expense of agriculture. A noted economist, Arcadius Kahan, called Soviet policy one of calculated subsistence for agriculture. Despite the increased attention given agriculture by Khrushchev and Gorbachev, the Soviet Union still suffers from inadequate mechanization, low fertilization, skilled labor shortages, and poor transportation. With about 75 percent more sown land in the early 1960s, the Soviet Union produced only about 63 percent of the United States' crop of major grains. By 1980, Soviet farm output reached 80 percent of that of the U.S. but with a much higher investment of labor and capital: eight times as many farm workers as the U.S. (23 percent of the work force) and five times the capital investment (one-quarter of all investment capital). Only under extremely favorable climatic conditions can the Soviet Union feed its population.

Khrushchev's attempts to raise agricultural production failed because they were primarily restricted to tilling new, marginal virgin land and trying one short-term project after another in order to raise production, instead of undertaking long-term efforts to modernize farming methods and provide adequate machinery and fertilizers. The post-Khrushchev planners have invested more in agriculture and raised the wages of agriculture workers, but despite their efforts, Soviet food needs cannot be met. From 1971 to 1973, the average growth of Soviet agricultural output was only 3.4 percent. The failure of the Soviet grain crop in 1972 necessitated huge grain purchases from the United States.

Brezhnev shifted even more investment funds to agriculture at the expense of the consumer-goods industry; agricultural investment increased from about 19 percent of total government investment in the early sixties to about 24 percent between 1976 and 1978. Much of this increased investment went to enlarge livestock herds and for land reclamation and improvement. But for ideology's sake, Brezhnev did not attempt to reduce the amount of collectivized land, which is much less productive than the privately owned plots due to mismanagement and an excessively overcentralized allocation of resources.

Soviet planners have been faced with another major agricultural problem—the migration of agricultural workers, especially the young, to the cities. A 1967 survey showed that 65 percent of those described as job transients were under thirty years of age. The Communist youth organization, *Komsomol,* has not been able to slow this migration. A 1966 survey of the Smolensk region showed that the number of *Komsomol* members working on state farms had halved in five years; on collective farms it had dropped even more, from 21,043 to 8,778. In order to harvest vegetables, urban residents were forced to help with the harvest. Students often spent as much as six weeks in the fields during harvest time in the sixties. Still, much of the produce is not harvested; one-third of the potato crop in 1980 remained unharvested. Total potato output declined 12 percent from 1966 to 1980.

Gorbachev's reform of agriculture has been designed to increase local initiative by reducing centralized decision making. Profitability was to govern agricultural ventures. Farming units were permitted to sell all produce above an existing target at market prices. Gorbachev's policy of increasing leaseholding has encountered strong opposition from state-farm bosses, who fear their loss of power, and collective farmers, who do not want to give up their security for the free market. Gorbachev does not want to force farmers into private farming, but he intends to reduce collective farming where peasants work little for their wages. As Gorbachev remarked, "No fool is going to work on a lease contract as long as he can have a salary without earning it" (*New York Times,* 14 Oct 1988).

The disparity between the drabness of life on a rural collective and the livelier life-style possible in a larger city is symbolized by the difference in the clothing styles in each. So, in the sixties, the arbiter of Soviet men's fashions—in an attempt to keep them down on the collective—advocated a return to Cossack styles, with dashing boots, embroidered shirts, and flared trousers as an alternative to urban fashion trends.

Eastern European Agriculture

Agriculture underwent a deeper transformation than did industry in Eastern Europe after the war. Most land was first divided into state-owned and cooperatively owned sectors, with agricultural workers receiving a wage. These wages rose even more rapidly than industrial wages at first.

In an attempt to satisfy land-hungry peasants, land was distributed in small private plots immediately after the war. Later, as governments came under Communist domination, the land was either taken over by the state or organized into cooperatives. The cooperatives ranged from those where the peasant owns nothing and is paid a wage to those where property is individually owned but cooperatively farmed. Fierce peasant resistance to collectivization in Poland, combined with the leaders' reluctance to collectivize, led to the establishment of over 3 million small private farms. In Hungary, huge cooperative farms with productivity bonuses replaced almost all the state collective farms. In order to maintain the rural labor supply, peasants were not issued rural passports that permitted them to travel: Soviet peasants began to receive such passports only after 1974.

Population density on the land, the primary problem in the interwar period, retards the development of agriculture; one study fixed the population density in the private sector at forty to fifty workers for every 250 acres. While in Western Europe the agricultural population is well under 10 percent of the working population, as of 1982 it remained over 20 percent in all East European countries except East Germany (4%), Czechoslovakia (14%), and Yugoslavia (5%).

Collectivized agriculture has not provided the answer to East Europe's agrarian problems. By the midsixties, Poland's agricultural output had risen more than that of any other East European country because of its small farms, whereas output in collectivized East Germany, Czechoslovakia, and Hungary was actually lower than the 1938 production level. In the midseventies, a Polish farmer proudly remarked, "It is amusing to us to see high-ranking Russian officers going home carrying sacks of potatoes." Among the countries with collectivized agriculture, only Romania has shown a slight increase in agricultural production since the war. Collectivized agriculture in Yugoslavia provides a higher yield mainly because the most fertile land is in large state farms in the Vojvodina area north of Belgrade, whereas individually owned farms (not larger than twenty-five acres) are located in infertile mountainous terrain. Since the midseventies, only Hungarian agriculture has continued to increase production sufficiently to meet its country's needs. The Polish practice of keeping food prices low in order to satisfy industrial workers led to low agricultural prices, reduced output, and black marketeering. In 1980, all Eastern European countries except Hungary imported more grain than they exported. Of course, official trade figures do not include the enormous underground economy in Eastern Europe. Much of the agricultural output as well as some industrial products are sold on the black market. In Hungary, private plots, comprising about 12 percent of the arable land, produced most of the vegetables and fruit and about half of the pork and poultry in 1980. Most of the remaining produce and most of the grain is produced on cooperatives, where workers receive a salary and bonuses for exceeding production goals. This combination has made Hungary the only East European country able to meet its own food needs. Other Eastern European countries began to follow the Hungarian practices in the early eighties, especially after Brezhnev praised the Hungarian performance in 1981. But the real solution to the agricultural problem, free-market prices for produce, results in extreme opposition from populations accustomed to low agricultural prices. Higher wages for industrial workers could offset price increases but will also make industrial products less competitive in the world market. This dilemma will produce extensive suffering no matter how enlightened the reforms.

Living Standards

Economic changes have not brought about a standard of living in the Soviet Union and Eastern Europe anywhere near that of Western Europe. Throughout the seventies and eighties, the Soviet Union suffered from falling rates of productivity and excessive defense spending that reduced outlays for consumer goods and health care. As a result, the infant mortality rate rose dramatically in the seventies: it increased by more than a third between 1970 and 1975. Although better registration could account for some of the apparent increase, the infant mortality rate in 1980 was 230 per 1,000 live births, compared to 192 in the United States and 178 in the United Kingdom.

Male life-expectancy rates in the Soviet Union actually decreased 4.3 years between 1965 and 1980, according to Chesnais. J. C. Chesnais calculates that a Soviet and Japanese male could have expected to live about the same number of years in 1960 (66.2 in the Soviet Union, compared to 67.7 in Japan); but by 1980, Soviet male life expectancy had declined to 61.9 years compared to 73.6 years in Japan. The Soviet Union's poor economic performance in the eighties can only have increased this discrepancy.

In terms of equalizing income, the Soviet Union achieved a greater equalization than most of the West European states, with the exception of Scandinavia. Table 11-2 indicates that top managers, physicians, and lawyers in the Soviet Union were not paid the huge sums characteristic in the West in the sixties, but that political leaders received a much higher salary than the average worker. Mervyn Matthew's study of 1972 incomes calculated that a Soviet elite, comprising the top 0.3 percent of the Soviet population, received an official income of 3.1 to 3.8 times the average pay, compared to the top 3 percent's average income of 8 times the na-

Table 11-2   Base Wage Differentials in the Soviet Union, 1963 (U.S. dollars per year, before taxes)[a]

Cabinet minister, republic government	9,125
University professor	7,070
Factory director (machine building)	6,240
Doctor of science, head of department in a research institute	5,730
Master foreman (machine building)	5,028
Engineer (oil industry)	4,238
Technician	3,724
State-farm manager	3,530
Average for all workers and employees	1,445[b]
Lawyer	1,376
Physician	1,260
Coal miner	1,092
Steel worker	872
High-school teacher	824
Construction worker	746
Machine-tool operator	746
Textile worker	679
Office typist	588
State-farm worker	586
Collective farmer (1962)	574

[a] *Rubles converted into dollars at 1:1.11 ratio.*
[b] *Total wages received, including bonuses. Bonuses are not included in the other figures in the table.*
Source: *J. P. Nettl,* The Soviet Achievement *(New York: Harcourt Brace Jovanovich, 1967), 254. Reprinted by permission.*

tional average in the U.S. However, C. Morrison calculated that additional fringe benefits and income add an extra 100 percent to the Soviet elite's official income in the early eighties. Since Stalin renewed income differentiation in the early 1930s to promote production, Soviet leaders have apparently felt that wage differentials are necessary in an industrialized society. It is noteworthy that men constitute only 40 percent of physicians, probably because of the extensive training required and the comparatively low salaries. The lure of becoming a party bureaucrat, with its higher income and special perquisites in the form of better housing, food, and consumer goods (see below), is more appealing.

The concentration of Soviet resources on heavy industry and the armaments and space programs has left little for consumer goods. Until recently, Soviet leaders were little interested in providing consumer goods: Khrushchev asserted, "A person cannot consume, for example, more bread and other products than are necessary for his organism. . . . Of course, when we speak of satisfying people's needs, we have in mind

Table 11-3   Per-Capita Meat
Consumption in 1978 (in kilograms)

USSR	49
East Germany	68
Hungary	72
Poland	86
West Germany	87
United States	116

SOURCE: USSR: Facts and Figures Annual, *John
L. Sherer, ed., vol. 6 (1982), 298.*

not whims or claims to luxuries, but the healthy needs of a culturally
developed person.'' Soviet per-capita consumption of consumer goods
was only 40 to 60 percent of that in France, West Germany, and the United
Kingdom in 1962. It is unlikely that there has been any improvement in
this ratio since the 1960s. Between 1970 and 1978, Soviet annual rates of
growth of per-capita consumption trailed even that of the struggling
United States economy: the Soviet rate was 2.5 percent, compared to 2.7
percent for the United States. In comparison to the fifty telephones per
one hundred inhabitants in Western Europe in 1985, only Czechoslovakia,
Bulgaria, and East Germany had more than twenty.

Despite Brezhnev's efforts to raise meat consumption, Table 11-3
shows that Soviet citizens consume far less meat then do East European
and Western inhabitants. Another measure of economic well-being that
is more meaningful than monetary comparisons (the Soviet Union sets
the rate of exchange of the ruble) is the amount of work required to
purchase commodities. Radio Liberty estimates that in 1982 it cost a Moscow inhabitant 46.8 hours of work to purchase the same weekly basket
of consumer goods that it took a Washington, Munich, Paris, and London
inhabitant 16.3, 20.4, 19.4, and 22.5 hours, respectively, to purchase. The
Soviet journal *U.S.A.* estimates that in 1988 the average Soviet inhabitant
worked 10 times longer than the average American to buy a pound of
meat, 4.5 times longer to buy a quart of milk and 3 times as long to buy
a pound of potatoes. Forty percent of Soviet households existed on less
than one hundred rubles a month (a ruble was officially being exchanged
at six to the dollar in 1989, but its real worth was about ten cents).

It is, of course, important to remember that consumer goods are more
equally distributed in the Soviet Union than in France, West Germany,
and the United Kingdom. For example, in housing there are few socially
and economically differentiated neighborhoods like those in the West; the
special housing and *dachas* of the powerful and influential are an exception. The size of a dwelling usually depends on the size of the family.

Since rents are low—only about 12 percent of an individual's income was spent on rent in 1982, compared to 51, 24, 39, and 28 percent, respectively, for an inhabitant of Washington, Munich, Paris, and London—there are fewer economic barriers to entry into certain neighborhoods than there are in the West. The living space per capita is, however, much lower in the Soviet Union than in the West: it was only about 10.3 square yards per capita in 1979.

As in Western Europe, the standard of living varies considerably among East European countries, being highest in East Germany, Czechoslovakia, and Yugoslavia. Tito boasted in 1974 that every fifth Yugoslav had a car. Typical Yugoslavs spent only 37 percent of their income on food and drink in the midseventies, compared to over 50 percent in the early sixties. There is little doubt that these figures would not be so favorable if many Yugoslavs had not become guest workers in more affluent countries in the north.

Within Yugoslavia there is a radical difference in the standard of living between north and south. The north, with a standard of living near that of Austria, resents having to help the underdeveloped areas of Macedonia and Montenegro in the south. In Czechoslovakia the standard of living varies too, being much lower in the primarily agrarian Slovakian east.

Regional differences have been a long-standing problem in Eastern Europe, especially in Czechoslovakia and Yugoslavia. During the interwar years, the Bohemian-Moravian areas in Czechoslovakia, like Croatia and Slovenia in Yugoslavia, had much more developed economic areas and considerably higher standards of living than other sections. The inhabitants of the Czech lands also held most of the government positions during the interwar years and in the postwar Communist government.

As in the Soviet Union, the Eastern European countries have offered low-cost housing and services. In East Germany and Hungary, apartments and houses cost an average of $14.50 per month, public transportation costs are a fraction of those in the West, and medical services are free. However, the low costs are often offset by poor quality goods and inadequate housing. Many apartments lack bathrooms, kitchens, and other features common to housing in Western Europe.

Because consumer goods are still expensive and of poor quality, visitors from Western Europe often find that their clothing attracts interest and sometimes prospective buyers. East Europeans must normally wait for extended periods to obtain consumer goods. A Bulgarian in 1984 had to wait twenty years to receive an automobile that had to be paid for in advance. Hungarians flooded into Austria in 1989 to buy consumer goods because of the scarcity and poor quality at home. An East German who fled to West Germany in 1989 complained that he had waited ten years to receive a car he had paid for in 1979.

Status

Despite Soviet and East European efforts to upgrade the status of the worker, the gap between theory and practice remains. The prestige of many jobs is little different from that of the same positions in the West. Service-class jobs, especially those of the new technocracy, continue to be more respected. A Hungarian woman's choice of a lower paying administrative position over that of a textile worker became a cause for concern among Communist officials in 1973. Industrial progress naturally demands highly trained experts; their jobs are more prestigious and their incomes higher.

An increase in leisure time is one device used by Eastern European countries to meet workers' demands for a life-style similar to that in the West. Every worker now receives one month's paid vacation per year. Factory-owned resorts in the mountains and on the Baltic and Black seas give workers the kinds of vacation they could only dream about fifteen years earlier; an East German worker could spend two weeks on the Baltic for as little as $20 in the early seventies. Eastern European travelers, overwhelmingly academics who bolster their income by teaching in the West, are being seen in increasing numbers in the West. However, even when Eastern Europeans are permitted to travel outside their country the West is still too expensive for most of them.

The Role of Women

Despite the egalitarian ideals of communism, women possess no more real power in the Soviet Union then they do in the West. The 15-member Politburo, headed by Brezhnev, had no female members. Only 8 women are among the 287 full members of the Central Committee of the Communist party. Men head all the government ministries and committees. Women are, however, well represented in the professions—about 70 percent of Soviet doctors and 79 percent of all school teachers are female. But these are low-paying professions that are not desired by men. The heads of hospitals and schools are almost always male. Women comprised 51 percent of the work force but two-thirds of them were involved in manual labor in 1980. Women's hourly pay of about 68–70 percent that of men is lower than in most Western European countries.

Women still occupy an inferior place in the home. Even among those who hold jobs on the outside, most still do all the housework. And because they lack labor-saving devices and seldom go out to eat, their household work is much more arduous than in the West. The comment of a divorced woman—one of three marriages ends in divorce—captures the frustration felt by many overworked women, "I doubt that I will ever marry again.

Soviet vacationers driving up to a cottage in a resort area near Kiev. (Camera Press London)

Why should I? Having a husband is like having another baby in the apartment.''

Added to the household duties are the ubiquitous lines in the shops. Soviet women have been found to spend as much as two hours each day waiting in lines and a 1985 average of twenty-seven hours a week on shopping and housekeeping, compared to six hours for men. A Polish survey found that the amount of time queuing increased from sixty-three to ninety-eight minutes a day between 1966 and 1976. It is true that child-care centers leave wives free to work, but this often simply means that a woman works both day and night without the satisfaction that comes with raising her own child. Except for the annual vacations, leisure is an unknown concept for Eastern European women.

Women have also suffered at the hands of central planners. With only one factory producing condoms and a very limited supply of birth-control pills, women choose to undergo from four to six abortions in their lives rather than face increasing poverty. A 1985 estimate of only official abortions placed them at 2.08 for each birth.

Social Structure

Postwar economic modernization and Communist-inspired social changes have transformed the East's social structure. In the Soviet Union the former ruling classes were destroyed during the interwar period. In Eastern Europe they lost their privileged positions after 1945.

Poland provides a clear example of the decline of a former ruling aristocracy. Those aristocrats who did not flee Poland as World War II drew to a close lost both their property and their political power. Some are now part of the professional and service classes. Perhaps the best example of this transformation is the experience of the famous Potocki and Radziwill families.

In the interwar period, the Potocki family owned 9 million acres of land and eighteen towns, and they employed countless peasants. When the Communists expropriated their land after the war, one member of the family, Ignacz Potocki, became a common laborer. But he had had a superior education and by the late 1950s the government's fear of the former aristocracy had declined. So Potocki, who was an expert on medicinal springs, became chief geologist of the Ministry of Health and Social Welfare. Many of the prominent Radziwills have also found employment—as engineers, accountants, and book publishers.

Hungary and Romania, which had had large and wealthy aristocracies, experienced a similar social revolution. But in Bulgaria, Yugoslavia, and Albania, where land was owned primarily by the peasants, little social transformation occurred.

All the Eastern European countries were primarily agrarian—60 to 75 percent of the working population was engaged in agriculture at the end of World War II. The nationalization of industry therefore had far less impact on the social structures than did the destruction of the landed aristocracy. Only in Czechoslovakia and East Germany did the nationalization of industry displace a significant segment of the population.

Changes in Education

Nowhere have the social changes been more dramatic than in education. Some Eastern states were ruthless in their determination to eliminate social privilege in education. In the fifties, university quotas were introduced for each social group throughout Eastern Europe. In East Germany, which Ralf Dahrendorf called the first modern society on German soil, at least half the student populations in all secondary schools had to be workers' and peasants' children. This requirement, along with the elimination of private property, succeeded in eliminating the grasp of the former elite on advanced education. By 1963, one-third of all university students and half the students in technical colleges came from working-class families.

Table 11-4   Percentage of Manual
Workers' Sons in Higher Education

	1960	1964
Yugoslavia	56.0	53.3
East Germany	–	40.0
Czechoslovakia	39.3	37.9
Romania	36.6	31.5
Poland	32.9	35.0
Bulgaria	–	28.0
Great Britain	25.0	–
Italy	13.2	15.3
France	5.3	8.3
West Germany	5.2	5.3

SOURCE: *UNESCO*, Access to Higher Education
(Bucharest, 1968), 49.

This change has meant that a much larger percentage of professors, judges, generals, and industrial managers now come from working-class backgrounds. In comparison with the West, especially France and West Germany, Table 11-4 shows clearly that the number of children from laboring-class backgrounds in universities was much higher in Eastern Europe in the sixties.

However, Soviet and East European leaders have retreated from the view that working-class children should have preference in higher education. Soviet leaders argue that all citizens are now socially equal. Though preferential points are still allocated for social origin, points are also allocated for political attitude and for work experience obtained after secondary school. This system permits influential *Nomenklatura* families to gain preferential treatment for their children. These practices have tended to favor the children of the elite. In 1971, children of blue-collar workers—numbering about 60 percent of the population—comprised 36 percent of those in higher education, compared to almost 60 percent for children of white-collar workers. East Germany dropped the 50 percent clause in the late sixties in order to provide sufficient competent managers for its rapidly industrializing economy. By 1981–1982, only 10.2 percent of Soviet youths entering the university were rural residents. In Poland, working-class children comprised 39.1 percent and peasant children 24.2 percent of those reaching higher education in 1951–1952 but only 24.8 percent and 12.2 percent, respectively, in 1976–1977. The proportion of the working class in the population increased from 39.3 to 40 percent during this time, while the peasantry decreased from 36.7 to 30.4 percent. Only Czechoslovakia has continued to increase the proportion of children from workers' homes in advanced education.

Higher education is becoming more selective, with only 11 percent of Polish and 7 percent of Czechoslovakian youths of the appropriate age group entering higher education, figures much lower than the proportion entering higher education in the United States and most Western European countries. As in the West, the children of the elite have higher aspirations than those below them and prepare themselves in special courses for the entrance examinations. In Poland in 1976–1977, 60 percent of teachers' and researchers' children had such preparation, while only 25 percent of workers' children received similar preparation. In spite of this trend to select future leaders from a more privileged sector of society, the number of children from working-class homes still considerably exceeds that of the West.

The Elite

Critics of the Communist regimes have charged that a new elite class has replaced the former elites throughout Eastern Europe. Central to the question of a new class is the distribution both of rewards and of power. Is there, in fact, a small privileged elite that siphons off a major part of the wealth and privileges of the Soviet Union and Eastern Europe? Has the Communist ideal that what each person gets is determined by his or her need been changed so that what each person gets is determined by his or her relationship to the ruling elite? Is power monopolized at the top in a totalitarian fashion, or is it distributed among various groups within the society? In sum, have the promises of Communist society been realized?

There is no escaping the fact that a new ruling stratum has replaced the old ruling classes. But it is similar to the old ruling groups primarily in its monopoly of political power and privilege, not in its monopoly of wealth. No individuals in the East compare with millionaires in the West. Property and inheritance are limited to personal real estate and belongings, and it is impossible to profit from personal savings; therefore, inherited wealth cannot be the basis for a new capitalist class. But what of the concept of a new class popularized by Milovan Djilas, a close associate of Tito and formerly vice president of Communist Yugoslavia? If the new-class label is restricted to those who exercise political power and benefit more than others from their favored position, then the theory has considerable validity. Top political, administrative, military, and economic officials have such elitist privileges as special stores, paid vacations at select sites, and preference in education and jobs for their children.

Marshal Tito became highly critical of the life-styles of some people in the Yugoslav ruling stratum. In 1973, he said it was time for Yugoslavia to rid itself of the deformations that had "brought shame to a Socialist society." To avert the development of a new "oppressive class," Tito stole a page from Chairman Mao's book. He removed about 100,000 members from the League of Communists and ordered all elected officeholders

FURTHER READING

Several edited studies have been particularly helpful in the preparation of this chapter: Pierre Kende and Zdenek Strmiska, ed., *Equality and Inequality in Eastern Europe* (1987); Henry W. Morton and Rudolph L. Tokes, eds., *Soviet Politics and Society in the 1970's* (1974); and Seweryn Bialer, ed., *Politics, Society and Nationality inside Gorbachev's Russia* (1989). The Morton-Tokes's study contains recent information on many social and political issures. The Kende-Strmiska volume provides several excellent studies of education (Janina Markiewicz-Lagneau), political power (Strmiska), and social mobility (Strmiska).

The views expressed by Alex Inkeles and Raymond A. Bauer in *The Soviet Citizen* (1959) are still voiced in more recent works. They maintained that Soviet citizens accepted the Soviet way of life even though they rejected certain leaders. They wanted the security that came with collectivism, central planning, comprehensive socialization, and single-party rule. More recent studies of Soviet society are John G. Eriksen, *The Development of Soviet Society* (1970), and David Lane, *Politics and Society in the U.S.S.R.* (1971) and *Soviet Economy and Society* (1985).

Criticisms of Soviet society from Soviet citizens include the sharp denunciations of Andrei Amalrik, *Will the Soviet Union Survive until 1984?* (1970), and Aleksandr Solzhenitsyn, *One Day in the Life of Ivan Denisovich* (1970) and *The Gulag Archipelago* (1974). For less polemical criticisms, see Roy Medvedev, *On Socialist Democracy* (1975) and *Let History Judge* (1971). The most important non-Russian criticism came from Milovan Djilas in *The New Class* (1957) and *The Unperfect Society: Beyond the New Class* (1969). In *The New Class,* Djilas contended that a new privileged group of party officials reaped the major rewards in Communist society and refused to institute true communism since it would destroy their privileged position. In *The Unperfect Society,* Djilas maintained that Communist ideology was disintegrating and was no longer accepted even by Communist leaders as a means of social organization. As a disillusioned former Communist vice president of Yugoslavia, Djilas was an early advocate of democratic socialism in Communist countries. Inequality in the Soviet Union can be studied in Mervyn Matthews's *Privilege in the Soviet Union* (1978) and in C. Morrison, "Income Distribution in East European and Western Countries," in *Journal of Comparative Economics* 8 (2), 121–38. A recent examination of corruption in the Soviet Union by Konstantin M. Simis, *USSR: The Corrupt Society* (1982), provides strong evidence of widespread corruption in Soviet society. Much of his evidence comes from his seventeen years experience as an advocate in Soviet trials.

The standard work on the Soviet economy is Alec Nove, *The Soviet Economic System,* 2nd ed. (1980). Outstanding studies of the Soviet economy under Gorbachev are Jerry Hough, *Opening Up the Soviet Economy* (1988); Marshall I. Goldman, *Gorbachev's Challenge: Economic Reform in the Age of High Technology* (1987); and Padma Desai, *The Soviet Economy: Problems and Prospects* (1987). A highly critical study of Soviet economic practices is provided by Jan Winiecki, *The Distorted World of Soviet-Type Economies* (1988). A dated but still valuable study is David Granick's *The Red Executive: A Study of the Organization Man in Russian Industry* (1960). Four recent studies of the Soviet economy are Paul R. Gregory and Robert C. Stuart, *Soviet Economic Structure and Performance*, 2nd ed. (1981); Holland Hunter, ed., *The Future of the Soviet Economy: 1978–1985* (1978); Morris Bornstein, ed., *The Soviet Economy: Continuity and Change* (1981); and Trevor Buck and John Cole, *Modern Soviet Economic Performance* (1987). For Khrushchev's agricultural policies, see Martin McCauley's *Khrushchev and the Development of Soviet Agriculture: The Virgin Land Programme, 1953–1964* (1976). McCauley believes that Khrushchev's error was not in planting virgin lands but in doing it in excess. For economic comparisons with other countries, see *Radio Liberty Research* and *USSR: Facts and Figures Annual*.

The Soviet worker can be studied in A. Brodersen, *The Soviet Worker* (1966); Robert Conquest, ed., *Industrial Workers in the U.S.S.R.* (1967); and Emily Clark Brown, *Soviet Trade Unions and Labour Relations* (1966).

For Soviet women, see Feiga Blekher, *The Soviet Woman in the Family and in Society* (1979); Alena Heitlinger, *Women and State Socialism* (1979); Alastair McAuley, *Women's Work and Wages in the Soviet Union* (1981); and Gail W. Lapidus, *Women, Work, and Family in the Soviet Union* (1982).

Details concerning the health problems in the USSR can be found in Christopher Davis and Murray Feshbach, *Rising Infant Mortality in the USSR in the 1970s* (1980). The revealing comparative figures on child mortality used in this chapter can be found in J. C. Chesnais, "La Durée de la Vie dans les Pays Industrialisés, *La Recherche*, 14 (147), 1040–48. Three accounts of Soviet life by journalists are Hedrick Smith, *The Russians* (1976); Robert G. Kaiser, *Russia: The People and the Power* (1976); and David Shipler, *Russia* (1983). All contend that the classless society is a myth in the Soviet Union, that Soviet industry is inefficient, and that the Soviet population is influenced by a pervasive collectivist mentality. All agree with Inkeles and Bauer that Soviet citizens equate freedom with danger and disorder and believe the state has given them the security they yearn for by providing cheap housing, sufficient food, guaranteed employment, free education and medical care, and pensions for the old and disabled. Much good information on living conditions can be found in Abram Bergson and Herbert Levine, eds., *The Soviet Economy: Toward the Year 2000* (1983).

There are few studies in English on Eastern European societies. A dated but valuable broader synthesis of politics and society is Ghita Ionescu's *The Politics of the European Communist States* (1967). Ionescu argued that the West underestimated the extent of political dissent in Eastern Europe in the sixties. He claimed that the Eastern European countries had an embryonic form of pluralism in the sixties and predicted that they would continue to become more democratic and less communistic. Nenod Popovic, in *Yugoslavia: The New Class in Crisis* (1968), applied the Djilas thesis to Yugoslavia. Jan F. Triska, ed., in *Communist Party States* (1969), looked at the nature of Communist rule throughout Eastern Europe. Some important articles are contained in Stephen Fischer-Galati, ed., *Eastern Europe in the 60's* (1963): Wayne Vucinich's contribution questioned some of Djilas's assumptions, he maintained that a new middle class of technocrats was numerous in Eastern Europe and that Djilas's static picture of Eastern European societies needed revision. For more recent information, see Stephen Fischer-Galati, *Eastern Europe in the 1980s* (1982), and Walter D. Connor, *Socialism, Politics, and Equality: Hierarchy and Change in Eastern Europe and the USSR* (1979).

There are many more studies of the Eastern European economies. An important study of the workings of Comecon is Michael Kaser's *Comecon: Integration Problems of the Planned Economies* (1965). There are many studies of the Yugoslav economic system, especially of the workers' councils. Competent studies are Jeri Kolaja, *Workers' Councils: The Yugoslav Experience* (1965); M. J. Broekmeyer, ed., *Yugoslav Workers' Selfmanagement 1947–64* (1968); and Ichak Adizes, *Industrial Democracy: Yugoslav Style* (1971). For a recent discussion of Yugoslav self-management, see Duncan Wilson's *Tito's Yugoslavia* (1979). John Michael Montias, in *Economic Development in Communist Rumania* (1967), has detailed Romania's attempts to establish a diversified economy.

The general works listed in the bibliography following chapter 7 contain information on economics and society in the other East European states. Jean Edward Smith, in *Germany Beyond the Wall* (1967), describes the rapid economic growth in East Germany and the transformation of society. See also A. Zauberman, *Industrial Progress in Poland, Czechoslovakia and East Germany, 1937–1962* (1964), and J. F. Brown, *The New Eastern Europe* (1966) and *Eastern Europe and Communist Rule* (1988). An important recent collection of essays on the Eastern European worker is Jan F. Triska and Charles Gati, eds., *Blue-Collar Workers in Eastern Europe* (1981). Changes in the Hungarian economy since the economic reforms of 1968 are excellently treated in Paul Hare, Hugo Radice, and Nigel Swain, eds., *Hungary: A Decade of Economic Reform* (1981).

See the Further Reading section of chapter 13 for political studies of recent events.

12 1968: Year of Crisis

To speak of repression in the case of an institution possessing no "physical" repressive power, such as a university, may seem paradoxical. This repression is part of the very functioning of the institution, its structure, which makes the student passive, because he interiorizes its norms and requirements. . . . This passivity kills all real desire and all creative spirit, the expressions of a non-alienated life.

Daniel Cohn-Bendit, in *The Action-Image of Society*
by Alfred Willener

We have introduced the specter of liquidation of the absolute power of the bureaucratic caste, a caste introduced to the international scene by Stalinist socialism. . . . But bureaucracy, even if it has not the dimensions of a class, still shows its characteristics in anything that concerns the exercise of power. It takes preventive measures to defend itself and it will do so to the bitter end. . . . We do not endanger socialism: to the contrary. We endanger bureaucracy which has been slowly but surely burying socialism on a worldwide scale.

"The Luxury of Illusions"
Prague Reporter, 31 July 1968

The internal hierarchy is to be abolished. Every employee, no matter what his job, will receive the same pay . . .

French workers' pamphlet
Assurance Générale de France, 1968

On its way toward the affluent society, Western Europe was shocked by a series of unexpected student-led demonstrations and strikes in 1968 that ultimately brought into question much of what Europe's leaders had been trying to achieve since 1945. Before the riots began, a long period of political passivity and increased consumerism had led some political scientists to suggest that the political calm could only be explained by an "end of ideology" brought about by the inappropriateness of radical solutions in the modern welfare state. The complacent attitudes of students in both Europe and the United States during the 1950s seemed to support the "end of ideology" theory. Although American students became more active in the early 1960s in response to the civil rights movement and then to the Vietnam War, Europe's students remained quiet. Even if students had been dissatisfied, no one expected that their activities could harm the stable, advanced European societies, let alone nearly bring down the government in France.

When unrest did erupt, it was not confined to Western Europe. In Czechoslovakia, students and reform-minded Communist party members overthrew an ossified bureaucratic leadership and blew a breath of fresh air into the party before they themselves fell to Soviet forces in late 1968. Despite the obvious political differences between France and Czechoslovkia, both had come to be perceived by the demonstrators as authoritarian, bureaucratic states that were unresponsive to the needs of the citizenry.

Danger signals, had the political community been alert to them, had already begun to appear in Western Europe by the early 1960s. Dissatisfaction and unrest, first evident in Italy, were directed at the overcrowding in universities, the outdated curriculum, and the authoritarian attitude and archaic teaching methods of the professors. The medieval university, where students could select and fire professors, provided a model for students dissatisfied with the overcrowded, bureaucratic Italian universities. In 1967, the ratio of students to professors in Italy was 105 to 1, as against 13 to 1 in the United States and 23 to 1 in French universities.

The problem was one not merely of numbers but also of the attitude of European professors. A privileged, small professorial elite opposed increasing the number of full professors and making curriculum changes, espcially those aimed at instituting new disciplines such as sociology and psychology. Sociology was being taught in faculties of architecture, because of its relevance to urban planning, but professors in general refused to acknowledge it as a genuine discipline.

Student Unrest in Italy and Germany

As early as 1965, students rioted at the University of Milan and the University of Trent, demanding reforms in the curriculum and a voice in university government. The most militant students at Milan were those in the faculties of architecture, where courses on sociology were taught. At Trent, where the only faculty of sociology existed, students demanded that the university be more closely related to the demands of the modern world. Clearly, the professors had been correct in fearing the consciousness-raising potential of sociology.

Neither the Italian nor the German student movement seriously challenged the stability of their respective governments. Unrest was expected even less among German students than among Italian students. Most Germans were satisfied to share in their country's growing prosperity. In fact, a major reason advanced for Germany's prosperity was the docility of its population. The stereotypical German students were passive information gatherers who would later take their places as good bureaucrats. While the stereotype may have been true for a large segment of the population, it did not fit the considerable number of university students who, according to one interpretation, wanted to atone for their elders' past submissiveness to authority.

Radicalism was at first restricted to a few students who had American connections: Karl Dietrich Wolff had taken part in civil rights marches and anti–Vietnam War demonstrations in the United States, Rudi Dutschke (Red Rudi) had an American wife, and Ekkehart Krippendorf had studied in the United States. German and other student movements borrowed the methods as well as the language of American protesters: "sit-in," "teach-in," "establishment," "military-industrial complex." But, in time, the German student movement spread to a much larger group of students and developed its own ideological positions. Among the many primarily German and European reasons for student dissatisfaction were the extreme authoritarianism of full professors, the failure of European universities to change their antiquated curricula, and a widespread dislike of the bureaucratized ruling structures.

Throughout Europe, extremist student groups lashed out at established authority and a growing consumerism that they felt manipulated the poor and filled the pockets of the rich. In their minds, modern society had destroyed all that was noble in people by channeling their desires solely to material possessions. Primarily from middle-class backgrounds, the student radicals perceived a wide gap between their own background and that of the lower income groups. Their model was not existing Communist parties in the West or East, since they rightly observed that these were bureaucratic, authoritarian entities (see Daniel Cohn-Bendit, *Obsolete Communism*); instead, they chose Che Guevara, Fidel Castro, Ho Chi Minh, Mao Tse-tung, or Leon Trotsky, all of whom represented rebellion against such perceived evils as U.S. imperialism, Communist bureaucratization, and inequality. This radical fringe would have been of limited effectiveness had it not become intertwined with the protests of a larger group of students concerning conditions within European universities— and had the political authorities not disregarded their legitimate protests.

German Student Protests

In 1966, the formation of the Grand Coalition—a political partnerhsip between the Christian Democrats (CDU) and the Social Democrats (SPD)—ignited the first German student protests. Student leaders of the German Socialist Students' Federation (SDS) felt betrayed by the Social

Democrats' actions. They now considered the SPD an integral part of the establishment and therefore uninterested in reform.

The students gave voice to their discontent in widespread protests against the Shah of Iran's repressive regime during his visit to West Berlin in 1967. Underlying this outburst was hostility over German and American support of the shah. The death of one student, Benno Ohnesorg, in the riots steeled the students in their determination to bring down the establishment.

The next target was the conservative newspaper-magazine empire of Axel Springer, whose publications had viciously attacked student leaders such as Rudi Dutschke. When Dutschke was shot by a deranged man at Easter, masses of students rose against Springer and succeeded in disrupting the distribution of his newspapers and magazines. This seemed to promise even greater successes in the future. But unlike French students, who almost toppled the Gaullist regime, German students confined themselves to discussing revolution and engaging in isolated minor confrontations.

The students' inability to act on a major scale has been interpreted as reflecting the German inability to act decisively or, more correctly, as resulting from insufficient public support. Older Germans, with their memories of postwar shortages, were afraid of any challenge to the stability of the government. So an SDS member had good reason to say, enviously, "It isn't that the French students are stronger; it's just that the public is more sympathetic."

Although German students were unable to mount a serious challenge to government policies, they did achieve important changes in the universities. They now have a share in university governance and have impelled most professors to change their teaching methods. As a result of chaotic disturbances in the universities during the height of the turmoil, many professors decided to leave the classrooms for good. And it is now commonplace in German universities to have student-suggested courses in which professors are participants rather than lecturers.

Protest in France

Until 1968, French universities remained so calm that students from Italy and Germany began to doubt the presumed revolutionary mentality of the French. Yet when the explosion came in 1968, it rocked not only the universities but also the Gaullist government. A number of extreme-left student groups—Trotskyites, Maoists, and anarchists—had existed since early in the decade. But they could speak for only a minority of the students and had no support at all among the remaining population.

Another surprising thing about the events of 1968 was that they came at a time of unquestioned prosperity and national grandeur. De Gaulle and France played a far greater role in the world than was justified by the nation's resources. Why, then, did the student-led protests in France spread to a much larger segment of the population than elsewhere and lead, despite a resounding election triumph in late 1968, to de Gaulle's resignation?

The immediate causes of protest in France were little different from those in Italy and Germany. For French students the Vietnam War became a symbol of the misplaced priorities of all military-industrial complexes, including the Gaullist regime. Especially annoying to students was de Gaulle's concentration on foreign affairs and his failure to respond to the often deplorable conditions in the universities. Classes at the famed Sorbonne sometimes had nearly a thousand students enrolled; those students who did not arrive early enough had to listen to lectures on closed-circuit television or buy copies of the lectures. The curriculum was filled with obsolete courses. There was little attention to sociology, modern social problems, or career preparation for those not going on for advanced degrees.

Students directed their dissatisfaction at the French Ministry of National Education and the local faculty governing bodies, which, in their opinion, were more interested in training a few researchers than in preparing the mass of students for less exalted careers. In response to student demands for relevance and participation in determining curriculum, the Ministry of Education fell back on tradition and repression. Another major issue grew out of the ministry's attempt to reduce overcrowding in the universities by making examinations more difficult. Therefore, the student demand for an end to examinations was an attempt to prevent the selection of only the gifted few for advanced degrees.

The Events at Nanterre   Paradoxically, the protests began at the new university at Nanterre, which had been established to relieve the overcrowding at the Sorbonne. Despite its excellent facilities and lower student-teacher ratio, Nanterre became the center for student dissatisfaction because it gave students a greater opportunity to question and sometimes embarrass their teachers. Classes were interrupted often by questions about the Vietnam War or Franco's Spain. Young instructors and assistant professors, having only recently completed the traditional course of instruction, were hard put to answer these questions. Many of the younger faculty members were won over to the idea of reform of the educational system. Moreover, the location of Nanterre near one of the shantytowns housing immigrant laborers promoted debate beyond purely university and academic matters. The contrast between the students' almost entirely middle-class backgrounds and the living conditions they saw around them convinced many students that the government was impervious not only to the need for change in the university but also to the plight of the poor.

The first incident occurred in November 1967 when sociology students at Nanterre, one of the few universities with a separate sociology faculty, resisted the introduction of a reform plan—called the Fouchet Plan—by the Ministry of Education. Student opposition to the plan foreshadowed the later more violent conflict over the role of the student in university governance. Although the Fouchet Plan responded to some student complaints by providing one course of study for those pursuing the *license* (roughly equivalent to our bachelor's degree) and another for those going on for advanced degrees, the course of study was lengthened by one year for some students. However, it was not merely the Fouchet Plan that aroused dissatisfaction. Both the Ministry of Education and the deans of the faculties refused to let students discuss the changes or participate in the faculty committee governing the School of Sociology that debated the plan. This incensed the students and triggered the eruption. The Nanterre protest failed, but it paved the way for the more violent reaction that was to come because it convinced student radicals that a moderate demand for a student voice in university governance was doomed to fail.

During the four months following the initial incident at Nanterre, student radicals (*enragés*) gradually brought together the four major issues of what came to be called the March 22 movement: opposition to Gaullism, rejection of the organization and structure of the university system, student freedom, and protest against the Vietnam War. While the Maoists and Trotskyites concentrated on the Vietnam issue, Daniel Cohn-Bendit led other students at Nanterre against all forms of administrative, political, intellectual, and sexual repression.

Cohn-Bendit's support for sexual freedom was a part of the much larger issue that students should be free to decide their own living conditions on campus. It was also a challenge to the repression that Cohn-Bendit found throughout society. Cohn-Bendit also struck out at the ossified, bureaucratic French Communist party, which he considered unresponsive to demands for change. His campaign instilled a desire for action into a left that had theretofore limited itself to the discussion of revolutionary objectives.

When the university attempted to expel Cohn-Bendit, the conflict enlarged beyond the revolutionary left. First the Sociology Department Assembly, composed of faculty and students, came out in support of Cohn-Bendit. Gaining confidence as they picked up student and faculty support, student leaders became more outspoken and disruptive. When the Vietnam Committee leaders were arrested on March 22, students invaded and occupied the administration building at Nanterre.

From this point onward, many rooms at Nanterre became meeting places for student groups engaged in discussing the university structure, Vietnam, and student-worker relations. By April, many instructors and assistant professors had joined these discussion groups. This breakdown in the traditonal relationships among faculty members unnerved the dean of the Faculty of Letters. Then student leaders proposed two anti-Imperialist days for May 2 and 3 at Nanterre, and a rightist student group began gathering support for an attack on the student radicals. At

The courtyard of the main building of the Sorbonne in Paris, France, filled with left-wing demonstrators during the student protests of 1968. (Magnum Photos)

this point the dean decided to close the university on May 2. With this decision, Nanterre ceased to be the center of agitation. The supporters of the March 22 movement then moved to the Sorbonne and the potentially more volatile Latin Quarter.

The Events at the Sorbonne   The protest at the Sorbonne might have been confined to the university community had not the violent reaction of the police enlarged the scope of the "events of May" to other groups in the society. Cohn-Bendit and other leaders of the March 22 movement had been notified that they were to face the Disciplinary Council of the University of Paris on May 6. More than four hundred leftist students including the March 22 movement leaders, met at the Sorbonne on May 3 to discuss their course of action at Nanterre. The rector at the Sorbonne, acting on the advice of the Ministry of Education, decided to call in the police in the hope that such a move would break the back of the student protest movement.

The sight of students being thrown into police vans on university grounds spread the protest beyond the original student activists, since a centuries-old tradition guaranteed the security of students within university walls and the police had not entered any university grounds since 1791.

In the Latin Quarter that night, police battled thousands of students who were demanding that the imprisoned students be freed. Three days later, on Bloody Sunday, thousands of students and faculty sympathizers armed with cobblestones battled police around the Sorbonne. Although 435 policemen and an untold number of demonstrators were injured, battles continued day after day in the Latin Quarter.

From May 3 to May 13, the protest movement was predominantly a student struggle, fought out in the streets. As the injury toll mounted, public opinion swung to the students. The police were stymied. The more they attacked, the greater grew the number of demonstrators and the popular support for the insurrection. The government turned a deaf ear to student demands to remove the police, open the faculties at the Sorbonne, and grant an amnesty to the imprisoned demonstrators. The confrontation continued.

Ultimately, on the Night of the Barricades—May 10 to 11—students surrounded the Sorbonne and the police with makeshift barricades. The barricades symbolized the students' refusal to abandon the Latin Quarter to the police and provided the psychological boost to keep the protest alive. The police attack on the barricades, followed by beatings of students in the police vans and at police stations, had several repercussions: it launched the general strike of May 13, it brought on the government's capitulation, it triggered the student occupation of the Sorbonne, and it spread the protest far beyond the original student nucleus.

From Student Protest to General Strike It was at this point that the French upheaval went beyond the student uprisings elsewhere. Whereas German students had had to face the wrath of workers, French students got their support. This cannot be explained by wages alone since the French workers were not content to accept a wage increase negotiated on May 27. What is more, neither the Communist party, nor the CGT (*Confédération Générale du Travail*), usually dominated by it, had approved of the workers joining the students.

Workers, especially the young ones, were protesting their lack of decision-making power in an ever more complex bureaucratized world. Among other things, they were asking for greater delegation of authority—the right of comanagement—just as the students were. French industry, led by the major federation of French employers, the *Conseil National du Patronat Français* (CNPF), resolutely supported its traditional authoritarianism. Most industrialists, with CNPF backing, had refused to set up or empower the factory management–workers' councils, *comités d'entreprise,* that had been established under de Gaulle after the war. Although these councils had no real share in management decisions but were limited to overseeing welfare activities and conferring with management, by 1965 only 6,000 of the 25,000 firms had complied with a 1945 ordinance to establish them. During the demonstrations, the *Confédération Français et Démocratique de Travail* (CFDT), a labor union with strength among both blue- and white-collar workers, made its position plain:

> The student struggle to democratize the university and the workers' struggle to democratize industry are one and the same. The constraints and institutions against which the students are rebelling are paralleled by even more intolerable forms in factories, or worksites, in offices and workshops. . . . Industrial and administrative monarchy must be replaced by democratic institutions based on self-management.

Some of those who joined in the protest were white-collar workers who also desired a change in the bureaucracies that governed them. Striking workers at the *Assurance Générale de France* (AGF), the second-largest French insurance company, demanded that those in positions of responsibility "be accountable for their actions to the entire staff," that they be subject to dismissal "by those who have appointed them," and that AGF property and stock become "the property of all, managed by all."

To protesting workers and intellectuals, the Gaullist regime seemed the prime example of an overbureaucratized, technocratic, soulless institution. With the Communist party becoming a part of this mammoth bureaucracy, workers saw little hope for change. Workers' slogans during the uprising, such as "Down with alienation," and "Comanagement," expressed their sense of estrangement.

The strike of producers and journalists at the nationalized French television stations characterized the rebellion of many, including young physicians and other professionals, and showed that the events of May were not restricted to students and workers. Television producers saw the May riots as their opportunity to end the centralization of programming and to gain a measure of local autonomy. Everywhere it was the same—a reaction against the centralization of authority that had stripped the individual of his right to make decisions. As former premier Pierre Mendès-France explained in 1968:

> The dispute is not simply over personalities or institutions. It also dramatizes the determination of Frenchmen no longer to be considered impotent subjects in a harsh, inhumane, conservative society, but rather to perform their own role freely in a society they can look upon as really their own.

With the power of the workers thrown into the fray, the Gaullist regime was soon on the verge of collapse.

On May 13, a twenty-four-hour labor strike brought Paris to a standstill. Nearly 300,000 people marched in a Paris without transportation, electricity, or postal service. Beginning on May 15, throughout France workers occupied factories, set up strike committees, even established worker management of factories. Everywhere the organization and management of the firms were criticized more than the workers' material conditions. Signs appeared proclaiming, THE BOSS NEEDS YOU—YOU DON'T NEED HIM. By May 17, nearly 10 million workers were out on strike and hundreds of young workers had joined the demonstrators in the streets. Action committees and student soviets sprang up all over France. The massive worker response finally forced the Communist party to support labor's demands for reforms. Even the Socialist party, led by Mitterrand, joined the protest movement when it appeared that the Gaullist regime could be toppled. Under duress, the government negotiated a settlement with the CGT that increased wages substantially. But when the rank and file refused to accept the agreement, the nation was at a standstill. Mendès-France and Mitterrand offered an alternative government, but the Communist party refused to cooperate with them.

De Gaulle's Counterattack   Until May 30, when de Gaulle finally acted, the protestors had good reason to believe that the government would fall. Except for the beleaguered police in the streets, little had been heard from the government. When de Gaulle left Paris on May 29, many expected him to relinquish power. Only his close associates knew that he had gone to West Germany to assure himself of the support of French troops stationed there.

Some of the causes for the discontent were not clear to the government when de Gaulle began his counterattack. He was inclined to the belief that worker demands for higher wages and student excesses were primary causes of the unrest. In any case, he had no intentions of tolerating what he considered to be anarchy or allowing his plans for French grandeur to be put in jeopardy.

After visiting the commander of the French troops in West Germany, de Gaulle returned to Paris and announced new parliamentary elections for June and firm measures to end the anarchy. In a television address on May 30, in order to rally all anti-Communist forces to his side, he unjustly accused the Communist party of instigating the outbreaks. Then he presented France with a choice: communism or Gaullism. As the students feared, de Gaulle's pleas were answered with massive support from most of the bourgeoisie and from the provincial areas. Immediately following his speech, 1 million French, including many from the provinces, staged a mass demonstration in Paris in favor of de Gaulle. This outpouring of support demoralized the rioters. Workers ended their occupation of factories, and students left the colleges they had seized. De

Gaulle arrested radical leaders and outlawed leftist student groups. The same forces that rallied to de Gaulle, which had been afraid to speak out during the height of the crisis, gave de Gaulle an impressive majority in the June elections; Gaullists increased their representation in the legislature from 200 to 299, while the left's representation dropped from 194 to 100.

De Gaulle's victory was short-lived. Within a year he felt it necessary to resign. His popularity had begun to fade even in the formerly strong Gaullist areas, and even his own party opposed his authoritarianism and concentration on foreign rather than internal affairs (see chapter 13 for a fuller explanation). The Gaullists remained in power for five years more, losing the presidency in 1974, partly as a result of a changed attitude in France brought about by the events of 1968. During the presidency of de Gaulle's successor Georges Pompidou, national priorities began moving toward happiness (*bonheur*) and away from grandeur. This in itself meant greater attention to pressing domestic problems and less attention to France's world mission.

For the students and workers, the results of 1968 could be measured with greater accuracy: University students gained many of their demands. Overcrowding was relieved by increasing the number of universities from twenty-two to sixty-five. Students achieved a measure of joint management in most universities. Greater autonomy, although much less than what students had fought for, permitted universities to avoid some of the rigid centralization of instruction under the Ministry of Education. The more radical demands for the abolition of exams and an end to the Ministry of Education itself were not granted.

Laborers received increased pay following the riots (see chapter 9), but they were still among the lowest paid in Western Europe. Workers also won the right to be represented through their unions on the governing boards in some enterprises; union representatives were given some free time to carry out union duties during working hours. Although workers did not achieve joint management, which was so important an aspect of their demands in 1968, they did receive flexible hours and a relaxation of the strict factory discipline. French managers, incapable of overcoming their hierarchical conceptions of factory relations, resolutely opposed giving workers a share in factory management.

Unrest in Czechoslovakia: The Prague Spring

Although there are many differences between the unrest in the West and in Czechoslovakia in 1968, there was one major similarity: the revolt against centralized, bureaucratic, authoritarian structures. Under the leadership of Antonin Novotny, Czechoslovakia had instituted rigid centralization by the early 1960s. Even though two Communist parties existed in the country, one in Slovakia and one in the Czech lands, all areas of the country were ruled dictatorially from Prague. Economic growth was slowed by rigid planning and resource allocation. No important decisions of any kind could be made without the approval of the Communist party in Prague.

Novotny was quite popular when he came to power in 1957 because he had rid the party of Stalinists, but his brand of authoritarian national communism soon became as oppressive as the Stalinism before him had been. Changes in Moscow, however, soon weakened his control over the party. The Soviet Union's continued denunciation of Stalin, Khrushchev's desires to decentralize economic decision making at home, and Yugoslav decentralization provided support for Czech reformers. The cultural division of the country into Czech and Slovak segments further weakened centralization.

Soviet denunciations of Stalinism had also encouraged Czech intellectuals to challenge Stalinist dogma at home. Czech philosophers began to undermine the Stalinist system through the study and discussion of such unorthodox Marxists as Antonio Gramsci and Herbert Marcuse. They turned also to Marx's *Economic and Philosophical Manuscripts* where they found a humanist Marxist alternative to Stalinism. Marxism with a "human face" began to appeal to Communist leaders wishing to legitimize their party's leadership. Historians began to weaken Stalinism by a frank investigation of the country's recent history. Czech and Slovak writers and film makers managed to conceal clever satires of the Stalinist leadership from censorship. By the time the authorities adopted harsh measures against the Writers' Union in late 1967, it only increased the resentment of reforming party members who had already been influenced by the criticism. This intellectual opposition would combine with desires for economic reforms and decentralization demands to slowly undermine the Stalinist leadership.

Slovak demands for economic decentralization soon received support from some Czech Communist party members who sought to overcome a severe economic crisis that had begun in 1962. Because of the decentralization in the Soviet Union, Czech and Slovak reformers felt they could try similar reforms at home. The Slovak Communist party ousted its Stalinist leader, Karol Bacilek, in 1963 and replaced him with the reformer Alexander Dubček. From 1963 until 1968, Novotny and the conservatives fought a losing battle against the reformers.

The conservatives' Achilles' heel proved to be the country's economic weakness. Led by economic expert Dr. Ota Sik, the reformers forced Novotny to accept decentralization of the economy in 1966. The reformers had managed to convince party members that excessive planning, excessive resource allocation, and inattention to the consumer-goods industry were responsible for Czechoslovakia's economic ills.

Novotny had been trying to fulfill Czechoslovakia's assigned role in Comecon as the producer of heavy industrial goods and had neglected to develop light industry. The economy had also suffered from a typical East European economic policy: instead of improving factories to overcome low output, Novotny merely built new factories and thus spread raw materials and labor even thinner. The reformers, following changes already instituted in Yugoslavia and the Soviet Union, succeeded in pushing through a system of profit accountability whereby industrial production could be measured more accurately (see chapter 11).

In November 1967, Novotny's position as party chairman received a decisive jolt. His savage suppression of student demonstrators from Charles University in Prague protesting dormitory living conditions brought widespread sympathy for the students and strengthened the party reformers. The reformers, who joined with the Slovaks to form a majority in the Central Committee of the party, compared Novotny's treatment of the students to his opposition to all reformers within the party. With his base of support eroded, it was a simple matter to replace Novotny as party chairman in December 1967. The selection of an outspoken reformer, Dubček, as his successor as first secretary indicated the extent of the reformers' victory. In March 1968, Novotny lost his position as president of Czechoslovakia to a moderate, the military hero General Ludvik Svoboda. The reformers' April 1968 action program was an attempt to legitimize the Communist party by making it defend its actions in public forums. As Dubcek said, "Authority must be renewed, it's never given to anyone once and for all." The program guaranteed the freedoms of assembly, organization, and movement and the protection of minority rights and personal property. It also intended to open up decision making outside the party in order to promote initiative at the local level.

With Novotny gone, a relaxed and joyous mood set in throughout the country. By June 1968, the changed attitude was immediately evident. Caught up in the euphoria, Czechs informed visitors that they needed American economic and diplomatic aid, not military help. The press, carried away with its new-found freedom, was given to exaggerating the changes contemplated by the new leadership. There was discussion of a viable political opposition and a political system that, to the rest of the Communist world, smacked of Western parliamentary government.

This euphoria turned out to be one of Dubček's major problems. Had he tried to prevent such discussion—and he may not have been able to do so—he might have lost the support of his countrymen; but unless he controlled the enthusiasm, he risked losing the support of the Soviet Union. Dubček was never able to free himself from this dilemma. To illustrate Dubček's difficulties, most newspapers published an extremely liberal manifesto, "The Two Thousand Words," written by the most liberal elements in the country. The manifesto promised military support to Dubček if other East European countires or the Soviet Union should invade, and it questioned the achievements of communism in Czechoslovakia. When Dubček did not publicly denounce this manifesto, the other

Eastern European states, all of them Warsaw Pact members, assumed that he approved it.

Despite Dubček's repeated protestations of loyalty to a Communist-dominated state, his actions hardly served to allay fears in other Eastern capitals. In April, Dubček permitted non-Communist political groups to form. Although he assured Moscow that these organizations would not become independent political parties but would be a part of the Communist-dominated National Front, it is easy to see why the Soviets would be suspicious. Furthermore, the Communist party promised to bring to trial all those responsible for the Stalinist-inspired political trials in the 1950s, a move that threatened to incriminate Soviet officials. Some papers had in fact demanded an investigation into Soviet involvement in the apparent suicide of Czech foreign minister Jan Masaryk during the Communist coup in 1948.

From April until the Soviet invasion on August 20, 1968, the "Czechoslovak experiment" became hopelessly entangled with Polish and East German fears that a similar "democratic" contagion might spread to their countries, and with Soviet fears that Dubček's policies might eventually lead Czechoslovakia out of the Warsaw Pact. As early as March, Poland's leader Władysław Gomułka had been upset by students' shouts of "We want a Polish Dubček." But East German party secretary Walter Ulbricht was not merely upset, he feared that his weaker authoritarian regime could be overthrown by similar reformers.

Czech leaders had already established contacts with West Germany in order to open trade relations between the two countries. The Soviet Union was willing to permit more internal liberalization in Czechoslovakia than in East Germany or Poland, but was afraid that Czech reformers might eventually demand an independent foreign policy similar to that of Romania. Soviet hard-liners conjured up visions of an anti-Soviet alliance of Yugoslavia, Romania, and Czechoslovakia.

Certainly Soviet military experts had much more to fear from a Czech withdrawal from the Warsaw Pact than they did from Romanian disaffection. Not only did Czechoslovakia border on Western Europe, but its withdrawal from the Warsaw Pact would have cut Eastern Europe in two and would have severely complicated military strategy in case of war with the West. The Czech reform was also ill-timed. Stung by the Soviet humiliation in Cuba in 1962, the Sino-Soviet imbroglio, Albanian support for China, and Romania's withdrawal from the Warsaw Pact, Soviet hard-liners were adamant in their opposition to Czech liberalization and possible loss to the Warsaw Pact countries.

Soviet and East European leaders, with the exception of those of Romania and Czechoslovakia, began their offensive against Dubček with the Warsaw Letter of July 14–16, ordering Czechoslovakia to reestablish the dictatorship of the Communist party or face invasion. Dubček stoutly rejoined that the Communist party was still in control, and he convinced the Soviet leadership. Still, it took a meeting between Dubček and Soviet leaders at Cierna in Slovakia to avert the intervention of Warsaw Pact armies that just happened to be on maneuvers in Czechoslovakia at the time.

Even though Dubček convinced the Soviets that the Communist party was still in control and that Czechoslovakia had no intention of pulling out of the Warsaw Pact, East Germany and Poland were not convinced. These two states demanded a meeting of all East European leaders at Bratislava in Slovakia on August 3. At that meeting Dubček was forced to sign the Bratislava Declaration promising not to go beyond the Polish reforms instituted by Gomułka in the late 1950s.

Between the Bratislava meeting and the invasion on August 20, several decisions by Dubček were seen by other Communist governments to have violated the Cierna and Bratislava agreements. When Tito and Romanian leader Nicolae Ceauşescu were given warm receptions in Prague, this was taken to indicate that Dubček was not going to adopt the attitude of other East European states toward Yugoslavia and Romania. More damning was a Czech draft of new party statutes permitting the existence of factions within the Communist party. Such actions hardly convinced Ulbricht and Gomułka that Dubček was opposing ideological heresy even in the Communist party.

However, Soviet leaders may already have decided on intervention as early as the Bratislava meeting. To Soviet leaders, the advantages of an invasion seemed to outweigh the disadvantages. They realized that they would be sharply criticized in the international press for a time, but they were convinced that it would not last much longer than the 1956 outburst following the invasion of Hungary.

Because of the policy of détente with the United States, with its recognition of mutual spheres of influence, Soviet leaders did not fear American intervention. On the other hand, the military and political example that Czech disaffection would have established was intolerable to many Soviet leaders.

After Dubček had been taken into custody by invading Soviet forces, President Ludvik Svoboda refused to appoint as new premier a conservative opponent of Dubček's and a man already approved by the Soviets, Alois Indra. The adoption of passive resistance by most of the population further frustrated Soviet designs to make the invasion appear to have been no more than a change of government. Some Czechs did throw Molotov cocktails or stones at Soviet tanks, but for the most part they merely tried to place obstacles in the way of the Russian advance. Svoboda's refusal to negotiate with the Soviet Union until Dubček was released probably saved Dubček's life, but nothing could be done to save the Czech experiment. Leaders subservient to Moscow were soon installed in office—Gustav Husák as party secretary and Lubómir Strougal as prime minister—press censorship was renewed, and Soviet troops were kept on Czech soil to protect the country against "imperialism."

Common Protest Themes

Many themes united the protest movements of 1968. Students in Paris and Prague lashed out at a repressive society and yearned for greater participation. Political repression was more direct and more in evidence in Czechoslovakia; but French students, workers, and intellectuals had similar feelings of frustration and powerlessness under Gaullist paternalism.

Although the French state did not engage in direct repression, it did centralize decision making at the top in all administrative, economic, and cultural institutions. In the eyes of the Parisian demonstrator, there was little difference between a Communist party bureaucracy in Prague and the bureaucratized institutions in France, including the French Communist party.

In both countries, demonstrators hoped to weaken or destroy the isolated bureaucratic structures with participation from below. Czech students' desires for greater intellectual freedom, in combination with the antibureaucratic efforts of economic reformers, brought down the government. Similar objectives in France nearly toppled the Gaullist regime in May 1968; contributed to the subsequent disenchantment with de Gaulle's authoritarianism, even among Gaullist deputies; and compelled his resignation in 1969.

FURTHER READING

Although a large number of works have appeared on the 1968 French upheaval, only a few are of major importance. Probably the best general coverage is in Adrien Dansette's *Mai 1968* (1971). The most complete coverage of the workers' role is provided by Pierre Dubois et al., *Grèves Revendicatives ou Grèves Politiques* (1971). On the role of the Communist party, see Daniel Cohn-Bendit's left-wing denunciation, *Obsolete Communism: The Left-Wing Alternative* (1968), and Richard Johnson's balanced study, *The French Communist Party versus the Students* (1972).

A highly critical treatment of the student rioters can be found in Raymond Aron's *The Elusive Revolution* (1968).

Four generally favorable treatments of the actions of the rioters are Daniel Singer, *Prelude to Revolution* (1970); J. J. Servan-Schreiber, *The Spirit of May* (1969); Alain Touraine, *The May Movement: Revolt and Reform* (1971); and Alfred Willener, *The Action-Image of Society* (1970). Singer believes the 1968 upheaval proved that a full-scale Socialist revolution is still possible in the developed Western countries. He maintains that there were valid reasons for the upheaval in France. He unfortunately spends much of his time arguing for revolution and outlining the proper revolutionary strategy to achieve a Socialist society.

J. J. Servan-Schreiber argues that the upheaval was caused by French cultural and social rigidity. This theme is similar to the one presented by Michael Crozier in *The Stalled Society* (1973). Touraine feels that the upheaval was a legitimate response to the advanced capitalist societies and their managers, who manipulate and control in an authoritarian manner all aspects of society. The events in France were therefore merely one instance of many possible revolts against postindustrial societies. Willener believes that a combination of political and cultural resistance gave the upheaval its intensity. The student demands for a new culture included action, egalitarianism, anti-authoritarianism, self-management, and imagination.

The most comprehensive treatment of the Czech upheaval is H. Gordon Skilling's *Czechoslovakia's Interrupted Revolution* (1976). A short treatment by an expert on Czech history is Z. A. B. Zeman's *Prague Spring* (1969). Eyewitness accounts are provided in *A Year Is Eight Months: Czechoslovakia in 1968* (1970), and Zdenek Mlynar, *Nightfrost in Prague: The End of Human Socialism* (1980). While William Shawcross has provided some insights into the character and policies of Dubček in *Dubček* (1970), a full understanding of his role may never be available because of the lack of information, especially on his meetings with Soviet leaders. Two studies that attempt to place the Czechoslovakian revolt into a broader perspective are Vojtech Mastny, *Czechoslovakia: Crisis in World Communism* (1972), and William I. Zartman, *Czechoslovakia: Intervention and Impact* (1970). The role of the press can be followed in Frank L. Kaplan's *Winter into Spring: The Czechoslovak Press and the Reform Movement, 1963–68* (1977). Kaplan contends that the press served as one of the primary factors in bringing about Soviet intervention as well as bringing about the reform movement. Milan Simecka's *The Restoration of Order: The Normalization of Czechoslovakia* (1984) is a sound analysis of the period after the uprising. Zdenek Suda provides an excellent history of the Communist party in *Zealots and Rebels: A History of the Communist Party of Czechoslovakia* (1980).

For the Soviet decision to invade, see Jiri Valenta, *Soviet Intervention in Czechoslovakia, 1968: Anatomy of a Decision* (1979), and Robin Edmonds, *Soviet Foreign Policy: The Brezhnev Years* (1983).

13 Eastern Europe and the Soviet Union in the 1970s and 1980s: The Quest for Legitimacy as Ideology Fails

How the Polish people and the Hungarian people will decide to structure their societies and lives will be their affairs.

Mikhail Gorbachev, 5 July 1989

The Soviet Union and Eastern Europe have experienced three major phases since 1968, with Soviet directives or experiences the predominant influence in the first and third phases and indigenous East European developments decisive in the second stage. The first phase ensued immediately after the suppression of the 1968 Czech uprising when the Soviet Union sought to shore up its Eastern European Empire through a carrot-and-stick approach. Adherence to the Warsaw Pact and Comecon were stressed, and any attempts to challenge the supremacy of the Communist parties or to develop political pluralism were rejected. To make such a policy palatable, the Soviet Union encouraged consumerism through subsidies and Western credits in order to legitimize Communist regimes through an improved standard of living and to divert attention from the absence of political freedom. Although these policies succeeded in the early 1970s, the serious worldwide economic downturn after the midseventies coupled with the failures of economic planning in the Communist bloc brought huge debts and economic chaos to Eastern Europe.

The second phase emerged in the late seventies in Poland and Hungary. The economic downturn and political immobilism of the leadership permitted opposition groups to form openly and challenge the Communist elite, and this began the rejection of the Soviet economic model of centralization and one-party dictatorship. A third phase began about 1985 with the coming to power of Mikhail Gorbachev in the Soviet Union; the further development of the Polish Solidarity movement in the eighties, with its extensive political consequences; and the rejection of Communist party leadership throughout Eastern Europe. As will be discussed below, these phases have resulted primarily from a long-term social transformation of the elite; the failure of the centralized Communist socioeconomic model, with its attendant political consequences; and the emergence of internal opposition movements.

The Brezhnev Years, 1964–1982

Although little is known of the deliberations that gained Leonid Brezhnev leadership of the party after Khrushchev's removal as general secretary, his subsequent activities indicate that he was chosen by the Politburo because he was a good party man who would respect the rights and privileges of party members. This so-called "respect for cadres" attitude inhibited reform since it was very difficult to replace ineffective party functionaries with reform-oriented members. Brezhnev immediately ended the division of the party into agricultural and industrial branches, thereby restoring authority to local officials. Still, his quest for institutional stability did not exclude economic reform. He continued to stress an increase in the production of consumer goods, a policy some have called "goulash communism," in order to raise living standards and support for the government. However, the lack of political change continued to slow a shift from producer to consumer goods.

Brezhnev was immediately confronted with a growing division in the Communist world. China had become an independent center among Communist nations as a result of its struggle with Khrushchev and Albania, and Romania had used the Sino-Soviet rift to gain increasing autonomy. But Brezhnev was not prepared to permit an East European country to end the monopoly of a Communist party, as the Warsaw Pact invasion of Czechoslovakia was to show (see chapter 12). After crushing the Czech revolution in 1968, the Soviet Union promulgated the so-called Brezhnev doctrine. By claiming that the autonomy of any Communist party or state was limited by the interests of "socialism," the Soviet Union reserved the right to intervene in "Socialist" countries to protect "Socialist" gains. The Soviet Union now had established a principle upon which to base Soviet intervention in Eastern Europe, and Brezhnev had secured his position atop the Soviet ruling elite. With Eastern Europe cowed after the Czech invasion, West German recognition of the existing East German borders and increasing economic and cultural exchanges with the West, Brezhnev was able to concentrate attention on areas other than Eastern Europe in the early seventies.

Brezhnev's greatest legacy would undoubtedly be the enhanced foreign role of the Soviet Union. The enormous increase in military spending, often at the expense of the consumer-goods industry, made the Soviet

Union a military equal of the United States. The 1972 SALT negotiations with the United States on military hardware acknowledged this parity. With their feelings of military inferiority receding and their sphere of influence apparently secured—West German recognition of the East German borders and the crushing of the 1968 Czech uprising—Brezhnev moved toward détente with the West.

From the beginning, a misunderstanding existed between the Soviet Union and the United States over détente. While the United States thought détente prevented the Soviet Union from challenging the United States outside the Soviet sphere of influence, the Soviet Union thought it meant seeking a relaxation in relations with the United States and Western Europe but continuing competition for influence and position throughout the world. The Soviet Union thought the competition, called "separatism" by some experts on Soviet policy, justified since the United States had frozen the Soviet Union out of Middle East peacemaking efforts and was challenging the Soviet Union in such places as North Vietnam and along the Soviet Union's southern border. In their opinion, Iran, which had been heavily armed by the United States, and Afghanistan were within the Soviet sphere of influence. Since the United States could challenge them in these areas, the Soviet Union reasoned that they could challenge the United States in Africa and Latin America. As it became clear to the Soviet Union that the United States perceived separatism to be inconsistent with détente, the advantages of détente began to be outweighed by the disadvantages. Finally, with the American move to befriend China (the Soviet Union hoped détente would isolate China), the American Senate's failure to ratify the SALT II arms treaty, the American opposition to Soviet treatment of dissidents and Jews, and Brezhnev's failure to obtain the American economic credits and technology he hoped would flow from détente, the Soviet Union lost interest in détente with the United States. However, Brezhnev and the Western Europeans continued to pursue détente since the trade ties and technological exchange between them made it almost indispensable (see chapter 14). With American president Ronald Reagan's attacks on Soviet policy after 1980, the gap between the Soviet Union and the United States widened until Gorbachev came to power in 1985.

The Soviet Union's Eastern European Empire became an increasing economic and military burden in the midseventies. The 1975 Helsinki Accords, which Brezhnev hoped would confirm Soviet hegemony in Eastern Europe through Western recognition of existing borders, were subsequently used by the West to demand greater autonomy for Eastern Europe. But the biggest shock to Brezhnev and the Politburo was the Polish Solidarity movement that began in the late seventies.

Added to the difficulties caused by the growing Polish unrest in the early eighties was a continuing Soviet war against Afghan rebels and enormous economic difficulties in every Eastern European country. With its own economy suffering severely (see chapter 11), the Soviet Union became—during Brezhnev's final years—a mighty military empire, threatened increasingly by its economic weaknesses and the continuing dissent and dissatisfaction among its many components.

In the midst of this tumultuous period, Brezhnev died. The political machinations that resulted in bringing Yuri Andropov to the post of party secretary in November 1982 demonstrate the effectiveness of the one major achievement of the party in the post-Stalin period—collective leadership. The choice of Andropov over Brezhnev's longtime friend and collaborator Konstantin Chernenko was made possible by political maneuvering prior to Brezhnev's death. When Andropov was appointed to the Central Committee secretariat in early 1982, he became one of four men who held positions in both the Politburo and the party secretariat and was thus in an excellent position to succeed Brezhnev. Andropov's attempts to reform the economy by increasing labor productivity were cut short by his death in February 1984. Although Mikhail Gorbachev had the support of the Andropov faction to succeed Andropov, Gorbachev apparently agreed to let Chernenko take the reins as general secretary in order to avoid a battle in the Central Committee. The Chernenko faction also agreed to continue Andropov's economic reforms. Chernenko, at age seventy-two, became the oldest man to become general secretary, surpassing Andropov's record by four years. His early death prevented him from making any impact on Soviet policy.

The Gorbachev "Phenomenon"

Chernenko's death on March 10, 1985, brought Gorbachev to power. Gorbachev's policies of "new thinking" (*novoe myshlenie*), "restructuring" (*perestroika*), and "candor" (*Glasnost*) have unleashed forces in the Soviet Union and Eastern Europe that many in the Soviet leadership may find intolerable, especially where they challenge Soviet dominance or the Socialist egalitarian model. His new thinking includes an openness about internal affairs and efforts to "democratize" internally when necessary in order to obtain efficiency. He is particularly intent on breaking down the excessive centralization of economic decision making and eliminating bureaucratic inertia.

There are long-term precedents for Gorbachev's domestic reform efforts. Khrushchev's failed reforms, as well as the limited reform efforts of Brezhnev and Andropov, are evidence of earlier attempts at reform that could not be realized due to internal obstacles. As Andropov's second secretary, Gorbachev had been responsible for economic reforms, and it was expected that he would continue such efforts once he took power. Gorbachev benefits from a long-term transformation of Soviet society that provides a growing technical elite who are impatient with the Soviet Union's technical backwardness.

Mikhail S. Gorbachev, Communist party general secretary since 1985, was elected president of the Soviet Union in March 1990 for a five-year term and reappointed general secretary of the Communist party at the Twenty-eighth party conference in July 1990. (Wide World)

Gorbachev brought an entirely new tone to international affairs as well. In foreign affairs his new thinking includes removing the nuclear threat, international interdependence and cooperation, and "reasonable sufficiency" in armaments. These views, articulated at the Twenty-seventh Party Conference in 1986, were soon followed by deeds. The past Soviet foreign policies of Stalin and Brezhnev were criticized, Soviet troops were pulled out of Afghanistan, agreements were reached with the West over reducing intermediate-range missiles in Europe, and extensive on-site verification was permitted.

Gorbachev is instituting his reforms slowly in order not to alienate his conservative opposition. Before the Twenty-seventh Party Conference, he concentrated on increasing discipline and investment and reducing alcoholism. When he began to restructure economic activity by promoting

Gorbachev's policies of openness and restructuring made it possible in February 1990 for thousands of Soviet citizens to demonstrate in Moscow against the Communist party's monopoly of power. (Wide World)

incentives, he reassured conservatives by promising them that reforms would save socialism. Reform is also being tied to a more efficient, stronger military. Gorbachev argues that the previous system was undermining Soviet defenses.

It was only when Gorbachev's attempts to restructure the Soviet economy encountered political and bureaucratic opposition that he began to stress openness and democracy in order to spread economic decision making outside the party and bureaucratic elite. Without political reforms, Gorbachev's economic reforms will fail just as those of Khrushchev and Premier Aleksey Kosygin did in the mid-1960s. He announced democratization in early 1987 and claimed, "It is either democracy, or social inertia and conservatism; there is no other way, comrades." But attempts to decentralize decision making and inject profit incentives and wage differentiation into the Soviet economy have met opposition from entrenched interests and workers who oppose the growing inequality in a Socialist economy. Such opposition is driving Gorbachev even further toward political reforms that will make it possible to realize his economic reforms.

The political reforms began in June 1988 when a new Congress of People's Deputies was established to select members of the Supreme Soviet, which debates issues and vetos government appointments. This two-stage election process and the fact that only two-thirds of the Congress is elected from candidates previously approved by the party does not make it a democratic body in the Western sense. But the fact that the Congress's debates are both open to the public and are reported to the public brings many issues into the open that previously would have been decided exclusively by the party. In June 1989, the Supreme Soviet showed some limited authority when it rejected eight of the seventy-one party candidates for the ruling Council of Ministers headed by Prime Minister Nikolai I. Ryzhkov. Gorbachev's moves in the early 1990s to strengthen the powers of the presidency indicate that he may utilize this new government structure to circumvent Communist party conservatives and gain the support of the modernizing elite to institute his programs. The party's dramatic renunciation of its monopoly of power in February 1990, in effect a rejection of Lenin's dictatorship of an elite revolutionary leadership, appears to be another stage in Gorbachev's disassociating himself from a weakened party. Gorbachev was appointed to a five-year term as president by the Parliament in 1990 in order to free him from the opposition in the Communist Politburo. The Communist party cadres are, however, still powerful in 1990 and could block these moves. If he succeeds, Russia will have a more Western-style presidency and the Communist party, which is now seriously weakened by division between reformers and hardliners and is breaking up into provincial parties, will become only one of many competing political groupings.

The impact of *Glasnost* and *perestroika,* no matter what happens to Gorbachev, will likely make a permanent return to the past impossible. The social transformation of the population, which has made many of Gorbachev's reform efforts possible, will probably also keep the Soviet Union moving in the direction of reform. The political and economic transformation of Eastern Europe that Gorbachev's reforms have furthered will also be difficult to contain unless the Soviet Union is willing to return to the repressive policies of Stalin or Brezhnev. Gorbachev's pronouncement, "How the Polish people and the Hungarian people will decide to structure their societies and lives will be their affair," indicates that he is willing to permit Eastern European countries a wide latitude in deciding their own affairs. These affairs, as we will see below, may go further than Gorbachev and the Soviet elite expected or desired. But any Soviet attempt to intervene directly will be extremely costly to the Soviet Union in terms of their own reform movement and their new image throughout the world.

Soviet leaders must also contend with dangerous Separatist movements in the Baltic states (Latvia, Lithuania, and Estonia) and among its Muslim and Turkish populations. The decisive election victory of a Lithuanian independence movement, the Sajudis Popular Front, in the Soviet Union Union's first sanctioned multiparty elections in February 1990 set the stage for the Lithuanian declaration of independence in March. Latvia followed with its own declaration of independence in April 1990. Estonia began a more gradual withdrawal from Soviet jurisdiction in April but has not officially declared its independence. Internal problems may make it impossible for the Soviet Union to deal affectively with Eastern Europe or even retain their authority within their own country.

Poland: Solidarity and Beyond

Stemming from workers' resentment of a government that brutally put down labor strikes in 1970 and 1976, the Solidarity union movement eventually challenged and broke the Communist party's monopoly of power in Poland and threatened Communist parties elsewhere. The government of Edward Gierek (1970–1980), that replaced the Gomułka regime after the 1970 strikes, successfully lulled the population by providing ample consumer goods in the early seventies. Underwritten by Soviet subsidies and Western loans, this consumer policy collapsed in the midseventies when Western loans were reduced and Soviet energy prices were increased. When Gierek attempted to cut budget deficits by raising the price of necessities in June 1976, workers' protests forced a rescinding of the price increases the next day. The government's use of force destroyed the support Gierek had built up by his consumerist policy and began a widespread self-government movement, the so-called Self-organization of Polish Society. This antigovernment movement was bolstered by the selection of the archbishop of Craków, Karol Cardinal Wojtyla, as Pope John Paul II on October 2, 1978. When the pope visited Poland in June 1979, the massive outpouring of support for him further stimulated the movement for self-government. The enthusiasm for the Catholic church and the Self-organization movement contrasted sharply with the scorn accorded the government. The Gierek regime fell when it foolhardily attempted to raise meat prices to overcome a rapidly increasing government indebtedness.

The major strikes of August 1980 brought a change in government. Gierek was replaced by Stanislaw Kania; but more important, authority began to shift from the Communist party to a workers' organization that had emerged out of the Self-organization of Society movement, Solidarity. At first the party was forced to make concessions to Solidarity because of the threat of strikes that would cripple an already weak economy. The workers, led by Lech Wałesa, won the unprecedented right in a Communist country to strike and organize independent trade unions. The government also agreed to let the state radio broadcast Catholic Sunday Mass as well as agreeing to a series of concessions that opened the government to closer public scrutiny of its activities.

By January 1981, Solidarity had become more than a labor union. With 10 million members and a National Coordinating Council newly elected by regional councils, Solidarity had become an alternative to the government. Faced with the overwhelming popularity of Solidarity, the Communist party could only delay and make limited concessions they did not intend to honor. Solidarity was torn between the moderates and radicals, or "cautious" and "audacious," as one commentator (Martin Malia) called them; the moderates sought to gain their ends through negotiation, while the radicals thought only confrontation would be effective. When further agitation forced the party to recognize Rural Solidarity in March 1981, the regime came near to collapse. Solidarity, led by the moderates around Lech Wałesa, called off any action for four months in order to let the party recover and avoid possible Soviet intervention. Although Soviet efforts to depose the party secretary Kania failed in June, the threat of intervention prevented radicals from gaining control of the movement. Still, Solidarity's proposal for self-management in heavy industry struck at one of the sources of party strength by removing the appointment of industrial managers from the party and putting it in the hands of the workers. In the initial phase of the struggle between the party and Solidarity from August to December 1981, Solidarity challenged the very basis of Communist authority. With the unprecedented meeting of Solidarity's National Congress in September 1981, it had become a real alternative to the party and a threat to Communist systems throughout Eastern Europe. From this point on, Solidarity threatened direct appeals to the masses if the party did not act on such issues as self-management. Solidarity's acceptance of a limited self-management offer led the more radically oriented National Congress to propose that a Council of Economic Control share power with the party and the Catholic church. The party, led after October 1981 by General Wojciech Jaruzelski (prime minister between February and October), proposed a National Front that would have reduced Solidarity and the church to minor partners in a ruling triumvirate. Jaruzelski succeeded in forcing Solidarity into the "radical" demand for democratic elections in December. Apparently, having decided upon the use of military force even before December—the organization of the military takeover required long-range planning as well as Soviet cooperation since the Russians controlled much of Poland's military logistics—Jaruzelski merely needed further evidence of Solidarity's radicalism in order to convince the military to follow him. The Soviet Union obviously pressured Jaruzelski—who was sympathetic to Moscow in any case—to use Polish troops to put down a movement that destroyed Communist authority. Jaruzelski's imposition of martial law and a military dictatorship in December 1981 demonstrated the bankruptcy of party rule and the widespread support for Solidarity.

Although outlawed, Solidarity survived and grew underground. While Jaruzelski felt strong enough to lift martial law in 1983, he could not obtain the support of the Polish population, despite many concessions, nor could he solve Poland's burgeoning economic problems. With no means of solving the economic crisis without cooperation from labor and apparently with Gorbachev's approval, Jaruzelski opened talks with Lech Wałesa and Solidarity in February 1989. These "Round Table" talks produced an agreement to set up a new one-hundred-member Senate with veto

Lech Wałesa, leader of Solidarity, lifts his arms in celebration after the organization signed an agreement with the Polish government in August 1980 allowing independent labor unions. (Alain Dejean—Sygma)

power over all legislation, to permit 35 percent of the seats in the lower house (*Sejm*) to go to the opposition and to establish a new office of president who would be chosen by Parliament. Solidarity granted the Communist party a majority in return for a promise to move to fully competitive elections in four years and a popularly elected president in 1995. The government calculated that these concessions were necessary to secure economic cooperation from the public and foreign aid. The Communists also calculated that Solidarity would become a junior partner in a Communist-led coalition government and would have to share responsibility for economic reforms that would initially bring unemployment, higher consumer prices, and a hold on wage increases.

The government's expectation that Solidarity would not be able to organize an effective campaign in time for the elections proved to be wrong.

The June 1989 elections produced a resounding victory for Solidarity: union-backed candidates won 99 of the 100 seats in the Senate and all of the 161 *Sejm* seats set aside for the opposition. But an even more humiliating result was that of the 299 *Sejm* seats allotted to the Communists and their allies, only five party members gained the required 50 percent of the votes needed although they were running unopposed. Those failing to gain the required vote included the prime minister, Mieczyslaw Rakowski, and interior minister, Czeslaw Kiszczak. In order to save the Round Table agreement, Solidarity and the government coalition reached an agreement to elect the rejected candidates in a runoff election. The government also failed to gain Solidarity's participation in a governing coalition led by the Communists that would have made it possible to impose the necessary economic reforms. Although Jaruzelski ultimately obtained sufficient votes for the presidency (all of the required 270), it was only because of Solidarity's maneuvering in order to save the compromise with him.

The most remarkable change came in August 1989 when the Communists, unable to gain a majority in the *Sejm,* permitted a Solidarity-led cabinet. Although Solidarity leaders would have preferred to wait until they could form a government on their own, they bowed to strong popular sentiment to form a coalition government with the Communists. The Solidarity prime minister Tadeusz Mazowiecki formed a cabinet with eleven Solidarity, four Communist, four Peasant, and three Democratic party members. Mazowiecki has had extreme difficulty in solving Poland's economic problems. Although Poland has obtained some loans and technical assistance from the West, the attempt to establish free-market mechanisms will bring about extreme hardship before it can become effective. Poland must also compete with other East European countries for the necessary financial support.

Poland's future could be changed radically by Gorbachev's replacement with a hard-liner in the Soviet Union. Left alone, Poland appears headed toward a multiparty political democracy. Solidarity itself will experience a multifaceted division, including a traditional Roman Catholic branch and a secular liberal branch. In order to gain some legitimacy, the Communist party changed its name to Social Democracy in late January 1990. However, there is such popular opposition to the former Communist leadership that Social Democracy will probably not play a major role in future governments. A January 1990 opinion poll found that less than 3 percent of the country intends to vote Communist in coming local elections. There is also a competing Union of Social Democracy party with which the former Communist party must compete. The Solidarity led government's economic plan to save the Polish economy will divide Solidarity members. Solidarity has in fact been tied to the large unproductive industries, such as coal mining and ship building, and therefore will probably split over any reforms that may require eliminating inefficient industries. Poland's attempt to establish a free-market economy has also divided those who wish to move slowly and those, including Wałesa, who want an accelerated strategy.

Hungary

Party secretary János Kádár's transition from villain to father figure continued in Hungary with the New Economic Mechanism (NEM) after 1968. Although Kádár had crushed the opposition to the Communist dictatorship after the 1956 rising, he began to relax the heavy hand of authoritarianism before 1968 with a relatively liberal travel policy, increasing economic freedoms, and public discussion of issues. Peasants, given freedom to till private plots and sell their produce, forgot the brutal reimposition of collectivization between 1959 and 1962. Both Khrushchev's de-Stalinization and the economic reforms continued by Brezhnev supported Kádár's relaxation. But it was the former NEM with its transfer of much decision making from centralized agencies to the factories, local self-management of the collective farms, and a partially free market that brought a greater measure of well-being to Hungary than to other Eastern European countries and greater popular support for the Communist party than anywhere else in Eastern Europe (see chapter 11 for details). These reforms became a model for some of Gorbachev's post-1985 reforms.

But the time was not yet ripe for such innovative changes in Eastern Europe. Pressure from the Soviet Union and from Hungarian workers who did not approve of the wage differentiation introduced by the NEM brought about the suspension of many NEM policies between 1972 and 1978. Against the economic logic of the NEM, workers' wages were raised by the party's Central Committee, and fifty large enterprises were put under the direct administration of the Council of Ministers. Some of those responsible for the NEM lost their places in the party leadership. When the worldwide oil crisis brought higher energy prices and the Western recession reduced orders for Hungarian products, the Hungarian economy went into a tailspin. By 1988, Hungary's foreign debt had increased to $20 billion from only $1 billion in 1970, or $1,500 per capita. Budapest's image as a showplace of the East suffered a corresponding collapse. When these economic difficulties continued in the early eighties, Kádár lost the admiration that he had built up with such difficulty after 1956 and the Communist party lost the claim to legitimacy it had gained in the sixties.

The worsening economic situation apparently convinced party officials and the Soviet Union to permit Hungary to renew its economic reforms after 1978. Party reformers such as Karoly Nemeth, Ferenc Havasi, Miklos Nemeth, and Imre Pozsgay took over important functions within the party. The reformers argued that economic advance needed political freedom to free up decision making and pushed through many reforms in the early eighties as Kádár's health slipped. Society and even the Communist party fragmented in the mideighties as economic difficulties multiplied and as reformers and conservatives clashed. Many of the economic reforms, with their emphasis on increasing output and profits, caused economic dislocation and unemployment. Attempts to decrease the foreign debt led to import restrictions, consumer goods shortages, and a dimming of Hungary's image.

Supported by Gorbachev's reforms in the Soviet Union and his oft-repeated emphasis on letting Eastern Europe find its own way to socialism, the Hungarian reformers slowly gained control of the government. In May 1988, Kádár relinquished his post as first secretary to Karoly Grosz; and two leading reformers, Rezso Nyers and Imre Pozsgay, were promoted to the ruling Politburo. But Grosz's ineffectiveness led to the naming of Miklos Nemeth as premier in early 1989, with Grosz retaining the party leadership. Grosz's position was further weakened in June 1989 when a four-member Presidium—including Grosz, Nyers, Pozsgay, and Nemeth—took over party leadership. When the reformist majority changed the name of the party to Socialist in October 1989, a small right-wing broke away and renamed itself the János Kádár Society. Pushed by reformers, the Parliament changed the name of the country to the Republic of Hungary, dropping the word People's, and voted 333 to 5 to adopt the "values of both bourgeois democracy and democratic socialism." A completely new constitution is to replace this modified consitution sometime in 1990. Although the Hungarian Communists had been responsible for instituting many reforms, they gained only about 5 percent of the vote in The April 1990 elections. The Communists have also split into the Hungarian Socialist party and the more hard-line Hungarian Socialist Workers' party. The center-right Hungarian Democratic Forum received 43 percent, the Alliance of Free Democrats received about 20 percent, and the Independent Smallholders party about 16 percent of the vote. Following the elections, Democratic Forum put together the first completely noncommunist government when they joined with the small holders and the Christian Democratic party in a center-right coalition.

Any governing coalition will face enormous reconstruction problems. The introduction of market forces will produce unsettled economic conditions at the same time that political reforms take place. As in Poland, the joy that should come from the demise of the dictatorial Communist regimes is overshadowed by a fear of what lies in the future.

East Germany: From Communist Orthodoxy to "Unification"

After losing 3 million people to the West between 1945 and 1961, the building of the Berlin Wall permitted East Germany to halt the emigration of its skilled work force and achieve by far the best economic performance in the Eastern bloc in the sixties. This so-called economic "miracle" (see chapter 11) was overshadowed, however, by the West German economic resurgence that continued to undermine the leadership of hard-line party secretary Walter Ulbricht. But Ulbricht's New Economic System for Planning and Management (NES) gained the support of many through its decentralization of economic decision making. Ulbricht's opposition to increased contacts with West Germany during the early stages of détente and Willy Brandt's *Ostpolitik* (or Eastern policy) led the Soviet Union to demand and obtain his replacement in May 1971.

East Germany's international isolation ended in September 1971 with the Berlin Accords, signed by Berlin's occupying powers and not by East Germany. These accords forced East Germany to increase contacts with West Germany and permitted West Berliners to make regular visits to East Germany. Forced to deal with the West Germans, East Germany then made its own agreement, the Basic Treaty of November 1972 with West Germany. The German Democratic Republic (GDR) gained West German de facto recognition, something it had always sought, and in 1973 admission to the United Nations.

The new first secretary, Erich Honecker, took a more pragmatic, technocratic approach to policy than Albricht. But he tried to limit the impact West German tourists, television, and trade would have on his regime by curtailing contacts as much as possible. In order to counteract the West German's land-of-plenty image, Honecker concentrated on raising living standards, increasing the supply of consumer goods, improving housing, and enhancing the East German image through athletic excellence. At the same time there was an increased stress on preserving the Communist monopoly of political power through enhanced ideological training, the supression of dissent, and criticism of Western materialism. Despite some economic success, Honecker's restriction of intellectual freedoms limited his regime's popular acceptance.

With few natural resources, East Germany was hit hard by the worldwide energy crisis in the seventies. West German tourist money and economic subsidies helped counteract some of the consequences of high-energy costs and convinced Honecker that the West German contacts were worth continuing when détente waned in the late seventies after the Soviet invasion of Afghanistan.

Gorbachev's drive for reform in the Soviet Union and the messages he relayed to the East German leadership during his visit to commemorate the fortieth anniversary of the German Democratic Republic proved to be instrumental in the massive peaceful protests that forced Honecker to resign in October 1989. Gorbachev's message to Honecker that the Soviet troops in East Germany would not take part in any suppression of popular discontent was leaked to the public. He also encouraged reform-minded Communists to oust Honecker. The East German leadership was therefore in a weakened position in late 1989 and feared its own troops would join the protesters. Gorbachev's encouragement of the reformers bol-

The Berlin Wall, seen here under siege by West Berlin demonstrators, served as a symbol of the Cold War and, later, of East German economic and political failure. It was opened in November 1989. (Wide World)

stered the internal opposition that had been building since early in the year. Honecker later admitted that he was responsible for rigging the May 1989 local elections that covered up a large protest vote against his regime and initially led to extreme frustration and desperate attempts by East Germans to leave the country. The pent-up anger against the Communists and the lure of a better life in West Germany led to a massive flight to the West through Hungary and a rapidly deteriorating economy. The Honecker government used police force against the demonstrators until October 9, when it was suddenly called off. Why force was no longer used is not clear. But it is doubtful that any force would have succeeded against the massive number of demonstrators and Russian opposition to the use of force. On October 18, Honecker resigned.

In November 1989, an interim Communist government opened the Berlin Wall in the hope that it would stem the exodus of the East German population to the West. But as the exodus continued at the rate of about 2,000 a day and the economy continued to deteriorate, East German leaders were forced to turn to West Germany for aid. These contacts received support from continuous demonstrations of East Germans for unification with West Germany. In order to distance itself from past policies, the Communists changed their name to the Party of Democratic Socialism and admitted opposition groups to the government. The emergence of indigenous reform parties such as the New Forum quickly lost out to the East German branches of the West German Social Democrats and Christian Democrats. Although opinion polls predicted that the Social Democrats would win the March 1990 elections in East Germany because of the greater support for their social policies, the Christian Democrats and the two small parties won 48 percent and the Social Democrats only 22 percent of the vote. The Christian Democrats' emphasis on national unification appealed to a private East German yearning for German national greatness that was never eradicated from individual consciousness by the Communists. The Christian Democats formed a coalition government with the Social Democrats in April 1990 in order to negotiate a union with West Germany. Financial integration started in July 1990 when East Germany accepted the West German mark as their official currency. Unless the Soviet Union objects, all-German elections will be held in December 1990.

Czechoslovakia: From Winter to Spring Again

The suppression of the Czechoslovak reform movement in 1968, the so-called Prague Spring, produced the most dejected, sullen population in Eastern Europe. Gustav Husák, placed in power in April 1969 by the Soviet Union, purged those who had not already fled and stripped the population of all political responsibility. In order to gain some meager legitimacy, Husák instituted a policy of consumerism to divert attention from the loss of political freedoms. With aid from the Soviet Union, the government directed funds toward improving the material condition of the population. Those owning cars increased from 1 in 17 in 1971 to 1 of 8 in 1979. The number of weekend homes, *dachas,* increased from 128,000 in 1969 to 225,000 in 1981. Government officials overlooked a large illegal or second economy that provided the population with additional goods and income. Much of the population sullenly accepted a materially improved but depoliticized life-style. As a young construction worker remarked, "We don't look forward to much, and we don't trust anyone" (*Time,* 18 April 1988).

Only in the midseventies did the Husák regime begin to experience any concerted opposition. A parallel or alternative culture led by two groups of intellectuals, Charter 77 and VONS (the Committee for the Defense of the Unjustly Persecuted), kept up a discussion of public issues despite persecution. Many dissidents, such as Vaclav Havel, published their criticisms from prison while others, Milan Kundera and Josef Skvorecky being the most famous, criticized the regime from exile. By avoiding any direct denunciation of the regime and publishing their thoughts in the Underground press, these intellectuals provided an alternative culture to the official one.

Beginning in the midseventies, the Czechoslovakian economy began to suffer severely because of high-energy costs and shortages. The situation worsened in the late seventies due to failed investment policies that left 30,000 industrial projects uncompleted in 1981. Severe shortages of consumer goods forced the government to divert funds from investment in order to prevent inflation and stem social unrest. Husák's failed policies finally led to his downfall in 1987. His successor as general secretary, Milos Jakes, promised "restructuring" but instituted no meaningful reforms.

Popular opposition to the Communist regime jelled on November 17, 1989, when a student-organized demonstration in Prague was brutally broken up by riot police in Wenceslaus Square. Students had been actively organizing opposition for over a year in youth clubs; in Underground publications; in discussion clubs; and, together with intellectuals, in literary magazines. The police action ignited strikes at Charles University and among actors supporting Vaclav Havel. Havel and his supporters in Charter 77 joined on November 20 with other opposition groups, including members of the People's and Socialist parties, to form Civic Forum, the later governing movement. When the enormous demonstrations beginning on Monday, November 21, came off without government intervention, the right of the popular masses to organize and voice their complaints had been established. The government was probably unsure of the loyalty of its armed forces. But more important, obtaining even a Communist majority ready to defend the failed system with force would have been difficult. The Civic Forum, involved in the most open discussions imaginable in the Magic Lantern Theater, used the support of the demonstrations, they often chanted "Long live the Forum," to force a meeting with the government on November 23. The Forum leadership was also aware that Gorbachev had been pressing the Czech leadership to implement reforms. Forum received further support through the daily press conferences that were broadcast worldwide to admiring audiences.

On Friday, November 24, Forum's image was further enhanced when Alexander Dubček, the leader of the 1968 Prague Spring, joined the revolutionary forces. Immediately after Dubček's address to the crowd in Wenceslaus Square, Jakes and the entire Communist Politburo resigned. The final blow to the Communist leadership came on November 27, with a successful general strike and an agreement by the government to negotiate with Forum. These negotiations led to the Communist government's agreement to delete the leading role of the Communist party from the constitution, remove Marxism-Leninism as the basis of education, and form a coalition government with Civic Forum. After November 29, the Slovak liberation movement, Public against Violence (PAV), joined with Civic Forum. Round table discussions between Forum, PAV, and the Communist party led to a Communist-led coalition government (only eight of the twenty-one ministers were Communists) and the resignation of President Husák on December 10. Havel's election as president on December 29 capped off the meteoric rise of Civic Forum. As an umbrella-protest organization, Forum could become a party or break up into many parties. In the June 1990 elections, Civic Forum won 53 percent of the vote for the Czech legislature (House of the People) and its Slovak counterpart, Public Against Violence (PAV) won 32.5 percent of the Slovakian legislative vote. The Communists won only 13.6 percent of the vote in the Czech lands and 13.8 in Slovakia. Forum and PAV are expected to form a coalition government with the Christian Democrats who won 12 percent of the vote in the Czech lands and 19 percent in Slovakia.

Czechoslovakia is probably best positioned of all the East-Central European countries to solve its economic problems. It does not have a huge foreign debt ($320 per capita in 1988), it had started to move away from rigid central planning before the November upheaval, and it has now begun to move toward a free-market economy.

Bulgaria: The Dutiful Ally

Bulgaria has been the only East European country not to oppose Soviet hegemony in any way. Bulgarian loyalty resulted from a friendship stretching back into the nineteenth century (see chapter 7) and complementary economic interests. Bulgarian concentration on light industry, agriculture, agricultural industry, electronics, and tourism fit in well with the Soviet economic plans for Eastern Europe. The Soviet Union supplied Bulgaria with heavy industrial goods, oil, and investment funds.

Politically, Bulgarian developments mirrored those in the Soviet Union. Both Communist party leaders Georgi Dimitrov and Vulko Chervenko dutifully followed the Stalinist nationalization and collectivization of industry and agriculture under a strict Communist party rule. When Khrushchev called for an Eastern European division of labor in the sixties, Bulgaria, under its new party head Tudor Zhivkov, obligingly complied. Zhivkov also used Khrushchev's denunciation of Stalin in 1961 to eliminate the Stalinists such as Chervenko from party offices. Zhivkov's rule of over thirty-five years (1954–1989) was characterized by what Joseph Rothschild describes as "autocratic yet accessible and with a common touch" that suits the Bulgarian egalitarian social tradition. Although the Bulgarian economy experienced steady long-term growth, it began to encounter serious energy and technological obsolescence problems in the eighties. Soviet oil supplies and investment funds also dried up as the Soviet Union had to seek funds externally for its own reforms. Bulgaria's attempts to Bulgarize all its minorities, especially the forced emigration of many ethnic Turks, produced international opposition to Zhivkov's regime.

In response to change throughout the Soviet bloc, the Bulgarian Communists appear to have made only a minimal amount of change in order to prevent the rise of any popular opposition. The removal of Zhivkov from power on November 10, 1989, and his subsequent indictment for inciting ethnic hostilities and for corruption and mismanagement, permitted his successors to blame him for all Bulgaria's ills. The party's surrender of its legal monopoly of power in January 1990 was another move by the new party leader Alexander Lilov and head of state Petar Mladenov to establish party legitimacy. The party's attempt to bring opposition groups into the government in February 1990 failed when they all refused to join a Communist-led coalition government. The opposition groups realize that they can only lose by joining a coalition: any government successes would be claimed by the Communist majority and any failures would have to be shared by all coalition partners. The lack of a democratic tradition in Bulgaria and the weakness of opposition groups such as the Agrarian party and the Union of Democratic Forces led to a Communist, now renamed Socialist, party victory in the May-June elections. The Socialists won 211 seats and the Union of Democratic Forces, a coalition of 16 parties and organizations, won 144 seats in the 400-seat Parliament. The party's control of the media will also prevent the opposition from effectively campaigning. However, a stagnating economy could cost the Communists some support. Significant change in Bulgaria appears to lie far in the future.

Romania: The Collapse of the Last Stalinist Bastion

Romanian opposition to Soviet hegemony began in the 1960s during the last years of Gheorghiu-Dej's leadership and continued under his successor, Nicolae Ceauşescu (1965–1989). Khrushchev's desire for a division of labor among Comecon countries relegated Romania to that of raw-materials supplier and light-industry manufacturer. Popular support for the Communist party's drive for a fuller economic development produced a government legitimacy seldom obtained among East bloc governments. Romania's independent course received further support from the Sino-Soviet split. Not only were China and Romania still following a Stalinist course, but China also opposed Soviet interference in the affairs of other Communist countries. Romania also did not provide Soviet leaders with sufficient reason for a military intervention. Although Romania refused to cooperate fully economically, it maintained strict one-party rule, thus providing no ideological heresy; and it did not withdraw from the Warsaw Pact but only refused to participate in maneuvers. Romania's finest hour came when it refused to participate in the invasion of Czechoslovakia in 1968. Although Ceauşescu despised the direction the Czech reforms were taking, he wanted to uphold the rights of Communist countries to develop as they saw fit. The rapid economic development in the sixties and growing contacts with the West, for economic reasons, brought Romania and Ceauşescu international acceptance.

The seventies and eighties were to produce another image of Romania. Ceauşescu's Stalinist attitudes and growing megalomania led to the loss of popular legitimacy and international respect. As the Soviet Union developed more reformist practices, with a relaxation in the Communist domination of power, Ceauşescu became even more despotic in order to maintain power. Ultimately, he came to trust only family members whom he placed in important government positions. Rothschild has described his rule as "dynastic socialism" to distinguish it from that of other Communist countries.

Any legitimacy Ceauşescu's regime possessed turned sour in the late seventies when energy and capital shortages led to a ruthless austerity program. Rationing of energy was enforced by secret-police squads sent out to enforce compliance. Naturally, the Soviet Union was not inclined to offer extensive aid to save such a maverick. Ceauşescu turned to draconian measures to halt the decline. In order to increase Romania's traditionally low agricultural productivity, Ceauşescu attempted to replace all small farming plots and some 8000 small villages with huge agroindustrial centers where production would presumably be more efficient. They were also intended to eliminate ethnic-cultural differences, such as the Hungarian and German settlements in Transylvania. He also attempted to proletarianize cities such as Bucharest by destroying the old bourgeois quarters and replacing them with huge Socialist housing developments with no private bathrooms or kitchens. In order to increase the population, Ceauşescu forbade all forms of contraception. Medical units were stationed in factories to detect pregnant women and penalize them if no birth occurred. Women who did not conceive by age twenty-five had to pay an additional tax of between 10 to 15 percent of their salary. These policies increasingly isolated his regime from society, from the West, and from the Gorbachev regime. Ceauşescu reduced the foreign debt to a low $50 per capita by 1988 by exporting almost everything that was not tied down, but this also caused mass misery by producing many shortages.

Such conditions produced a reaction like no other in Eastern Europe and have continued to influence the postrevolutionary situation. Instead of large, peaceful demonstrations and limited retaliatory violence by the Communist regimes typical elsewhere, Romania experienced savage government reaction. The revolutionary period began when government troops and security agents, the *Securitate,* massacred hundreds of demonstraters in Timisoara on December 17, 1989. The demonstraters had protested the treatment of a minister and police brutality against a small group of people who tried to protect the minister. The crowd eventually marched to Communist party headquarters where they were ruthlessly broken up by the *Securitate* and police. Ceauşescu apparently wished to avoid the fate of other East European regimes and chose to follow the Chinese policy of massive repression. That the regime lasted only four days longer, however, apparently resulted from the extremely hostile popular resentment of his rule. After returning from a scheduled trip to Iran, Ceauşescu delivered an arrogant radio and television speech on December 18 in which he took responsibility for the government action against those he termed "hooligans" and "Fascists."

His speech on December 21 in Bucharest to a crowd that Ceauşescu had packed with his supporters revealed to him the popular hostility to his regime and steeled the resolve of all those who opposed him. After some preliminary favorable responses from his supporters, student-led chants of "Ceauşescu the dictator" were spontaneously picked up by most of the crowd. Ceauşescu fled the scene but was captured by the military. Four days later, on December 25, Ceauşescu was executed by forces of the Council of National Salvation. Violent confrontations then took place between the army and the hated *Securitate* until the latter were either killed or driven into hiding. This council later set up a 253-member provisional Council for National Unity that acted as a Parliament until national elections in May 1990. These elections gave the National Front 80 percent of the vote. Although the Council of National Salvation contends that it had been established six months before Ceauşescu's downfall, it appears that this may be only a ploy to reestablish the legitimacy of the Communists who make up its membership. Despite the fact that the

Communist party relinquished its legal monopoly of power, the continued dominance of the Council of National Salvation has brought about frustration and attacks by those who want the immediate establishment of more democratic forces. Opposition groups such as the Union of Democratic Forces, the Social Democratic party, and the Agrarian party did not have enough time to mount effective campaigns for the May elections. Since the Communist-dominated Council of National Salvation controls the media, oppositions groups did not get adequate national exposure. Still, hatred of the Communists is so intense among students and intellectuals in Romania that it is doubtful that the National Salvation government can soon quiet the opposition. Crowds now chant, "Everything is the same as before" and "We didn't die for socialism, we died for real democracy, Western democracy." A real revolutionary atmosphere still exists in Romania and many solutions are possible, including a military dictatorship to quiet the unrest. The hatred and anger that were a part of the Ceauşescu regime will not dissipate quickly.

Yugoslavia: From Tito to Turmoil

Although the growing fragmentation that engulfed Yugoslavia in the 1980s appears on the surface to be primarily the result of Marshal Tito's death in 1980, it had its origins as far back as the fifties, and Tito is partially responsible for it. The self-management system instituted in 1952 (see chapter 2) increased local authority by decreasing centralized economic decision making. Since the fifties, a battle between reformers and conservatives has become entangled with ethnic-provincial allegiances: in broad terms, the reformers have sought decentralized decision making and are associated with the more economically advanced northern regions of Slovenia and Croatia, and the conservative centralizers have found their main strength in Serbia.

Since the self-management system was originally conceived as an ideological counter to Soviet pressures in the period 1948–1952 and has continued to serve as a justification for the Yugoslav system, it cannot be lightly discarded no matter how poorly the economy performs. Its justification was that self-management brought the worker to the center of economic-political decision making and was therefore a much more advanced form of socialism than the Soviet system. The League of Communists took on the role of guide and teacher rather than undisputed decision maker.

Several decisive battles were decided in favor of the reformers in the sixties, while the economy improved steadily and provided Yugoslavia, predominantly Croatia and Slovenia, with the highest standard of living in Eastern Europe. A new 1963 constitution gave increased autonomy to local enterprises and administrative units (communes) at the expense of federal, central authority. It paved the way for major reforms, known as "the Reform" by Yugoslavs, in 1965. The Reform introduced mainly market mechanisms for the economy, cut out government subsidies for weak enterprises, and moved to integrate the Yugoslav economy into the world market. The immediate economic dislocation caused by the Reform led to a massive migration of Yugoslav workers to Western Europe and to their enrichment in comparison with those who stayed at home. Conservative opposition to these reforms was dealt a severe blow when the centralist Serbian-oriented vice president Rankovic fell from power in 1966. His fall gave the reformist forces renewed momentum and further restricted federal power. However, the reformist forces' aggressive promotion of efficiency (Croatia, Slovenia) versus equality (southern Yugoslavia) and local autonomy, led Tito to purge them in 1971. He was later to remark that he should have used this occasion to tame the "eight little autarchies." But the constitution had just been amended in 1970 to give prime authority to the six republics and two autonomous provinces. The federal government retained authority over foreign policy, defense, and some financial and monetary policies. Decentralization was expanded even further with the 1974 constitution that reduced the federal government's domestic duties to primarily that of arbitrator among the republics and provinces and gave Kosovo and the Vojvodina veto rights over federal decision making.

A change in the self-management system in 1966, with the aim of bringing workers into the decision-making process and of reducing the managerial-technocratic monopoly of local power vis-à-vis local party officials, added to the decentralization of power. Tito apparently believed that self-management so designed would reduce ethnic particularism by breaking up the solidarity of ethnic blocs. The result of this reform was ineffective, inexperienced work councils that had to depend on the technocratic-managerial elite. When the economy turned down in the late seventies and eighties, self-management began to be viewed as a sham.

The mideighties brought a renewed debate between reformers and conservatives with the economic decline. With local enterprises enabled to negotiate loans, Yugoslavia's indebtedness increased rapidly to over $20 billion. These loans were in many cases ineffective since there was no centralized Yugoslav market and local enterprises often lacked the capability to compete internationally.

The solution worked out for Tito's successor contributed to the decline of the center. Unable to groom a true "Yugoslav" successor and aware that a Serb or Croat would not be acceptable as a long-term leader, Tito promulgated the "standing rules" for collective leadership in October 1978. Leadership was to be rotated: the presidency of Yugoslavia and the party were to be rotated annually among the republics, and the prime ministership was to be rotated every four years. Such limited continuity in leadership coupled with strong powers of the republic areas limited the effectiveness of the central government. As the government immobilism worsened and the economic problems grew, the decentralization achieved earlier came increasingly into question. Some demanded recentralization, while others demanded even more free-market mechanisms and greater provincial autonomy. Changes in 1988 increased the amount of land an individual could hold privately from ten to thirty hectares (approximately twenty-five to seventy-four acres), granted the right to strike, and increased private enterprise. But the economic problems increased nationalism and enhanced the possibility of a conservative solution. A strong national Serb leader, Slobodan Milosevic, encouraged Serbs to dream of a greater Serbia by limiting the autonomy of Kosovo and the Vojvodina. At the same time the reformist provinces of Croatia and Slovenia moved toward an even freer economy and greater independence from the center. After the Yugoslav League of Communists voted to permit a multiparty system on January 22, 1990, the Slovenian Communist party broke away from the national party on February 4 and renamed its party the Party for Democratic Renewal. Despite this Communist transformation, the Slovenian multiparty elections in April 1990 produced a separatist majority and a decisive defeat for the Communists. A coalition of six parties, called EMOS, won 55 percent of the vote for the social-political chamber. The Communist party finished third, behind the Liberal Party, with only 20 percent of the vote. Two weeks later, a center-right Croatian Democratic Alliance, advocating autonomy for Croatia, won 70 percent of the vote for Croatia's social-political chamber. The Democratic Alliance's stress on Croatian nationalism appears to have been the decisive issue, since the Communists also advocated a democratic system and autonomy for Croatia.

The present prime minister, Ante Markovic, has moved rapidly to modernize Yugoslavia's economy. He moved to gain international convertibility for the dinar on January 1 by tying it to the West German mark. He has also attempted to open the country to heavy foreign investment by permitting 100 percent foreign ownership of business and 99 percent ownership of banks. He contends that Communist party squabbles are secondary since the Communists represent only a small portion of the population. However, his economic reforms may not have sufficient time to work before Yugoslavia is pulled apart by its ethnic differences. It appears that a total Yugoslav solution is impossible short of a military coup or a massive civil war between north and south. But Yugoslavia's demise has been predicted before and has not come to pass.

Conclusion

While the overthrow of authoritarian regimes in 1989 was aided by Gorbachev's policies and his sometimes timely interventions, the main impetus for change came from within these countries. All the upheavals except that in Romania were marked by massive peaceful demonstrations

EASTERN EUROPE
(EAST–CENTRAL EUROPE)

Tallinn
ESTONIA

LATVIA
Riga

LITHUANIA

Vilnius

Moscow

EAST
Berlin
GERMANY

POLAND

Warsaw

U.S.S.R.

Nov. 1989, Berlin Wall opened
March 1990, Free elections

1980, Solidarity formed
August 1989, Solidarity–led government

(Gorbachev 1985–)
Feb. 1990, Communist party renounces
monopoly of power

Prague
CZECH
AND
SLOVAK
FEDERATIVE
REPUBLIC

Dec. 1989, Havel
elected president

March 1990,
Free elections

REPUBLIC
OF
HUNGARY

Budapest

ROMANIA

Dec. 21–25, 1989, Overthrow of
Ceaucescu

YUGOSLAVIA

Belgrade

Bucharest

Jan. 1990, Multi-party system
April 1990, Free elections in Slovenia
April-May 1990, Free elections in Croatia

BULGARIA

Sofia

Jan. 1990, Communist party renounces
monopoly of power

Tirane
ALBANIA

0   250   500

Scale of Miles

against the leadership. The widespread opposition to the Communist leadership had long existed. For instance, Vaclav Havel wrote of the double life characterized by a public support but private disdain for the regimes. Once the populations perceived that some possibility existed to overthrow the regimes, the private side was given vent in the massive demonstrations. The fact that no major counterrevolution occurred except in Romania can be attributed to the Communist hierarchy's loss of faith in their right to rule. They no longer thought the system worth defending. Communist central planning and thought control contained the seeds of its own destruction.

Further Reading

Scholarly works on recent developments in the Soviet Union can be divided into those having a positive view of the reform efforts and those expecting failure and a return to a more oppressive system in the Soviet Union and Eastern Europe. Those studies with a more positive assessment include the works of Jerry F. Hough, *Opening Up the Soviet Economy* (1988) and *Russia and the West* (1988), and Moshe Lewin, *The Gorbachev Phenomenon: A Historical Interpretation* (1988). Both contend that long-term economic and social trends are supportive of reform efforts and that any reversion to an oppressive system would be temporary since it would fly in the face of the social transformation of the country. Basile Kerblay's *Gorbachev's Russia* (1989) also stresses the social transformation that has primed the Soviet Union for reform. Donald R. Kelly's *Soviet Politics from Brezhnev to Gorbachev* (1987) is a clear, thorough analysis of political change. Paul Marantz's *From Lenin to Gorbachev: Changing Soviet Perspectives on East-West Relations* (1988) argues that real changes and a lively internal debate concerning Soviet foreign policy indicate that Gorbachev is earnest about change and that reform has spread beyond Gorbachev himself.

Studies that are pessimistic include Zbigniew Brzezinski, *The Failure of Communism* (1988), and Judy Shelton, *The Coming Clash* (1989). Shelton believes that the Soviet leadership is losing its ideological hold and that it cannot produce economic improvement soon enough to legitimize itself.

Excellent studies of the Soviet economic reforms include Jerry Hough's book cited above; Marshall I. Goldman's, *Gorbachev's Challenge: Economic Reform in the Age of High Technology* (1987); and Mark R. Beissinger, *Scientific Management, Socialist Discipline, and Soviet Power* (1988).

Outstanding studies of the intricate ties between external and internal politics include Seweryn Bialer, *Stalin's Successors: Leadership, Sta-*

bility and Change in the Soviet Union (1980) and The Soviet Paradox: External Expansion, Internal Decline (1987), and the Paul Marantz study cited above.

Competent general studies of Eastern Europe are Stephen Fischer-Galati, ed., *Eastern Europe in the 1980's* (1981); Karen Dawisha, *Eastern Europe, Gorbachev and Reform: The Great Challenge* (1988); and Adam Bromke, *Eastern Europe in the Aftermath of Solidarity* (1985). Two excellent studies that have provided much information and insight in this chapter include Joseph Rothschild, *Return to Diversity: A Political History of East Central Europe since World War II* (1989), and J. F. Brown, *Eastern Europe and Communist Rule* (1988). A recent solid study of the Balkan countries is Barbara Jelavich, *History of the Balkans, vol. 2, Twentieth Century* (1983).

For Poland, see the works cited in chapter 7 and Timothy Garton Ash, *The Polish Revolution: Solidarity* (1985). An interesting first-hand account is provided by *A Way of Hope: An Autobiography*, by Lech Wałesa (1987). For a recent history of Polish events, see the current literature in the *New York Review of Books, The New Republic, Contemporary Review, Foreign Affairs*, and *Atlantic*. Martin Malia's "Poland: The Winter War" in the *New York Review of Books* (18 March 1982) is especially informative. Neal Ascherton's *The Polish August: The Self-Limiting Revolution* (1982) provides a good description of revolutionary events from August 1980 to July 1981. The most recent events are analyzed by Timothy Garton Ash in the *New York Review of Books*.

For recent Hungarian affairs, see Charles Gati, *Hungary and the Soviet Bloc* (1986); Bennet Kovrig, *Communism in Hungary: From Kun to Kadar* (1979); and Hans-Georg Heinrich, *Hungary: Politics, Economics and Society* (1986).

A fine study of the domestic and foreign policy of the German Democratic Republic is A. James McAdams's *East Germany and Détente: Building Authority after the Wall* (1985). David Childs's *The GDR: Moscow's German Ally* (1983) is a sound study.

For Czechoslovakia, see Milan Simecka's *The Restoration of Order: The Normalization of Czechoslovakia* (1984). J. F. Brown's *Bulgaria under Communist Rule* (1970) and John D. Bell's *The Bulgarian Communist Party from Blagoev to Zhivkov* (1986) are indispensible. For Yugoslavia, see Slobodan Stankovic's *The End of the Tito Era: Yugoslavia's Dilemmas* (1981). For an outstanding account of the history of the self-management system, see Harold Lydall's *Yugoslav Socialism: Theory and Practice* (1984). Nora Beloff's *Tito's Flawed Legacy: Yugoslavia and the West since 1939* (1986) and Steven R. Paulowitch's *The Improbable Survivor: Yugoslavia and Its Problems, 1918–88* (1990) demystify Tito's role in the formation of the Yugoslav state after 1945 and provide a more realistic assessment of Tito's responsibility for Yugoslavia's present dilemmas.

14 Political and Economic Trends Since the 1960s in Western Europe

The Old Testament prophets did not say, "Brothers, I want a consensus."

British prime minister Margaret Thatcher in response to the presumed British consensus in support of the welfare state

European economic and social renewal in the sixties provided strong support for the political status quo. Conservatives in Western Europe and Socialists in Scandinavia continued their decades-long rule during this long period of economic resurgence. But the economic downturn that began in the early seventies, described below, helped unseat incumbent political parties throughout Europe as electorates voted for change. A leftward trend that had begun in Western Europe in the sixties as a result of relaxed East-West tensions and a growing Socialist political moderation accelerated rapidly in the seventies. The apparent moderation and national-centered policies of some Western European Communist parties, or "Eurocommunists" as they were called for a brief period in the seventies, gained them some additional support. Europeans no longer thought that a vote for a Communist candidate was necessarily a vote for Moscow. The continued relaxation of tensions between East and West and Europe's desire to pursue an independent foreign policy had promoted a policy of détente, or increased understanding and contacts, between Western Europe and the Communist world. These contacts, especially the economic ones, were maintained or even enhanced despite the United States–Soviet animosity in the early eighties. Gorbachev's assumption of power again relaxed East-West tensions and permitted a resumption of contacts.

As a Western European economic crisis deepened in the late seventies, incumbent political parties either lost office or had their majorities sharply reduced. In Great Britain, West Germany, Norway, Sweden for a time, and the Benelux countries, parties on the left either lost power or influence. In France, Italy, Spain, and Greece the moderate Socialist left gained power or reduced the Conservative hold on political office. In all Western European countries the Communist parties lost support beginning in the late seventies due to Soviet actions in Afghanistan and Poland; Socialist parties' successes at the polls; and a popular rejection of a radical leftist program of more extensive welfare, higher taxes, and more nationalization of business enterprises. Political changes in the major Western European countries are described more fully below.

End of Authoritarian Government in Southern Europe

The fall of three authoritarian governments in the seventies—in Portugal, Spain, and Greece—had broad significance for both the inhabitants of those countries and for Europe as a whole.

Portugal   Most remarkable was the overthrow in Portugal. In 1974, the seemingly impregnable rightist dictatorship of Premier Marcelo Caetano, successor to Antonio Salazar, was suddenly overthrown in a coup d'état carried out by junior army officers and a few sympathetic generals. These officers had been forced to serve repeated tours of duty in Portugal's African colonies of Angola, Guinea-Bissau, and Mozambique; they had received low pay and few promotions; and they had been given inferior equipment with which to fight Soviet-armed guerrillas.

To make matters worse, a new government policy permitted university students to obtain second-lieutenant's bars after undergoing a short course at the military academy. This debasement of their own stature was what drove the officers to form the *Movimento des Forces Armades* (MFA), or Armed Forces movement, which was responsible for toppling the Caetano regime.

The political views of these young officers had been shaped by constant contact with disgruntled Portuguese university students who had been compelled to serve in Portugal's African territories and by captured African guerrilla leaders who convinced many of the officers that they were no less manipulated and suppressed than the native Africans. The students and captured guerrilla leaders, many of them Communists, persuaded these junior officers that only a thoroughgoing change in Portuguese society and leadership would improve the position of the military. This explains the strong Socialist-Communist sympathies of the original military leadership.

These captains and majors became convinced that they could not win the colonial wars and that they were going to be blamed for the defeat in Africa, as they had been blamed for the loss of Goa to India in 1961. At that point they began to question their support for what they believed to be a corrupt, inefficient, reactionary government in Lisbon that was prepared to sacrifice the army in order to save itself.

The revolt in April 1974, euphorically dubbed the "Carnation Revolution" because the revolutionaries wore carnations (the new symbol of socialism), brought to power General António de Spínola. He had recently been dismissed from his post as the army's deputy chief of staff because he had openly urged the political democratization of Portugal and an end to the costly colonial wars in Africa. Because of Spínola's widespread popularity among the Portuguese population, the MFA threw its support to him in order to achieve some respectability for the military junta.

The government of Spínola, filled with Conservative older officers, stood well to the political right of the MFA leaders who had planned and carried out the military coup. Although Spínola and the twelve-man Co-ordination Committee of the MFA immediately began to disagree over colonial and domestic policy, the MFA did not want to replace him until it had secured its own power in Portugal. Spínola opposed granting immediate independence to Guinea-Bissau and Mozambique and giving the Communist party a role in the government, both of which were MFA policies.

Spínola lost the first round when the MFA forced him to accept a member of the Coordinating Committee sympathetic to the Communists, Vasco Gonçalves, as prime minister. When the MFA and the Communist party forced Spínola to cancel a rally of his supporters in September 1974—considered a coup attempt by the MFA—Spínola resigned the presidency. He apparently hoped he would be called back to power; not an impossibility, when the Communist influence among the military leadership was overcome by the country's predominant Conservative and Center forces.

Portugal's military leaders have been guided by their conviction that a powerful Parliament, dominated by the Socialists and parties to their right, would halt the military's policy of nationalization and impede the movement toward greater equalization of wealth. But the Communist party had supported the military's economic and social program, and it therefore exerted a major influence on the military leadership until November 1975. At that time the removal of the Communist-backed Gonçalves because of Western pressure, coupled with the opposition of more conservative military leaders, led military units sympathetic to the Communists to attempt a coup. Its failure reduced Communist influence among military leaders and in the country as a whole.

Nationalization of the Communist-dominated television and radio stations and reorganization of the Communist-influenced, state-owned press severely weakened the Communists. The now-moderate Council of the Revolution, the executive authority led by General Francisco Costa de Gomes, acted rapidly to remove leftist military officers from the armed forces.

The authority of the military has declined as a result of the ideological differences among military leaders and the parliamentary election victories of the Socialist party (led by Mário Soares) and the bourgeois parties. The Socialist victory in the April 1976 parliamentary elections and the demand for a return of parliamentary government put the Socialist party in a dominant position in the newly formed legislature. The Socialists shared power with the newly elected president António Ramalho Eanes, the army chief of staff who had won 61 percent of the presidential vote in the June 1976 elections. Before the 1982 constitution, the government was responsible to the president.

The results of the 1976 election showed how far the political leadership had moved to the right since the revolution. A once-popular leftist military leader, Major Otelo Saraiva de Carvalho, received only 16 percent of the presidential vote, whereas Eanes, who was responsible for crushing the rebellion of leftist military units, won easily. The original revolutionaries, whose goal was a complete revamping of society, were now disillusioned and powerless.

Power began to shift toward the right after 1976. But a series of minority governments between 1976 and 1987 produced weak administrations and caretaker governments. The 1987 elections provided a dramatic change when Anibal Cavaco e Silva's center-right Social Democratic party gained an absolute majority of the votes and seats in the legislature. Cavaco, who had headed a minority government since 1985, was aided by the disunity of the left, a rapidly improving economy, and low energy prices. The Communist party faded to only 12 percent of the vote in 1987. A two-party system may be forming as the Socialist party gained 22 percent of the vote in 1987 and recent polls indicate that their support has risen to about 36 percent of those polled. Although Portugal has experienced rapid economic growth since 1985, it is still the poorest country in Western Europe. But increasing investment from the EC, which it joined in 1986, and the Common European Market coming in the nineties may give Portugal's economy the boost that it needs. Portugal hopes it can become the California of Europe by concentrating on semiexotic produce, high-technology goods, and tourism.

Spain In terms of its size (38 million inhabitants) and ultimate importance in any possible European union, democracy's gain in Spain was the most significant south European transition. General Francisco Franco, supported by the Catholic church, the army, and the fascistic Falange movement, made only enough concessions in his decades-long authoritarian government to avert rebellion. Many liberals were appeased in the 1960s by the relaxation of press censorship, the abolition of military courts, rapid economic advances, and the election of an opposition comprising one-sixth of the Parliament. Even before Franco's death in 1975, reform movements among more progressive members of his regime, younger army officers, and the Catholic Opus Dei movement supported a relaxation of authoritarianism. Through a long process of negotiation with opponents of Franco, these more moderate supporters of Franco prepared the way for a surprisingly smooth transition to democratic government under Franco's hand-picked successor, King Juan Carlos, and his prime minister, Adolfo Suarez González. Elections in 1977 gave power to a Union of the Democratic Center (UDC), with Suarez González as prime minister. The Socialists (PSOE), perceived as moderate by most voters, received a very substantial 28.5 percent of the vote. The Communists (PCE) received only 9.3 percent of the vote because of their radical image.

Spanish reverses resulting from the economic slump that began in Europe in the midseventies temporarily undermined some of the popular support for democratic rule. Some Spaniards looked back nostalgically at Franco's last years, which had seen rapid economic growth. The economic problems, combined with Basque Separatist terrorism and increased crime, gave the army sufficient excuse to attempt two coups to "restore order." The last one, in February 1981, was beaten back only by Juan Carlos's stout defense of democracy and his prestige among military leaders. Another result of the economic slump and political turmoil was the discrediting of the ruling UDC. In the October 1982 elections, the Socialists, under the leadership of Felipe González, won decisively. With 46 percent of the vote and 201 of 350 seats in the legislature, the Socialists promised to modernize and democratize Spain. The election itself represented the surmounting of another hurdle on the way to true democratic government. There was fear worldwide that the military would not permit the Socialists to take power. But the Socialists' moderate program combined with the devastating Communist defeat—they dropped from 11 to 4 percent of the vote—apparently persuaded the military to give the Socialists a chance. In fact, 22 percent of the military in Madrid voted Socialist. Another factor was the strength of the rightist Popular Alliance party, which gained 105 seats in the 1989 elections and 106 seats in the 1989 legislature. The military undoubtedly thought that the PA would serve as a brake on any possible Socialist excesses. The Socialists' continued moderation and the almost total collapse of the Communist party (the United Left received only 7 seats in 1986 but recovered slightly to 17 seats in 1989) have brought about a political calm, which some refer to as a trivialization of politics, similar to political life in much of Western Europe.

Few expected that the Socialists would still be ruling in the nineties. But favorable international economic trends, especially a lowering of oil prices and a reviving worldwide economy, and the disunity of parties on the right have led to a long tenure for González's Socialists. The Socialists lost seats in both the 1986 elections (from 201 to 184) and in the 1989 elections (from 184 to 176) due to their austerity program to stem a too-rapid economic growth. The efforts to dampen economic growth (about 5 percent a year) in order to control inflation have reduced it from 24.5 percent in 1977 to about 7 percent in 1989. These efforts unfortunately increased unemployment (about 18 percent in 1989) and held down wages. While labor is unhappy about these developments, most Spaniards are basking in a new-found affluence brought about by the rapid modernization. This modernization picked up even more in the late eighties after Spain joined the EC and as massive investment from the United States and Western Europe accelerated growth. Spain's relatively low wages and the pending 1992 single market in Western Europe have encouraged countries to locate more of their manufacturing there. Spain appears to have escaped its authoritarian past. Even the problem of Basque terrorism seems to be on the wane as most Basque people are demonstrating against terrorism. Now Spain's major problem will be to control an ever-expanding economy and manage its integration into the EC.

González has also proved to be a moderate in foreign policy. Although public-opinion polls indicated that Spaniards were opposed to continued membership in NATO and the Socialists had opposed Spain's entry in 1982, González convinced Spaniards to approve Spain's membership in 1986. González calculated that NATO would help modernize his military forces and speed Spain's integration in the EC. He gained approval by getting NATO to agree not to store nuclear weapons in Spain and by convincing the United States to reduce its military presence there. The Separatist movements continue to trouble Spain. Although Catalonia, the Basque country, and other regions were granted autonomy in 1980, Basque terrorism for complete independence has continued. While Spanish democracy is therefore still under some stress, Spain appears to be in the democratic camp to stay.

Greece Greece might well have followed the Western European political pattern had it not been for a military coup in 1967. Prior to the military takeover, a center-right coalition under Konstantinos Karamanlis had given way to George Papandreou's Progressive Center Union (EPEK) in 1964. Papandreou could have formed a coalition government with the EDA, a Communist Front organization, but chose instead to call an election in which he gained a majority for the EPEK. The army, sensing in Papandreou's victory a challenge to its authority, took a stand in opposition to the EPEK. When it became clear that the EPEK would win the 1967 elections, the army carried out a coup d'état and set up a right-wing military dictatorship. Papandreou and other center-left politicians were forced to flee the country.

Despite worldwide criticism, often led by Greeks in exile, the military maintained its dictatorial rule. An abortive attempt by the deposed King Constantine to overthrow the military junta ended with his flight into exile. During its years of authoritarian rule, the military junta tried to establish Greek suzerainty over Cyprus to satisfy the Greek majority on the island and the Greek Nationalists at home. When its attempt to oust the ruler of Cyprus, Archbishop Makarios, brought Greece close to war with Turkey and close to civil war, the junta was forced to recall Karamanlis in 1974. Karamanlis's center cabinet, which restored the 1952 constitution, won victory in the 1975 elections. Since a 1974 plebiscite had abolished the monarchy, Greece was prepared for a full-scale return to democracy.

The government of Karamanlis, fraught with continuing economic problems, quickly lost the parliamentary majority it had enjoyed in 1974–1975. Karamanlis's one major achievement was arranging Greece's membership in the EEC in 1981.

After years of political fragmentation and weak coalition government, Andreas Papandreou's Panhellenic Socialist movement (PASOK) won a decisive victory behind an anti-NATO, anti-EEC, Greece-for-Greeks, Socialist program in 1981. As in the major European countries, much of his support came from those who desired change rather than from those attached to any specific program. With 172 of the 300 seats in Parliament, PASOK had the necessary majority to implement its program. However, the enormity of Greece's economic difficulties forced Papandreou to go slowly with his socialization programs. After some initial wage and welfare increases, which only added to Greece's high inflation, he adopted a pragmatic economic program that emphasized economic recovery rather than social welfare. His threats to pull out of NATO were not carried out, primarily because the United States would have found it necessary to strengthen Greece's major opponent, Turkey, in NATO if Greece left. This would threaten the Greeks in Cyprus where 20,000 Turkish troops were stationed to protect the Turkish minority.

PASOK won the 1985 parliamentary elections but with a reduced majority of twenty-two seats. Severe economic problems forced Papandreou to impose austerity measures and limit his anti-American, anti-EC policies in order to obtain economic aid. These measures produced popular dissatisfaction and reduced PASOK's popularity. The Papandreou government fell in 1989 after party members were implicated in a series of financial scandals and Papandreou's own personal relationship with a mistress, whom he divorced his wife for and married in July 1989, came to light. The June 1989 elections produced a coalition government of center-right New Democracy and the Communist-dominated Alliance of the Left and Progress. Once this coalition finished its investigation of the corruption charges against the Papandreou government, it called a new election for November. Though indicted for its role in the corruption, Papandreou's Socialists gained 3 seats in the legislature (from 125 to 128) as did New Democaracy (145 to 148). The Communist-led Alliance, however, dropped from 28 to 21 seats as a result of their cooperation with the right. New Democracy would have won a majority except for a change in the electoral system in June 1989 that made it more difficult for any party to win a clear majority. Another election was avoided only by the formation of an all-party government on November 21. Elections in April 1990 gave New Democracy 150 of the 300 seats in Parliament and Papandreou's Socialists 123 seats. With the support of one independent rightist, New Democracy has now excluded the Socialists from the government and perhaps brought the Papandreou era to an end.

Europe's Foreign Policy Independence

The independent foreign policy initiatives begun by Gaullist France in the sixties accelerated in the seventies as United States policy vacillated, as European contacts with the Soviet Union and Eastern Europe increased, and as Europeans sought to reduce their economic and diplomatic dependence on the United States. While foreign policy measures will be discussed in further detail in the sections on each country, the general outline can be summarized here.

A strong initial impetus for an understanding or détente with the Soviet Union came from the United States–Soviet confrontation in Cuba in 1961–1962. When Khruschev was forced to withdraw Soviet missiles from Cuba by an American blockade in 1962, the way was prepared for an understanding. Having come so near to war, both sides now moved toward reducing the tensions that had brought them to the brink. Only one year after the crisis, they agreed to ban the testing of nuclear weapons in the atmosphere, sea, and outer space. Moreover, the emergence of China as a new superpower in the sixties demanded that the two superpowers bury their differences to meet this new challenge.

There were also compelling domestic reasons for the Soviet move toward détente. In order to develop their economy fully, Soviet leaders wanted to reduce defense appropriations—possible only if an understanding with the United States could be reached—and to obtain financial and technical aid from both the United States and Europe. Commitments in Vietnam made the United States desirous of achieving a *modus vivendi* with the Soviet Union. Events after the Czech invasion in 1968—which proved to be only a mild setback to the policy of détente—indicated that the Soviet Union had become a status quo power.

In addition to a multitude of cultural and economic agreements with the West, the Soviet Union became one of President Richard Nixon's staunchest supporters during his unsuccessful attempt to escape the consequences of the Watergate scandal. Afraid that a new president might reverse the Nixon policy of détente, the Soviets charged that anti-Soviet forces in the United States were hoping to use the scandal to change American foreign policy. In the 1974 national elections in France, the Soviet Union favored the ultimately victorious Liberal party candidate, Valéry Giscard d'Estaing, over the candidate of the left coalition, François Mitterrand, on the grounds that Mitterrand's election might lead to turmoil in France and thus upset the many economic and diplomatic arrangements between the two countries.

Western Europe's foreign policy also reflected the relaxation in international tensions. As the apparent need for American military protection lessened and contacts with the East increased, Western European countries began to shape their own foreign policy. De Gaulle pulled France out of NATO, and West Germany formulated its own *Ostpolitik* (Eastern foreign policy). Europe's tendency to pursue a more independent policy was promoted in the seventies by the economic exchanges with the East, the hope that increased contacts would modify Soviet behavior, the United States' military and foreign policy failures (Vietnam and Iran), and continuing economic weaknesses. When the new United States president Ronald Reagan attempted to return to a policy of confrontation with the Soviet Union after 1980, he encountered the stiff resistance of much of Europe. In 1982, the refusal of France, Italy, Britain, and West Germany to stop the shipment of high-technology goods to the Soviet Union to build a gas pipeline to Europe forced the Reagan administration to drop its opposition to the shipments. An embargo on such goods to the Soviet Union would have affected 96 percent of West German exports to the Soviet Union but only 18 percent of American exports. Obviously, Western Europe had much more invested in détente than the United States. Not even the Soviet invasion of Afghanistan in 1979 and the Soviet-backed suppression of the Polish Solidarity movement in December 1981 altered seriously what Europeans considered to be an essential understanding with the Soviet Union.

Gorbachev's initiatives (described in chapter 13) further reduced East-West tension and led to a weakening of both the Warsaw Pact and NATO. The United States and the Soviet Union began a gradual scaling down of their military weaponry after 1985 as the economic burden of keeping up the arms race and modernizing the Soviet economy proved to be too much for the Soviet economy. Once arms reductions began, Western European countries pushed for even greater reductions in order to reduce tensions and the possibility that their countries might become future battlegrounds. Increasing economic ties, especially between West Germany and Eastern Europe, also reduced tensions.

European Problems: The End of Rapid Economic Growth

Europe's major problem has been the economic slump begun in 1973, and its consequences. After two decades of rapid economic growth, Europe faced an economic crisis that no longer responded to Keynesian economic measures (see chapter 4). Almost every European nation described itself as being particularly susceptible to this tenacious economic malady, referred to variously as Englanditis, the Dutch disease, le mal Belge, etc. . . . But there were common causes for the slump. The recession resulted from high energy costs, which began with the quadrupling of oil prices between 1973 and 1975; increased competition from low-cost, high-technology countries; popular economic and social expectations; and governments' bungled attempts to overcome the crisis.

Although high energy costs have often been singled out as the major cause of the European crisis, the British and Dutch experiences indicate that it may not have been. British North Sea oil and Dutch North Sea gas made them self-sufficient and even net exporters of energy. Still, they suffered as much as the other European countries from the crisis. Also, in the first years of the oil-price increases, the West Germans were able to overcome the high energy costs by an aggressive export policy to the OPEC countries. Moreover, the Japanese, with almost no domestic energy sources, overcame the high costs of energy through conservation and increased exports. The answer then is much more complex than excessive energy costs.

A more important factor may have been Europe's decline in productivity and loss of technical superiority in comparison with newly industrialized states. The once clear superiority of European automobiles, steel, and capital goods no longer existed. Sweden, which had held 7.5 percent of the world's export market in 1961 (primarily due to its high-quality products), saw its share slip to 3 percent in 1976. Higher cost Volvo and Saab automobiles no longer had the clear superiority over Japanese cars they once did. Only West Germany's huge favorable trade surplus ($81 billion in 1989) still provides the EC countries with a favorable balance of trade. After only a $3 billion deficit in 1978, the EC had a combined $28.5 billion deficit in 1979 before recovering to a near balance in 1987.

In order to come to grips with the economic consequences of the slump, governments often exacerbated the problems. To meet the social problems caused by the crisis, many governments ran huge budgetary deficits that fueled inflation. To keep living standards from falling, governments continued to support wage and benefit increases with extensive borrowing. Such borrowing increased inflation by bidding up the price of capital and reducing the amount of money available for industrial investment. Decreased investment—it dropped from 4 percent of the national income in 1970 to 2 percent in 1982—reduced the West's technological superiority over Japan, South Korea, Brazil, and other developing countries. It became almost impossible to stop the economic slide since the alternative seemed to offer only economic suffering and political disaster for incumbent parties. But continuing economic problems eventually led to a change in attitude among electorates. They began to vote incumbents out of power if they failed to balance budgets and bring inflation under control.

Beginning in the late seventies, European governments began to impose austerity measures—price and wage controls, higher taxes and interest rates, curbs on government spending—in order to bring down inflation. Even the new Socialist government in France, after an initial period of deficit spending, had to follow Great Britain, Italy, Holland, and Belgium in imposing austerity measures. Unfortunately, the short-term consequences of such measures have been higher unemployment and reduced government investment in industry. Ultimately, austerity measures are intended to bring down inflation, reduce manufacturing costs by holding down wages, and therefore increase exports. Such policies still may not be able to increase exports sufficiently due to the continuing competition from the much lower cost, high-technology countries. It will also require a very costly industrial modernization for which there are limited funds. Recovery will undoubtedly be very slow and is unlikely to produce the economic benefits enjoyed by Europeans in the sixties. The most optimistic economic outlook forecasts continuing EC growth rates of only 2 to 3 percent into the nineties, compared to 5 percent for the period 1950–1972. Europeans, as well as Americans, are going to have to accept a new economic reality that will reduce expectations and may even reduce the standard of living in some countries. Already labor has been forced to postpone wage and cost-of-living adjustments in order to save jobs. Despite this somewhat pessimistic outlook, Europeans are still enjoying a standard of living much above that of most of the rest of the world.

West German Political Transition

West Germany provides one of the earliest examples of the political transition outlined in the introduction to this chapter. After the German Social Democratic party (SPD) dropped its revolutionary program in 1959, it slowly increased its representation in the *Bundestag,* as Table 14-1 shows, first at the expense of the Christian Democratic party (CDU) and its Bavarian affiliate the Christian Social Union (CSU) and later of the Free Democratic party (FDP). The election gains in the 1960s show clearly the result of the SPD's adoption of a reform rather than a revolutionary program.

Despite outspoken student criticism of SPD opportunism, the majority of the newly enfranchised voters cast their ballots for the SPD. The SPD first gained a share of power in 1966 as a part of the coalition put together by CDU chancellor Kurt Georg Kiesinger. It was Kiesinger who wanted the SPD in the coalition because the FDP would be unwilling to support the strong economic measures he considered necessary to bring Germany out of a recession. Also, he did not want the CDU to shoulder all the blame for the unpopular tax increase he was going to institute. The co-

Table 14-1 *Bundestag* Seats

Party	1957	1961	1965	1969	1972	1976	1980	1983	1987
CDU-CSU	270	242	245	242	225	243	226	244	223
SPD	169	190	202	224	230	214	218	193	186
FDP	41	67	49	30	41	39	52	34	46
Greens	–	–	–	–	–	–	–	27	42

alition solved the economic problems by raising taxes, cutting military spending, and encouraging investment.

An unfortunate aspect of the economic crisis and the coalition was the growth of right-wing radical groups. An extreme Nationalist group, the National Democratic party (NPD), with many former Nazis as members, won forty-eight seats in provincial elections in 1967. Although it won another twelve seats in 1968 by playing on the fears of those who had been upset by the student demonstrations, the return of economic stability soon halted the NPD growth. Moreover, once the CDU was in opposition after 1969, voters registered their complaints by voting for the CDU rather than for the NPD.

In foreign policy, West Germany, under Kiesinger, began to break away from American tutelage. With Brandt as foreign secretary, the first steps were taken to establish normal diplomatic relations with the East. But it was not until Brandt became chancellor in a coalition with the FDP that West Germany's *Ostpolitik* (Eastern policy) began in earnest. Brandt's policy went beyond the reopening of diplomatic relations with East European states to the recognition of East Germany and an acceptance of the boundaries set up between Poland and East Germany after World War II.

This recognition, vehemently opposed by German Conservatives and never even contemplated by earlier Christian Democrats, convinced most East Europeans that Brandt was sincere in his efforts to normalize relations with the East. The possibility that his *Ostpolitik* might ultimately lead to a reunification of the Germanies was looked upon with considerable trepidation by other Western European countries.

Brandt remained in power until 1974, when he stepped down because of his disappointment with the failure of European unification, the slow pace of social reform, and the discovery of an East German spy among his advisers. His successor, Helmut Schmidt, representing the technocratic element in the SPD, was ideologically far from the postwar revolutionaries' brand of socialism or even Brandt's dedication to the concept of social improvement. Brandt had told the German people to prepare for the long-term social reforms he was contemplating, whereas Schmidt spoke only about the solution of present problems. Schmidt claimed, "I'm not a visionary and I'm skeptical of all the visionaries. Germans have an enormous capacity for idealism and the perversion of it." One of his first moves was to drop several of Brandt's reform proposals, but in an effort to satisfy the left wing of the party, he decided to push Brandt's proposals for giving workers a say in the management of large businesses.

Schmidt's concentration on resolving economic problems produced immediate dividends in overcoming an economic slowdown brought on by the shortages and high cost of oil from 1973 to 1975. Germany overcame the shortages and trade imbalance by cutting its oil use 20 percent and by increasing exports to the OPEC countries sufficiently to wipe out a

10-billion-mark deficit in three years. Germany was not to suffer serious economic difficulties again until 1979.

The economic slump did influence the 1976 elections. Before the extent of Germany's recovery became apparent, the voters returned the CDU-CSU to its legislative levels of the sixties and reduced the SPD-FDP coalition to only a ten-seat majority in the lower house (see Table 14-1). Although the governing coalition recovered in the 1980 elections to a forty-four-seat majority, divisions between the coalition partners and within the SPD curtailed the SPD's room for maneuvering and increased the FDP's influence far beyond its parliamentary numbers.

The political differences within the parties and between them reflected the social transformations at work in German society since the sixties. The SPD had become deeply divided between an increasingly influential left wing and a traditional moderate right wing. Schmidt, who leaned more toward the right, had to relinquish party leadership to the only person able to pacify both wings, former chancellor Willy Brandt. The left, primarily an outgrowth of the New Left movement of the sixties, was opposed to nuclear energy and weapons, to NATO, and to economic growth and industrial society. Since the right wing of the SPD and the SPD's perennial coalition partner the FDP supported all these things, the government often found it either impossible to act or had to make short-term compromises on many important issues. While Schmidt walked a tightrope between these two factions, the SPD was losing support on both the left and the right. When Schmidt had to compromise on social welfare to satisfy the FDP, the SPD lost labor and left-wing supporters. His inability to stop the growth of unemployment—7.5 percent in 1982—was the result of pressure from the SPD right and FDP to keep down expenditures and inflation. In June 1982, the SPD had to cut back government borrowing, an anti-inflationary action, in order to satisfy the FDP. Also, strong pressure from the public and the CDU-CSU to stem radicalism was countered by the left wing of the SPD as undemocratic.

The FDP, the so-called dog-wagging tail of West German politics, was in coalition with the SPD from 1969 to 1982. This coalition was held together by the lack of alternatives, a fear of change, the distribution of patronage, and the pressure from holders to high-level jobs made possible by the SPD government. The more free-market FDP blocked an extension of welfare, a growth of the national debt, and any extension of a labor voice that went beyond the then current codetermination practice in industrial management. Of course, much of the SPD right, as well as Schmidt, were happy with these "compromises." But increasing disagreements over the means to deal with an economic slump led the FDP to leave the governing coalition in October 1982. When the FDP's demand for reduced welfare expenditure was rejected by the SPD, the governing coalition became deadlocked. When Schmidt demanded that the FDP acquiesce, they left the coalition and joined with Helmut Kohl's CDU-

CSU bloc to form a new majority in the *Bundestag*. A number of local-election losses had also convinced many FDP deputies that the German public was moving to the right and a coalition with the CDU would be in their own best interest.

The SPD had long profited from a lack of unified opposition from the CDU-CSU. Both the head of the CDU, Helmut Kohl, and of the CSU, Franz Josef Strauss, lacked Schmidt's popularity and had strong opposition within their own parties. CDU-CSU losses in the 1980 elections constituted a rejection of the CDU's authoritarian chancellor candidate Strauss and his policies. With Strauss no longer the chancellor designate, however, the CDU-CSU presented a more united front in the 1983 elections and under Kohl's leadership increased their seats in the legislature from 226 to 244.

A new political group that changed the direction of West German politics in the eighties was the Ecologists or "Greens." Originally an environmental group, the Ecologists were closer to the left of the SPD in that they opposed economic growth, atomic energy and nuclear weapons, and parts of the Atlantic Alliance with the United States. Their similarity to the left of the SPD cost the SPD political support. But division within the Greens limited their development to that of a rival to the two main parties. They were divided between those who wished to take government positions (realists) and those who wished to remain an opposition party (fundamentalists), believing that any political participation would compromise the movement's principles. The 1983 elections confirmed the new CDU-CSU/FDP coalition by giving the CDU 244 seats, the FDP 34 seats, the SPD 193 seats, and giving the Greens their first political representation with 27 seats.

Parliamentary elections in January 1987 reconfirmed the shift to the CDU-CSU/FDP coalition. As Table 14-1 indicates, the elections showed a further loss of seats for the SPD, whose traditional labor constituency continued to decline as a portion of the population. Also many youths who had previously supported the SPD switched to the Greens or the CDU-CSU/FDP. Since the SPD had moved more toward the political center most left-leaning youths began to support the Greens. An even larger number of youths became conservative CDU voters. There was a general feeling that the CDU-CSU/FDP could better manage the economy in difficult economic times. The CDU also profited from increased economic-cultural ties with Eastern Europe after 1985. The SPD's decision to shift more toward the center in order to increase its vote had in fact lost it votes to the Greens. The CDU lost votes to the FDP due to Franz Josef Strauss's attack on détente, which was being championed by the FDP and was popular with a public interested in lowering East-West tensions and increasing contacts with friends and relatives in East Germany. Brief upsurges in voting for the neo-Nazi National Democratic and the Republican parties appear to have been primarily reflections of rural discontent over the reduction in farm subsidies necessary for European integration in 1992 and the resentment of foreign workers. Although the CDU is now dominant, it will have to alter its appeal in the future since its primary support has traditionally come from dwindling groups: farmers and small-town residents. The incorporation of East Germany into a united Germany could ultimately result in greater support for the Socialists unless Kohl succeeds in his quest to become the "unification" chancellor. The East Germans appear to support the SPD's greater commitment to social welfare, but the Nationalist euphoria resulting from unification under the CDU could indeed increase the latter's support.

Germany's economic problems of the last decade have been less a result of internal policies and more a result of foreign competition. In 1982, the Japanese controlled 95 percent of the once-strong German photography market, 11–12 percent of the automobile sales, and they were making strong inroads in many other areas. The smooth sailing with high economic-growth rates and low unemployment that Germans had come to expect in the fifties and sixties was no longer possible. Germany was and is still facing a problem common to advanced industrial societies in competition with countries that have high technology but lower labor costs. Yet the Germans remain the leading exporting nation by a large margin. In 1987, West Germany exported $294 billion worth of goods, compared to $250 billion for the United States and $231 billion for Japan. As previously noted, their 1989 trade surplus of $80 billion topped all countries. And with 1992 fast approaching, the Germans are feverishly preparing to adjust to the new large European market. Many believe that the reduced internal barriers will most benefit the extremely efficient German firms. But European integration may be slowed as much of West Germany's investment may now be directed toward East Germany if the move to unification continues.

How the Germans would react to a future curtailment of expectations has been a topic much discussed in the foreign press. Some believe that the Germans are incapable of making the compromises that the British have had to make. But those who support the Greens have already made the decision to live in the future with less. German democracy has also endured savage attacks from right and left and survived. While the extremism of both radical fringes—especially the violent countercultural Baader-Meinhof gang and the neo-Nazis—and the government's sometimes violent response to them led some to question the German's commitment to democracy, Germany withstood the shocks and seems now firmly in the democratic camp. The unification of the two Germanies, predicted to be completed with all-German elections in December 1990, will probably increase German national feeling. The slogan "We are somebody again" indicates that a united Germany will want to play a much larger political role than West Germany has played in the past. Of course, to pull the East German economy up to the level of West Germany's would take between $300 and $650 billion, according to experts. But once that was accomplished, a united Germany would have a much greater potential than other European nations.

French Political Transition

In France the establishment of the Fifth Republic under the powerful presidency of de Gaulle upset the traditional political balance between right and left. Both the fortuitous economic situation and de Gaulle's adept handling of the Algerian rebellion swung support to the right during the 1960s. In the 1964 presidential elections, the Gaullists alone received 44 percent of the vote, whereas the Left Federation of Communists and Socialists, headed by François Mitterrand, got only 31 percent of the vote.

Despite the election success, de Gaulle's popularity had already begun to decline by 1964. His blocking of British entry into the EEC in 1963 made many French turn their backs on him. Others dropped their support when it became apparent that de Gaulle wished to reduce French democracy to a facade. A growing number felt that France should not try to develop an independent nuclear military deterrent but should concentrate on domestic problems.

The elections began to shift toward the left after 1964. In the 1967 parliamentary elections, the Gaullists' vote declined from over 50 percent of the total in 1962 to 38 percent. The overwhelming Gaullist victory in 1968 following the student-worker riots proved a temporary response, reflecting the belief of many voters that their only choice was between Gaullism and communism. The election victory only temporarily overshadowed the shortcomings of de Gaulle's regime. With his policies often verging on megalomania—for example, his refusal to consult his own ministers on issues under their jurisdiction—most Frenchmen breathed a sigh of relief when he retired in 1969. He retired when his referendum on limiting the Senate's power and composition and granting regional governments more authority was defeated. While de Gaulle expected that the decentralization proposal would be sufficiently popular to help overcome opposition to reducing the Senate's power, he interpreted the referendum's defeat as a rejection of his own authority.

De Gaulle's successor, Georges Pompidou, continued many Gaullist policies but stripped them of their authoritarian character. He was not too proud, as de Gaulle had been, to devalue the franc and thereby increase French exports. He also gained popularity by dropping French opposition to British entry into the EEC. But Pompidou's policies, after this promising start, lost momentum. French political theorists, such as Michel Crozier, began to write about France's "blocked" or "stalled" society. They contended that France's sociopolitical structure—many conservative small farmers and shopkeepers and a politically dominant and inflexible bourgeoisie—blocked any significant reform. Adding to

Pompidou's woes were a deteriorating economy, the Arab oil embargo, and his own failing health. After his death in 1974, the possibility for a United Left—Communist and Socialist parties—election victory appeared likely because of the unpopularity of the Gaullists. However, the French still remained true to that old stereotype that their heart is on the left but their checkbook is on the right by electing as their next president Valéry Giscard d'Estaing, the technocratic Liberal party candidate of the center-right. The handsome, youthful-looking Giscard had run a Kennedy-style campaign. Although more elitist than de Gaulle, he ran his campaign as a man of the common people. Still, his margin of victory over the United Left candidate, the Socialist Mitterrand, was only 1.2 percent of the popular vote.

Giscard d'Estaing's presidency began with much promise. Operating under his slogan "Change without risk," he pushed through many Liberal reforms with the support of the left; he lowered the voting age to eighteen, reduced state control over the media, imposed a capital-gains tax on the rich, and liberalized divorce and abortion laws. Still, France's tax system remained one of the most unfair in Europe with excessive indirect taxation. Giscard continued an independent foreign policy as had his two predecessors, but he was less opposed to the United States than de Gaulle had been and more committed to Europe. Giscard, in fact, admired the openness of American society and hoped to move France in that direction.

Because of a worsening economic situation and the growing popularity of the left at the departmental and municipal levels, a victory for the United Left appeared imminent in the 1978 legislative elections. But a split in the left brought about by the Communist party's fear of aiding a rapidly growing Socialist party under Mitterrand—the Socialists outpolled the Communists for the first time in the 1978 election—weakened them on the eve of the elections. In addition, the old fear of the left, nurtured by Giscard during the election campaign, helped give the right 51.5 percent of the vote and a legislative majority of eighty-nine seats. After Giscard's triumph, he began to lose popularity due to his inattention to needed domestic reforms and a reversal from his earlier populist style to an almost de Gaulle–like regal style. But the economic problems— energy shortages, high inflation, and unemployment—were even more decisive in reducing Giscard's popularity.

The stage was set for one of the most remarkable political turnabouts in postwar France. Starting with a new Socialist party in 1971—the old SFIO disbanded in 1969—Mitterrand's Socialists became the dominant party on the left in 1978 and in the National Assembly in 1981. Mitterrand's election to the presidency in 1981 by a 51.8 to 48.2 percentage margin over Giscard was as much a rejection of Giscard as an endorsement of the left in that many French were merely voting for a change. Certainly the Gaullists' lukewarm support of Giscard was an important factor. Instead of uniting against the left on the first presidential ballot, the Gaullists had run their own candidate. Giscard's 28 percent of the vote in the first round rather than the predicted 36 percent did not provide him with a sufficient springboard for the second round. But Mitterrand's victory also resulted from changes in French society and a transformation of the French left. The social groups who have traditionally supported the right—farmers, small shopkeepers, the wealthy bourgeoisie, and non-working women—have declined relatively in comparison with those who tend to support the left—salaried workers and wage-earning women. Even more important has been the shift from the Communists to the Socialists. In the National Assembly elections, the Socialist party's vote jumped from 16.5 percent of the popular vote in 1968 (the SFIO) to a commanding 37.5 percent in 1981. The Communists slipped from 20 percent in 1968 to only 16.2 percent in 1981. Some of this resulted from the Communists' abandonment of the United Left. About one-quarter of the traditional Communist voters who still believed in a United Left switched to Mit-terrand in the 1981 elections. Also, the Communists' return to a more hard-line, pro-Moscow position—leader Georges Marchais refused to condemn Soviet actions in Afghanistan—cost the Communists support. French voters were also less fearful of the left once they realized that a smaller Communist party would have limited influence over the decisions of any left-of-center government.

National Assembly elections, brought about by Mitterrand's dissolution of the Conservative-dominated Assembly, resulted in an absolute majority for the Socialists: 288 of the 491 seats. The Socialists' majority in the National Assembly would have permitted the Socialist premier, Pierre Mauroy, to govern without the Communists. However, Mauroy included them in his government, four of forty-four cabinet posts, in order not to appear to be the one responsible for the breakup of the United Left and also to keep the support of many blue-collar workers who were members of Communist-dominated trade unions.

Mitterrand began his first term of office in traditional Socialist fashion; he increased the minimum wage, expanded social benefits, added a man-datory fifth week of paid vacation for salaried workers, reduced the work week to thirty-nine hours, imposed higher taxes on the rich, and nation-alized the major banks. While these policies were popular among all but the rich, they exacerbated the economic difficulties.

In 1982, Mitterrand switched to an austerity program in order to reduce the huge budget deficit and high inflation. Emphasis was now placed on modernization rather than socialization, encouraging new private enter-prises, and reducing public expenditures. Especially alarming to the left wing of the Socialists was the rejection of the policy that automatically adjusted wages upward as prices rose. While these policies began to lower the inflation rate, they increased unemployment as firms reduced work forces and government support dwindled. Unable to support such a free-market program, the Communist ministers left the government in 1984.

François Mitterrand found it necessary to adopt free-market economies and reduce socialist measures in order to stimulate the country's economic growth and
fight inflation. (Reuters—Bettmann Newsphotos)

Since these economic policies had stirred up some resentment, the Socialists lost the 1986 parliamentary elections to a center-right coalition.
With 31 percent of the vote and 215 seats, however, the Socialists remained the largest party in the Assembly. For the first time the Fifth
Republic had a president who did not represent the majority in the National Assembly. Mitterrand still had two years left of his seven-year term
and he refused to resign. Mitterrand's appointee as premier, the neo-
Gaullist Jacques Chirac, pursued economic policies not too different from
those of the previous administration. He speeded up the economic modernization of French industry through more rapid privatization and reduced government expenditures. But he differed from Mitterrand in limiting immigration, increasing police powers, and reducing the wealth tax
introduced by the Mauroy government. This period of cohabitation, a
president and premier from different political groupings, came to an end
in 1988 when Chirac lost to Mitterrand in the presidential elections. Mitterrand had gained much support by appearing to stand above politics

while Chirac had alienated many in the day-to-day running of the government.

The June 1988 parliamentary elections increased the Socialist Assembly seats to 276 and reduced the center-right's to 258. Some of this slim majority was due to Mitterrand's public plea not to give the Socialists an overwhelming majority since it might strengthen the left-of-center forces too much and threaten his programs. The Communists won only 27 seats and became even more marginalized in French politics. The extreme right-wing National Front of Jean-Marie Le Pen dropped from 33 seats to 1 due to a change in the electoral system away from proportional representation to a first-past-the-post system. It appears that the two moderate-right parties, Rassemblement pour la république and Union pour la démocratie française (RPR and UDF), and the Socialists will each continue to command about 20 percent of the vote. Some view this development as the normalization of politics, that is, it is becoming similar to politics in other West European countries, while others see it as the banalization or loss of distinctiveness of political life. Certainly the policies of the two main political groupings differ little. The new premier, the Socialist Michel Rocard, pursues policies that differ little from those of Chirac. Rocard claims that the Socialists are left-wing Democrats in the tradition of George McGovern in the United States. The center-right might favor more privatization than the Socialists, but they are one in their modernizing, deflationary policies. The center-right also approves more restrictive policies concerning immigration, civil rights, and the freedom of information.

In foreign affairs, Mitterrand took a tough stand against Soviet actions in Afghanistan and Poland and pledged to support the Atlantic Alliance politically, although he would not participate militarily in NATO. He supported American missile deployment in Europe since he believed this would deter a Soviet attack with conventional weapons. But Mitterrand thinks that American economic imperialism is as dangerous as Soviet militarism. He has also idealistically committed France to increased aid to the Third World since he believes that North-South problems are more important than East-West problems. France's primary foreign policy problem is one of adjusting her vision of grandeur with her declining ability to cut an independent path in international affairs.

Italian Political Transition

The growing importance of the Socialist left is nowhere more apparent than in Italy, even though the left's political fortunes have been hindered by its ideological divisions. The Socialists (PSI) and Communists (PCI) have refused to cooperate on the national level, although they cooperatively rule many regional and local areas in Popular Front governments, thereby preventing the left from exercising an effect on politics and society commensurate with its popularity. The non-Communist left, although

Table 14-2   Seats in the Italian Chamber of Deputies

Party	1958	1963	1968	1972	1976	1979
Communist party (PCI)	140	166	171	171	227	201
Socialist Party of Proletarian Unity (PSIUP)	–	–	23	0	–	–
Socialists (PSI)[a]	84	87	91 (PSU)[a]	61	57	62
Social Democrats (PSDI)	22	33	–	29	15	20
Republicans (PRI)	6	6	9	151	14	16
Christian Democrats (DC)	273	260	265	265	263	262
Liberals	17	39	31	20	5	9
Monarchists	25	8	6	0	–	–
Neo-Fascists (MSI)	24	27	24	56	35	30
Others	5	4	–	8	4	18

[a] *The PSU (United Socialist party) existed from 1966 to 1969. In 1969, it divided into the PSI and the PSDI.*

sharing in center-left coalition governments between 1963 and 1969—the Christian Democrats' (DC) "opening to the left"—never had the strength to alter the policies of the ruling DC majority significantly.

The center-left coalition failed to meet the expectations of the public. In five years it had done little to modernize Italy's schools, hospitals, or law courts. The public, primarily the lower classes, suffered from poor public transporation, inadequate housing, and the lowest wages in the developed European countries. The nationalization of electricity, a major achievement of the coalition, aided the former owners and only burdened the government. A plan to decentralize administration by setting up regional administrators did not become effective until the early 1970s. Nor had Italy yet begun to profit from two agreements Fiat made to build car factories in the Soviet Union and Poland.

Unfortunately for the Socialists, only the DC gained political favor from the coalition. In the 1968 elections, the United Socialist party (PSU)—formed when the PSI and the Social Democrats (PSDI) merged in 1966—lost twenty-nine seats. As Table 14-2 shows, twenty-three seats were won by the Socialist Party of Proletarian Unity (PSIUP), the former left of the PSI that had broken away in protest against PSI leader Nenni's cooperation with the DC. These changes and a Communist party gain indicated that the trend to the left had not ended. The losses led the PSU to break up in 1969; in protest against the coalition, the PSU split into the former Socialist (PSI) and Social Democrat (PSDI) factions. Although a majority of the PSI remained loyal to the new DC premier, Mariano Rumor, his unwillingness to meet their demands reduced the coalition to a policy of muddling through. In 1972, the center-left coalition collapsed.

The political fortunes of the PCI improved remarkably in the seventies, especially on the local level. Local election victories in 1970 increased the PCI's control from the so-called Red Belt of Emilia-Romagna, Tuscany, and Umbria to six of Italy's twenty semiautonomous regions and most of the major cities from Naples northward. The lack of corruption among Communist officials, the support of young voters, an increasingly less ideologically oriented program, and the continued immobility and corruption in the DC-dominated national government were primarily responsible for the Communist gains.

During the sixties and seventies, the Communist leadership under Palmiro Togliatti and Enrico Berlinguer emphasized a Eurocommunist position with the expectation that it might gain them a share of power—that much discussed "historic compromise"—with the DC. Eurocommunists stressed a peaceful path to socialism rather than a Leninist seizure of power. They also sought to distance themselves from Moscow, especially after the 1968 crushing of the Czech revolutionaries, by emphasizing their national roots. Throughout the seventies, Communist parties attempted to join with other left or center parties to gain a share of power. The PCI even dropped its opposition to NATO and the Catholic church. Although the PCI never gained the historic compromise, despite gaining 34.7 percent of the popular vote in the 1976 parliamentary elections, they did cooperate with DC-led governments from 1976 to 1979 by supporting them, or at least by not opposing them, in the legislature. Their quest was damaged in 1978 when Aldo Moro, their DC interlocutor, was assassinated by the Red Brigades. When the PCI's demand for cabinet positions from the DC for their continued support was rejected in 1979, the PCI withdrew their support from the government and it collapsed.

After 1979, the PCI fared less well. It lost 4 percent of its popular vote in the 1979 elections because some on the left thought it had moved too far toward the center, while some on the right were not convinced that it genuinely supported democratic government. Also, the PCI lost votes to the more aggressive and less ideologically narrow Socialists (PSI) and Radicals (PR). The PCI's shift in 1979 to a possible "left alternative" government—PCI and PSI—was rejected by a PSI leadership that had visions of replacing the PCI as the power on the left.

The PSI resurgence was one of the most notable political occurrences in the seventies and eighties. After the failure of the political alliance with the PSDI in the late sixties, the PSI remained in the shadow of the PCI until the late seventies. It often cooperated in center-left governments with the DC and as the weak partner in Popular Front governments with the PCI on the local and regional level. But a more pragmatic, reformist leadership under Bettino Craxi gave the PSI greater popularity and more political clout. Following 1979, the PSI became the DC's major coalition partner and the PCI's main nemesis. The PSI challenged the PCI's stated allegiance to democracy and the Western Alliance by constantly challenging them to clarify their objectives. They also became more attractive to a less ideologically inclined electorate by rejecting further nationalization of property, a centralized direction of the economy, and labor demands for increased wages and benefits. It was the Craxi-led government from 1983–1987 that abolished the *scala mobile* (wages tied to rising costs); reduced expenditures for health and social security; and increased utility costs, transporation fares, and luxury taxes. While unpopular to most laborers, these changes were supported by most of the electorate.

As Italian society became more secularized (passage of the divorce and abortion bills) and less polarized socially and politically (breakdown of political subcultures and decline in party identification), more flexible broadly based parties profited at the polls. These changes also accounted for the growth of the PSI and the Radical party with its left libertarian program of unilateral disarmament, legalization of drugs, women's liberation, and antinuclear-arms policy.

While these transformations were reshaping the left, the ruling DC party was being weakened by Italy's economic weaknesses and political unrest. It was held responsible for not stopping the economic and social conflicts in the seventies that led *La Stampa* of Turin—one of Italy's leading newspapers—to declare in 1974; "Italy is shaken by turbid ferment; it runs the risk of becoming a country on the outskirts of civilization and reason." As Italy was shaken by strikes, student unrest, violence from left and right fringe groups, corruption, high inflation, and energy shortages, the DC governed—some would say muddled through—with minority governments and shaky majority coalitions that fell in rapid succession. The DC's monopoly of grass-roots patronage and power and a strong economy in the fifties and sixties had diverted attention from the internecine battles between left and right within the party and the political shortcomings of DC leadership. But the enormous difficulties, beginning with student riots and the general strike in the late sixties, exposed the near political paralysis of the DC. The DC's ineffective and sometimes corrupt rule—the revelation of the United States' financing of the DC in the sixties and the Lockheed Aircraft Corporation's bribes to DC politicians in 1970, to name a few—contributed to the political and social turmoil since corrective action could not be taken. Extreme rightist (the neo-Fascist Black Order, Third Position, and Armed Revolutionary Nuclei) and leftist (Red Brigades, Front Line, and others) groups struck with increasing ferocity at Italy's leaders and against each other with little fear of reprisal. The most sensational case was the kidnapping and execution of former premier Aldo Moro in 1978 by the Red Brigades. DC leaders, often very capable parliamentary managers such as Giulio Andreotti, Mariano Rumor, and Aldo Moro, put together short-term, primarily left-center governments in the seventies that managed to provide some order but little direction. Their perennial problem was the formation of political programs that excluded the PCI—always the second largest party in Parliament—but had sufficient strength to make and execute policy in the face of PCI opposition.

Economic and political changes decreased social and political unrest in the eighties. A growing materialism reduced leftist radicalism. A continuing decline of the industrial working class reduced the PCI's normal constituency, while the growth of the service class increased support for center and right parties. The PCI loss of twenty-six parliamentary seats in the 1979 elections, another three in the 1983 elections, and another twenty-one in 1987 reduced their effectiveness and made them more willing to compromise. The growing strength of the PSI and PR provided the DC with more flexible coalition partners and may permit the DC, assuming they can agree among themselves, to implement long-term reform programs rather than the typical makeshift ones designed to secure a ruling coalition. But the future may continue to lead away from the DC monopoly of power. Although the number of DC parliamentary seats has declined only slightly since 1979, they have lost some of their power and patronage at the local and provincial level to the PCI and PSI. In addition, one of the pillars of DC power, the Roman Catholic church, has lost influence in Italy. In an overwhelmingly Catholic country, the church was unable to prevent the passage of laws permitting divorce (1972) and abortion (1980) or a revision of the fifty-five-year-old concordat that ended Roman Catholicism's status as the state religion (1985).

Still, the DC, as the largest party, maintains its national dominance through the "five parties" system. Since 1979, when the PSI decided to participate in governments without the PCI, Italy has been ruled by coalitions comprising the DC, PSI, PSDI, Liberals, and Republicans (PRI). With the premier always coming from one of these five parties, Italy has in some respects obtained a relative continuity. For example, Giulio Andreotti, who formed a DC-led cabinet in July 1989, has been prime minister six times and held senior cabinet posts in twenty-eight of the forty-five postwar governments. These parties combined in the mideighties to reduce the Communists' control of local government: the PCI lost almost all mayoralties except that of Bologna. But these five parties have not been able to forge a government sufficiently strong to resolve the problem of political instability and immobilism.

Italy has also shown a resiliency and strength that few foreign observers thought possible. Confronted with extensive political violence in the seventies, especially the Red Brigades' assassination of Aldo Moro in 1978 and their unsuccessful kidnapping of an American NATO general in 1982, Italians rallied behind the government and the radical left was seriously weakened. However, it appeared that these problems worried foreigners more than they did Italians. Italians have learned to live with a measure of economic and social unrest and corruption that would totally disrupt other societies. Such an attitude indicates a popular acceptance of the conflicts, albeit somewhat exaggerated, endemic in democratic society.

In 1989, the PSI was in a position to play a major role in Italy's political future. The possibility of a left alliance of PCI and PSI is a slim possibility even with the changes in Communist governments in the Soviet bloc and the continuing move of the PCI toward the political center. A left-coalition government would probably necessitate that the socialists become the main left party in order to be electable, and this they will not attain soon. The PSI-initiated dialogue with the PCI in 1989 may also prod the DC into major concessions to the PSI in order to prevent a left coalition from taking power. Craxi's demand for a more powerful presidency, similar to that in France, is a distinct possibility no matter which coalition emerges. The PCI has already expressed an interest in a strengthened executive, and the DC might have to agree to it in order to prevent a left coalition. Such an executive could remove much of the political instability that has characterized Italian politics since 1945. If the strong economic growth of the eighties continues, a strengthened central government might be able to deal with the serious imbalances of wealth between north and south, with inflation, and with the large national debt.

The Vatican

While Italy has suffered from the lack of decisive leadership in the postwar period, the Vatican was blessed with strong leadership. The most momentous pontificate was undoubtedly that of Pope John XXIII (1958–1963) who brought about one of the most dramatic departures from Roman Catholic tradition. Pope John's policy of updating (*aggiornamento*) the church to bring it into step with twentieth-century developments has correctly been called the "Johannine Revolution." While it responded to some Catholics' call for a modernization of the church, it alienated many Catholic conservatives who thought the changes too far-reaching. His 1959 call for an Ecumenical Council to promote Christian unity was unexpected. Many thought his pontificate would be short and uneventful due to his advanced age when selected (seventy-seven). Protestants were receptive to the ecumenical movement because of Pope John's engaging personality and sincerity and his sending of observers to the World Council of Churches meeting in 1961. In addition, the fact that the Vatican Council, which first met in autumn 1962, contained a large majority of clergy in favor of ecumenism did not escape the attention of other Christian denominations. Delegates rejected many of the proposals that had been prepared by the Curia due to their more conservative nature. Finally, Pope John's encyclicals captured worldwide attention and widespread approval among Christians. *Mater et Magistra* (Mother and Teacher), issued in July 1961, expressed deep concern for social and material welfare, peace, international reconciliation, and political rights. His next encyclical, *Pacem in Terris* (Peace on Earth), covered much of the same ground as *Mater et Magistra,* but it was addressed not just to Catholics but to "all men of good will." It supported the United Nations, upheld political independence, and called on the rich countries to aid the poor

Pope John Paul II, shown here celebrating outdoor mass in Lucerne, Switzerland in June 1984, has traveled widely since his selection as Pope in 1978. (UPI—Bettmann Newsphotos)

ones. He lifted the ban on cooperation with unbelievers whose objectives might be beneficial to mankind. Thus, he removed the ban on Catholic support for the left. In practice, he did not oppose the Italian "opening to the left" that brought Socialists into the government in the 1960s.

Pope John's death in 1963 did not stop the ecumenical movement or reforms in the church. His successor, Pope Paul VI (1963–1978) supported ecumenism by seeking reconciliation with other Christians: his visits to leaders of the Eastern Christian churches in Constantinople and Jerusalem brought a new spirit of cooperation among them. He also pushed through many reforms initiated by his predecessor: the papacy would share more power with bishops, the authority of the Curia was reduced, and the Mass would be celebrated in the vernacular. But the liberals did not get all that they wanted. Pope Paul's 1987 support for the practice of clerical celibacy led many clergy to leave the priesthood. A year later, Pope Paul ruled against the use of contraception in *Humanae Vitae* (Human Life).

After the thirty-four-day reign of Pope John Paul I, the College of Cardinals in 1978 shocked the world by choosing a non-Italian as pope. Pope John Paul II, formerly Archbishop of Cracow, has attracted great attention due to his own charisma and his support for the Polish Solidarity movement. Thus far, his policies have tended to be more conservative than those of Pope John XXIII and Pope Paul VI. He has supported traditional practices for the clergy and laity, stressed papal authority in doctrinal matters, and restricted liturgical experimentation. But his involvement in world affairs has been more like that of Pope John XXIII and Pope Paul VI. He has traveled extensively and has exhibited a common touch similar to that of Pope John XXIII. His sociopolitical policies have been rather ambivalent. On the one hand, he has supported social justice; but on the other, he has restricted the social and political activities of the clergy. He is perhaps concerned that the clergy will become too concerned with worldly issues to the detriment of their religious duties.

In Italy, the Vatican has lost some ground, partially due to John Paul's more limited interest in domestic politics. In 1985, the new concordat with the Italian government, described above, accepted the civil court's right to adjudicate marital annulments and agreed that classes in religious doctrine would no longer be obligatory in the schools. In practice, one hour of religious instruction or an alternative hour of instruction in some other area has become the rule. Although only 25 percent of Italian Catholics attend Sunday Mass, the church still wields major influence in their lives. All major occasions, such as baptism, marriage, and burial take place in the church. But a growing secularism tied to modernization is robbing most of the church functions of their original significance.

British Political Transition

Britain experienced one of the most remarkable political transitions in its history after 1965. After about thirty-four years of general agreement concerning welfare state policies, the Conservatives under Margaret Thatcher turned radically to a self-help, antiwelfare position after 1979.

In the sixties, Britain experienced a slight shift to the left. Conservative party supporters soon discovered that they had little to fear from the Labour party and Prime Minister Harold Wilson, elected in October 1964. Almost as many labour as Conservative members of Parliament had gone to the "proper" schools. Wilson, a former Oxford economics don, represented the right reformist wing of the Labour party. Its left wing, desiring a fully socialized economy with the nationalization of all industry, was in the minority.

Wilson chose to fight the economic problems through the traditionally Conservative policies of cutting back on government spending and increasing taxes. After he received a larger majority in the 1966 parliamentary elections, Wilson reduced government spending on both military and welfare programs. Both the increased social security payments and the freezing of prices and wages angered workers and the left wing of the party. Labour popularity declined even further when Wilson was forced to devalue the pound 14 percent to raise British exports and reduce imports; devaluation raised the price of such necessities as bread.

By 1969, devaluation had started to have the desired effect: instead of deficits, the economy had a sizable surplus. But when Wilson called an election in an attempt to take advantage of the improved economic conditions, the attempt failed. The Conservatives, led by Edward Heath, won a thirty-seat majority in 1970. It seems the economic improvement was not as apparent to an electorate that had suffered through the economic emergencies and devaluation.

For the next four years the Conservatives tried to end inflation and put the economy on a healthy footing. Instead, Prime Minister Heath had to declare a state of emergency five times in less than four years in office. Moreover, the confrontations between Heath and the coal miners brought serious disruption to Britain's economy and a loss of support for the Conservatives. Labour, under Wilson, returned to power in February 1974. With only a small majority, Wilson was not able to act decisively to overcome the economic problems. He resisted the left wing's demands for more nationalization by pointing out the precariousness of Labour's majority.

While Labour ruled in Britain from 1974 to 1979, the party underwent a political transformation that seriously reduced its effectiveness. The left wing of the party grew in strength as the labor unions, becoming more militant in the face of economic adversity, threw their support to a more radical political program. Contending that private industry had failed to make adequate capital investments, the left wing—led by the Labour industry manager, later energy minister, Tony Benn—planned for massive nationalization of Britain's largest companies. Heath derisively referred to Benn as "Commissar Benn" and to his department as the "Gosplan Department" in an obvious reference to the Soviet planning procedures. But the left did not stop with Benn's program. It moved on to a more radical position, a "Socialist transformation" of society that included the nationalization of Britain's two-hundred largest corporations, the abolition of all elite institutions—including "public" (i.e., private) schools and the House of Lords—withdrawal from NATO and the EEC and unilateral disarmament. As Labour moved in this leftist direction after 1974, a moderate right wing first lost influence within the party and eventually left the party in 1981 to form the new Social Democratic party. Wilson was one of the first victims of this party turmoil. Unable to forestall this widening gap in Labour, Wilson resigned as party leader and prime minister in 1975. His successor, James Callaghan, was equally unsuccessful in overcoming this division in the party.

While these battles were going on within the ruling party, Britain continued to experience serious economic problems, growing Separatist movements in Scotland and Wales, and violence between Catholics and Protestants in Northern Ireland. Crippled by the internal divisions, Labour could only muddle through. In fact, one of Britain's most decisive acts, the positive referendum (67 percent) on British participation in the

EEC in 1975, came about because of Wilson's desire to forestall a split in the Labour party by removing the EEC decision from the badly divided party. Meanwhile, Britain's economy continued to stagnate. In June 1976, the pound's value dropped to $1.71 on its way down to nearly $1.00 as worldwide confidence in the pound declined. Inflation twice topped 20 percent, and unemployment passed the one million mark by the midseventies. Even more humiliating was the necessity in 1974 to borrow massively from the International Monetary Fund to meet government expenditures.

With the Separatist movements in Scotland and Wales and Catholic-Protestant violence in Northern Ireland added to the dismal economic outlook, many began to speak of "Englanditis" to describe Britain's unique problem. After winning nine parliamentary seats in 1974, Scottish Nationalists, who were convinced North Sea oil would permit them to do better on their own, forced the Labour government to consider some form of autonomy, since Labour needed their votes in Parliament. By moving slowly toward compromises on Scottish and Welsh devolution, British unity was preserved by referenda in Scotland and Wales in 1979 for continued association with England. The Northern Irish turmoil was not so easily resolved. Large-scale violence between Catholics and Protestants forced Britain to suspend Northern Ireland's Parliament in 1972 and establish direct rule from London. Since then, violence has continued between the Irish Republican Army (IRA) and Protestant extremists, with the British army caught in the middle. In the late seventies, the IRA extended the violence to England with the expectation that it would force the British to grant Catholics greater rights in Northern Ireland. (For a fuller explanation of the Ulster problem see chapter 16.)

In 1979, the British electorate gave the Conservatives a whopping forty-three-seat parliamentary majority and brought the first female prime minister, Margaret Thatcher, to power. The election was both a reaction against Labour's ineffectiveness and the power of labor unions, and a vote for change. Thatcher, or, as she has often been called, "the Joan of archconservatism," offered law and order, lower taxes, less government intervention, fewer welfare programs, and an end to inflation through control of the money supply. Her election signaled a major change in direction for Britain. Until 1979, both Labour and the Conservatives had accepted the welfare state and public ownership that had been ushered in after the war. The consensus on welfare state policies had become known as "Butskellism" after the Tory R. A. Butler and Hugh Gaitskell, the Labour leader. Butskellism aimed at reducing inequalities in income, education, housing, and health care. But rapidly rising inflation, continued strikes, and industrial uncompetitiveness gradually undermined the consensus. The year of the elections was particularly bleak: popularly known as the winter of England's discontent, Englanditis was exaggerated by numerous strikes that paralyzed the country. Thatcher was also aided by a steadily decreasing percentage of laborers in the voting population, who tend to support Labour, and a left-right division in the Labour party that reduced its effectiveness.

The unemployment and cuts in services introduced by Thatcher's budget-cutting monetarist policies (high interest rates to reduce inflation and decreased government expenditures) reduced her popularity during her first three years in office. Just when it appeared that she might lose the next election to Labour, her policies finally began to work. The inflation rate began to drop, and North Sea oil began to bring much-needed capital to the British Treasury. But it was Thatcher's dramatic recapture of the Falkland Islands from Argentina that restored British pride and permitted Thatcher to call for elections and to win again in 1983. Thatcher claimed the Falklands victory put the Great back in Britain. The single-member-constituency election procedure gave the Conservatives 61.1 percent of the seats but only 42.4 percent of the popular vote, Labour 32.2 percent of the seats but only 27.6 percent of the vote, and the Liberal-Social Democratic Alliance only 3.5 percent of the seats but 25.4 percent of the vote (the Alliance ran second to the Conservatives in 256 constituencies). So, the popular vote gives a better indication of Conservative popularity.

With a much enhanced Commons majority, Thatcher could now forge ahead with her self-help, antiwelfare state policies. She lowered taxes on wealth and property, stepped up the privatization of industry, sold municipal housing units to former renters, cut subsidies to inefficient industries, continued her attacks on labor unions, and brought down inflation from nearly 20 percent to about 3 percent in 1986 with her monetarist policies. Unemployment rose from 4.2 percent in 1979 to 13.3 percent in 1983, after which it leveled off to between 9 and 11 percent as many inefficient factories went out of business. Thatcher can point to many economic successes. British Steel, for example, moved from a $3.3 billion loss in 1980 to a $758.5 million profit in the fiscal year ending in 1988 by reducing the number of factories and jobs—the chairman of British Steel said, "You've got to be able to fire a shotgun down the shop floor and not hit anyone" (*New York Times,* 5 December 1988)—and adding performance bonuses. British Steel's pretax production costs are the lowest in the world. As a whole the British economy has grown at about a 3 percent rate in the eighties or a rate better than other industrialized countries.

In 1987, Thatcher became the first prime minister in modern British history to win a third consecutive term, with the conservatives winning 43 percent of the votes (376 seats) against a divided opposition. Labour, weakened by internal divisions and its unilateral disarmament position, gained 32 percent of the votes but only 208 seats because of the concentration of its votes in certain constituencies. The Liberal-Social Democratic Alliance obtained only 22 percent of the votes (22 seats) because of internal divisions and the resultant lack of a coherent program. Voting reflected the division in Britain between the poor industrial north, where Labour dominated, and the rich commercial south, where the Conservatives won decisively. The Thatcher revolution has extended beyond her destruction of Butskellism. She also undermined the power of the labor unions in Britain and even restricted unions' right to strike. She has strengthened national against local government and reduced the autonomy of universities and local school authorities. Her stress on self-reliance and the individual severely weakened the decades-old British devotion to equality and the community as a whole. While some believe Thatcher has gone too far in her denigration of dependency, even some in her own party, there are many who have profited from the economic revival. Two-thirds of Britons owned their own homes in 1988, compared to one-half in 1979, and voters' real income was up by 25 percent over 1979. Thatcher's economic success has led Labour, under Neil Kinnock, to accept much of the Conservative economic philosophy. We may be seeing the return to two-party competition in Britain but one that will reflect the revolution that Thatcher has brought about in the British economy and consciousness.

Thatcher's popularity began to fade in 1990 as the inflation rate rose to about 10 percent and the growth of real GNP was predicted to decline from the low 2.5 percent in 1989 to only 1.9 percent in 1990. Many economists are contending that the country seems on the verge of a recession. Although respected, Thatcher is not loved by the public. Thatcher added to her unpopularity by her arrogant treatment of her associates. She now appears to be in a minority in her own party. A 1989 opinion poll gave her an approval rating of only 24 percent, the lowest of any prime minister in fifty years. Still, one must not sell her short. She is the only modern prime minister to be elected to three successive terms.

Political Transition in the Smaller Nations

Among the smaller European countries, a political shift toward the left occurred in the sixties. But in the seventies, a turn back toward the center began as electorates expressed their displeasure with the economic slump, higher taxes, and the possibility of more extensive welfare measures from Communist or far-left Socialist parties. The moderate Socialist parties became an oft-chosen coalition partner as they became more reform oriented.

Belgium, Luxembourg   In Luxembourg, three parties, the Christian-Social People's party, the Socialist Workers' party, and the Democratic or Liberal party have dominated the political coalitions. Although the Christian-Social and Liberal parties tend to support a free-market economy more than the Socialists, all three support the social welfare measures introduced since the war. The Communist party has experienced a two-decades decline, primarily because it did not adopt a more moderate Eurocommunist position. Major socioeconomic conflicts have been avoided through the cooperation of the labor unions, business, and government. Although Luxembourg has not experienced the severe economic problems of the other Benelux countries, it adopted austerity measures and cut taxes in the mideighties in order to control inflation and unemployment and keep the economy strong.

After heading several center-left coalition governments since 1979, Belgium's prime minister, Wilfried Martens, formed a center-right coalition in 1982. His Christian Democratic–dominated government imposed an austerity program in order to deal with the economic slump. Government subsidies to industry and wages were cut, the Belgian franc devalued, consumer prices frozen, and tax incentives for industrial investment raised. With inflation decreasing and trade back in balance by 1984, Martens returned to office after the 1985 and 1987 elections. Although the 1987 elections produced a Christian Democratic–Socialist–Flemish–Nationalist coalition, economic retrenchment continued. In fact the Socialists stressed the ethnic issue rather than traditional socioeconomic issues. The Belgian Communist party's stubborn adherence to an orthodox Leninist position led to its exclusion from Parliament after 1985. Continued austerity measures reduced the inflation rate below 2 percent in 1989 and brought an economic growth rate of about 3 percent. But Belgians had to accept increased unemployment as inefficient firms failed and successful ones became more lean. Belgian's other major problem remains the Flemish-Walloon split. In 1988, Brussels became the third major administrative area joining French Wallonia and Flemish-speaking Flanders. Most Belgians hope that this granting of further local autonomy will make it possible for the Dutch- and French-speaking inhabitants to live together in one state. The central government's jurisdiction now includes only foreign affairs, defense, justice, social security, and monetary policy.

The Netherlands   In the Netherlands, moderate center-right or center-left governments have alternated in power during the last decade. When Labor withdrew from the center-left government in 1982 due to their refusal to support cuts in public spending, an interim government headed by the Christian Democrats was formed. A center-right government of Christian Democrats and Liberals took power after elections in September 1982 and implemented cuts in government spending, taxes, and government employees, as well as ending the indexing of wages and welfare benefits. Although these austerity measures were painful, the public returned this center-right government of Ruud Lubbers to office in 1986. But the Lubbers government fell in May 1989 when it failed to respond energetically to environmental issues. The Communist party lost its three parliamentary seats in 1986 and is no longer represented. The September 1989 elections returned a Labor-led center-left government.

Scandinavia   In Scandinavia, a popular dissatisfaction with the costly social welfare programs, high taxes, and government spending swept the Socialists from power in Sweden from 1976 to 1982, in Norway from 1981 to 1986, and in Denmark from 1982 on. Although there was widespread satisfaction with Scandinavia's high standard of living, the taxation rates of near 70 percent of income that were needed to support the costly social welfare programs spread dissatisfaction. Since the late seventies, Danish voters have shifted their ballots toward parties in the middle of the political spectrum rather than the left, producing a political standoff between right and left. The result has been a series of minority governments in the eighties. The radical Communist and Left-Socialist parties have lost all political representation in the eighties. Since 1982, Poul Schluter of the Conservative People's party has served as the first non-Socialist prime minister since the interwar period. But his center-right coalition government rules as a minority government. Political dissatisfaction has been expressed recently in the increased representation for the Progress party. It gained sixteen seats in the 1988 elections on a program of reduced taxes, government spending, and bureaucracy. But its extreme antiwar, anti-immigrant position has kept it from any government coalition. Denmark's citizens will have to decide if they wish to continue to pay high taxes—they increased to 51 percent of GDP under Schluter—to support the extensive welfare system. The vote for the Progress party indicates that they may be leaning in the direction of lower taxes and reduced welfare benefits.

Sweden In Sweden, where the Social Democrats lost the prime ministership in 1976 but remained the largest party, squabbling among the three non-Socialist parties gave the Socialists an opportunity to return to power in 1982. But it is not the same Social Democratic party that held power before 1976. They have moderated their views in order to accommodate the party to this new public consensus. The late party leader and prime minister Olaf Palme led the party toward moderate wage agreements, reduced taxes, and a postponement of a proposed wage earners' fund, which probably cost the Social Democrats a victory in the 1976 and 1979 elections. The fund, to be taken from payroll taxes and company profit taxes, was to be used to buy company shares so that trade unions would eventually take over Sweden's major companies. In a country that has had what most Swedes consider to be a healthy mix of social welfare and private enterprise, the wage earners' fund proposal seemed to threaten a system that works well in spite of recent economic reverses. Since Palme's assassination in 1986, Ingvar Carlson has headed up a Social Democratic coalition with the moderate Communists. In the 1988 parliamentary elections, the Social Democrats slipped from 159 to 156 seats, and the Communist party rose from 19 to 21 seats. The three main non-Socialist opposition parties lost 19 seats (171 to 152). Carlson's promise to lower income-tax rates and provide a sixth week of paid annual vacation was more appealing than the opposition's tax-cut proposals.

Sweden's high standard of living (second only to that of Japan) and low unemployment rate (1.7 percent in 1988) may have been other important factors in Carlson's success. The election of twenty Greens to the *Riksdag* marks the advent of environmental issues as an important consideration in future elections. Sweden is facing increasing economic difficulties as a result of its full-employment policy, extensive welfare system, and labor attitudes. Although Swedes work an average of only thirty-one hours a week, their absentee rate is the highest in Western Europe. Sweden's share of the world market has declined 4 percent a year beginning in 1988. The remedies for Sweden's economic ills will be unpopular. Carlson's government fell in February 1990 when his austerity package failed to win approval. Labor refused to agree to a wage freeze. An income-tax reduction to 50 percent did pass in 1989, but indirect taxes were raised to maintain revenue. This backing away from the egalitarian society many Swedes cherish met stiff resistance. A needed reduction in the number of public employees, now one-third of the work force, to obtain a more market-oriented economy also faces much opposition. Sweden will find it difficult in the future to overcome the economic advantages enjoyed by the new high-technology, low-cost countries unless employment and wage policies can be altered and the extensive welfare system cut back in order to increase investment funds for industry.

Norway   Norway's disunited Labor party lost power in the 1981 elections to a coalition of Conservative, Christian People's, and Center parties. The electorate apparently tired of high taxes, excessive public spending, and declining industrial efficiency. After five years of Conservative rule, Labor returned under the popular leadership of Gro Harlem Brundtland. Labor, though divided over Norway's relationship with the EC and NATO, continued to rule until September 1989, primarily due to Brundtland's personal popularity and an austerity program that reduced the inflation rate. She has promoted the progressive image of Scandinavia by choosing eight female cabinet members. Women have comprised 34 percent of the legislature since 1985. The Labor party requires that 40 percent of its candidates for public office be women. The 1989 elections produced a much-increased vote for the tax-cutting, reduced-welfare Progress party and prevented either Labor or the three non-Socialist Moderate parties from obtaining a majority. Since neither Labor nor the moderate Conservatives wish to cooperate with the Progress party, government instability will exist until the next elections.

Austria   In the midst of all of this political fragmentation and governmental instability in Western Europe, Austria has been a model of stability. Until 1966, Austria was ruled by the two main parties, the People's party and the Socialist party, under a proportional representation system that alternated members of these parties in the various bureaucratic posts and in the cabinet. After a brief period in opposition (1966–1969), the Social Democrats, led until 1983 by Chancellor Bruno Kreisky, ruled alone until 1986. Both Austria's avoidance of the worst aspects of the post-1972 economic slump and the flexible "catch-all nature" of her political parties have led to her political stability. Neither party adheres strongly to an unbending ideological position. Since Austrian labor has held down its wage demands because of a system that permits labor to arbitrate wages and prices cooperatively with government and industry— the so-called social partnership—Austria's labor market has been extremely calm. Also, the Social Democrats have concentrated as much on establishing a modern industrial state as on social welfare. The party's fear that higher taxes would reduce economic investment made it refuse to shift ever more of the tax burden onto the wealthy.

Austria's long-running success story was interrupted in the eighties by the election of Kurt Waldheim to the presidency in 1986 and by increasing economic problems. Waldheim, the former secretary general of the United Nations, doggedly clung to the presidency despite intense international and internal pressure that he resign after it was disclosed that he had concealed his role as an SS officer in World War II. This controversy has led to Waldheim's isolation and instigated a national soul-searching concerning Austria's role in the National Socialist era. Added to Austria's woes is an economy that has turned flat because of over-employment, excessive bureaucracy, and technological obsolescence. Looming in the future is Austria's relationship to the European Community. If Austria does not join the EC, it may lose a large part of its foreign market; but if it joins, it may encounter overwhelming competition by more efficient Western European industries. Franz Vranitsky, the reformist Socialist chancellor in a coalition government with the People's party since 1986, has moved to modernize outdated industries and reduce government expenditures. If Vranitsky is successful in his attempt to fine-tune the Austrian economy and Austria is able to overcome Soviet objections to its membership in the EC, Austria's economic future should be bright.

FURTHER READING

Those interested in further information should consult the many periodicals that provide the most recent information. I would recommend the following periodicals: *Foreign Affairs, The Economist, Contemporary Review, The New Republic, New Left Review*, the *New York Review of Books*, and the many publications of the Organization for Economic Cooperation and Development. Especially helpful are the OECD *Observer* and the annual surveys of member nations. Newspapers I found helpful were the *International Herald Tribune*, the *New York Times*, the *London Times*, and foreign newspapers too numerous to mention.

For French history, I would recommend the following books: Gordon

Wright, *France in Modern Times,* 4th ed. (1989); John Ardagh, *France Today* (1987); William G. Andrews and Stanley Hoffmann, *The Fifth Republic at Twenty* (1981); D. L. Hanley, A. P. Kerr and N. H. Waites, *Contemporary France: Politics and Society since 1945* (1979); Michel Crozier, *The Stalled Society* (1973) and *Strategies for Change: The Future of French Society* (1982); and Dorothy Pickles, *Problems of Contemporary French Politics* (1982). For a critical view of Mitterrand, see Daniel Singer, *Is Socialism Doomed? The Making of Mitterrand* (1988). A more positive view is provided by George Ross, Stanley Hoffmann, and Sylvia Malzacher, eds., *The Mitterand Experiment: Continuity and Change in Modern France* (1987). David S. Bell and Byron Criddle, in *The French Socialist Party: Resurgence and Victory* (1984), argue that the Socialist party had no alternative but to pursue the strategy it did: to transform itself into a presidential party with the aim of obtaining the presidency.

I found the following books helpful for recent British history: Andrew Gamble, *Britain in Decline* (1981); Anthony Sampson, *The Changing Anatomy of Britain* (1983); David Coates, *Labour in Power* (1980); David Childs, *Britain since 1945* (1979); Alan Sked and Chris Cook; *Post-War Britain* (1979); Geoffrey Smith and Nelson W. Polsby, *British Government and Its Discontents* (1980); Richard Rose, *Politics in England,* 3rd ed. (1980); R. M. Punnett, *British Government and Politics,* 4th ed. (1980); and Samuel H. Beer, *Britain against Itself: The Political Contradictions of Collectivism* (1982). Peter Jenkins's *Mrs. Thatcher's Revolution: The Ending of the Socialist Era* (1988) is a fine study of Thatcher that grudgingly gives her her due. But he laments Britain's new emphasis on efficiency and individualism and what Jenkins considers to be an unconcern for the less fortunate. Dennis Kavanagh's *Thatcherism and British Politics: The End of Consensus* (1987) is a solid description of the transformation of British policy and outlook under Thatcher but again is critical of her style and lack of compassion. Labour is expertly covered in Eric Shaw's *Discipline and Discord in the Labour Party* (1987). Shaw believes the strong contract with the labor unions to be Labour's major obstacle to challenging the Conservatives.

For the Federal Republic of Germany, I would recommend Kendall L. Baker, Russell J. Dalton, and Kai Hildebrandt, *Germany Transformed* (1981); David P. Conradt, *The German Polity* (1978); Karl H. Cerny, *Germany at the Polls* (1978), Lewis Edinger, *West German Politics* (1986); and Arnold Heidenheimer and Donald Kommers, *The Governments of Germany* (1975). Two sound studies of German foreign policy are Wolfram F. Hanrieder, *Germany, America, Europe* (1989), and Diane Rosolowsky, *West Germany's Foreign Policy: The Impact of the Social Democrats and the Greens* (1987). A study that argues that West Germany has not done enough to promote European integration is Simon Bulmer and William Paterson, *The Federal Republic of Germany and the European Community* (1987). A recent analysis of West German economic policy since

1945 is provided by Jeremy Leaman, *The Political Economy of West Germany, 1945–85: An Introduction* (1988). Peter J. Katzenstein's *Policy and Politics in West Germany: The Growth of a Semisovereign State* (1987) is a sound political analysis. Henry Ashby Turner provides a comparison of East and West Germany since the war in his *The Two Germanies since 1945* (1987). Two suggestive, stimulating views of the German character are provided by Walter Laqueur, *Germany Today: A Personal Report* (1985), and John Ardagh, *Germany and the Germans: An Anatomy of Society Today* (1987).

For Italy, the following books were instructive: Norman Kogan, *A Political History of Postwar Italy: From the Old Center-Left to the New Center-Left* (1981); Donald L. M. Blackmer and Sidney Tarrow, *Communism in Italy and France* (1975); Giuseppe Di Palma, *Political Syncretism in Italy: Historical Coalition Strategies and the Present Crisis* (1978); and Alan S. Zuckerman, *The Politics of Faction: Christian Democratic Rule in Italy* (1979). Joe LaPalombara's *Democracy, Italian Style* (1987) provides a stimulating and very positive assessment of Italian politics and culture. Spencer M. DiScala's, *Renewing Italian Socialism: Nenni to Craxi* (1988) is a sound description. For papal affairs, see Francis X. Murphy, *The Papacy Today* (1981), and J. Derek Holmes, *The Papacy in the Modern World, 1914–1978* (1981). Donald Sassoon's *Contemporary Italy* (1986) is an important interpretive survey of politics, economics, and society.

For the Scandinavian countries, see M. W. Childs, *Sweden: The Middle Way on Trial* (1980); W. G. Jones, *Denmark: A Modern History* (1986); Jurg Steiner, *European Democracies* (1986); Arne Selbyg, *Norway Today* (1986); and the readings following chapter 5. For the Benelux countries, see E. H. Kossman, *The Low Countries* (1978); J. Fitzmaurice, *Politics of Belgium: Crisis and Compromise in a Plural Society* (1983); Charles Wilson, *Profit and Power* (1978); and Paul Marque, *A Short History of Luxembourg* (1976).

The move from authoritarianism to democracy in Spain is best described in Paul Preston's *The Triumph of Democracy in Spain* (1986). Preston emphasizes changes among Franco Moderates that made the transition to democracy possible. Paul Share, *The Making of Spanish Democracy* (1986), also points out the importance of changes within the Francoist dictatorship that smoothed the way to democracy. A competent recent study of Franco is Juan Pablo Fusi's *Franco: A Biography* (1988). For Portugal, see Robert Harvey, *Portugal: Birth of Democracy* (1978). Political events in Greece are excellently described by Richard Clogg's *Parties and Elections in Greece: The Search for Legitimacy* (1988). For a good comparative study of Austria and Switzerland, see Peter J. Katzenstein, *Corporatism and Change: Austria, Switzerland, and the Politics of Industry* (1984).

15 Thought and Culture Since 1945

Is it not barbarous to write poems after Auschwitz?

Theodore Adorno

After the experiences of World War II—the mass exterminations, the bombing of civilian centers, the atomic bombing of Japan—a pervasive cultural pessimism settled over continental Europe in the immediate postwar period. For if the land of Goethe and Bach could carry out the atrocities of Auschwitz, what hope was there for mankind in general? Only after extensive soul searching could Europeans, especially the Germans, begin to seek answers to this paradox. Except for those who remained loyal to some form of Marxism, Europe's intellectuals first turned against all ideological systems, all attempts at understanding the whole, to a distrust of all "facts" and "knowledge." This existential attitude was most evident immediately after the war in philosophy and literature.

A broader cultural-intellectual influence that transcended the war experience continued to transform cultural endeavor, particularly the arts, in the postwar period. This so-called modernist movement was a search for novelty and a rejection of the cultural forms that had dominated the nineteenth century. Building on the late-nineteenth-century rejection of Enlightenment rationalism, a modernist avant-garde revolted against realism and figuration in art, against story and representation in literature, and against ornament in architecture. Some of the artistic elite rejected the modern industrialized, bourgeois world. An iconoclastic avant-garde (Dadaists, surrealists, etc.) purposely produced works that upset or could not be enjoyed by the bourgeoisie. The result was a distancing of the artistic elite from society and a division between high and popular culture.

By the 1960s, a postmodern attitude began to supplant the modernist perspective. But it was not a complete break with modernism as can be borne out by its affinity with certain giants of the period such as Sigmund Freud, Friedrich Nietzsche, James Joyce, Pablo Picasso, Arnold Schönberg, Samuel Beckett, Anton von Webern, Jorge Luis Borges, and the surrealists. This postmodern impetus was to take many forms as it was, to a large extent, a reaction against individual modernists; against the international style in architecture (Le Corbusier, Mies van der Rohe); against abstract expressionism in art; and against any philosophical attempts to seek unity or wholeness. The postmodernists' turn to popular culture (pop art, op art, etc.) has multiplied the forms and made it difficult to distinguish high art from kitsch. The postmodernists, to an exaggerated degree, believe they are constricted by existing cultural patterns and by history; therefore, their attempts to escape these perceived constraints goad them on to even greater breaks with the past.

These culturally innovative trends have revolutionized art and music but have captured only a small avant-garde in literature. While a literary avant-garde experimented with language forms in order to break previously accepted modes of communication, the mainstream continued to be concerned about plot and narrative. The constant search for novelty, or "free invention" as its practitioners termed it, produced many new styles in rapid succession and ultimately resulted in fragmentation. Emerging out of this artistic morass in the seventies was a trend back to representation, story, and history. A closer study of philosophy and the various arts will reveal these dominant trends.

Philosophy

Existentialism   Existentialism was an appropriate response to the war and postwar pessimism. Although existentialism had been formulated long before the war in the works of Søren Kierkegaard, Friedrich Nietzsche, Martin Heidegger, Edmund Husserl, Karl Jaspers, and others, it gained broad intellectual acceptance only in the postwar period due to a widespread skepticism and disenchantment among intellectuals on the Continent. To these intellectuals, World War II seriously undermined any rational attempts to understand the world. The existentialist rejected all systems based upon a mechanistic understanding of the universe, such as rationalism and positivism. In this absurd, incomprehensible world only an ultimately skeptical philosophy such as existentialism could give meaning to existence. If, as the existentialist claimed, all facts were suspect, all knowledge relative, the individual was alone and isolated in a world without meaning. Existential man, according to its most outstanding postwar exponents, John-Paul Sartre and Maurice Merleau-Ponty, had to find his own meaning in this meaningless world.

Sartre's major work, *Being and Nothingness,* maintained that with God and reason both dead, the only course left open to man was an individual adjustment to an absurd existence. To free oneself from such a meaningless existence, one must make choices and act on them. Acting creates values or, as Sartre explained, essence. Man is essentially what he makes of himself. Existence is given meaning through commitment, and for Sartre this commitment was to communism. Sartre had, by this choice, given the very individualistic philosophy of existentialism a broader social base. Even when he became aware of the shortcomings of Communist regimes—the Stalinist concentration camps, the suppression of the 1956 Hungarian Revolution, etc.—he maintained his allegiance since, in his opinion, communism was ultimately superior to capitalism. Sartre's adamant defense of communism eventually weakened existentialism, since many of his followers, including Merleau-Ponty who had once defended Stalin's Moscow trials of political opponents, could no longer accept his position. Sartre's close associate Albert Camus broke with him over his commitment to communism. Camus retained the existential distrust of abstract ideas and ideologies that, in his opinion, produced hatred and suffering. Camus moved, however, from the absurdity of existence concept, best argued in *The Stranger,* to an exaltation of the everyday pleasures in life.

But by the fifties, the lack of effective action by the existentialists, their internal haggling, and rapid economic advance in France had reduced the support for such a "meaningless" philosophy. Many intellectuals were no longer able to accept Sartre's gloomy view of existence, his extreme rejection of bourgeois society, and his doctrinaire commitment to communism. The legacy of existentialism is, on the one hand, a healthy skepticism; and on the other, cynicism, defeatism, and apathy.

In the Anglo-Saxon world, an analytical school influenced by Ludwig Wittgenstein mounted a similar assault on understanding the whole in the fifties. According to its credo, since the world of language is divorced from the world of fact, any attempt to understand the world is folly; one can only make up myths. The best one can do is minutely examine phenomena in order to get rid of error, purge ambiguity, clarify, and define.

Structuralism   Once existentialism was undermined, no major movement emerged to replace it for over a decade. Only in the sixties did another notable philosophic movement, some say only a method or viewpoint, emerge. Called structuralism, it differed from existentialism in that it viewed man less as a free agent. Structuralists maintained that man's choices were determined by the existing structure of the basic units in a society. By understanding the relationship of the various units, rather than by understanding the content of phenomena, truth would emerge.

Claude Lévi-Strauss, the anthropologist and father of structuralism, held that all societies have similar underlying mental structures—apparent in their myths—that guide them. Phenomena could be analyzed, he maintained, by reducing them to their simplest components. He rejected the view that some societies are more advanced than others since all can be reduced to these essential structures. He thus rejected the idea of historical progress from primitive to advanced stages of civilization. Although the key that would unlock these essential components of all societies had not yet been found, Lévi-Strauss influenced scholars in many fields to search for underlying structures. The psychologist Louis Lacan sought to unravel the unconscious as one would a text, believing the key to both to lie in the structure of language. We can, according to Lacan, understand Freud's meanings more clearly by studying his use of language. Even many who refused the structuralist label approached their work from a structuralist point of view. The Marxist Louis Althusser attempted to uncover economic structures, class situations, and polarization in the societies he studied.

In language studies, structural analysis had preceded Lévi-Strauss by many decades. Before World War I, the Swiss linguist Ferdinand de Saussure had begun to experiment with a science of language, and his work served as the groundwork for the modern study of structural linguistics. Building on Saussure's pioneering work, postwar linguistic structuralists—Roland Barthes, Noam Chomsky, etc.—posited that language is composed of elements that logically relate to each other. Since this relationship orders one's thoughts and therefore determines one's ideas, what one says or writes determines what one thinks rather than the opposite. Here again, one's thoughts are ordered by these underlying relationships that are little perceived consciously. Language leads to classification and classification is oppressive. One can achieve understanding only by uncovering these internal relationships. While the structuralists hoped to impose order on what they considered to be the anarchy in thought brought on by existentialism and its demise, they frightened away many intellectuals who viewed structuralism as imposing a deterministic order on reality. Moreover, Lévi-Strauss's failure to find those "universal mental structures" diminished the appeal of structuralism.

Poststructuralism In the subsequent poststructuralist or postmodernist era, philosophy became exceedingly fragmented and specialized, although tending to focus on linguistic and conceptual analysis. The poststructuralists typically ventured beyond structuralism to a critique of language, history, truth, time, space, and existence that broke existing boundaries even more than structuralism had done. They rejected attempts to understand anything in its entirety. Therefore, most opposed any totalizing view of history, such as Marxism, or any search for coherent patterns, such as the structuralists' search for a common code underlying all languages. Jacques Derrida, a French philosopher of language, attempted to achieve an original structuralist aim—the complete destructuring of language. He read important philosophical texts of his contemporaries and "deconstructed" many of their basic assumptions.

Derrida, Foucault, and Barthes were all poststructuralist to the extent that they did not believe in universal, timeless mental structures, as had Lévi-Strauss, but contended that thought patterns change over time. Foucault, for example, argued that societies' codes of knowledge are constantly being transformed. Most poststructuralists undermined the original structuralist search for universal recurring patterns by giving thought and language a historical dimension. Lévi-Strauss called them ministructuralists. On the other hand, Derrida contended that Lévi-Strauss had not gone far enough in his study of myths since he had not attempted to find out if all myths are equivalent. Derrida, as well as other poststructuralists, believed that many of the basic tenants of modernism were already outmoded and therefore not "modern" even when first presented. In other words, modernism preserved much that was traditional, according to the poststructuralists. Therefore, they wanted to examine all the underlying assumptions of modernism in order to get at reality.

Marxism   In the period of intellectual fragmentation after 1960, Marxism experienced a revival. Marxism in its totalitarian, Stalinist form was rejected and replaced by a Western liberating, emancipatory Marxism—the humanistic Marx of the early manuscripts rather than the economic determinist of *Das Kapital*. The Frankfurt school of social theorists, led by Theodor Adorno, Max Horkheimer, and Herbert Marcuse, joined with the followers of the Italian Antonio Gramsci and the Hungarian Georg Lukács in emphasizing Marx's cultural message. Marx, in his early writings, they maintained, had pointed out that capitalism had not only alienated man from his work through mass-production techniques but had also undermined his cultural values. Marcuse extended Marx's theories to modern society, where he held capitalism had created materialistic automatons or one-dimensional cultural philistines. Marcuse's quest to free man from both political and sexual oppression and thereby restore his true nature was especially attractive to the New Left. These "humanistic Marxists" tended to downplay revolution in favor of gradualism. Gramsci had stressed that the first stage should be an attack on capitalist culture and only later an alteration of politics. Some Marxists rejected this stress on the young Marx. Louis Althusser argued that revolution would not just come about gradually but had to be prepared for and organized. To Althusser the real Marx was the Marx of *Das Kapital*. By the seventies, Marxism had become hopelessly splintered as intellectuals and the New Left fashioned their own Marxism to fit their specific situation.

One notable attempt to save Marxism in the face of the poststructuralist onslaught on any unifying theory has been that of Jurgen Habermas. Against the poststructuralists' rejection of all attempts to find any coherent patterns in history to understand the whole, Jurgen Habermas is seeking to restore a Marxist holistic view of history. Habermas fears that much poststructuralist thought, especially that of Foucault and Derrida, threatens to undermine political democracy through its rejection of Enlightenment rationalism. Despite Habermas's efforts, the philosophical avant-garde continued to be dominated by a neo-Nietzscheanist, poststructuralist attack on any attempts to find wholeness in the 1980s.

Literature

Although no new literary genre arose in the immediate postwar period to challenge such modernist giants as James Joyce, Thomas Mann, and André Gide, two trends or moods became widespread. Immediately after the war, a common theme among writers was a disgust, a repugnance, with European civilization brought on by fascism and the war and by the economic and moral poverty of the prewar period. These essentially existentialist writers concentrated on the meaningless, bleaker aspects of life. Novels dwelt on such themes as crime, inhumanity, poverty, despair, and cultural pessimism. Although this trend never vanished completely, another mood became dominant in the late fifties. It rejected the values and attitudes associated with the affluent society, mass consumerism, and complacency that had become typical in Europe in the sixties. By the seventies, literature began a retreat from social concerns toward private individual themes. These directions in literature were overshadowed in some countries, France in particular, by the postmodern-poststructural critique of language that raised questions of form and structure above questions of content. This movement's emphasis on difference and hostility to any coherent view of phenomena promoted the present extreme fragmentation in literary modes.

The immediate postwar period produced an outpouring of socially committed, "engaged" writers. In the first postwar decade, the message of most was an existential one. In France Albert Camus, Sartre, and Simone de Beauvoir searched for meaning in what they regarded as an absurd, incomprehensible world. They passionately attacked the bourgeoisie, whom they held responsible for all the world's ills, by writing novels the latter would not understand or enjoy. They tended to emulate the unconventional surrealist novelists of the interwar period. Although these existentialists failed to transform radically the form or language of the novel, they did alter the content away from traditional entertaining plots and character portrayal to what they considered to be a realistic depiction of man's sorry condition. However, Sartre and de Beauvoir soon turned away from the novel, since they did not believe that this form was effectively imparting their message. Sartre turned to the theater and de Beauvoir to more scientific investigations of the human condition (*The Second Sex*) and direct attacks on the Fifth Republic.

German writers such as Günter Grass, Heinrich Böll, and Wolfgang Borchert described the moral and political bankruptcy of Germany by bringing Germans face-to-face with the excesses of the Nazi period and the war. Borchert described the despair and loneliness of a soldier returning home after the war in *The Man Outside*. In the *Tin Drum*, Grass had a dwarf tell about the moral inadequacies of the middle class before and during the war. Both in the *Tin Drum* and in *Dog Years*, Grass demythologized the Nazi period by showing how vulgar and ludicrous the

Nazi officials and sympathizers had been. Grass also became actively involved in political and social causes and thereby rejected the traditional German separation of the artistic and political communities. Böll concentrated at first on the physical and psychological toll wrought by Nazism and the war in *Acquainted with the Night* and *House without Keeper*. But he soon turned his pen against bourgeois social climbing and what he perceived as a crude materialism in *Billiards at Half-Past Nine* and *The Clown*. His *Group Portrait with Woman* describes how a woman's life is destroyed because of bureaucratic insensitivity and concentration on power and money.

The most outstanding German dramatist, Carl Zuckmayer, described anti-Nazi resistance in *The Devil's General* and *Chorus in the Pyre*. The two other most noted playwrights writing in German were Swiss: Max Frisch and Friedrich Dürrenmatt. Frisch's and Dürrenmatt's themes included man's failings after the war. In their many plays, inhumanity, greed, complacency, cowardice, and weakness were ever-recurring themes.

In Italy, Alberto Moravia, Cesare Pavese, Carlo Levi, Elio Vittorini, Vasco Pratolini and others adopted a stark neorealism to depict the moral, political, and social shortcomings of Italy before and during the Fascist period. Levi's *Christ Stopped at Eboli* revealed the economic and social problems of southern Italy. A Fascist opponent exiled to Eboli experiences the grinding poverty that is endemic in the south. Many, Elio Vittorini and Vasco Pratolini among them, adopted a Communist perspective in their novels about the economic and social problems of the working class. In *Hero of our Time,* Vittorini's main character's murder of his mistress is depicted as a logical outcome of his bourgeois sociopolitical upbringing. Existentialism had little influence in postwar Italian literature. Perhaps their greater optimism shielded them from the existential despair felt by their French counterparts.

In the first postwar decade, Great Britain produced no new literary movement of note. The major writers—George Orwell, Graham Greene, Evelyn Waugh, T. S. Eliot, and E. M. Forster—were very individualistic and therefore not part of any school. Communism was not only not a major influence as it had been on the Continent, but it was attacked by George Orwell in *Animal Farm* and *Nineteen Eighty-four*. Perhaps the absence of past social and political problems on the scale of those on the Continent and the postwar welfare state reforms of the Labour government limited the despair or need for action felt by many continental intellectuals. These factors, combined with a British dislike of abstract philosophical speculation, could also have been the reason for the lack of an existential literary movement with its rejection of past values and experiences.

In the late fifties, a notable group of British writers joined in the criticism of the affluent society. A group identified as the "angry young men," or "kitchen-sink school," alienated by the developing consumerism and continuing class distinctions, lashed out at the type of society the welfare state was producing. Still, most confined their anger to what they viewed as the shortcomings of the welfare state, without calling for its overthrow. While writers such as Kingsley Amis poked fun at class pretensions in *Lucky Jim*, Alan Sillitoe, in *Saturday Night and Sunday Morning*, and John Osborne, in *Look Back in Anger*, went beyond criticism of class barriers to depict a working-class world devoid of real meaning.

In the sixties, a new generation dissatisfied with the reforms of the welfare state and distraught over the spread of nuclear weapons and the widening Vietnam War turned to a more radical opposition to the government. Repelled by this New Left onslaught, some turned in the other direction. In *Lucky Jim's Politics*, Kingsley Amis rejected his former antigovernment position and attacked political socialism. Doris Lessing expressed her disenchantment with communism in her cycle of novels, *Children of Violence*, and in her celebrated exploration of the political, psychological, and sexual revolutions of our time, *The Golden Notebook*. But most writers clung to the New Left movement both in Britain and on the Continent. Their intellectual mentors were the neo-Marxists Herbert Marcuse, George Lukács, and Antonio Gramsci. Their common theme was man's alienation in a world of plenty. Most looked to the early humanistic Marx for inspiration. Marcuse, in *One Dimensional Man*, argued that mass-consumer society satisfied man's material needs but not his intellectual and cultural needs. He and his followers struck out at what they viewed as an alienating, dehumanizing world.

Literature experienced a major change in the fifties when a French avant-garde began to experiment, as James Joyce and Borges had done earlier, with the form, writing, and theory of the novel. These "new novelists"—Alain Robbe-Grillet, Michel Butor, Claude Simon, and Nathalie Sarraute—disengaged the novel from its previous attempts to understand the past or present. Writers now sought to describe things as they appeared and did not seek a deeper underlying meaning or try to influence their audience to act. Character development and narrative form typical of the traditional novel were sacrificed to a detailed investigation of time, memory, and object. Sarraute, for one, concentrated on minutely describing the many sensations that direct our lives. For these writers literature was anti-intellectual, anti-ideological. Robbe-Grillet spoke for them all when he stated, "We no longer believe in depth." To them the search for meaning in life served no purpose and should be abandoned.

Robbe-Grillet has been the most influential of these "new" novelists. The content in his works existed merely to draw attention to their form and procedures. His repetition of key sentences with slight variations, in such works as *Project for a Revolution in New York*, was intended to deaden any emotional response from the reader. In *Project*, the continued repetition of a torture eventually robs it of its tragic nature. Such an

phaville (1964), Godard attacked mechanization itself; in *Weekend* (1967), the meaninglessness and materialism of bourgeois existence; and in *Every Man for Himself* (1980) and *Slow Motion* (1980), sexual degradation and economic exploitation. Some of these French films became so experimental, so much a personal creation, that they were viewed by only a few avid cinema fans.

German Filmmakers Most noteworthy since 1965 has been the renaissance of the German cinema. After two decades of producing escapist, imitative films, Germans such as Volker Schlöndorff, Rainer Werner Fassbinder, Werner Herzog, Wim Wenders, and Margaretta von Trotta began to produce imaginative, unconventional works in which directors developed their own personal style in the French (*auteur*) manner. Schlöndorff's *Young Torless* (1966) and the *Tin Drum* (1979) received international acclaim. The former, an adaptation of Robert Musil's novel, juxtaposes the psychological strains of life in a boys' school and life in Nazi Germany. The *Tin Drum*, an adaptation of Grass's novel, shared the Grand Prix Prize at Cannes in 1979. Schlöndorff's films have intricate political and social themes; *The Lost Honor of Katharina Blum* (1975), based upon a Heinrich Böll novel, studies the destructive effect the press can have on individuals.

Fassbinder's films have an equally strong social message. They normally deal with the downtrodden, the underdog, and the oppressed. *Katzelmacher* (1969) and *Ali: Fear Eats the Soul* (1973) treat foreign workers in Germany. Perhaps to exorcise the domination-dependence relationship among homosexuals, Fassbinder has treated homosexuality in a number of films: *The Bitter Tears of Petra von Kant* (1972); *Fox and His Friends* (1975); and *In a Year of 13 Moons* (1979). Shortly before his death from drugs in 1982, he finished *Lili Marleen* (1981) and *Lola* (1981). One of his most successful films commercially, *The Marriage of Maria Braun* (1979), suggests that Germany had to prostitute itself morally to achieve economic recovery in the postwar period.

Concerned with human failings, Werner Herzog dramatizes our unquestioning adoration of technology and rationalism. His *Stroszek* (1977) deals with what he regards as the plastic cheapness of much of American culture.

Bergman and Buñuel While this national approach to the postwar cinema has exposed the major trends in the cinema, it has omitted two giants of the screen, Ingmar Bergman and Luis Buñuel. Although Bergman's very individualistic style makes his work difficult to categorize, his themes of interpersonal relationships, evil, suffering, death, and the meaning of existence raised the cinema to new heights. In one of his greatest movies, *The Seventh Seal* (1956), a medieval knight gambles with Death in order to have time to consider the value of living. Organized religion was relentlessly attacked as an instigator of death—the Crusades, the Inquisition, etc. In *Wild Strawberries* (1957), the main character, an old doctor facing death tries to determine if his life has been of any use. Some of Bergman's later films, such as *Cries and Whispers* (1973), returned to the theme of death and reassessment of life. *The Virgin Spring* (1959) treated the subjects of youthful innocence, evil, and retribution. A daughter's rape and murder are revenged by her father in a most brutal manner. Some of Bergman's later films are masterful studies of interpersonal relationships. In *Persona* (1967), he dealt with the relationship between a nurse and a mentally disturbed actress who has refused to speak for years since she believes that existence is meaningless.

Excessively pessimistic about man, Luis Buñuel has been a constant critic of the Catholic church and social institutions. In *Belle de Jour* (1967), a whorehouse is depicted as a place of genuine passion in contrast to marriage where passion is shown as artificial. In *Viridiana* (1961), he pointed out the uselessness of faith and charity. In *The Discreet Charm of the Bourgeoisie* (1973), Buñuel poked fun at bourgeois pretentions and objectives.

East European Filmmaking   There has been also a great outpouring of imaginative cinema in Eastern Europe since Stalin's death. Although nationalized, the film industry served here as a forum for social criticism and ideological exchange during periods of de-Stalinization. The Polish, Czech, and Hungarian cinemas experienced unusually productive and creative periods during political thaws in the fifties and sixties. In Poland, Andrzej Wajda's neorealist films—*A Generation* (1954), *Canal* (1956), *Ashes and Diamonds* (1958)—established his reputation as one of Europe's major directors. In the sixties and seventies a number of major directors emerged but were forced out of Poland by re-Stalinization: Roman Polanski, Jerzy Skolinowski, etc.

Even more impressive has been the profusion of world-renowned, innovative Czech films and directors. Building upon a strong prewar film tradition and profiting from the liberalization of the midsixties, a Czech new wave produced such award-winning films as Elmar Klos and Jan Kadar's *Shop on Main Street* (1965) and Jiri Menzel's *Closely Watched Trains* (1966). Menzel's film combined humor and tragedy in the coming of age of a boy both politically and sexually in Nazi-occupied Czechoslovakia. Kos and Kadar's *Shop on Main Street* also mixed humor and seriousness. The main character, a Chaplinesque figure, shuns work and respectability during the Nazi occupation. As an Aryan controller in a Jewish widow's button shop he is forced to decide whether he will protect the old woman from being sent to a concentration camp or protect himself. His vacillation ultimately leads him to unintentionally murder the woman and then hang himself out of guilt. The political crackdown after 1968 forced Kadar, Jasny, Forman, and others to flee the country and thus stifled much of the creativity of the Czech cinema.

Hungary's major contribution to the cinema came during the political thaw from 1953 to 1956 and the unexpectedly relaxed rule of János Kádár after 1956. As in Czechoslovakia, the Hungarian directors, especially Andras Kovacs and Miklós Jancsó, were extremely innovative in form and technique. Both attacked the debilitating influence authoritarianism, political terror, and bureaucracy have on creativity: Kovacs, in *Difficult People* (1964) and *The Stud Farm* (1979); Jancsó, in *The Round Up* (1965), *Silence and Cry* (1968), and *Red Psalm* (1972).

Only Yugoslavia, of the other East European countries, produced films that compare with the creative cinema of Western Europe. Severely limited by censorship, Soviet filmmaking has not measured up to that in other East European countries.

Postmodernist Filmmaking Although many film modes existed side by side in the eighties, an international postmodernist genre has emerged with the films of Hans-Jurgen Syberberg, Jean-Jacques Beineix, and Hugh Hudson. These films employ what Andreas Huyssens describes as double coding—the mixing of high-cultural and popular-cultural modes and the past with the present. Syberberg's *Parsifal* (1984) attempted, according to Jim Collins, to "interconnect simultaneously" many German cultural traditions. He juxtaposed Richard Wagner's opera *Parsifal,* a high-cultural mode situated in Germany's mythic past, with the contemporary experience. The nineteenth-century opera is tied to the medieval Parsifal myth and the myths surrounding Nazi Germany. Beineix's *Diva* (1981) mixed the mass cultural-detective mode with the elitist-opera mode in order to demonstrate how different discourses shape reality. The intertwining of the two modes culminates in the final scene when opera star and male "commoner" embrace on stage. These postmodernist directors view such mode mixing as necessary to make sense of today's fragmented discourses.

Art and Architecture

Art Art and architecture followed somewhat the same path as the cinema. Immediately after the war a neorealist, engaged art was dominant. Artists such as Bernard Buffet, Bernard Lorjou, and Claude Venard depicted the human condition in a realistic manner. However, the neorealist goal of describing the human condition was soon overcome by an avant-garde, nonfigurative, abstract, art-for-art's-sake movement that resembled in many ways the "imaginative" cinema that emerged in France and spread throughout Europe.

Postwar abstractionism rejected those abstract artists schooled in the prewar period—Picasso, Braque, Chagall, and the sculptors Giacometti and Brancusi—who still worked with figures or images, even though these might be greatly distorted. Art was to create a new reality through the use of materials, colors, and form. No former aesthetic or social guidelines were to deter the artist from creative expression. The American abstract expressionism of Jackson Pollock and Willem de Kooning in which the artist sought existential self-realization through action—by throwing or frantically brushing paint on a canvas—was very influential in Europe. The European tachist group, led by Jean Fautrier, Georges Mathieu, Pierre Soulages, Nicholas de Stael, and Karel Appel, strove for self-definition in the nonrepresentational use of color and form. Meaning or images would appear on the canvas without any premeditated image in mind. The canvas became a space in which to act rather than to compose. Some rejected imagery completely in an attempt to divorce art from subject matter or the artist's feelings. Such paintings—those of the Frenchman Yves Klein are a good example—might be one solid color. A similar minimalist movement in sculpture reduced objects to their simplest minimal shapes. The British minimalist sculptors, Anthony Cato and Philip King, reduced everything to geometric forms.

But even greater attacks on traditional conceptions of art were to emerge in the sixties. Popular (pop) art, begun as an attack on the products of mass culture by some and an open acceptance by others, rejected existing aesthetic standards by depicting common objects such as beer cans, cereal boxes, and many other objects from popular culture. To many it symbolized the bankruptcy of modern art.

It was also rejected by a group of optical (op) artists who disliked any social commentary in art. Led initially by Victor Vasarely in France and by Bridget Riley in Britain, the op artists explored optical reactions and movement by employing color shadings and geometric patterns repeatedly. A number of op artists, especially those with strong science backgrounds, were interested in the application of science and technology to art.

While much of the public could accept op and pop art as legitimate artistic movements, they could not accept such art movements as earth art that involved moving huge amounts of dirt in remote areas or wrapping buildings in plastic as serious art. Nor was conceptual art—staged events or happenings rather than a physical object—accepted by most of the public as art, no matter how creative.

In reaction to these experimental forms in postwar art, the 1970s produced superrealism and neo-expressionism, which constituted a return to some of the major concerns of nineteenth-century figurative painters, such as representational forms, light, and the mixing of colors. But contemporary painters in these genres differed from their predecessors in that they used excessive amounts and kinds of color; thus, they are often called violent figurative painters. The Italians Sandro Chia, Enzo Cucci, and Francesco Clemente, and the Germans A. R. Penck, Rainer Fetting, Markus Lupertz, and George Baselitz are a few of the leading superrealist and neo-expressionist artists. While a few Americans were painting in these styles, they generated a greater response in Europe. This may have

Bridget Riley. *Current,* 1964. Synthetic polymer paint on composition board, 58⅜ × 58⅞ inches. Collection, The Museum of Modern Art, New York. Philip Johnson Fund. A fine example of op art.

Sandro Chia. *Water Bearer,* 1981. Oil and oil pastel on canvas, 206 × 170 cm. Collection, Tate Gallery, London. One product of the increased interest in super-realism in the 1970s and 1980s. (Courtesy of Sperone Westwater Gallery, NY)

ended New York's domination of avant-garde painting. Although it is impossible to determine if any style is dominant at this time, it is clear that those who paint in a representational mode are no longer ostracized by the artistic community as they were in the fifties and sixties. In some regards, painting has returned to a form of art that the public never deserted. The most popular artists of the postwar period continued to be the giants of the interwar period, such as Picasso and Chagall.

Architecture   The dominant architectural style of the immediate postwar period harkened back to the early twentieth-century views of such architects as Walter Gropius and Mies van der Rohe concerning freestanding crystalline shafts. Termed *international style* or *functional,* these modernist glass skyscrapers were constructed throughout the industrial world. All aspects of the buildings were to conform to their essential function, which meant that structures were to be simple and unadorned. Hans Scharoun's Philharmonic Concert Hall in Berlin concentrated all building materials on achieving perfect acoustics. Skyscrapers were normally unadorned glass structures with no decoration.

In the early fifties, a new style, new brutalism or monumental formalism, began to overcome the international style. It rejected the customary sleek glass wall of the international style for a rough, sculpted appearance, usually in concrete, and exposed structural components. Le Corbusier, the world-renowned architect working primarily in France, had already experimented with sculpted components on some of his essentially international-style structures. But in the fifties, he created some of the most impressive examples of this new style. His church, Notre-Dame-du-Haut at Ronchamp, France, is a good example of the sculpted, rough look of monumental formalism. Other Europeans—Eugene Beandouin, Marcel Lods, Pier Luigi Nervi, Joern Utzon, Viljo Revell, Eduardo Torroja, and Felik Candela, among others—soon took up this new style. Torroja and Candela erected large sculpted umbrella roofs with cavernous interiors that could be infinitely divided.

In the seventies, a postmodern style began to replace modernism. The postmodern continued modernism in its use of contemporary building techniques and materials, but it added decorative ornamentation and historical symbolism. Charles Jencks described it as "double coding" or the combination of elite-popular and new-old. These postmodernists argued that the modernist style did not communicate effectively with the public and was, therefore, alienating. Some observers date the death of the modernist style with the rejection of cheap fabrication typical of many of the alienating functionalist housing blocs of the sixties. One of the best European examples of the postmodern is the Neue Staatsgalerie in Stuttgart, Germany. In the United States, the postmodernist style can be seen in Philip Johnson's AT&T building in New York with its Chippendale pinnacle. A few architects have turned to a late modernist style, epitomized

The Neue Staatsgalerie in Stuttgart, Germany, is a good example of postmodernist integration of past architectural motif and modern technological advances. (Peter Walser. Courtesy of the German Information Center)

in the Pompidou Center in Paris, which is still dedicated totally to the new.

In residential areas, attention concentrated on the site and the use of natural materials. City architects attempted to separate motor traffic, shopping, and residential areas. In business areas, more attention was paid to relieving the austerity created by numerous glass skyscrapers. This was achieved by building parks, garden atriums in large buildings, and breaking up the flat glass facades with concrete or steel geometric forms.

Music

As with painting, postwar serious music must be divided between that which is in most demand by the public—romantic, classical—and that being written by postwar composers—total serialism, electronic music or *musique concrète,* and aleatory or chance composition.

Although the music of the postwar avant-garde was not well received by the more tradition-bound public, it did have strong ties to the past. Total serialism was a logical outgrowth of the serial (twelve-tonal) compositions of the interwar Vienna school—Arnold Schönberg, Anton von Webern, and Alban Berg. Total serialists viewed themselves as architects or engineers of sound who were bringing structure and organization to music. Schönberg had first hit upon the concept of serialism in the twenties as a means of bringing system to a triumphant, intuitive atonality. He attempted to arrange the twelve notes of the chromatic scale in a fixed order. The twelve-tonal serialism employed by such composers as Pierre Boulez, Olivier Messaien, René Leibowitz, and Karlheintz Stockhausen was in some regard a way to bring back order as well. Messaien established scales of pitch, duration, and loudness in his composition, *Mode of Durations and Intensities.* In 1948, Pierre Schaeffer adapted electronic music to natural sounds to produce what has been termed *musique concrète.* Karlheintz Stockhausen carried such experimentation a step further to electronic-sound synthesis. Stockhausen and Boulez in Europe and the American John Cage soon jettisoned the order so sought after following the war when they began to compose chance or choice compositions. Since little order was provided for sounds and music in their compositions, music was what happened to occur at each performance. In one of Cage's works, *Silent Sonata,* no sounds are made. In Europe, Stockhausen and Boulez composed similar chance or aleatory works that left a great deal up to the individual musician cr freed him, as they would have it, to be creative. A musician could choose his own tempo, measure, or pauses, etc. In Stockhausen's *From the Seven Days* (1968), each score was a prose poem that provided only general instructions for the musicians.

While the fifties had experienced a continuation of serialism, the expansion of electronic music, and the beginnings of chance or aleatory music, the sixties produced such a multiplicity of musical forms that it is virtually impossible to isolate any dominant trends. There are those who have gone back to the diatonic harmony of the romantic and classical periods (Samuel Barber, Michael Tippett), and those who are still experimenting with electronic aleatory music (Boulez, Stockhausen), serialism (Milton Babbitt), chance (Cage), and revolutionary Socialist music (Hans Werner Henze, Luigi Nono). The future seems to promise diversity rather than integration.

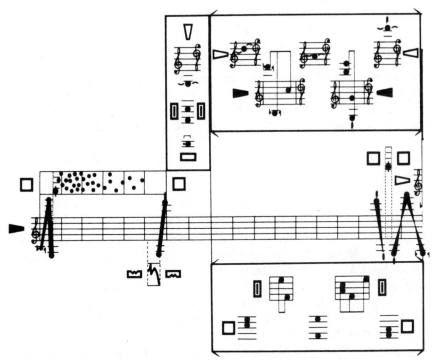

This section from the score of Karlheintz Stockhausen's *Zyklus* shows to what extent contemporary composers have departed from traditional forms of musical notation. (©Universal Edition (London) Ltd., London, 1960. Used by permission of European American Music Distributors Corporation, sole U.S. agent for Universal Edition.)

Culture and the Popular Media

A worldwide youth culture began to emerge in the sixties characterized by the various forms of rock music, television, blue jeans, mass consumerism, and hedonism. What is often termed *Americanization* is more aptly understood as an extension of the postmodern condition throughout the economically advanced world. The multiplication and commodification of cultural forms is now a worldwide phenomena. An influential youth culture first emerged in the United States but has since spread to Europe and other economically advanced areas. This youth culture, exemplified by such rock groups as the Beatles, the Who, and the Rolling Stones, spread even beyond economically advanced areas as youth culture was spread by the media and an increasing number of international travelers. Its internationalism is apparent in a 1989 dance craze, Lambada, a French digital production of a Bolivian melody and Brazilian rhythm performed

by a Senegalese-French band. In the sixties and seventies, an antiau-
thoritarian, antimilitary, and antiheirarchical youth culture emerged. It
sanctioned drug use (the Beatles' "Lucy in the Sky with Diamonds"
advertised LSD) and sexual liberation, and it poked fun at bourgeois materialism and conformism. This cultural milieu was stronger in countries
like England and the United States where the generational gap was more
pronounced than on the Continent. With the development of punk and
acid rock in the eighties, the early rock groups now appear tame. In fact,
much of the support for early forms of rock music comes from the middle-
aged who look back nostalgically to those years of protest against racism,
the Vietnam War, and "establishments" everywhere.

Summary

The present proliferation of cultural modes and discourses has brought
dismay to cultural conservatives such as Adorno, Lyotard, and Baudril-
lard. Such conservatives believe the absence of a dominant *zeitgeist*
means cultural chaos as well as the loss of belief and authentic social
relationships. But postmodernists believe that this plethora of cultural
modes has not led to a decline in values or in social relationships. They
contend that the existence of many credos does not mean that people do
not have any cultural values. The recent resurgence in religious belief
seems to support their position. They also differ on the mass media. The
critics contend that the mass media has led to the decline of narrative,
but the postmodernists find mininarrative even in rock-music videos and
in the television serial. Essentially the conservatives yearn for a dominant
cultural ethos while the postmodernists relish what they consider to be
the richness of cultural heterogeneity.

FURTHER READING

Few comprehensive surveys of thought and culture since 1945 exist.
The most complete is Roland N. Stromberg's *After Everything: Western
Intellectual History since 1945* (1975). A good background for the period
is provided by H. Stuart Hughes's *The Sea Change: The Migration of
Social Thought, 1930–1965* (1975).

Modernism and postmodernism can best be studied in Stromberg, and
Andreas Huyssen, *After the Great Divide: Modernism, Mass Culture,
Postmodernism* (1986); Christopher Butler, *After the Wake: An essay on
the Contemporary Avant-garde* (1980); Hal Foster, ed., *The Anti-Aes-
thetic: Essays on Postmodern Culture* (1983); Jim Collins, *Uncommon
Cultures: Popular Culture and Postmodernism* (1989); and Charles
Jencks, *What Is Postmoderism?* (1987).

World War II attitudes. Once the Soviet lid was lifted, earlier nationalistic and anti-Semitic attitudes reemerged. These attitudes may diminish after the euphoria associated with a greater self-determination dies down.

Terrorism

Terrorism remains a disruptive but declining phenomenon in most countries except Northern Ireland. The turmoil in Northern Ireland (Ulster), in Cyprus, and in the Basque region of Spain originated before World War II. The Ulster violence can be traced back to a centuries-old conflict between the native Catholic Irish and the primarily English and Scottish Protestant settlers. Whether its source is essentially socioeconomic (as asserted by the Irish Republican Army, the IRA) or religious (as asserted by the British and the Ulster Protestants), the enmity has been a part of the European experience for generations.

After the imposition of direct British rule in Ulster in 1972, desperation drove the IRA to extend the terrorism to the streets of London. Unable to overcome the Protestant majority in Ulster, led since 1971 by Ian Paisley and the Democratic Unionist party (DUP), and confronted by British tanks and soldiers, the IRA hoped to paralyze both the Ulster and British governments in order to attain its goals of equality for the Ulster Catholics and the incorporation of Ulster into the Irish Republic. In October 1982, a renewed round of violence began after elections to a new Northern Ireland Assembly designed to be a first step in restoring local self-government. Catholic candidates all refused to participate because, as they argued, the Protestant majority in the Assembly would deny Catholics any role. But the recent violence is only an exaggerated phase of the continuing hostility in Northern Ireland. Efforts at reconciliation have been thwarted by divisions among the Catholics and Protestants as well as between the two. Not one Catholic or Protestant group can speak for all Catholics or Protestants and therefore neither Sinn Fein (the political wing of the IRA), the Catholic Social Democratic and Labor party (SDLP), the DUP, or the Official Unionist party (OUP), among others, can effectively represent each side during negotiations. Britain's two-part strategy has not yet borne fruit. One part is the 1985 British agreement with Ireland that gave the Irish Republic a consultative role in Northern Ireland but permitted Ulster to remain a part of the UK as long as the majority of its citizens desired it. The second part made Ulster semiautonomous by creating a local assembly. The Unionists' fear that this assembly was a first stage in taking Ulster out of the United Kingdom led all fifteen Unionist MPs to resign their seats in the British Parliament in December 1985. In June 1986, Britain dissolved the assembly and relied solely on the Anglo-Irish intergovernmental conference. The number of deaths from political violence increased to sixty-two in 1986. No end is in sight for the violence and divisions.

In Cyprus the conflict between the Greek and Turkish inhabitants centers on the Turkish Cypriote charges that they are a mistreated minority, in both an economic and political sense, and the Greek Cypriot desire to incorporate Cyprus into a larger Greece. After Cyprus achieved independence from the British in 1960, a complicated political arrangement agreed to in a compromise between Greeks and Turks was the basis for a division of responsibility in local government. This broke down in 1963 when the Greeks tried to take over, and hostility was minimized only through the presence of a United Nations peacekeeping force.

A 1974 attempt to oust the Cypriot president Archbishop Makarios and join the island to the Greek mainland to satisfy Greek Nationalists led to a Turkish invasion of Cyprus and an intensification of the civil war. Only the presence of Turkish troops in Cyprus and the fall of the military junta in Greece have preserved a modicum of peace on the island.

In Spain, Basque Separatist terrorism against Madrid is the result of a long-standing Basque desire for more autonomy or independence for the four Basque provinces, over against the former Franco regime's desire to eliminate the Separatists. The conflict is ultimately a matter of the linguistic and cultural uniqueness of the Basque regions and the failure of previous Spanish rulers to integrate the area fully into the Spanish nation. The granting of greater autonomy in the early eighties reduced the violence and may ultimately pacify the region.

While these conflicts may be among Europe's major problems, they are not of recent origin, nor are they more violent than the terrorism of political extremists that has spread throughout the world in the last decade.

Discontented and Conformist Youth

Newspapers have referred to Europe's rebellious youth as the new "lost generation." Their aimlessness, despair, cynicism, and occasional violence is met with incomprehension by most of the older generation. Especially troublesome during the last few years has been the youth occupation of buildings, random violence, and sharply increased deaths from drugs. The police were kept busy in Germany and the Netherlands in the early eighties evicting squatters from their "homes." In staid Zurich, Switzerland, youths broke windows and set buildings afire when Swiss authorities closed a youth center that police claimed had become a center for the distribution of drugs. In France, youths shocked their elders by stealing cars, racing them through cities, and then burning them—called "moto rodeos" by the youths. The authorities are perplexed by the apparent aimlessness of their activities. It does not have as clear a purpose as the youth protest of the sixties. Then, youths were in revolt against colonialism and imperialism (Algeria and Vietnam) and against bureaucratization (1968); they were also prorevolutionary. Except for the neo-

Fascist groups, today's youthful rebels are apolitical and anarchistic. They reject Marxist organization as well as that of their own governments. As one said, "Who wants to hear about organizing when we want to undo the organization."

Some of the discontent can be explained by the unemployment that accompanied the economic slump in Europe after 1973. The number of idle youths increased rapidly. In 1982, youth unemployment topped 20 percent throughout Europe. With nothing to do and little prospect for work, some youths have given in to hopelessness and cynicism. These youths developed an anger at what they consider to be the welfare state's preoccupation with order, cleanliness, and economic security. They feel deserted and isolated. There are a few who have joined radical fringe groups, such as the Maoists, the German Red Army Faction, the Italian Red Brigades, the neo-Fascists, etc., but many alienated youths have simply stopped supporting any objective. Their lives have become a meaningless welter of drugs, video games, and rock music. They live for today and do not believe that tomorrow is worth preparing for.

In contrast to this rebellious minority is a conformist majority who are usually at peace with existing society. Although dissatisfied with some educational policies and the shortage of meaningful jobs, most Western youth accept existing society. They have joined in demonstrating only to protest the unresponsiveness of rigid bureaucracies or governments' excessive use of police force. Of course, youths in Eastern Europe have played a major role in toppling the Stalinist regimes (as described in chapter 13).

Bureaucracy

There can be little doubt that the authority of national governments and their executive branches increased since 1945. In France, the constitution of the Fifth Republic is a clear example of a strengthened executive. This increase of executive power has occurred in most European states. As populations and economies have grown, economic and social problems have become more complex, and national governments rather than local governments have tended to deal with them. These vast, impersonal, centralized bureaucracies are more often than not unresponsive to local and individual needs. Senior civil servants often withhold undesirable information from their superiors in order to avoid disturbing consequences, or they engage in conspiracies against their superiors. Executive branches of government have much larger staffs and resources than do the legislatures and have therefore taken more and more authority into their own hands. Legislatures, besieged with bills, overwhelmed with duties, and lacking in resources, have done nothing to keep a rein on the growth of executive authority. Adding to the confusion has been the growing influence of interest groups in decision making. Legislators and administrators have been beset with demands and pressure from ecologists, numerous business and agricultural lobbies, labor groups, women, and others. In Sweden, Austria, and Holland, labor, government, and business cooperatively decide government policy in the economic and social sphere. A special Dutch Social and Economic Council exists for this purpose in the Netherlands. These bodies have a great deal more knowledge about their situation than do legislators. Popular discontent with the remoteness of decision making and big government's increasing inability to resolve local problems led in the late seventies to moves to decentralize decision making. Italy, France, Spain, Britain, and Greece have increased decision making at the local and regional level in order to bring the government more in touch with local problems and to avoid fueling agitation for divisive independence movements.

Loss of European Distinctiveness

The unprecedented material rewards of the new Europe have undermined unique European life-styles. Some Europeans speak of a decline of Frenchness or Germanness and a rise of materialism that they equate with the American way of life. Increasingly, Europeans have discussed measures to preserve the European quality of life. At the same time, other Europeans have recommended that Europe adopt many American economic and business practices in order to be able to compete with American companies.

Even a casual observer can note the American influence on Europe's languages in newspapers and on television. But, there is a distinct difference from country to country in the extent of the use of English. As might be expected, in France the inroads are relatively slight; admitting the reality of *le weekend* was a major step for them. But is is going to be difficult for Europeans to avoid the cultural homogeneity that is a by-product of economic modernization and the close economic ties among European nations and between Europe and the United States. Europeans now have their own fast-food cafés—McDonald's restaurants are a common sight—and European youths are not only attracted by American music, films, TV shows, and fashions but have developed their own Euro-versions.

On the other hand, Europeans no longer feel inferior, as they did in the fifties, when American economic and technical superiority was unquestioned. Now Europeans believe they have caught up if not surpassed the United States in technology and economic well-being. Europeans point to the technical inferiority of American products, especially automobiles, with undisguised pride. As a Frenchman told Anthony Sampson in 1983, "I remember when I first went to America thirty years ago. Everything looked bigger, newer, faster. Now everything looks shabbier and older than here." This changed attitude offers much promise for improved relations between Europe and the United States. With Europeans no longer feeling inferior, they can more readily accept the American presence in Europe without thinking of United States economic and cultural imperialism. This new-found pride should also lead Europeans to be less dependent on the United States as is already evident in many European economic and foreign policy initiatives. It is perhaps now more proper to view both Europe and America as in the forefront of the Westernization of the world. Many of those in the forefront of change in Eastern Europe wish to obtain the benefits of Western economic advances. Recent opinion polls throughout Eastern Europe found that West Germany was the most popular economic model rather than the more socially egalitarian Sweden.

Looking to the Future

The apparent end of the Cold War has reduced Europeans' fear of war, especially a nuclear war, and opened the way for Europe to reallocate its resources to deal with many pressing domestic problems. These additional funds should make it possible to address pressing ecological problems. If recent elections in Scandinavia can be viewed as a harbinger of things to come, ecological issues will be one of the major political issues of the turn of the century. Another important issue will be achieving economic equality and greater political representation for women. The advances made by many Scandinavian countries have already provided a model for the rest of Europe and the world. The forging of European economic integration in the nineties will make it possible to attack ecological, gender, and other problems on an all-European scale. Europe's future, barring a counterrevolution in the Soviet Union, looks bright.

Index